The Wagn

The Wagners

THE DRAMAS OF A MUSICAL DYNASTY

NIKE WAGNER

Translated by
Ewald Osers and Michael Downes

Weidenfeld & Nicolson
LONDON

First published in Great Britain in 2000
by Weidenfeld & Nicolson

First published in Germany in 1998
by Insel Verlag, Frankfurt am Main und Leipzig

A CIP catalogue record for this book
is available from the British Library.

ISBN 0 297 64315 0

Typeset by Selwood Systems, Midsomer Norton

Set in Minion

Printed in Great Britain by
Butler & Tanner Ltd, Frome and London

Weidenfeld & Nicolson

The Orion Publishing Group Ltd
Orion House
5 Upper Saint Martin's Lane
London, WC2H 9EA

CONTENTS

ILLUSTRATIONS

between pages 140–141

The programme for the Bayreuth Festival in 1969, listing the directors since Richard Wagner founded the festival in 1876 (Hartmut Zelinsky, *Richard Wagner. Ein deutsches Thema*, Berlin, 1983. © Medusa Verlag, Berlin)
Richard Wagner (Richard Wagner–Nationalarchiv Bayreuth)
Cosima Liszt (Richard Wagner–Nationalarchiv Bayreuth)
Wahnfried, 1874–1945 (Private collection)
The house in April 1945 after bomb damage (Bernd Mayer archive, Bayreuth)
Wagner's hall at Wahnfried in 1958 (Richard Wagner–Nationalarchiv Bayreuth)
The hall today (Photo: Wilhelm Rauh, Bayreuth)
Franz Liszt by Jean-Auguste Dominique Ingres
Marie D'Agoult by Théodore Chassériau
The Liszt children, by Friedrich Preller (Richard Wagner–Nationalarchiv Bayreuth)
Eva, Isolde, Siegfried, Daniela and Blandine with Hans Richter (Private collection)
Winifried and Siegfried in 1916 (Private collection)
Siegfried with his wife and children, 1925 (Bayreuth Festival Guide)
The 'Wahnfried youngsters' with their guardian Tietjen (Private collection)
Gertrud Reissinger photographed by Wieland (Private collection)
Verena, painted by Wieland (Private collection)
Wolfgang and Wieland in 1938 (Private collection)
Winifred with Adolf Hitler (Private collection)
The Festspielhaus on the Führer's birthday, 1939 (Bernd Mayer Archive)
Friedelind Wagner (Photo © Feldscharek)
Wolfgang and Wieland (Bildarchiv Süddeutscher Verlag, Munich)
Franz Wilhelm Beidler (From *Cosima Wagner-Liszt* by Franz Wilhelm Beidler, Pendragon-Verlag, 1997)
Gertrud and Wieland (Photo: Ernst Gebauer)

vii

Wolfgang and Ellen (Private collection)
Wieland with his children (Photo: Siegfried Lauterwasser)
Wolfgang with his children (Photo: Ernst Gebauer)
The Lafferentz children with their aunt Friedelind, their grandmother Winifred
    and their mother Verena (Photo: Siegfried Lauterwasser)
Wieland with his wife, Gertrud (Photo: Ernst Gebauer)
Wieland with his lover Anja Silja, at a rehearsal for *Lulu* in Stuttgart in 1960
    (Photo: Fritz Peyer, Hamburg)
Act III of *Siegfried* in Wieland's production, 1952–59 (Photo: Siegfried
    Lauterwasser)
Act III of *Siegfried* in Wolfgang's production, 1960–64 (Photo: Wilhelm Rauh)
Eva Wagner (Photo: Thomas Doorn)
Katharina Wagner (Photo: *BUNTE*)
Eva and her daughter, Antoine (Photo: Klaus Tritschel, Bayreuth)
Wieland Lafferentz and Verena (Photo: Sulzer, Salzburg)
Nike and her daughter, Louise (Photo: Klaus Tritschel, Bayreuth)
Wolf Siegfried Wagner, in 1982 (Private collection)
Gottfried Wagner, in 1997 (Photo: Zoller)
Wolfgang Wagner (Photo: Jean Loup Debionne for *BUNTE*)
Gudrun Wagner, in 1997 (Photo: Manfred Otzelberger, Bayreuth)
Daphne Wagner, part of the new generation at Bayreuth (Photo: Emil Perauer,
    Munich)

ACKNOWLEDGEMENTS

My German is very difficult to translate. So first, and with the utmost appreciation, I would like to thank those who spared no pains to render my 'typically German' (or perhaps 'terribly German') text into English. The work of Ewald Osers provided the basis for this translation. Most of all, however, I would like to thank Dr Michael Downes, who devoted himself to the book in an unusually knowledgeable, patient, and meticulous manner. His work was far more than translation, involving as it did total comprehension of the material, in order to reshape it for this updated English edition. As the author, I am particularly indebted and especially grateful to him.

The ladies at Weidenfeld and Nicolson, publishing director Rebecca Wilson and assistant editor Catherine Hill, have been wonderfully helpful. I would like to thank both of them for their energy and understanding – knowing as I do the difficulties of working with foreign authors!

I leave mention of my friend George, Lord Weidenfeld, until last, but it will be clear from the preface how closely he is involved with the genesis of this book. We are linked by the city of Vienna, and have met time and again at the Bayreuth Festival. I thank him with all my heart for his confidence in me, which enabled me to keep the project of this book in my mind over the years, and at last to see it bound between two covers in reality.

FOREWORD

Richard Wagner and his now numerous descendants obstinately remain news, in a way that is not true of any other artist and family. The music-dramas for which he is above all remembered are perhaps more popular than they ever were, even though singers capable of doing justice to the chief roles in his mature works are rarer than they have ever been – a situation which means that every opera house is eager to mount Wagner's works, but finds it almost impossible to do so. Meanwhile the context of those dramas, the intentions of their creator and the climate of opinion in which they were written, is the subject of intense critical and scholarly or pseudo-scholarly debate. That is in large part due to the two indisputable facts that Wagner was anti-Semitic, and that Hitler passionately admired his work, though not at all because of Wagner's personal views, or because he thought that the dramas have an anti-Semitic subtext. Nonetheless, many people find it hard, and it seems increasingly so, to ignore the possible connections between Wagner, the man and his work, and Hitler's racial views and policies.

Oddly enough, in the decades following the Second World War this was not the case: there was a huge amount of discussion of Wagner, as there has been since his works were first produced, but very little of it concerned his political views or the political implications of his works. Gradually, however, the extent of the involvement of Wagner's descendants in extreme right-wing politics has become apparent. It was always known that Hitler was a regular attender at the Bayreuth Festival, and that Winifred Wagner, widow of Wagner's son Siegfried and organiser of the Festival after his death in 1930 until the last 'War Festival' in 1944, was a close friend and admirer of the Führer. And it had always been clear that when her two sons Wieland and Wolfgang re-opened the Festival in 1951 it was with the intention of giving it a drastically new, de-politicised look. But it was only later that the degree to which the sons themselves, and many other aspects of life at Bayreuth, were implicated in the Nazi movement, became clear. Perhaps, too, it took longer than people expected for the full horror of what Hitler accomplished to sink in. Whatever the reason, interest in Wagner's supposed influence on the Nazi *Weltanschauung* has gained momentum during the last twenty years, and some commentators on the composer seem to find little else of interest to write about.

At the same time, the Wagner family and its inheritance, always disputatious in a highly public way, has been behaving with lavish dysfunctionality. After the family's second genius Wieland died in 1966 at the age of 49, his younger, adminstratively gifted brother Wolfgang took over as sole director, and has been in charge for 34 years. He is now older than any male Wagner has been before, but still insists on clinging to power, until he can get his way and secure the succession for his second wife Gudrun, whose gifts closely resemble his own. There are numerous opponents, within and outside the family, of this idea, and the author of this brilliant book is one of the leaders of the opposition. She is one of Wieland's children, described by him, she tells us, as 'superfluous', but evidently devoted to many aspects of his work. She received a training in literature and philosophy, and wrote about the Viennese cultural critic (and self-hating Jew) Karl Kraus, under the direction of the great humanist teacher Erich Heller. Nike Wagner is at home in a formidable range of disciplines, very much in a certain German way, and not at all in a characteristic English one; one might compare her range and her intensity with that of Susan Sontag. In this book, which seems to me the most brilliant written about Wagner for several decades, she bites off an enormous amount and contrives to chew it all with grace and wit, while her learning is never in doubt. The first half is devoted to a study of the dramas of Wagner, from *Der fliegende Hollander* to *Parsifal*. She takes for granted a sophistication of approach on the part of the reader which is challenging and exciting, and the reward is a feast of new insights. As, in a fairly broad sense, a Freudian, and one who realises to what a degree her great-grandfather was too, she analyses the dramas as creative explorations of universal tensions within the family. That is not her sole concern, but the relations between parents and children, undeniably a major element in Wagner's plots, take centre stage. What is amazing is the freshness with which this not unfamiliar ground is covered. However much more there is to the works, and Nike Wagner makes no claim to be exhaustive, she establishes Wagner's greatness as a singularly unillusioned and balanced prober of the torments and glories of family life.

The second part of the book is just as fascinating. Nike shows how over and over again certain patterns of relationship have led to conflicts and denunciations, as well as passionate attachments and loyalties. The Wagners have lived out their feelings with a relentlessness and honesty which would almost qualify them for major roles in the founding father's dramas. The happiest period the Wagners have known was that in which the composer himself was alive: he was a wonderful husband and father however much he may have been a troublesome man to the rest of the world. He commanded a devotion which no one in his family was in the least reluctant to give him, because to be a member of that circle was so obviously to be uniquely privileged. After his death disputes of one kind and another broke out, sibling rivalries surfaced, and his widow was unable to maintain the lack of favouritism to her children which was so notable a feature of Wagner as a parent. Nike Wagner traces the often ugly, always riveting and sometimes very moving history from Wagner's death to the present, alluding freely to Wagner's dramas, and without contrivance. She genuinely shows how Wagner's myths arise from history, and how the particular history of his progeny has been an obsessional living out of the myths. She deals with utter candour and unsparingly, but without deluges of recrimination, with the attachments of her family to Hitler. Finally, she puts her cards on the table: she wants to have a part in the succession. Whatever her administrative skills, no reader of her book can doubt that she has an understanding of the dramas which qualifies her for a leading position in an institution where fresh air is desperately needed.

MICHAEL TANNER
Cambridge
October 2000

PREFACE

Many years ago I met Lord Weidenfeld at the Hotel Sacher in Vienna. I was still working on my book about Karl Kraus and the Viennese Modernists at the time. As a publisher, however, what Lord Weidenfeld wanted was a book on the history of Richard Wagner's family: a dynastic history, 'something like the story of the Rothschilds'. I thought it an excellent idea, but I had 'more important' things to do just then, being entirely immersed in the *fin-de-siècle* world of his own former native city of Vienna.

Over the years the Bayreuth material worked away in me – or rather, in my mind the past history of the Wagners kept clashing with the story that was still going on. Old griefs and memories mingled with the events of the present. Historical and intellectual material accumulated and was stored away; it was gradually infiltrated and leavened by new ideas and perceptions. With every visit to the festival in summer, and through the family's constant discussion of itself, of art, politics, and all its neuroses, this material became ever richer, more varied and more extraordinary.

However, the less it resembled the kind of material of which dreams are made – and dreams are always circulating around the family theatre on its green hill – the more heavily it weighed. The passage of time played a part. Everything living grew older, was frozen into rigidity: the family residence of Wahnfried was transformed into a museum, the family inheritance was entrusted to a foundation, and the artistic direction of the festival ground to a halt. Furthermore, the next generation was being thwarted. *Die Walküre*, Act III, Scene 1: an old man bars the way . . .

So what was I to do with the weight of my family history?

Every sense of impotence has its own fruitful dynamic. At first all my energies were channelled into an intellectual preoccupation with the works of Wagner. I wrote my essays; the music I had heard as a child called out for study. But something else still goaded me. Perhaps the family history was a fifth part of the *Ring* cycle, an addition to the tetralogy? It was certainly fantastic enough: first a part of living European cultural history, then suddenly very German, then opening out to the wider world again – always in parallel to the political history of the time, following every fold in its drapery, and at the same time forming new folds of its own.

By indirect routes, I had arrived at the place Lord Weidenfeld had wanted me to reach on that occasion in Vienna. I wrote the family history. It fascinated me as if it really were the story of another dynasty such as the Rothschilds. But it was my own story too, and affected me deeply in its dialectic of near and far, the strange and the intimate. Perhaps, in line with the oldest of educational precepts, one's aim should be to discover what is strange in oneself, and oneself in what is strange. And at the end, it seems to me, that was what I did discover. At this point the narrative leaves the safe ground of observation from a distance, and moves into a very personal confrontation with the present.

NIKE WAGNER
October 2000
Vienna

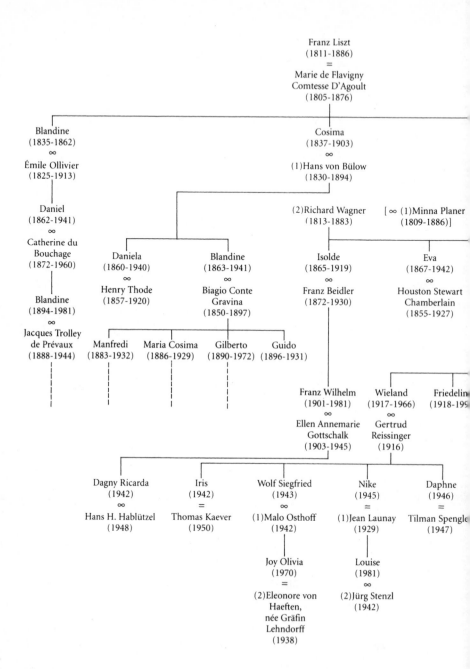

Franz Liszt
(1811-1886)
=
Marie de Flavigny
Comtesse D'Agoult
(1805-1876)

Blandine
(1835-1862)
∞
Émile Ollivier
(1825-1913)

Cosima
(1837-1903)
∞
(1)Hans von Bülow
(1830-1894)

Daniel
(1862-1941)
∞
Catherine du
Bouchage
(1872-1960)

(2)Richard Wagner
(1813-1883)

[∞ (1)Minna Planer
(1809-1886)]

Daniela
(1860-1940)
∞
Henry Thode
(1857-1920)

Blandine
(1863-1941)
∞
Biagio Conte
Gravina
(1850-1897)

Isolde
(1865-1919)
∞
Franz Beidler
(1872-1930)

Eva
(1867-1942)
∞
Houston Stewart
Chamberlain
(1855-1927)

Blandine
(1894-1981)
∞
Jacques Trolley
de Prévaux
(1888-1944)

Manfredi
(1883-1932)

Maria Cosima
(1886-1929)

Gilberto
(1890-1972)

Guido
(1896-1931)

Franz Wilhelm
(1901-1981)
∞
Ellen Annemarie
Gottschalk
(1903-1945)

Wieland
(1917-1966)
∞
Gertrud
Reissinger
(1916)

Friedelin
(1918-199

Dagny Ricarda
(1942)
∞
Hans H. Hablützel
(1948)

Iris
(1942)
=
Thomas Kaever
(1950)

Wolf Siegfried
(1943)
∞
(1)Malo Osthoff
(1942)

Nike
(1945)
=
(1)Jean Launay
(1929)

Daphne
(1946)
=
Tilman Spengle
(1947)

Joy Olivia
(1970)
=
(2)Eleonore von
Haeften,
née Gräfin
Lehndorff
(1938)

Louise
(1981)
∞
(2)Jürg Stenzl
(1942)

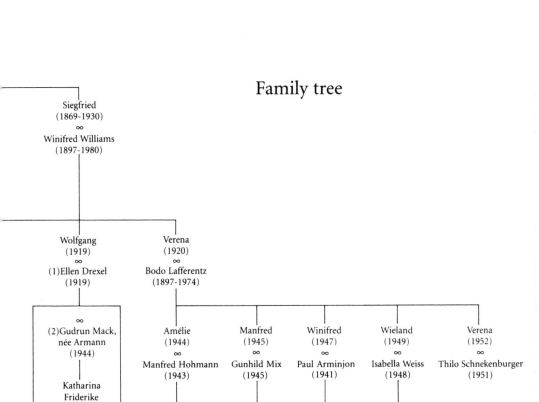

Daniel
(1839-1859)

Family tree

Siegfried
(1869-1930)
∞
Winifred Williams
(1897-1980)

Wolfgang
(1919)
∞
(1)Ellen Drexel
(1919)

Verena
(1920)
∞
Bodo Lafferentz
(1897-1974)

∞
(2)Gudrun Mack,
née Armann
(1944)

Amélie
(1944)
∞
Manfred Hohmann
(1943)

Manfred
(1945)
∞
Gunhild Mix
(1945)

Winifred
(1947)
∞
Paul Arminjon
(1941)

Wieland
(1949)
∞
Isabella Weiss
(1948)

Verena
(1952)
∞
Thilo Schnekenburger
(1951)

Katharina
Friderike
(1978)

Christopher
(1984)

Leif
(1979)

Verena Maja
(1970)

Eva
(1945)
∞
Ives Pasquier
(1950)

Gottfried
(1947)
∞
(1)Beatrix Kraus
(1950)
∞
(2)Teresina Rossetti
(1955)

Wendy
(1973)

Matthias
(1981)

Antoine Amadeus
(1982)

Eugenio
(1985)

INTRODUCTION
Bayreuth and the Wagners

*What is it, you sleek creatures, that glitters and glistens
there?* – Das Rheingold
Alone then glows the Grail . . . – Parsifal

BAYREUTH – THE GEOGRAPHICAL LOCATION – LIES AT A CROSS-
roads: strategically located between Munich and Berlin, Paris and Prague.
Before the two World Wars, it was at the centre of Germany and Europe;
after the partition of Germany, it was relegated to a marginal position,
but it has now been restored to its place at the heart of the reunited federal
Länder. It is a place of history: a former residence of margraves, shaped
into an architectural jewel in the eighteenth century, with a château and
a rococo theatre, a hermitage, fountains and grottoes. It is a place of
literature: its sandstone houses, onion-topped church towers, beer cellars
and delightful hills have been much described, and it inspired both the
Romantic Jean Paul and the anarchist Max Stirner. It is a place of politics,
bearing the scars of its involvement in wider German events. It was badly
bombed in the last war, and has suffered too from the questionable
aesthetics of municipal reconstruction: it now rejoices in the banality of
motorway flyovers and shopping arcades.

Bayreuth – the symbolic location – is the centre of the annual Wagner
festivals, and its Wagner Theatre is a shrine to the art of a single composer.
It is this that has defined the town for the wider public: Bayreuth, to the
world, is synonymous with Wagner. The Festspielhaus, established by

1

Richard Wagner and built to his precise plans, has presided over the town on its famous green hill for over a hundred years. In this building, constructed in the simple style of a factory as a deliberate contrast to the ornate and opulent court opera houses of the period, Wagner's works are performed every summer to an audience from Germany and beyond.

The reason for this exclusive identification of the town with the mission of its summer festival – the perception that Bayreuth 'belongs' to Wagner, more completely, for example, than Salzburg belongs to Mozart – lies in a peculiar interplay of real, historical factors with imaginary, spiritual and mythological ones. This interaction of contradictory forces is similar to that found in Wagner's scores, in which at some points a dynamic plot is linked to music which creates a timeless present, and at others music drives the plot forward when the action is in danger of being lost in reflection. The Wagner–Bayreuth nexus (we can call it Wagner's Bayreuth to distinguish it from the geographical Bayreuth) is formed from a similar integration of contradictions: the antithesis between reality and consciousness, between history and myth, generates a certain dynamism – albeit one that is checked by the eternal recurrence of the same works.

Wagner's Bayreuth is the product of a constant collision between real and unreal elements: between the reality of a festival town in the present and the past, and an image in the collective consciousness. The fusion is not so complete, however, as to make the constituent parts of the phenomenon impossible to analyse. In one sense, for example, the Festspielhaus is nothing more than a festival theatre, a seasonal operatic enterprise with all that that entails: problems of staff and casting, stage sets and lighting designs, union agreements and safety regulations, a box office and computers, often in need of repair. The Festspielhaus is a cultural business. As such, of course, it does not stand in isolation, but has always operated in conjunction with the rest of society, with its rights and powers, its wishes and demands. Even though it took shape rather magically before the composer's eyes, once upon a time, with the unreality of a folly, there still had to be a real king of Bavaria, and behind him a Bavarian state budget, to bring the whim to life. There had to be willing town fathers, private benefactors, associations prepared to undertake the pilgrimage, as well as a circle of propagandists, paladins and pressmen.

2

All this has since changed only insofar as the structures of those political institutions, businesses, and media outlets that surround the Festspielhaus have themselves changed.

The real Bayreuth was and is linked to its context, and to the conditions which that context offers or dictates. It forms part of political history and reality, and of the cultural evolution of the nation. For in Wagner's Bayreuth, culture is defined first and foremost as German: cultural identity is reflected and confirmed through the image of the German nation. This has much to do with the composer's own understanding of himself, even if this self-understanding is not always clear from his operas and writings. Wagner regarded his theatrical revolution as both an allegory of, and a stimulant to the reshaping of German culture as a truly national art.

The continual repetition of Wagner's works, the almost incredible continuity with which they have been staged – from the days of Ludwig II, across two World Wars, to the present – signals the continuity, simultaneously disturbing and reassuring, of a particular strand of German history. This history reveals itself through the quasi-monarchical succession of the festival directorship, with its reigns and regency periods (this interpretation is no more and no less justified than any other attempt to humanise the historical process by emphasising the role of 'kings and queens'). Each new era of festival history brings its own drama and excitement, regicides and usurpations, revolutions and new beginnings. If the story of Bayreuth can indeed be understood as a microcosm of a broader political history, then the defining feature it shares with the outside world is its preoccupation with power – understood both as possession and as the ability to command. This preoccupation is also present, of course, in Wagner's work. Given that *Der Ring des Nibelungen*, that *summum opus* whose very execution demanded its own theatre, is concerned above all with the transfer and exercise of power, the preoccupation may justifiably be labelled as the *Ring*-principle – and the *Ring*-principle may in turn be identified with Wagner's Bayreuth.

The *Ring*-principle plays itself out through contestation and power struggle, both within the family and against various outside forces. Even the core of the Festspielhaus, the stage, has become an arena in which rivalries

3

are fought out, particularly since the late 1930s, when the tendency for directors to try to stamp their own identity on the Wagnerian stage was first established. The stage becomes the arena in which artistic capabilities and reputations are tested. In this way, it assumes a revelatory character, exposing subtleties and deficiencies of character: success or failure there can affect a contender's position in future leadership struggles. The stage is never a purely aesthetic domain: it projects the glittering symbol of the golden ring deep into the structures of political power.

It is not the dominance of the *Ring*-principle alone, however, that causes Bayreuth to be identified as 'belonging' to Wagner; after all, every opera house, every political party, every sizeable business experiences similar power struggles. There is another aspect of the Ring whose presence is exclusive to Bayreuth, however: this is the mythical dimension, one which has been observed and described on numerous occasions. Emblematic representations of the Festspielhaus, particularly those dating from the beginning of the twentieth century, often show a mysterious light emanating from behind the theatre, surrounding it with a kind of halo: the house is literally radiant. Light, however, can have different iconographic meanings, and the light here is not the result of the sun of Enlightenment having been cast on the house; rather, it is an indicator of the mystical significance of the building. This is proved not only by the writings of Wagner's followers, who had always preferred a religious model of theatre to an intellectual and critical one; it is demonstrated also by the arguments of Wagner himself, who had always conceived of his theatre as a place where the renewal myth would be fulfilled, as a German equivalent of Delphi.

In contrast to the archetypal 'village church', situated in the middle of a community and therefore likely to engender a sense of the community belonging to its people, Wagner's theatre towers high above the town, framed by a dark pine forest, a sacred grove. The arrangement of the auditorium as an amphitheatre recalls the theatres of antiquity. The audience is squeezed together – imprisoned, almost, in mind and body – and drawn in to the total work of art, forced to surrender to what is happening on stage. The lowering of the orchestra pit turns the orchestra into a mysterious oracle, in line with Wagner's intention to create a 'Dionysian' effect (as correctly analysed by Nietzsche). The sound swells up in the

4

dark, seemingly without origin, so that the music seems to be a hallucinatory figment of the imagination; the simple timber structure is thus transformed into a theatre of orgiastic ritual. The mythical quality of the experience is further enhanced by Wagner's choice of subject matter – heroes and knights, gods, swans and dragons – which leads the imaginations of his audience back towards half-remembered legends.

Wagner's Bayreuth could not exist without this superstructure: the mythical Bayreuth is a constant companion to the real Bayreuth, anchoring it against the buffeting of struggles and upheaval. This quality of timelessness is symbolised by the Holy Grail, an image drawn from the Christian–Germanic myth that was Wagner's principal source. The Grail encapsulates all that is magical and sacred about Bayreuth; as in *Parsifal*, it is radiant, illuminating the entire community. Its radiance has a quite different quality to the seductive 'glitter' of its temporal counterpart, the Ring, since that brings disaster to whoever wears it. We can therefore identify a Grail-principle which stands alongside and opposite the *Ring*-principle; it is the interaction of the two principles that created and creates Wagner's Bayreuth.

The Grail-principle seeks to safeguard whatever is timeless, constant, mysterious. It was most strikingly personified in Wagner's life by his desire to use Bayreuth to lend a timeless, cultish character to his own work, an aim pursued most elaborately in relation to *Parsifal* itself, that 'farewell to the world' intended to be performed exclusively at his own theatre. This intention had repercussions beyond his own lifetime. The story of the 'Lex *Parsifal*' (Cosima Wagner's attempt to persuade the Reichstag to prohibit performances of the piece outside Bayreuth) and the Wagner family's use of the term '*Parsifal* theft' to describe the performances that took place in Amsterdam and New York before the expiry of the thirty-year copyright period are good illustrations of the interaction of the Grail-principle with the dynamic forces of progress, the collision of myth and history. It is a moot point whether we should condemn the act of abduction as an attack on the Holy Grail, or, in a more enlightened mood, welcome it as the demystification of the archaic in favour of progress, emancipation and democracy.

Wagner's Bayreuth was constructed from the combination of various elements of Wagner's work with physical characteristics of the Festspielhaus itself: the acoustic consequences of its architecture and its remote, elitist location. However, there is another important element that has allowed the Bayreuth myth to endure even in the most secular of times: this is Wahnfried, the Wagner family's private residence, symbolically situated in the centre of Bayreuth. This classical villa, adjoining the gardens of the margraves' palace, was a personal gift from King Ludwig; after Richard Wagner's death his widow Cosima lived there, and with her and after her, Wagner's children, grandchildren and great-grandchildren. Real as this villa was with its promising name,* its mythical significance was still greater. The inhabitant of Wahnfried was also the director of the festival: Wahnfried therefore came to symbolise the domestic history of the festival. Leaders were bred here, family alliances forged and enmities fomented; it was the home of that theatrical family whose family life was itself compelling theatre.

At one level, of course, Wahnfried is a physical inheritance, a town house with garden and outbuildings, and the *Ring*-principle operates at this level, too. However, it owes its mythical status to the unusual circumstances under which it is bequeathed: it is not just a legacy to be administered, but also a spiritual inheritance, a commitment that must be nurtured and passed on from generation to generation. The family guards an archive of European significance, and is obliged by the provisions of a legacy to 'ensure the festive performance of the works of Richard Wagner'. Admittedly, the text of this stipulation is found in the will of Siegfried Wagner, not Richard: there is no last will and testament in Richard's hand, and Siegfried himself had merely been charged by his father to preserve the legacy in an 'ethical [and] moral' manner. As he was only fourteen when his father died, his mother Cosima initially assumed the Bayreuth regency. On Siegfried's death his English widow Winifred would inherit both the Festspielhaus and Wahnfried. She in turn would be succeeded by their children, and so the pattern has continued.

Every family with an awareness of its own ancestry constructs its own saga. Precedents may be found in the impressive genealogical tables in the Bible, and royal and imperial houses have always sought to legitimise

---

*A literal translation of Wahnfried is 'peace from illusion'.

their authority by demonstrating the longevity and purity of their blood-line. The bourgeoisie rushed to emulate these examples, gaining a sudden interest in their family tree as soon as it became distinguished by property, or, as in this case, by artistic achievement. In most cases, the beginning of a dynasty is marked by a clear act of foundation, establishing a purpose within the family and a claim towards the outside world. In this case, that act was the laying of the foundation stone of the Festspielhaus, the moment at which the Wagners' history became clearly distinct from that of other composers' families. Ownership and operation of a festival theatre sent the family's prestige soaring, and bestowed a certain aura of spiritual superiority upon them.

Although they were not endowed with castles and coronets, only with debits and credits, the Wagners became likened to royalty in the public imagination, and various versions of their family saga were disseminated. Their actual history was so coloured by hearsay that reality became fairy tale, an archetypal nineteenth-century myth. Many elements of their story conspired to make it seem more like fantasy than reality: the presence of a king walking alongside the artist; the fact that the king was young, handsome and romantic and that the artist was a social revolutionary, refugee, émigré and notorious debtor; the fact, moreover, that there was a 'princess' in the shape of the slender Cosima, the product of a romantically illicit union between the most celebrated virtuoso and composer of his day, Franz Liszt, and a beautiful French countess. If we look closer to our own time, we find further elements of fairy tale in the Wagners' story. Siegfried, the son, married a destitute English orphan who, even as a schoolgirl, had yearningly drawn his profile in her exercise-books, like Cinderella with her Prince Charming. This couple was blessed with numerous children, among whom were the two brothers who, after war and destruction, saved the honour of the house. And the fairy-tale has not released us from its power, even today. After the tragically early death of the older brother, the younger set himself on the Festspielhaus throne to begin a reign whose length has reached supernatural proportions. And there he remains, the King Lear of the green hill.

Through the archives, as though through a trap-door, we enter the deepest vaults of this family fortress, the engine-room of the legend. We are forcibly reminded of the image of the Grail, which has to be unveiled by the heirs so that the old man, Richard Wagner, can live. The Grail must be made to radiate again and again so that fresh blood is pumped into the veins of his work. The lives of the executors, too, seem to depend on this ritual of unveiling and display, as though the fable told by *Parsifal* has been turned back on the family, shaping their lives and dictating their actions. Wagner's Bayreuth contains a rite for the family: a rite that must be repeated as a talisman against time and history. He who resides at Wahnfried must continually uncover the festival Grail: only in this way can the essence of the myth be preserved.

This account of Wahnfried emphasises the elements of continuity and stasis, but the house has also always witnessed the contradictory impulses of change, restlessness and movement. The laws of nature dictate that a family will tend towards diversification, development, division, a process from which younger members will emerge to challenge their elders. Thus the Grail-principle is challenged by its opposite pole, by elements of conflict and disagreement: the *Ring*-principle mercilessly intervenes whenever problems of inheritance and succession arise.

One such instance arose when Cosima sought to question the Wagnerian paternity of one of her daughters, Isolde, falsely claiming that her first husband, Hans von Bülow, was Isolde's father. There was considerable anxiety at Wahnfried that Isolde – given that name because she was born at the time of the Munich première of *Tristan*, when Cosima and Richard were still living together illicitly – would bring in her husband, the conductor Franz Beidler, as a potential heir to the Bayreuth throne. Cosima would not tolerate the presence of any rival to her son, Siegfried, so she claimed that Isolde had no Wagnerian blood in order to deny her any leverage with which to realise her family's ambitions.

This scandalous denial of entirely legitimate claims recalls the numerous thefts that take place in *The Ring*. The motif was to recur in the next generation of family history. The son of Isolde and Franz Beidler, Franz Wilhelm became a lawyer and writer, resident in Switzerland. After the Second World War, during which the residents of Wahnfried were seriously incriminated by their friendship with Adolf Hitler, Beidler proposed a complete reorganisation of the festivals under the direction of an international committee of respected writers, musicians and intellectuals.

Skilful intrigue by the Wagner brothers, Wieland and Wolfgang, ensured that he was marginalised and that his proposal was not even discussed. The brothers treated their sister Friedelind in a similar way: as the only member of the family to oppose the Nazis and to go into exile, she would have been the ideal candidate to reconstruct the festival – a genuine Wagner, yet untainted. But anyone who has grasped possession of the festival Ring does not relinquish it voluntarily. Wolfgang Wagner, the grandson, has guarded it since 1951, initially together with his brother, but since 1966 on his own. He has presided as Intendant for far longer than is sensible or desirable, and has placed a strain upon the tradition by disregarding the wishes and rights of younger members of the family. Intrigue has joined with obduracy to break, at least temporarily, the unwritten contract between the generations.

Historical conflicts such as these reveal the innate ambivalence of the opposing forces: the tensions that exist within, as well as between, the stasis of myth and the dynamism of history. Where the Grail-principle dominates for too long, a shadow is cast: ritual can become routine, repetition is in danger of stagnating into a celebration of the *status quo*. This is what happened in the period following Wagner's death, when Cosima was the guardian of the Grail. In the context of the mausoleum, where a weakened Grail-principle is sacrosanct, the morally questionable *Ring-* and robbery-principle reveals its necessity as a safeguard against bad myth; through death, it is a font of new life.

The two principles thus reveal their vital relationship with each other, perhaps even their interdependence. The similarities and the differences between them are present in their visual manifestations: they both contain the geometrical figure of the circle, but their differences are revealed when they are viewed in three dimensions. The circle of the Grail has depth and volume: it is a source of plenitude, of sustenance. The circle of the Ring, by contrast, appears as a narrow ridge: metaphorically, it can be linked to a mountain pass or a racetrack. Both these symbols may involve deception of the senses: the depth of the Grail may be a chimera, like that of the skies, while the circular track of the Ring creates an expectation of progress that may prove to be illusory. Nonetheless, Wagner's creation of the redeeming image of the Grail, after the orgy of destruction at the end of *The Ring*, is seen by many musical philosophers as the composer's last word – the victory of 'radiance' over 'glitter'. The fact that the two symbols have the circle in common demonstrates the interconnectedness of the composer's works, and his hope that his art would represent not the end of the world but its continuation.

The symbol of the circle is present everywhere in Wagner's Bayreuth: roundness is found as much in the topography of the festival landscape as in the spiritual dimension. The layout of the Wahnfried garden is circular; the view from the central room is of a circular fountain surrounded by a circular lawn. The avenue leading to the Festspielhaus describes an arc. Circles dominate the stage, too. With the benefit of hindsight, we can see that Wieland Wagner's 'New Bayreuth' stage space, perceived as revolutionary at the time, was in fact rooted in tradition: the magic circle became the archetypal idea underlying his production of the *Ring*, and, to an even greater extent, of *Parsifal*. The circle was also an important image for the followers of Wagner: the 'Bayreuth Circle', active in Wagner's lifetime as propagandists of his work, developed an ideology of cultish, nationalistic philistinism after the composer's death – their very name reveals their intellectual isolation. Their present-day successors, the 'Association of Friends of Bayreuth', identify themselves to one another by a small golden ring on their lapels, jocularly referred to as the 'Golden Sphincter'.

Wagner's dramas, together with the Festspielhaus, constitute a system which seeks to safeguard the timelessness of its own mythology; this state of affairs is merely reinforced by the annual repetitions of the festival and the associated cult of Wagner, now fanned by the international media. The driving force of the system, however, is provided by the family, by the Wahnfried idea: the family's activities are founded on their identification with their cultural heritage and their striving, following Goethe's injunction, to inhabit their inheritance, to realise it within themselves and make it radiant. However, these two complexes of ideas – we may refer to them in shorthand as the Festspielhaus and Wahnfried – never quite escape their own historicism; nor do they escape each other. In their ambivalence and their dialectical integration of the Grail-and *Ring*-principles, the theatre and the home, Wagner's Bayreuth and the family substance, are congruent with each other. The theatre of the

Wagners and Wagner's theatre are twin aspects of a single entity.

It is no accident, therefore, that the family will feature heavily in the following chapters, even those that focus on Wagner's works. The family dramas are inseparable from the music dramas. As if the subterranean power of the family had guided the author's pen, the essays increasingly drift from the objective and aesthetic into the subjective and private, until they culminate in an account of family history. The more musicological essays on Wagner's works, too, reflect family history, in that they record staging posts in the author's intellectual biography. They could not have been unaffected by father, mother or brother, by the ceaseless flow of family conversation – approving, ironic or mocking – that accompanied individual interpretations and reinterpretations of Wagner's theatre.

The author's participation in various dance groups between 1963 and 1965 furnished her with a sensual attachment to *Tannhäuser*, *Die Meistersinger* and *Parsifal*: the euphoric sense of scenic space which that experience provoked, normally the prerogative of old hands, has inspired her subsequent involvement with these works. Beginning in the 'New Bayreuth' of her father, Wieland, whose post-war spirit and imagery moulded her childhood and youth, an educational journey through the world – taking in musical and intellectual-Jewish America, philosophical circles in France and finally literary Austria – gave rise to new and different views on Wagner. These outside perspectives helped her to decode her own milieu and to shed some of her intellectual naivety. However, it also helped her to become more conscious of her happy childhood in the artistic environment of Wahnfried. The author's changing opinions and impressions of Wagner have acquired something of the quality of geological strata in her mind: the lower strata are hidden, but not destroyed, and a moment from the past often reappears suddenly to illuminate a preoccupation of the present.

Many of the essays on individual works reflect a personal or family involvement in a particular production, and some details on this autobiographical background may be useful. The author's brother, Wolf Siegfried, made an exciting reassessment of the values in *The Flying Dutchman* in a production of 1978, a time when even the most Romantic of operas were being exposed to a down-to-earth historical reading. Wieland nearly broke his teeth on the *Tannhäuser* problem, rather like the composer himself, who was unable to resolve the discrepancies within this work. The author's reflections on *Lohengrin* are more concerned with the general background of this opera, representing as it does a transition from French and German Romanticism to genuine Wagnerian music drama. In the background, however, are two experiences connected with the family: Wieland's unforgettable 1958 production in Bayreuth, notable for the beauty of its blue and silver sets, faithfully painted by the director's thirteen-year-old daughter, and Gottfried Wagner's 1996 production in Dessau, which endeavoured to demonstrate that the 'Hitler inside Wagner' was already present by the time of *Lohengrin*.

Der Ring des Nibelungen particularly interested the author because of the way in which a huge family psychodrama was hidden beneath the cloak of German mythology. It is scarcely necessary to spell out the innumerable resonances between this drama and the action played out in the family theatre; members of the family frequently identify themselves with characters from *The Ring*, and gain an understanding of their own conflicting emotions from the family struggles depicted there. As for *Tristan*, a revealing essay by Wieland, written in response to his own Bayreuth production of 1962, forms the background to the thoughts on the work presented here. Not only was that production one of his most successful, his essay on it is a remarkable document of suffering, written at a late stage of his terminal disease in the Munich clinic to which he had been moved in July 1966. The character of Tristan here provided the opportunity for Wagner's grandson to explore his own melancholy and depression. There are many inner threads between this slow death, this text and the 'twice-solitary death' contemplated here; the more recent stimulus for this essay was the 1992 production by Wolf Siegfried, Wieland's son and the present author's brother.

The subterranean interweaving of the works of Wagner with the history of the family is particularly relevant to *Die Meistersinger*. Wieland's post-war productions of *Die Meistersinger* represent stages in the growth of an awareness of the truth about Hitler's Germany, revealing how the first vague feelings of guilt were articulated: though rarely put into words, they were reflected in the images of the production. Wieland spoke out aggressively on the subject of the corrupted German Richard Wagner (but did he really know what he was saying?): 'Ever since 1945, the festival management, and the town of Bayreuth, have endeavoured to let this subject, fatal to the Bayreuth Festival, be forgotten.' The era of National Socialism was then too close to Wieland's still-young generation for the full extent of its horror to register. The fact that an event only begins to strike home after a lapse of time is an as yet unexplained paradox of 'coping with the past'. Though the present author's work is not directly connected with the persistent suspicion of anti-Semitism that has surrounded *Die Meistersinger* since 1945, it explores matters such as folly and wit in relation to the linguistic and psychological mechanisms of humour. An examination of the pleasure arising from 'wicked wit', from *Schadenfreude*, readily reveals analogies with the political sphere. The German word for folly – *Wahn* – frequently appears in Wagner's vocabulary, flickering between artistic and more questionable connotations. Despite the secure social structures shown in *Die Meistersinger*, this folly can at any time flip over into madness and chaos. Violence cannot be accurately defined or predicted. Hans Sachs' question – 'How in God's name did that come about?' – all too often applies to our world too, though we only ask it when it is too late.

How it came about that the Jewish Vienna of the turn of the century became the centre of the author's literary research, and her spiritual home too, is another question that is not easy to answer: it is a milieu far removed from Wahnfried. Admittedly, a thread does lead back to Wahnfried: Vienna at this time was the home not only of Karl Kraus, Sigmund Freud, Arthur Schnitzler and Hugo von Hofmannsthal, but also of Adolf Hitler. This fact may illuminate the attempt to understand the unfortunate connection between Richard Wagner's anti-Semitism and the anti-Semitism of the cultured Jewish bourgeoisie. *Parsifal* and the phantasm of purity, translated into a private theology, provide an opportunity for reflecting on this paradoxical historical delusion. *Parsifal* is a personification of family tradition, but it is not an end. Traditions must at some stage be broken, and *Parsifal* will one day be seen in a new light, as the demands for progress dictate. Although the 'family spirit' has prevailed so far, even against the anti-traditionalism of Wieland Wagner, future interpretations of *Parsifal* must inevitably be coloured by life outside Bayreuth.

The second part of the book directly explores the family's history. First of all, there are two brief essays focusing on particular family members: Wieland and his mother, Winifred. There is good reason to single out these particular Wagners, even though both feature prominently in the general family history that follows: their attitudes and the opposition between them could be said to have defined 'Bayreuth' for the outside world in the decades following the war. Wieland Wagner's life at this time consisted of various attempts to escape from the family fortress: the stages of this journey are explored in the chapter on his 'negative life', with a little help from Hegel. The essay on Winifred attempts to understand the true nature of her relationship with Adolf Hitler, despite the fact that 'truth' is a strangely elusive concept where this particular woman is concerned.

The final seven chapters of the book aim to tell the history of the Wagner family in more or less chronological terms – although as the reader will note, chronology is forever disrupted by striking recurrences of themes and patterns of relationships between different generations, recurrences which it is the chronicler's duty to explore. Despite the violent upheavals recounted in this history, the family currently presents a strangely tomb-like aspect to the public: the phrase 'Wahnfriedhof' may be used to describe this phenomenon.* Since the conversion of the Festspielhaus into a public enterprise, supervised by a foundation, Wahnfried has become a museum. No member of the family has lived there for a long time. The present festival director, Wolfgang Wagner, lives in a private house in Bayreuth; the rest of Wagner's descendants are scattered throughout Germany, Europe and beyond. The *Ring*-principle seems to have had the final word: the twilight of the gods has descended. Although the Grail on the green hill is still regularly unveiled, its lustre has faded; it now has only the dim glow of the perpetual candle flame in the church. There are signs, though, that the story is about to enter a new phase, and the book ends with a brief consideration of some of the ways in which Bayreuth may begin to look forward again, after the long sleep of the Wolfgang era.

*In the original German edition, the title of the section of the book dealing with the family's history is WAHN/FRIED/HOF. It is impossible to make an effective English translation of this pun: Nike Wagner's invented word compresses numerous meanings of which 'Wahnfried' (the Wagner family home) and 'Friedhof' (the German for cemetery) are only the most obvious.

PART ONE

Wagner's Theatre

1

Wandering Jew or Exploiter? – thoughts on the *Dutchman*

THE FLYING DUTCHMAN IS NOT A SPECTRE, NOR SATAN, NOR
Ulysses – nor is he Ahasuerus, the Wandering Jew of the ocean. Why then
is he perceived in these abstract, mythological terms, both by Wagner and
by the other characters in his opera? What is the real significance of this
mysterious figure?

The sources of inspiration for *The Flying Dutchman* are well known.
In 1838, while he was still living in Riga, Wagner encountered both the
old legend of the ghost ship, and Heinrich Heine's treatment of the same
subject. The composer and the poet met a year later, when both were in
exile in Paris; with Heine's approval, Wagner went on to produce his
libretto. There is one major difference, though, between Heine and
Wagner: the poet ironically suggested that the Dutchman was saved *from*
a woman, while the composer – prefiguring the preoccupations of his
later works – presented a story of redemption *by* a woman.

The most interesting feature of Wagner's version is the angle from
which we see this so-called redemption of a guilty man: everything is seen
from the viewpoint of Senta, the woman who sacrifices herself. Everything
is filtered through her psyche, and the centre of the piece is her ballad, in
which the legend is told. The ballad symbolically binds together the whole
of time: the past is retold, the present is enacted, and hopes for the future
are expressed. Mysterious images from the Dutchman's tale – the blood-
red sail, the black mast and the pale suffering face – are summoned from

an apparently primeval age into Senta's home, where she and the other girls are at their spinning wheels. Despite the legendary, timeless character of this presentation, Wagner actually states that the Dutchman comes from the 'historical period of the voyages of discovery'. Heine is still more precise: he writes of a captain dressed in a Spanish-Dutch style, a buccaneering Mijnheer of the period of William of Orange. The historical period of the odysseys that are described is at least a century before the period in which the stories are actually told in the house of Daland, Senta's father. And on this period is superimposed the early nineteenth century, the period in which Heine and Wagner were working. The opera therefore interweaves three quite distinct historical periods. They have one thing in common, however: as Wagner put it after the event, in his 1851 'Communication to my Friends', each represents 'a break with an old world'.

The figure of the Dutchman, as described in Senta's ballad, dates from between the late-sixteenth and the mid-seventeenth centuries, the period in which the Low Countries were struggling for independence against Spain, and were themselves becoming Europe's principal trading nation. This period also witnessed the shift of trade from the Mediterranean to the great oceans, as well as the conquest of overseas territories: Ceylon, Java and the Cape Colonies. The new ways of life that resulted from these developments had a gradual but significant impact on the collective consciousness. The strange experiences of the seafarer were subsequently stylised to such an extent that the sailor became an archetype of existential suffering; this image particularly appealed to the romantic generation.

Another important cultural effect of colonisation was that events, in those distant parts of the world that had just been discovered, became converted into myths: this was the only way for those back at home to make sense of what could not otherwise be comprehended. How else could the inhabitants of isolated villages and coastal settlements under-stand the new opportunities of mastering and exploiting nature that the exotic colonies offered? Amazement at the fabulous treasure imported was accompanied by fear of the sea, and of the perils of venturing into the unknown. This is how stories of ships' kobolds, sea monsters, devil's curses and superhuman sea captains arose. These myths often had a particular fascination for the feminine psyche, because women were generally prevented from experiencing adventures at sea for themselves. This is why Othello held such a powerful fascination for Desdemona – 'she loved me for the dangers I had passed'. Similarly, in Heine's poem, the Dutchman scarcely needs to tell the girl of his 'most unheard-of suffering' on the 'immeasurable watery waste'. She had already read his sufferings in his face, and had so identified herself with them that she was ready to sacrifice her own life for him.

The personification of such projection and identification that Wagner gives us, in the form of an eighteenth-century sea merchant's daughter, is by no means hysterical, let alone schizophrenic. This is not only because to present such a clear-cut 'case study' would be artistically unsatisfactory. It is also because Wagner himself understands Senta as an ordinary woman in extraordinary circumstances: he describes her as a 'robust Nordic girl', whose 'vigorous madness' erupts only as a consequence of her total naivety. The composer's comments do not close the argument, however – the debate about Senta's psychological state remains open. Some features of her behaviour seem to invite the conclusion that she is 'disturbed': her enhanced empathy, her access to the alternative reality of the imagination, so anxiously suppressed by those around her, and the way in which she encourages her subconscious wishes to emerge into the open. Seen in another light, though, her words and actions may be understood as those of a typical young girl, who dreams of an exceptional man who will liberate her from the dull, predetermined life of her parental home, and from the stifling prospect of marriage to the honest but conventional Erik. The fact that her chosen lover is not a Prince Charming, but an embittered nihilist, reflects the cultural taboo on female erotic fixation: it must not be expressed directly, but it can be disguised as the Christian virtue of pity, if a suitably pitiable object is chosen. Alternatively, her choice can be seen as symptomatic of the period's taste for taciturn, brooding, violent heroes – think of Heathcliff, created only four years later.

If the morality of the stolid, patriarchal Daland was such that he found no problem in handing over his own daughter to a stranger in exchange for merchandise and money, then Senta's hopes of escape and fantasies of a better and more exciting life can also be understood as a reaction against her pragmatic, mercantile family. We must not be misled by the fact that she sits and dreams at her spinning wheel, apparently imprisoned as a daughter and a woman: this is no Penelope, not even for Wagner. The outward appearance of passivity – of a woman who is just waiting for her man – is a façade. In reality, she is very active, although most of the activity is conducted under the surface: she withdraws her affections from the wrong suitor, she follows her dream of a man, she identifies the reality when it appears, she fatally pledges him her loyalty.

But the interest of Senta's character is not solely psychological. She is also motivated by political and ethical concern: she embodies that Christian sense of justice which is uneasy at the brutal subjugation of other countries. This view of events really reflects the preoccupations of Wagner's own century: although reservations about the negative effects of colonialism were undoubtedly felt during the period in which the opera's events take place, they were not fully articulated until later. Senta's concerns are revealed in the imagery of the libretto: the prevalence of the colours black and red in her description of the ship of the dead, for example, are a visual index of her horrified reaction. A similarly apocalyptic view is present in Heine's description of the first steamships: 'They carry a dark fire in their chests and they sail against wind and weather. Their plume of smoke flutters like the black panache of the nocturnal horseman, their paddle-wheels are like huge circular spurs dug into the sea's wavy ribs, and the refractory foaming element has to obey their will like a horse – but very often the boiler bursts and the inner fire sears us.'

The attribution of monstrous, bestial characteristics to a machine was a common rhetorical strategy during the age of Heine and Wagner, reflecting a deep-seated alienation from the supposed benefits of technical progress. The period is characterised by the conflict between the economic drive of the industrial revolution, and the romantic opposition to its achievements. As the hold of atheism and rationalism became stronger, the arts reacted by staking out a domain where the irrational and the supernatural held sway: for example, the popular operas of this time – Fouqué and Weber, Marschner and Meyerbeer – are full of demons, naiads, witches, devils and vampires. The dramatic reappearance of these creatures is surely an expression of the century's fear of progress; new terrors are converted into an ancient, familiar, and often natural form, in order that the threat they represent can be conquered, and mankind reassured. Senta's visions, likewise, manifest the regressive, mystifying tendencies of the psyche in the face of industrial and technological upheaval. A similarly cataclysmic upheaval – from medieval to modern – is in fact contained within the legend of the Dutchman, and it was this that made it such an appropriate vehicle for the expression of contemporary fears. It offered the young Wagner the chance both to articulate his own historical position, and to conceal it.

Such reflections can provide the creative spark for a production, as Wolf Siegfried Wagner, the son of Wieland Wagner, and Wolf Münzner, Wieland's former assistant in Bayreuth, realised in 1978. In order to make the separate – but connected – levels of the narrative more apparent, they set the *Dutchman* in the period during which it was written and composed.

The Dutchman, in this production, was a cynical exploiter of distant colonies. This meant that his 'curse' was real, not metaphysical; it was the curse of loneliness, of remoteness from all human company during weeks and months at sea. The production demonstrated that the abstract ideas of the libretto – the immensity of time, space, and treasure, hinted at by Daland – had parallels in the real world: the oceans, the transatlantic possessions of the Netherlands, and their human and material resources. The Dutchman's homelessness and alienation were genuine, but they were the product of early capitalism, not of some mythical burden. His longing for the security offered by a woman's devotion was also genuine, but what this hard-nosed sailor sought, like so many of Wagner's male characters, was not love – and hence not *this* woman in particular – but his own personal salvation. Hidden behind this vague concept was a death-wish, all the more justified because death was his only means of escaping his self-alienating, modern existence. He vacillated between the satanic forces that drew him forward to discoveries and conquests, and the suffering that resulted from this inclination; he was neither wholly alive nor wholly dead. Expelled by the people to whom he became a stranger, he projected his misanthropic disgust even on to the means of his own success – the sea. The magical sequence of seven years, during which he was permitted to come ashore in order to 'work on his redemption' (as Heine put it), stood for his stubborn yet hopeless attempts to reintegrate himself into a lifestyle that had long since ceased to suit him.

He blamed his inevitable disappointment on the faithlessness of women: a truly fairy-tale reading of the situation. His end was consistent with his life – not very metaphysical. Instead of a heroic death and transfiguration, this production suggested a kind of accident; he became entangled in the ropes of his own ship, trapped in his own nets, and his slaves seized the opportunity for mutiny and cast him overboard.

And what of Senta? Wolf Siegfried's production placed her in exactly the same position at the end as she had been at the beginning. This simple image movingly suggested the timelessness of her psychological situation, identifying her as a typical young girl who had denied reality and lost herself in a dream of a mysterious, irresistible destiny. To a mind that is in this state, any object can become fabulous, as long as it provides sufficient nourishment for the imagination – whether by an adventurous past, an exotic exterior, or a hint of mysterious suffering, heroism or martyrdom. All of these the Dutchman of course provides, even if he himself is unworthy of the devotion she bestows upon him. But Senta's desire to experience the extraordinary, the absolute, also reveals her deeper need for liberation The symbol of this liberation, imbued with erotic associations, is the sea. In the prophetic dream which Erik dreams for Senta and holds up to her as a mirror of her own desires, she escapes with the 'pale man' out to sea, to freedom and death, because such desires are boundless.

In this production, the standard interpretations of Senta and the Dutchman seemed to have been entirely reversed. Traditional productions always emphasise the mystical timelessness of the Dutchman – but here he was pinned down, fixed to a particular time and place. Senta, on the other hand, is conventionally treated more realistically: direction and design often emphasise her bourgeois Norwegian origins. But here she is delocalised and raised into a symbol of longing, rebellion and self-realisation. Had not the director's great-grandfather described her as the 'woman of the future'? The future of the young revolutionary composer was also focused on freedom: he too followed his 'demon', the call of the wild, both in art and politics. Like Senta, he had a 'longing ... not for the old and familiar, for something to be regained, but for something new, surmised and desired, something unknown ...'

2

'Without any comfortable intermediate stage' – *Tannhäuser*

THERE IS A WELL-KNOWN ANECDOTE ABOUT THE FAMOUS Wagnerian conductor, Hans Knappertsbusch. He was famous for his dislike of rehearsals, and would often step on to the podium with the words: 'Gentlemen, you know the piece, I know the piece. So let's start.'

We all know *Tannhäuser*: those highlights, those barely Wagnerian remnants of old operatic numbers – arias, ensembles, even a finale complete with cabaletta. The Pilgrims' Chorus, the entry of the guests, Elisabeth's aria, the Song to Venus, the 'virgin's prayer' – we know them only too well, we love them, we hum along to them, albeit with a certain uneasiness. The situation of a man who cannot decide between two women – Elisabeth and Venus – is somewhat hackneyed. The central character is a staple of the romantic novel: the handsome hero who will not forego anything, who wants both sex and purity, adventure and security, an erotically exciting partner and a legitimate partner from his own class. Wagner covers this familiar figure and his romantic triangle with layers of pseudo-medieval, quasi-Christian wrapping, to create a confection of dubious historical and stylistic consistency. Though Cosima dutifully recorded that '*Tannhäuser* is as sacred to us as *Parsifal*', it is questionable whether we would be interested in this work at all, were it not for its electrifying music.

A work of art is regarded as such because, in spite of all its clichés, it retains a dimension that makes it mysterious once more – as if it possessed some inner inexhaustibility which asks to be probed again and again, and which astonishes us each time we investigate further. Sometimes this inexhaustibility lies in the perfection of artistic means, as in *Tristan*. On other occasions, interest resides in the very imperfections of a work, in a sense of inward or outward incompleteness, in unresolved tensions in the plot or music. This is certainly the case with *Tannhäuser*, to an extent that is unusual with the craftsmanlike Wagner, whom Thomas Mann rightly admired as an 'accomplisher'. Strictly speaking, *Tannhäuser* was never finished: it was a perpetual 'work in progress' for Wagner, returned to time and again. Frequent revisions – often necessitated by practical problems – followed the premiere of the work in Dresden in 1845: we can distinguish Dresden, Paris, Munich and Vienna versions. None of them represented the composer's final word: only a few weeks before his death, as Cosima's diaries tell us, Wagner declared that he 'still owed the world a *Tannhäuser*'.

The dissatisfaction felt by the composer of *Parsifal* for this work of his middle years has naturally excited much speculation among music-ologists. Did he sense that, on closer inspection, his *Tannhäuser* mixed too many different styles? Did it worry him that the Bacchanal and Venus passages revealed the experience of *Tristan*, that they were musically so much more sophisticated and chromatic than the rest of the piece, with its simple, archaic style? That the entry of the guests was set in an artificial, courtly style while *Tannhäuser*'s account of his meeting with the Pope foreshadowed the more fluid approach of his later music dramas? Was he troubled by the heterogenous musical identity of *Tannhäuser*, something of which neither *The Flying Dutchman* nor *Lohengrin* can be accused? Was this why he perpetually tinkered with his own handiwork in this piece?

Documentary evidence cannot give us entirely satisfactory answers to these questions, but it seems likely that Wagner was aware of the stylistic peculiarities and the unresolved tensions within this piece, and that it was this that led him to admit that he still owed it to the world. It revealed traces of former concerns which were not sufficiently sublimated, trans-formed into art, or resolved to satisfy Wagner – as musician, dramatist or man. What is lacking – to proceed with this somewhat Hegelian argu-ment – is the dialectical resolution in that dramaturgy of antitheses and contrasts from which Wagner built up this piece. *Tannhäuser* creates a world of black and white, night and day, heaven and hell, with very little in between these polarised extremes.

*

This chapter takes its title from Wagner's reminiscences about the Munich premiere of *Tannhäuser* in 1865, and the singer who took that title role in that performance, Ludwig Schnorr von Carolsfeld: 'As its fundamental feature I described to him the intensity of his delight as well as of his contrition, without any real comfortable intermediate stage, rather switching abruptly and resolutely.' This sense of 'discomfort', of stark clashes between contrasting emotions and contrasting worlds, is an important component of the '*Tannhäuser* problem': the audience as well as the hero is subjected to sudden, disconcerting changes of mood. That first Munich audience had to deal not only with this, but also the unexpected length of the piece: they were used to the cuts in the finale of the second act which Wagner had made in order not to overstretch Tichatschek, the tenor in the Dresden premiere, and they reacted coldly when forced to listen to the complete version preferred by Wagner. Moreover, they were seized with consternation at the intensity with which Schnorr sang Tannhäuser's cries of remorse ('Erbarm dich mein!' – Have mercy upon me!) and the image of insanity he projected when forced to part from Elisabeth. Even Wagner's more perceptive friends wanted the composer to return to what he himself called the 'earlier, more comfortable, more colourless and to me personally unsatisfactory concept' of *Tannhäuser*. Wagner and Schnorr, however, joined forces against this 'general effeminacy, and indeed dissipation … of public taste'; it is no accident that later the same year, Schnorr von Carolsfeld became Wagner's first and never-surpassed Tristan.

This episode demonstrates that the sharpness of the conflict between opposing forces in *Tannhäuser* is quite deliberate. In a fine study entitled *The Fundamental Figure of the Divided World in Wagner*, Friedrich Dieckmann argued that the principle of dichotomy – reflecting the political and cultural conflicts of the age – was crucial to Wagner's work. The terms of the dichotomy, and the form the conflict took, changed in each work, but the clash between worlds – a magical–mystical–romantic one and a historically real and locatable one – almost invariably ended fatally. *Tannhäuser* is a special case within this pattern. The Dutchman, Lohengrin and even the more fortunate Walther von Stolzing are personifications of a romantic ideal which invades everyday life: they inevitably find themselves in conflict with the 'real world' and end up either expelled as outsiders (*Dutchman* and *Lohengrin*) or integrated within it (*Meistersinger*). Tannhäuser, by contrast, embodies the contradiction between romantic and real worlds within himself. He is no emissary from outside, identified by a romantic symbol such as a swan or ghost ship, but a native, a singer of songs with a harp, just like his knightly colleagues. At the same time, however, he is a stranger, an outsider, a man caught between two hostile worlds – 'a stranger in both and related to both', in Dieckmann's words. This spells his ruin.

The fatal nature of the situation is caused by the fact that both worlds are real, with their own independent theatrical existence. The Venusberg (Venus Mountain), for example, is not just an illusion, or a fantastic symbol of the hero, but a reality in which other characters also share. Wolfram perceives it in the third act, when he pulls Tannhäuser back, so its existence is proved before witnesses. But the situation is also fatal for psychological reasons: Tannhäuser is unable to settle for either of the worlds. At the Venusberg he longs for the simple life and the immediacy of nature; on the Wartburg he is seized by nostalgia. Tannhäuser's means of dealing with the outside world leaves no way out. He is crushed between two spheres – and there is also a second death as a consequence. Elisabeth's act of self-sacrifice is no *Liebestod* – there is no togetherness or reconciliation: it is a lonely and sad death.

The unusually cruel way in which the familiar Wagnerian 'divided world' is laid out seems to me the most striking and fascinating aspect of *Tannhäuser*. This is mainly because it runs counter to the composer's general ideal that all contrasts, both musical and psychological, should be mediated. This idea is already discernible in *Tannhäuser* itself, though its consequences were explored more fully in later works. For *Tannhäuser* is not an 'early work', though its inconsistencies and peculiarities may tempt us to pigeon-hole it mentally in this way: it is a work that shows Wagner already en route from opera to music drama. For this very reason, it is fascinating to observe how the more mature composer played down and softened some of the more youthful, headstrong and harsh details of the work, even as he left its basic antithetical structure unchanged.

Let us take a closer look at the uncomfortable, mercilessly polarised world of *Tannhäuser*. Can the starkness of the clash between the worlds of Venusberg and Wartburg be attributed to the plot, which welded together two heterogeneous bodies of legend? Is it due to the auto-biographical motives that subconsciously guided the composer's pen, motives that can be discerned in the finished work as a dramatic subtext? Is it a function of the psychology of the hero, who even in 1846 was accused of 'pathological characteristics' by Eduard Hanslick, then still a supporter of Wagner? As we might expect, all three factors play a part, and we must consider them in turn.

Even the title of the work announces the dichotomy: in full it is *Tannhäuser and* (not '*or*') *the Contest of Song on the Wartburg*. Two groups of legends that have very little to do with one another are intertwined. The first of these is the legend of the knight Tannhäuser – recorded in *Des Knaben Wunderhorn*, but dating from earlier sources (and already given an ironic treatment by Heinrich Heine, just as the story of the Flying Dutchman had been). In the sources, Tannhäuser spent some time at the Venusberg, then tore himself away, but failed to receive absolution from Pope Urban. He never learned of the symbol of forgiveness – the withered staff once more sprouting leaves – because, in his grief and suffering, he returned to the Venusberg once more and disappeared there. The second source is the story of the minstrels' contest at the Wartburg, originating in Thur-ingian legend and related by E.T.A. Hoffmann in his *Serapionsbrüder*.

Apart from a few minute cross-references, there is no connection between the Tannhäuser and Wartburg stories, and hence no plot to unify the narrative. But without plot there can be no opera: Wagner therefore ties a dramatically effective knot by inventing a love affair between Tannhäuser and Elisabeth, the niece of Landgrave Hermann. However, the conflict between the two legendary worlds is so complete that this liaison cannot span the distance between them. Love, which might have acted as a mediator – the instrument of salvation, a bridge between the sinful and moral worlds – is not allowed to do so. This is not only because it is tainted, because Tannhäuser is a different man after his experiences in the brothel. It is also because Tannhäuser deprives love of the conditions it needs to flourish by destroying its social environment: irritated by the idea of courtly love, which seems to him mendacious, unworldly and intellectually lazy, he proclaims that the true nature of (male) love lies in sexual pleasure. By the code of the world in which he finds himself, he is now an outsider, a criminal. And the woman who loves him experiences his affront as a 'deadly blow'. She is now almost forced into the role of a saint, for whom love must mean *caritas*, intercession and renunciation. As Reinhold Brinkmann argued, Elisabeth represents an 'allegory of the Virgin Mary': after all, Tannhäuser breaks the spell of the Venusberg by invoking the name of the Virgin.

The extreme nature of her self-sacrifice matches the extremeness of Tannhäuser's sinfulness: only her martyrdom can atone for him. In death, the mediating forces of love can finally become effective: Elisabeth at least helps the sinning Tannhäuser to a merciful Beyond – in Christian terms, she saves him. The resolution of the conflict needed to be represented in one way or another, and Wagner chose to use the symbols suggested by the pious legend itself, since these would at least be readily comprehensible for his audience. The suggestion that this qualifies *Tannhäuser* as a Christian mystery play about guilt and punishment, about sin and redemption, is a dubious one. Although Wagner remarked, looking back on his work in 1851, that 'it gives me some pleasure to have, on one occasion, stood so stubbornly on a Christian point of view', it is questionable whether it was possible at this time to present a Christian ending without an element of artificiality. It seems more likely that Christian imagery is used as psychological metaphor: heaven and hell, for the Romantic era, represent extremes of consciousness, and the conflict between them often tears the soul apart. This explains the many 'torn heroes' of Romantic novels: one such novel, Ludwig Tieck's absurdly demonic *The Faithful Eckart and the Tannhäuser*, was one of Wagner's sources for this opera of romantic brutality.

The fact that the 'divided world' takes such an extreme form in *Tannhäuser* is not merely the passive result of Wagner's decision somewhat arbitrarily to link the two legends by inventing the relationship between the hero and Elisabeth. On the contrary, it is a deliberate strategy: the linking itself is carried out in a way that intensifies the conflict between the two worlds to the point of explosion. Some producers have tried to understand why Wagner deliberately heightened the violence of the work in this way. Such producers have often interpreted *Tannhäuser* in terms of a clash between the individual and society; they see the hero as a revolutionary artist, in conflict with the reactionary, ossified structures of a police state, whose rigid rituals crush all artistic originality and sensual spontaneity. This is a valid approach, of course, but it must be remembered that the piece was conceived *before* the revolutions of 1848, and the Dresden uprising in particular: *Siegfried*, rather than *Tannhäuser*, is the allegorical product of Wagner's career as a political revolutionary. If parallels need to be drawn with historical phenomena, it would perhaps be more enlightening to consider Wagner's attitudes to Paris, 'that distasteful soil of modern sensuality' where he had lived between 1839 and 1842. The Venusberg is surely a symbolic representation of the Parisian *paradis artificiel*, rather than a Christian projection of a hell of voluptuousness. I agree with Friedrich Dieckmann's argument that the Venusberg stands for 'Paris, Europe, the West': that frivolous, commercialised and corrupt world in which 'freedom, and also alienation' are more advanced than in 'provincial Germany with its comfortable backwardness'. Our interpretation of *Tannhäuser* may gain from a further investigation of the composer's Parisian experiences.

Wagner's autobiography, *Mein Leben*, gives a clear account of the situation. He is twenty-nine, living in Paris, leading a miserable life, doing all kinds of casual jobs in order not to go hungry. Driven by nostalgia for his homeland, he looks for a German subject for an opera. Having for a while considered Manfred, son of the Hohenstaufen emperor Frederick II, he comes across the story of Tannhäuser, which attracts him not by its 'historical aspect' or by its 'brilliant historical and poetic texture', but because Tannhäuser himself is a 'human being', an infinitely gripping and moving figure', an 'artist hungry for life'. In April 1842 he returns to Germany to rehearse his *Rienzi* in Dresden: he crosses the Rhine for the first time together with his wife Minna, he has 'bright tears in [his] eyes' and 'as a poor artist' vows 'eternal loyalty to [his] German fatherland'. His journey takes him past the Wartburg, which inspires him 'exceedingly warmly'. 'I immediately made a nearby ridge into my Hörselberg and thus, travelling along the valley, constructed the scene for the third act of my *Tannhäuser*'. Ten weeks later he proceeds to the concept of his libretto. The world to which he returns seems to him like home, full of nature and peace; it seems simple, genuine and pure; it seems German. His

Tannhäuser is 'a German from head to toe', he writes upon completing the opera to his friend Karl Gaillard, a French music critic. Resentment against France, against Paris – as the quintessence of outward show, of 'sensual pleasure-seeking' and entertainment, a city which did not wish to know about him but adored Meyerbeer – was deeply rooted in his soul. (Even decades later, with the Prussians outside Paris at the end of 1870, he looked forward with pleasure to the anticipated bombardment of the city.) Alongside his antagonism to Paris, Wagner seethes with outrage at Germany's division into a multitude of small states, and at the artistic narrow-mindedness and repressiveness of these statelets. 1848 is just around the corner.

We must not lightly dismiss the idea of reading *Tannhäuser* as a 'period piece', to use Dieckmann's phrase: as a resumé of Wagner's experiences between the incompatible worlds of Paris on the one hand, and Eisenach (location of the Wartburg) and Dresden on the other. Through the polarisations in *Tannhäuser* we can gauge how deeply Wagner must have experienced the differences between these worlds and their cultures. 'Things French', he wrote, had been 'instinctively repulsive' to him: 'in no way did I feel an inclination to acquire the French character for myself.' But there is also a certain ambivalence. Paris was at that time the cultural capital of Europe, where he wanted to succeed at all costs. After the visits of the little Saxon to the 'brilliant performances at the Grand Opera', he experienced, by his own admission, a 'lustfully flattering warmth' which 'excited in him the wish ... and indeed the certainty that he could yet triumph here'. In reality, he was still seeking his own identity; endeavouring, polemically and creatively, to create a specifically German art, opposed to the aesthetics of Italian and French art, whose 'outward effects', 'inner muddleheadedness' and triviality he despised. It is a satisfying irony that the greatest Parisian theatrical scandal of its era – a 'battle evening' that was nonetheless a 'triumph', in Wagner's own words – should have been provoked by, of all things, *Tannhäuser*.

The 'divided world' of Wagner's operas was informed not only by the external facts of the composer's life, but also by aspects of his own character, as he confessed in a famous letter. In 1859 – at precisely the time when he was reworking *Tannhäuser* in 'tristanesque' manner – he wrote from Paris to Mathilde Wesendonck, the woman who inspired *Tristan*: 'It is fundamental to my nature to switch rapidly and strongly between extremes of moods: the greatest tensions can scarcely do other than touch; therein often lies life's salvation. Basically, true art has no other purpose than to show these highest moods in their extreme attitude to each other.' Only a few lines later, however, he took his own ideas a stage further. The special nature of his music could in fact be attributed to the fact that it was concerned 'with mediation and intimate fusion of all elements of transition of outward moods into each other ... I would now regard my finest and most profound art as the art of transition, for my whole artistic web consists of such transitions – I have come to dislike the harsh and abrupt.'

This self-characterisation demonstrates Wagner's justifiable pride in his newly found mastery as a composer: a mastery shown above all in *Tristan*. It is interesting, though, that immediately after this passage in the letter he mentions not *Tristan* but *Tannhäuser*. He complained that a production in Berlin had cut the transition passage at the end of the second act, believing that it was a 'longueur'. As far as the composer was concerned, this passage perfectly mediated between the outburst of horror following Tannhäuser's confession and Elisabeth's intercession. *Tannhäuser* seemed to him to be particularly prone to being cut by insensitive producers – and it is easy to guess why he was so adamant that this should not happen. Because 'comfortable intermediate stages' are absent from the action, the brief orchestral transitions are vital to help the audience cope with the sudden turns of events: the rhetorical and psychological function of the transitions is to prevent the audience's attention from waning, to maintain a belief in the reality of the events on stage. The audience should, indeed must, be guided – and the transitions are the way in which this is effected.

The same letter to Mathilde also contains important revelations about the secret links between Wagner's psychological make-up and the qualities of his music. It discusses the tendency of the composer, whose temperament was clearly highly strung and explosive, simultaneously to attach such importance to the opposite tendency in his work: the smoothing over of the 'rough edges' of moods, the transition and mediation between contradictory emotions. His greatest wish as an artist was 'to be

31

understood', as his 'Communication to My Friends' makes clear. In order to achieve this, he had to learn to create conciliatory transitions between extreme emotions and moods; if he failed to do this, his audiences would be bemused and disturbed by the jagged edges and violent upheavals of his music, and would stop listening. His career was marked by the tension between his 'need for discharge of our innermost feelings' (in other words, the tendency to express unmediated extremes of emotions), and his realisation of the need for moderation.

This need did not only apply to his artistic work: his personal behaviour suffered from the same instinctive faults as his art, a fact illustrated by an incident from his social life. The same letter to Mathilde discusses a party that Wagner and she had both attended, where he had suddenly lost his temper and offended his friend, the architect Gottfried Semper, with a 'strongly worded attack'. Having immediately calmed himself down, he looked for a way of helping the conversation to resume on an even keel. His chosen strategy proved a spectacular failure, because he had decided that the best way of making peace was not 'falling silent', but continuing to talk; thus, instead of apologising for offending Semper, he ranted on, without comma or full stop, about his art. No one was able to interrupt, with the result that he no longer found anyone inclined to listen to him. Wagner, offended by the company's irritation, drew the childish conclusion that he would now avoid all parties concerned.

In the social sphere, he had failed to accomplish a 'transition' as a result of poor communication: in his music drama, he had to do better, if he wished to be understood. The fact that he was able to learn is proven by his development from *Tannhäuser* to *Götterdämmerung* – that perfect universe of mediation and reflection, where no musical detail stands alone, and no change is ever abrupt. But the 'magic of relation' for which Thomas Mann praised his music did not come naturally to him: it was hard won.

What then do his new insights into the nature of communication mean for *Tannhäuser*? Will the Wagner of *Tristan*, now revising the earlier piece, draw any conclusions from his new and more fruitful understanding of mediation? Will he construct bridges between the worlds of Venus and Wartburg? Will he achieve a harmonious unity between the opposing poles, musically if not dramaturgically? Certainly not! Admittedly, the addition of a few short transitional passages à la *Tristan* served to smooth over some of the more abrupt changes of mood, but by far the most significant change was the recomposition of the Bacchanal and the Venus passage from the first act, in Wagner's new, chromatically iridescent style. The effect of this change was the opposite of mediation: it both emphasised and widened the gap that already separated these sections from the music representing the medieval Christian world of the Wartburg. That music is left virtually untouched from the Dresden version, so that it is now all too clear that it originates from an earlier stage of his development.

Of course, the revision brings advantages too: in particular, the part of Venus is much more substantial and interesting than in the Dresden version. As Hans von Bülow admiringly wrote, Venus 'no longer is a stage Medea, but a veritable goddess of the first rank.' But the new stature of the goddess sets up a further element of conflict in the drama: she now has to be taken seriously as an opponent. Many connoisseurs of musical refinement have detected not only echoes of Isolde, but also anticipations of Kundry in the Venus of the Paris version. Perhaps Wagner had not entirely recovered from his passion for Mathilde Wesendonck, to whom he continued to write, confiding his every thought about the Paris *Tannhäuser*: something of her spirit certainly seems to infiltrate the new music for Venus.

The plot Wagner chose for *Tannhäuser*, and his own life at the time he conceived it, have both been shown to lack 'comfortable intermediate stages' – what then of the central character, Tannhäuser himself? Thanks to Wagner's dissatisfaction with the representation of the character on the contemporary stage, we have a wealth of evidence about his artistic intentions. Tannhäuser, he wrote in 1852, is by no means an 'unstable, weak and unmanly character, swaying one way and the other'. The whole drama would be incomprehensible if he were understood and acted as 'benign or conventionally pious with, at most, a few debauched inclinations'. Wagner continues: 'Never and nowhere is Tannhäuser something just "a little", he is everything fully and totally.' Superlatives abound: 'With the most extreme rapture he luxuriated in the arms of Venus', with the most complete conviction of the 'necessity' of what he is doing he breaks those fetters, 'with fullest unreservedness' he surrenders to the dictates of his innate nature and to 'the tearful outburst of a childlike religious repentance'. In the name of Elisabeth, the past and the future merge 'lightning-like as in a fiery stream which ... unites as a radiant star of a new life for him', then, his heart jumping with joy in 'happiest love of life, he rushes forward to meet his love'. 'Like a distant dull dream all the past lies behind him ... he scarcely remembers it'; however, he still has to fulfil his parting vow to Venus, to be her 'courageous champion' in the world. Wagner thus arrives at the logical conclusion that 'Tannhäuser, who is capable only of the most immediate expression of his most sincere and most direct emotions, is bound to find himself in sharpest conflict with [the Wartburg] world'. He promptly abandons all other considerations, and in his song in praise of Venus raises himself to 'the highest exultation', only, 'quite abruptly', to perceive 'a totally new phenomenon – the woman who sacrifices herself out of love for him'. From this point onwards, Wagner explains, Tannhäuser can no longer live without the intensity of his suffering equalling that of his earlier raptures.

'Fully and totally' – that is how Tannhäuser behaves, in everything he does and with everything he encounters: unreflecting, unremembering, only existing in the here-and-now of his emotions, no matter how contradictory these are. He is not unlike the young Siegfried, changeable, living only for the moment, amnesiac even without the aid of a magic potion; nor the young Parsifal, who runs away from his mother and forgets her. 'Deep oblivion has descended over today and yesterday', Tannhäuser declares as soon as he has escaped Venus. Who is this man? A psychopath, a manic-depressive, or an ultra-romantic artist? The divisions of the modern world seem to cut through him: as Baudelaire put it, 'Here two principles have chosen the human heart as their main battlefield – that of the flesh and that of the spirit, hell and heaven, Satan and God.' The divided world in which Tannhäuser moves – the mythological brothel of the goddess of love on the one hand, and the morally regulated, courtly Christian world of the Wartburg and the Pope on the other – is, at one level, simply a metaphor for the extreme polarisation of his inner life. But how did such an inwardly torn hero come to be conceived?

Wagner had long declared his disdain for the 'vacillating' operatic hero who dominated the contemporary Parisian stage: characters such as Arnold in Rossini's *William Tell*, or Meyerbeer's creations such as *Robert le Diable*, Raoul in *Les Huguenots*, or Jean in *Le Prophète*. This was the competition: these weaklings had to be artistically eclipsed. For a musician of the future, however, there could be no return to the hero of the eighteenth-century *opera seria*, who could still act with untroubled self-assurance. The heroes of Grand Opera could only be overturned through a radicalisation of their most prominent characteristic, their fluctuations of mood and attitude. Whereas the hero of Grand Opera assumed a variety of poses without engaging himself in any of them, the new hero had to commit his whole self to every action, every emotion, no matter how contradictory. Small wonder that the hero's character became irrevocably torn apart.

Wagner's plan, though born of a jealous and polemical attitude, was aesthetically successful. Through the radicalisation of his protagonists, his operatic work gained a stature that raised it above the *juste milieu* in Meyerbeer's Paris: in Tannhäuser, he created a hero greater than any seen there for many years, with the possible exception of Berlioz's Benvenuto Cellini. Although Meyerbeer's protagonists frequently found themselves in a tragic conflict, these rather passive figures never themselves personified a 'utopian will' whose force could transcend the context of their particular plot. Tannhäuser, who drains both the cup of pleasure and the cup of suffering to the dregs, is certainly consumed by such a 'utopian will', a fact that decisively distinguishes him from a Robert, a Raoul or a Jean. This will manifests itself in his search for salvation: in Wagner's words, his 'yearning for satisfaction in a higher nobler element', for 'the element of infinite love not existing on earth'. Although we previously characterised Tannhäuser's situation, slightly flippantly, as the common one of a man caught between two women, it seems unlikely that any woman could be 'the right one' for a character such as his, whose forced 'torment of the soul' contains some of the stuff of a saint. He would not be able to remain with any woman, because his thirst is in fact a spiritual and very selfish one. He wants *his* salvation – and he only *believes* that he can find it with women. In truth, woman's love – despite its ideal incarnations as a goddess and an angel – is not the love of God. There can be no help for Tannhäuser in this world.

Wagner, on the other hand, *could* be helped in this world. *Tannhäuser*, for him, was a superbly effective form of self-therapy, just as *Werther* had been for Goethe. By creating a character who embodied so many of his own extreme characteristics, he was able to externalise them and to deal with the 'misery within him'. Of course, creator and created are, in one sense, identical. Wagner, between 1842 and 1845, *was* Tannhäuser, he was him again between 1859 and 1861, and probably remained him, to a degree, for the rest of his life, given that he felt that he still 'owed' the world this work. For Wagner, too, followed every impulse 'fully and totally': he, too, was torn between competing ideals of what 'woman' should be.

Sigmund Freud admired the work of poets who had the courage to give voice to their subconscious: Wagner does the same thing, no less clearly. Tannhäuser's split image of femininity reveals much about the Oedipal conflicts of his creator. The Oedipus drama, which determines the psychological development of early childhood, and the remnants of which persist into adulthood, is played out within the nuclear family. The son has to kill his father, or else the father will kill him as a potential rival. The son loves his mother but, because of the incest taboo, is not allowed to do so; in order to love other women, he must free himself from her image. In the roaming sexual fantasies of the pre-pubescent boy, ideas of the pure and the sexual woman merge in the image of the mother. But because the mother belongs to the father, feelings of vengeance, hatred and guilt are also aroused. Tannhäuser is confronted with two symbolic father-figures against whom he attempts Oedipal rebellion, but in both cases he fails: in the personal father–son encounter with the Landgrave, he capitulates and accepts punishment for his offence; in the encounter with the super-father, the Pope, his submissiveness has fatal consequences. Wagner, as we know, regarded himself as 'fatherless': his father died before he was born, and for a while, he bore the name of his stepfather. The ceaseless recurrence of father–son conflicts in his work makes it clear that the deep-rooted problem could only be resolved at the artistic level. Wagner still has to practise 'healthy patricide': Lohengrin sacrifices his personal happiness to his distant father, Parsifal; King Mark's anger shatters Tristan; Siegmund falls victim to his stronger father. Siegfried at least manages to smash his grandfather's spear, but the only son who truly triumphs over a father figure appears in Wagner's last work, when Parsifal supersedes Titurel. Tannhäuser, by contrast, displays the impotence of the rebellious but doubly submissive 'guilty son'.

The fatherless son has a mother, of course. But not until *Parsifal* does the mother-figure openly appear. In *Tannhäuser* the subconscious idea of the mother is concealed beneath two conscious projections of the feminine: saint and whore. Compare with Kundry, Wagner's most psychoanalytically revealing character, in whom these two images of the feminine merge with unparalleled boldness. Kundry is sexual tool and Mary Magdalen in one: to the boy Parsifal she suggests the image of his mother while also trying to seduce him. She personifies the contradictory images of the mother, fused into one in the subconscious. In *Tannhäuser*, the double image of the mother is still neatly and firmly separate: the conscious mind, with its censorship, does not admit what the subconscious knows. Only Wagner's handling of these images reveals the conflict-generating psyche of the artist. He wants the pure and saintly woman to win the duel for the man she loves. Venus, though gaining stature through the work's revisions, must ultimately lose.

In *Tannhäuser*, then, we see a few flashes of Wagner's male fantasies: flickering flames which, in *Parsifal*, turn into eternal lights. The composer's yearning for redeeming purity, perceptible in *Tannhäuser*, drives him to extremes in his final work, in which a cult of sexual purity is unmistakably espoused. There, the seed sown in *Tannhäuser* brings forth the most bizarre blossoms of chastity. Although Wagner theoretically supported the Young Germany ideal of free sensuality, his final work expresses a reactionary condemnation of sensual pleasure – even though that pleasure is simultaneously celebrated and glorified by his music. In *Tannhäuser*, though, the conflict has not yet been resolved: the fact that the protagonist cannot decide in favour of either of the two faces of the subconscious mother-image is in keeping with the antithetical character of the work. There is no solution to the Oedipus conflict in which Wagner/Tannhäuser is embroiled, unless the act of representing it on stage is itself a solution.

Perhaps it is a pity that Wagner did not choose, for *his* Tannhäuser, the way out which Heinrich Heine provided in his poem. For Heine, champion of the Romantic Enlightenment, Venus simply provided sex with caring:

when Tannhäuser returned from Rome, she first of all served him with hot soup, then prepared a bath for him before retiring with him to bed! But Wagner, of course, was not a man of the Enlightenment, and he was not interested in 'comfortable' resolutions of conflicts. Instead, he initiated an art that was riven with oppositions – and this did not stop with *Tannhäuser.*

3

The universal poetry of *Lohengrin*

IN ITS DAY, *LOHENGRIN*, WAGNER'S 'ROMANTIC OPERA IN THREE Acts', was an icon of both avant-garde music and elitist taste – but it has long since become a cultural relic. In Germany at least, everybody first saw *Lohengrin* as a child, and its plot is as familiar as any fairytale. In the early twentieth century, in particular, it became so popular that its author almost disappeared behind it, rather as Heine did with his *Lorelei*. Few people seem to know the name of the composer of the bridal march, even though his greatest hit is played at nearly every wedding. But the popularity of the music has been accompanied by ridicule: Lohengrin, the Knight of the Swan, was the object of countless parodies and satires, right from the start of his existence. The best known examples are Hans Pfitzner's *Café Lohengrin*, Heinrich Mann's account of a visit to *Lohengrin* by the aggressive philistine Diederich Hessling in the novel *Der Untertan*, and Walter Slezak's collection of theatrical anecdotes, *What Time is the Next Swan?*

Our great-grandparents and grandparents could never resist the fascination of the romantic miracle which occurred in *Lohengrin*, despite its primitive stage mechanics. The tendency of various heads of state to identify themselves with the hero – from Ludwig II through Wilhelm II to Adolf Hitler – has made such miracles politically notorious. However, through jokes, anecdotes and quotations, this opera gradually became so lovingly integrated into our everyday lives, that its real aesthetic substance was lost behind its decorative paraphernalia. Unmistakable evidence of this popularity can be found on any stroll around a flea market in Germany or Austria. Along with plaster busts of Richard Wagner, there are always cups and plates bearing pictures of Lohengrin, sometimes accompanied by a stave with the notes of the 'forbidden question' motif – crockery for the musically literate. *Lohengrin* has long been a design cliché, a cultural logo.

This familiarity has often made it difficult for musicologists to arouse much interest in the piece. Reinhold Brinkmann admitted in 1979 that 'Everything has really been said about *Lohengrin*, as about so much else.' The following year, Michael von Soden expressed the same view: 'No significant controversies exist nowadays about the interpretation of this work – either on the stage or in exegesis and criticism.' In contrast to the Nibelungs' tetralogy, whose inner fragmentation continually provokes new interpretations on the stage, *Lohengrin* appears to be free from any conflicts or ambivalence that might resonate with our own *Zeitgeist*.

It was not always thus: the first performances were surrounded by controversy. Although the Dresden Kapellmeister completed the full score in April 1848, *Lohengrin* was not premiered in his home town, unlike *Rienzi* and *Tannhäuser*. Wagner's participation in the May Uprising and his subsequent political exile to Switzerland meant that his new opera was not performed until 1850 in Weimar, and then only with the assistance of his friend Franz Liszt. The social and theatrical revolutions of the time had a significant and possibly inspirational impact on *Lohengrin*, a fact invariably noted by commentators interested in Wagner's connections with contemporary politics. No one now seriously shares Thomas Mann's opinion that *Lohengrin* and the year 1848 are two separate worlds, linked at most by a certain nationalist enthusiasm. It is much more likely that the widespread contemporary outrage at social and political conditions became mixed in the young composer's mind with his own personal outrage at contemporary artistic life.

This is not necessarily to say that *Lohengrin* is a work that advocates political revolution: Wagner's politics were always ambiguous, even at this time of youthful fervour. Wagner on the barricades, and Wagner of the Dresden Patriotic Club, who wished to combine republican endeavours with monarchy; Wagner the friend of the anarchist Bakunin and co-editor of a revolutionary pamphlet, and Wagner for whom the only purpose of the revolution was to persuade the King of Prussia to see sense and entrust the affairs of the opera house to its conductor – all these are one and the same person, the romantic artist. The real enthusiasm of the composer and his works was for *artistic* revolution: Dresden provided the backdrop for a work which, while it did not make political revolution its subject matter, certainly initiated a revolution within the history of opera. *Lohengrin* bids a farewell not to feudalism, but to the old methods of constructing opera – a farewell, as Franz Liszt said in his legendary discussion of the work, to the 'entire adopted economy' of opera, to the principle of division into 'arias, romances, solos and tutti ... designed merely to let singers and melodies ... achieve effect.' Wagner did not create a blueprint for a better society, but he did create what Liszt called 'an entirely new work of its kind'.

We need somehow to see beneath the familiarity and untopical subject matter of *Lohengrin*, in order to understand something of the fascination which its music exerted on its original audiences. In his essay of 1971 on *Lohengrin*, Carl Dahlhaus made a remark which he did not pursue: 'The romantic opera, which culminated in *Lohengrin*, proved its worth as "universal poetry".' 'Universal poetry' was an ideal proposed by the early Romantics, who aimed to abolish all the boundaries between different art forms, including that between philosophy and poetry. Friedrich Schlegel stated that '[Universal poetry] comprises everything that is poetical, from the greatest – the system of art containing within itself several systems – down to the sigh, the kiss breathed by a child in artless song.' This grand design was probably never accomplished by any of the novels, stories, dramas or lyrical poems of the Romantics, impressive though individual examples by Novalis, Tieck, Brentano, Eichendorff and others certainly were. The problem for such writers was that their poetics aimed beyond what could actually be accomplished by words alone: their aspirations were inherently musical, as Tieck acknowledged when he stated that he hoped to transform his 'painfully earth-bound speech' into pure music.

This is almost what happens, as if by accident, in Schubert's Lieder or Schumann's poetic piano pieces, but the early operas of Wagner – *Die Feen, The Flying Dutchman, Tannhäuser* and *Lohengrin* – represent a more thoroughgoing and deliberate realisation of some of the aesthetic projects of the early Romantics. Everything seems to be connected with everything else, there are systems within systems, poetry is fused with music, philosophy with psychology, history with myth, legend with fairy-tale. They lived up to the ideals of Novalis (whose *Hymns to the Night* Wagner drew on in *Tristan*) that the spirit should recognise itself, time and again, in the created work: Novalis's dictum that 'theatre is man's active reflection of himself' applies to Wagner, more than to any of his other contemporaries. And the 'blue music' of *Lohengrin* – to use Nietzsche's phrase – has always been identified with Novalis's 'blue flower' of Romantic longing, more completely than anything else its composer created.

Despite this apparently cosy identity between *Lohengrin* and Romanticism, there is a conflict between the historically anchored action of Wagner's opera, and Romanticism's 'mind and taste for the infinite', as Schleiermacher put it. For *Lohengrin* is an aesthetic hybrid: a mixture of historical drama and fairy tale, of 'genuine' and 'invented', of 'real time' and timelessness. The framework is provided by the historical figure of King Henry I, the Fowler, who is trying to persuade the leaderless Brabantians to join in the campaign against the Hungarians. There are numerous fairy-tale elements: innocence persecuted, a miraculous apparition, a magic swan with a small gold chain, a wicked woman practising the black arts. Added to this we have a simple narrative structure, which clearly distinguishes between good and evil and records their clash. The central musical motif – the forbidden question – also has a fairy-tale character, expressing the superstitious idea that a person who unveils his identity also forfeits his magic power. The aesthetic conflict already inherent in this amalgam of historical drama and fairy tale is further intensified by Wagner's tragic ending: this may have been in keeping with the tradition of historical drama and of grand opera, but it was a jarring element within the conventions of fairy tale, which usually ends happily.

But theatregoers have never been worried by such contradictions. After all, there is nothing 'real' about the Middle Ages depicted in this piece: they are merely a colourful backdrop. Wagner himself made this point repeatedly, admitting that the German kingdom represented in the story was of only marginal significance. He was not at all interested in the anonymous medieval author who provided the only surviving source of the Lohengrin epic, apart from a few references by Wolfram von Eschenbach. The source text's discussions of genealogy, and its moral justification of the crusades on the grounds of the divine descent of Godfrey of Bouillon from the Chevalier du Cygne, were of no relevance to Wagner. He was more concerned with the 'primeval human poem' contained within it, which might help him to represent a universal and insoluble human conflict.

In Wagner's *Lohengrin*, the historical element is not of crucial importance, though it does lend a certain colour and glamour to the opera, and it sanctions the inclusion of trumpets and marches. It also helped Wagner to do something he loved, which was to represent a moment of historic change – here, a transition from one religion to another. The sorceress Ortrud is the daughter of an old Frisian king, and her intrigue against Lohengrin and Elsa is conducted in the name of the 'desecrated gods', Wodan and Freia. Like Romantic poets such as von Arnim, Novalis and Brentano, Wagner enjoyed using the Middle Ages as a framework: it allowed a nostalgic return to an idealised past of social cohesion and unity, which of course had never existed in this form. It was not the reality of history that really fascinated the Romantics, but its spirit.

In *Lohengrin*, as in the work of the Romantic poets, the clash of swords, the military herald, the nationalist bombast do not touch upon what is essential in the plot. This can be shown by examining the way in which Wagner's concept of the piece developed. In July 1845, the composer was taking the waters at Marienbad, in order to recover from the 'atmosphere of the theatre lights' in Dresden. Mentally, however, he was unable to relax: he used the time to write down a detailed plan for *Lohengrin*. Disappointed by the scantiness and shallowness of the source text, Wagner related how he freed the 'by now almost unrecognisable legend from the rubble and mildew of its poor prosaic treatment', and 'by [his] own invention and refashioning brought it back to its rich, highly poetical value'. He did so by drawing on an eclectic range of other sources: the Grimm Brothers' *German Legends*, which contained the children's story of the swan, Bechstein's collection of fairy tales, and various Dutch legends. The poeticisation and romanticisation of *Lohengrin* went hand in hand with its detachment from its original historical context.

'Everything poetic must be like fairy tale', demanded Novalis, and

Wagner abided by this law of 'univeral poetry': he infused and interleaved the medieval Christian and patriotic subject matter with fairy-tale elements, until little more than a plot framework and a few characters were left from the original historical material. Moreover, he added a fairy tale of his own invention: the character of Ortrud. For dramatic and poetic reasons, a dark counterpoint was necessary to the bright world he took from the sources, and the introduction of this sorceress brought several new elements to the drama. As a 'wild seer', Ortrud is still partially rooted in paganism and magic. She – unlike the supposedly more enlightened characters – realises that her 'white' opponent, Lohengrin, also operates with magical means, and that fear of losing his magical powers is the motivation for his repeated invocation, 'Never shalt thou ask me'. In inventing his own magical elements, Wagner abided by the rules of the genre: the ritual repetition of formulas is an important part of the fairy tale of all cultures and epochs, as is the attachment of a mysterious power to a name.

The language of fairy tale is superficially simple, but it is often also secretive, enciphered, signifying something complex. Objects have symbolic connotations, and characters often have allegorical significance. The Grail, for example, is always a symbol of holiness, of unearthly grace, of the ineffable, even though its external appearance can change. For Wagner, it was the ideal central symbol for *Lohengrin*, because the prohibition of questioning is integral to it. (Wagner's last work confirms that this was his understanding of the Grail: when Parsifal asks 'Who is the Grail?' he receives the reply 'This cannot be said.') In the earlier work, the Grail itself is still invisible, but its messenger, Lohengrin, is also its allegorical representative. He is a personification of an idea, rather than a flesh-and-blood human being: this is why he seems so strangely incorporeal, glassy, appearing and vanishing like a beam of light. Drawn across the water from a distant land by a fabulous beast, he does not assume control of his own actions, but behaves passively, as though he is a puppet of his father, Parsifal. But Lohengrin is also a god who wishes to become human through the love of a woman: this aspiration, doomed to failure, also belongs to the realms of fairy tale, and Lohengrin is in this respect a kinsman of Fouqué's Undine. Finally, he is also an allegorical representation of the ideal of the Romantic artist: this image implies 'being misunderstood', and out of joint with one's own society. Lohengrin thus has multiple meanings: he is a knight of the Grail and a god who cannot become human, but also a misunderstood modern artist.

If 'universal poetry' was the ideal that drove the early Romantic poets, then they took a fairly pessimistic view of their chances of realising it. Novalis, for example, wrote that 'Divinatory, magical, truly poetical persons cannot arise in conditions such as ours', and elsewhere that 'We seek the absolute everywhere and invariably only find things'. A further brief excursion into Wagner's biography is justified here, in order to try and understand the circumstances that prompted his attempt to succeed where others had failed.

Let us go back to 1845, and that summer in Marienbad. Wagner is working, in defiance of his doctors' orders. He feels 'light and cheerful' and, excited by the prospect of making money quickly, drafts a comic opera, *Die Meistersinger von Nürnberg*. But then something disturbs him: he experiences, as though from within, a prohibition on pleasure, and a resurgence of instinctive urges. Some mysterious inner command forces Wagner to abandon his cheerful subject. He is forced back towards the Middle Ages, towards tragedy and, we should add, towards Romanticism:

> No sooner had I stepped into my bath about the midday hour than I was gripped by such an urge to write down my *Lohengrin* that, unable to wait the hour necessary for my bath, I jumped out impatiently after a few minutes, scarcely allowed myself the time for dressing properly and, like a man possessed, ran to my apartment in order to put down on paper what was oppressing me. This recurred for several days until the detailed scenic plan of *Lohengrin* was written down.

A few years later, Wagner spoke rather dismissively of *Die Meistersinger* as an 'enjoyable little excursion into the sphere of the cheerful', the last attempt of a 'pleasure-seeking desire' to adjust to an 'environment of triviality'. He had felt 'passionately urged' to abandon it, in order to put himself into the 'nostalgically serious mood' of *Lohengrin*.

This creative impulse was unusually intense, even for Wagner; his reaction may be explained in part by his sense of identification with the subject. He explained in his 'Communication to my Friends' that he increasingly felt a 'manifestation of opposition' which could only express itself 'towards modern life as a yearning, and eventually as outrage, that is, as tragedy'. The composer found himself surrounded by doubts and criticism: the world around him did not believe in the 'absolute artist' or the revelation he could bring. The artist's radical subjectivity found no correspondence in the bourgeois world: 'emotion' was answered by 'reason', and to this extent its conditions of existence were tragic. *Lohengrin* was the artistic product of this train of thought, and its central character personified the dilemma: Lohengrin's greatest wish was to be 'accepted unreservedly and to be understood by emotion', but doomed to failure, he must return 'to his solitude, destroyed'. Lohengrin can be understood as a self-image of the Romantic artist: if one remembers his solitude, his endless travels, his 'exalted nature' and the aura of strangeness and remoteness that surrounds him, one realises that he contains virtually all the elements of this Romantic archetype.

How, then, do the other characters in the opera fit in to this interpretation? There is a tension between history and fairy tale here: the more historically rooted the character, the more difficult it is for him or her effectively to represent an 'idea'. Ortrud, of course, is drawn largely from fairy tale. She personifies the doubts which assail Elsa and which will destroy the happiness of this beautiful, good but naive girl. She must therefore be given the external appearance of a sorceress, a bad fairy. Her evil machinations begin with the removal of the heir to the throne and her king-making efforts on behalf of her own husband, and culminate in her psychological warfare against the next pretender, Lohengrin. Her grim figure contains a shattering revelation for the nineteenth-century Romantics: that women, too, might become politically active. 'A political man is distasteful', Wagner wrote to Franz Liszt, 'but a political woman is horrible.' Ortrud represents political intrigue and calculating pragmatism: this was part, but only part, of the rationalist spirit which resulted in a critical and sceptical attitude towards the artist, an attitude from which Wagner/Lohengrin believed he suffered. Ortrud is therefore the adversary of the 'divinatory man' Lohengrin – she is his female anti-Christ. In this role, as a pagan princess, Ortrud moreover personifies everything 'reactionary': Wagner describes her as 'concerned only with the old and therefore hostile to anything new'. He is oblivious, therefore, to the paradox of equating that attitude with the spirit of politics, given that it is Enlightenment thinkers rather than reactionaries who generally display the critical and sceptical attitudes that he associates with politics. He disregards this contradiction in his concern to create in Ortrud a figure representing everything that opposes the miraculous, innovatory power of the artist.

The allegorical weight of the drama is concentrated into Lohengrin and Ortrud: this means that the partners of the two protagonists, Elsa of Brabant and Count Telramund, inevitably appear somewhat two-dimensional in comparison. In 'Communication to my Friends' Wagner attempts a retrospective enhancement of the character of Elsa, by presenting her as Lohengrin's *anima*: the 'other part of his own nature', his 'subconscious awareness' and therefore his complement, a symbol of his yearning to be complete. Wagner could well be using the benefit of hindsight here, deliberately tailoring his argument in order to make Elsa fit into the pattern of redeeming heroines. This was the function which he now thought appropriate for the principal female characters in his operas, and it was one that had already been admirably fulfilled by Senta and Elisabeth, even though the theory was not in place at the time that they were created. In the opera, as distinct from Wagner's gloss on it, the most noticeable attribute of Elsa is her ability to dream, to create her own hallucinatory reality. She uses this quality as a strategy to convert her physical and political weakness into strength: she dreams so intensely that the hero of her dreams appears in the flesh. But she is nonetheless a somewhat helpless figure in the face of political intrigue: innocent, dressed in white, an unhappy daughter of a king. Despite this fairy-tale exterior, Elsa of Brabant is clearly outlined in Wagner's historical sources, as is Telramund – who in the opera is little more than an instrument for his wife, Ortrud. It is perhaps no coincidence that of the four principal characters, the two most clearly outlined in the source are also the weakest; this fact testifies to the Romantic predominance of fairy tale over history.

'The fairy tale is quite musical', Novalis wrote in his *Fragments*. If Wagner succeeded in translating the Romantic ideal of fairy tale into music in *Lohengrin*, then much of this success must be attributed to the extraordinary, magical effect of the Prelude to Act One: its numinous, ethereal quality conjures up an image of the distant Grail. It is interesting that there have been so many literary attempts to describe the effect of this piece, to translate the music back into words. This re-translation is not an abandonment of the Romantic programme, which regarded the total musicalisation of language as its poetic Utopia, but a paraphrase of it. It is an attempt to understand this musical image, which seems to achieve exactly what musicalised speech sets out to do: it creates a continuous stream of evocative sounds, insubstantial, abstract and pure. This is close to Novalis's ideal of 'Tales, without continuity, but with associations and dreams. Poems – merely well-sounding and full of beautiful words – but also without any trace of meaning or connection.' We may pursue this idea a little further, by comparing three accounts of the effect of the prelude by different Romantic writers: Wagner himself, Liszt, and Charles Baudelaire.

It is clear that Wagner understood the prelude as having some descriptive content, since he gave it the subtitle 'The Holy Grail' when he presented it on its own at the Zurich Festival Concerts in May 1853. However, the vessel containing Christ's blood is not portrayed directly here – as a Holy of Holies, as in *Parsifal*. Rather, it is evoked as a feeling, a counter-image of nostalgia which opposes a world of 'empty concern with gain and possession', a world which could not satisfy 'the human heart's indestructible desire for love'. The desire for love is projected by ecstatic imagination beyond the physical world, and ultimately attaches itself to a miraculous image, real but unapproachably distant: the musical suggestion of yearning is answered by the musical symbol of the Grail. And then the suggestion of movement enters the scene:

> To the ecstatic gaze of supreme, otherworldly longing for love, the clearest blue heavenly ether seems at first to thicken into a wonderful, barely perceptible, yet magically emerging apparition; in infinitely delicate lines, but with gradually increasing clarity, the miracle-offering flight of angels imperceptibly descends from radiant heights, escorting in their midst the sacred vessel.

This host of angels now pours the blessing over the 'beholder', then vanishes once more. Wagner's ecstatic prose is of course ultra-Romantic in style. At times, indeed, it is so overloaded with near-tautological descriptions of extreme pleasure – blissful shivers of delight', 'wonderfully sacred excitement', 'bursting with powerful longing', 'breath of most ineffable bliss and emotion' – that it almost begins to read like a parody of itself.

Wagner's vision of angels, who can become a little cloying, is replaced in Liszt's account by a huge, fantastic piece of architecture, a heavenly Jerusalem of the soul:

> Before our mind's eye arises this temple which, in the poet's eye, is a structure of unmouldering wood and golden gates, with thresholds of asbestos, with columns of opal, with window casings of onyx, with forecourts of precious stones – resplendent halls which may be approached only by those whose hearts are uplifted and whose hands are clean.

But Wagner, according to Liszt, does not show us this temple as it might be seen by the naked eye. Rather, it is 'mirrored by azure waves, reflected by iridescent clouds. A broad, dreamy descending of the melody, a fragrant ether surrounding the sacred image we are about to see . . .' As the opera continues, this unreal structure is overlaid with the equally unreal excitements of the soul, arising from the orchestra pit: 'From it rises the cry of hate, the rage of revenge, the whisper of love, the ecstasy of adoration. As though in a fragrant haze it sketches mystical dreams and colours proud urges with brilliant inks.'

Alongside his literary paraphrase of the prelude, Liszt makes some penetrating remarks about the aesthetic character of the whole opera: 'Everything unites, everything links together, everything escalates' – no musical detail can be separated from the whole. This method of construction makes new and particular demands on the listener, who is required to deploy an acoustic memory over a long period of time, to link together clusters of motives which are repeated and varied throughout the piece, if he wishes fully to understand the significance of the drama. As Liszt correctly observes, Wagner's music thus gives pleasure to the intellect as well as the senses: Romantic music is misunderstood if it is regarded as belonging solely to the 'sphere of vague emotions'.

The fact that Romantic art essentially depends on the acute functioning of the intellect, despite its association with the cult of the emotions, was well known to that famous musical connoisseur, Charles Baudelaire. The

French poet first heard the *Lohengrin* prelude at a concert of Wagner's music at the Théâtre des Italiens in Paris in 1860. He was already familiar with Wagner's account of the flock of angels, and Liszt's image of the reflected temple, and decided to supplement these paraphrases with his own account. The images received by Baudelaire's *âme poétique* are more abstract than those recounted by Wagner and Liszt – the poet describes images of dreams and dreaming. Freed from the 'fetters of gravity', he experienced the 'extraordinary pleasure characteristic of high-altitude locations'; this pleasure is accompanied by a feeling of total solitude and a sense of an infinite horizon, 'steeped in faint light, infinity itself'. He continues: 'Soon I had the sense of increasing brightness, an intensity of light growing at such speed that no dictionary could adequately describe this continual rebirth from brilliance and whiteness.' Movements of light guide the soul to ecstasy, raising it far above the earthly world: 'finally the experience of space extended to the last imaginable boundaries.'

When he heard the *Lohengrin* prelude, Baudelaire sensed an intimate artistic kinship between its composer and himself. Both, he believed, were unconcerned with the notional boundaries that had traditionally separated different art forms. Both were attempting to create an entirely new art, which would be synaesthetic – fusing together a range of intense stimuli, normally experienced by different senses. Baudelaire himself had already described this artistic vision three years earlier, in his poem 'Correspondances' from *Les Fleurs du Mal*:

> Like echoes from infinity drawn out
> Into a dappled unison of light,
> Beyond the dawn of day or dead of night,
> All scents, all sounds and colours correlate.

'Correspondances' envisages a world in which all that appears solid and substantial has melted away, to be displaced by a universal network of sound–colour relations. Perception of the world is transformed: its traditional foundations disappear. The *Lohengrin* prelude, if understood as a vision of a timeless, infinitely white space, breaks with all traditions and opens the door to an understanding of art that will lead through symbolism to abstraction. Baudelaire's understanding of the piece as 'white music' almost anticipates the ideas of Wassily Kandinsky:

White is like the symbol of a world where all colours ... have disappeared. That world is so high above us that we cannot hear any sound ... That is why white acts upon our psyche like a great silence, one that is absolute for us. Internally it sounds like a non-sound. It is silent, which is not dead, but full of possibilities. White sounds like a silence which can suddenly be comprehended. It is nothingness ... standing before the beginning, before birth.

Detached from its religious content and other specific poetic images, Wagner's music, to Baudelaire, is a non-image of absolute insubstantiality: it dissolves its hearers into a state of pure sensation and cognition, untrammelled by any specific content. Thus the door to the modern movement is open. It is beyond dispute that the peculiar sound-world of *Lohengrin* creates an intense visual impression, but the colours in which that impression have been clothed have changed. *Lohengrin* was traditionally described as being bathed in an ethereal blue, now Baudelaire identifies it with the essence of 'whiteness'. Later generations, though, turn Baudelaire's whiteness into its opposite, and describe *Lohengrin* in terms of a deep, nihilistic black.

At the very end of the nineteenth century, another French poet described his experience of the *Lohengrin* prelude. Paul Valéry was not a particularly enthusiastic Wagnerian, despite the fact that his youth had coincided with a period of notorious wagnérisme in France. He formulated his understanding in similar terms to those of Baudelaire, even though he proceeded from an entirely different aesthetic basis. He saw the prelude as exemplifying a state in which consciousness was fully receptive, fully aware of its own activity; pitches, durations and timbres were chosen, he believed, in order to evoke and maintain an idea of 'infinite expectation'. There is a paradox here: how can one hold on to something that is already infinite? The paradox reveals the difficulty of expressing the ineffable in art, either in language or in music.

The *Lohengrin* prelude, which fulfils Romantic desires almost to excess, is followed, lest we forget, by the opera: that conflict of ideas, in words and music. Wagner is not a symphonic poet, whatever the prelude may suggest, but a musical dramatist. He therefore has to deal with the problem of language, with the fact that language constantly refers back to a specificity of content that music continually seeks to escape – language contains an inherently anti-Romantic aspect. If the wordless overture represents the processes of the unconscious, then does the rest of the opera seek to bring music back to language and content, to revisit the unconscious with the assistance of the conscious mind? As Elisabeth Lenk speculates, does Wagner intend to 'step on land' with language, just as the Flying Dutchman did with a woman, because he has come to realise the horrors of an infinite existence on the seas of the unconsciousness? Why else would the characters in the opera continually interrupt the infinite melody of the orchestra with their limited and finite concerns?

It was one of the cardinal principles of the Romantic movement that music was the Romantic art par excellence, and that all poetry ultimately aspired to 'become music'. Wagner's own position was more complex and ambiguous: he was a double agent, acting on behalf of both music and language. His debate with Beethoven and his dispute with a critic of *Lohengrin* – conducted from exile in Zurich in the early 1850s – clearly show the point at which his divergence from orthodox Romantic thinking began. He has a different idea of language, a different understanding of what communication means.

While Wagner was working on *Opera and Drama*, which sought to define a new approach to the problem of reconciling words and music, he received an unexpected letter from a certain Adolf Stahr. His correspondent, who was the professor of classical philology at Oldenburg, reproached the composer for his monotonous and unrhythmical melodies in *Lohengrin*. Instead of taking offence, Wagner replied, as he described it, 'with a certain – hard to define – smile'. *Lohengrin* was a world away from what he was planning now, and he found it embarrassing to have a 'sloughed snakeskin' held up to him: he would prefer to see *Lohengrin* forgotten. From the heights of his new-found creative position, he did not entirely disagree with his critic: he conceded that at the time of composing *Lohengrin*, the 'primal kinship' between music and language had not yet been clear to him. The blame for this, however, should not be attributed to the music, but to the language and its as yet 'unformed verses'. In 1847, he had understood music merely as a 'full flowering of language', entirely in keeping with Romantic theory; music, for the Romantics, represented the continuation, advancement and enhancement of poetry. What mattered to him now, however, was dredging up the music that was already present within language, in order to achieve 'salvation' through the universality of emotion. At this point, therefore, Wagner began to distance himself from the Romantics: here began his journey from 'word poet', who elevated the text to the level of music, to 'tone poet', who 'redeemed' the text into its 'primal kinship' with music. The tortuous language and circuitous philosophising which mark all the texts dealing with this subject indicate the difficulty Wagner found in explaining this distinction in words.

In opposition to the Romantics, he had to justify his thesis that redemption into total emotion through symphonic or purely instrumental music was no longer a valid option for the consciously creative artist. He finds confirmation of this thesis in Beethoven, one of the few predecessors he admired. For Wagner, the crucial moment was the final movement of the Ninth Symphony, which brilliantly brought about a transition from pure music to word, fulfilling 'the need, felt by the musician, to throw himself into the arms of the poet'. Only then could the semantically fulfilled, 'redeeming melody' arise – even for a composer whose instrumental music was as inventive and profound as Beethoven's. The connection through the word, back to the intellect and 'awareness', was necessary in order to 'liberate' music.

After *Lohengrin*, Wagner's journey from 'word poet' to 'tone poet' brought about a different approach to the language of the libretti. Wagner realised that, as a prerequisite to creating the sort of text he wanted, he needed to organise language according to its musical particles, its vowels and consonants, in order to make it truly fluid. The language of a work of art had to be radically different from the 'poor language of everyday life': it should be understood as 'sound language', treated according to the nature of its constituent sounds. This required a return to the 'roots of language'. Wagner regarded the vowel as 'intensified sound', the stretchable, singable sound that produces the inner effect of the tone; the consonant, by contrast, encloses the vowel, and provides both its 'physiognomic exterior' and its ability to convey meaning. This new understanding of the structure of poetic language also implied an abandonment of the old method of end-rhyme, which merely satisfied the ear and pacified the mind, in favour of alliterative poetry. Alliteration helped the poet both to convey the identity of different emotions, by linking the initial letters of root-words, and to emphasise the contrast between them, by changing the vowel sounds. The mixed emotions involved in any situation could thus be economically and clearly conveyed: for example, Lust–Leid (joy–sorrow). This new form of speech opened up a universe of associations and emotions for Wagner, and brought language into a new relationship with music: henceforth, the musical tone was no more than the 'mother element' in which the 'accentuated and alliterated root word' was resolved.

When he replied to Adolf Stahr's criticisms, Wagner was able to inform him with pride that he had now completed the text of *Siegfrieds Tod*, and that his language now had that 'robust sensual connection necessary for music'. Speech music and musical speech now complement one another, like two equal but independent partners: from their structural kinship springs forth the through-composed music drama. *Lohengrin* had proved in retrospect to be the end as well as the culmination of romantic opera. The uncommitted, amorous entwining of 'tone, fragrance and colour' had to yield to the serious 'primeval kinship' of the myth. The passionate love affair, which ties a couple only temporarily, had to give way to an enduring marriage.

The principal subject of Wagner's correspondence with Stahr now became not the music of the opera, but its plot: in particular the ending, with the separation of the lovers. The issues debated were central to *Lohengrin*'s identity as a Romantic opera. There is a conflict here between the work's allegiance to the Romantic aesthetic, which dictated its attempts to arouse 'a sense and taste for the infinite' by means of an open form, and its need to obey the conventions of stage drama, which necessitate a structured plot with a clear beginning and end. Perhaps Wagner had chosen the wrong genre from the start, and should have written a novel, if he had wanted to fulfil the Romantic dream of 'universal poetry'? Had not Novalis expressly stated that only the novel could embrace all literary genres, all of history, both recorded and legendary, all the possible magical transformations of characters and events: that the novel alone could realise the dream of infinity in space and time? Should

Wagner have followed this road, leaving *Lohengrin* as a fragment, that model of completed incompleteness so beloved of the Romantics?

Fortunately for all concerned, Wagner did not write a novel, but solved his problem differently: not through form, but through content. Immediately after the premiere of *Lohengrin*, the concerned opera enthusiast Hermann Franck urged him to soften the conclusion of the work with its severe punishment: Lohengrin's departure and Elsa's death. The seeds of uncharacteristic uncertainty were planted in Wagner's mind, and he considered other possible endings: Elsa, for example, could depart together with Lohengrin. He chose to leave things as they were, but five years later the same question arose again, when Adolf Stahr wrote once more to suggest that Lohengrin could give up his magical powers for the sake of love: only in this way, he argued, could the audience be 'elevated from the vague dream symbolism of abstract transcendence'. Wagner should allow Lohengrin to become human, in order to humanise the myth. The composer hesitated again: he now thought that Stahr might be right, much to the concern of *Lohengrin*'s original champion Franz Liszt, who favoured the separation of the lovers. Wagner tormented himself with this for weeks, until suddenly matters became 'as clear as daylight' to him, and he sent a telegram to Liszt from his Swiss exile which read 'Stahr is wrong, Lohengrin is right.' That was the end of the affair.

Had Wagner yielded to the sentimental, bourgeois compromise suggested by his well-meaning advisers, *Lohengrin* would no longer have been 'universal poetry', and this most Romantic of operas would have been guilty of treason against itself. Of course, we are entitled to pity Elsa, made guilty despite her innocence and cruelly punished by death: in the medieval sources she does not have to die. And *Lohengrin*, by virtue of this merciless ending which left no hope of redemption, became the 'blackest' of Wagner's tragedies, in Peter Wapnewski's words. Had the composer shown pity for the pair of lovers, or had he tried to humanise the other-worldly nature of Lohengrin for the sake of human love, he would have destroyed his own dramatic situation, so skilfully constructed in the first place that it almost provided a textbook case of paradox. And only through the paradox can an inward openness of form prevail against the demands for closure articulated by dramatic convention. Only thus can something like pure emotion – whether we call it longing or, like

Novalis, the 'possibility of infinitely exciting pain' – be maintained in a floating equilibrium.

The road to within – proclaimed by the Romantics as the only way forward for poetry – is also, of course, the road towards the modern movement of psychoanalysis. If we apply a psychological approach to the end of *Lohengrin*, we find ourselves looking at the human foundations of the dramatic paradox. Seen in this light, the separation of Lohengrin and Elsa seems to have been inevitable from the outset, since it is the logical consequence of their inner motivations. For if Elsa's love is real, as her character leads us to assume it must be – if it is that warm-hearted, human, womanly love for which Lohengrin in his narcissistic solitude yearns – then she is bound to ask the question about his identity. Love demands certainty about its object, and cannot be content with abstraction. Lohengrin, on the other hand, seeks to be loved as a god: he wants love as blind trust, love given as a gift, love at no cost, love as total belief in him, no matter who he is – he prohibits the question in order to ensure Elsa's enslavement through love. Yet he also wants to be loved as a human being, to be redeemed. Such is the dialectic of male egotism, the crime for which Wagner eventually punishes his hero: he is not allowed to become human and retain his divine self at one and the same time.

A conciliatory conclusion would be false to the inner truths of these characters. Characters cannot escape from their own skins: Lohengrin is bound to seek the absolute and finds a mortal woman who wants knowledge, Elsa seeks a human partner and finds the absolute. In this respect the opera finally reveals aspects of a Romantic novel, one that concerns the split between the imagined and the real in the human ego. The dream can enter life, but life cannot enter into the dream. The dream, however, survives: Lohengrin returns to the distant land from which he came, and he will return, in 'strange airy form' (Novalis), to trouble women in their dreams.

'If I wanted to let go of Lohengrin, he had to go as he was,' Wagner stubbornly wrote to those who had tried to persuade him to change the ending. 'With total intoxication I submerged him in music; there was nothing else I could do. Thus at least I spared myself a rationalist opera.' This fate was certainly averted: *Lohengrin* is not a rationalist work, and the hero's immersion in music is perhaps the surest sign of its Romantic credentials as 'universal poetry'. But the work also contained the seeds of its own destruction: with this work, Wagner had taken Romantic opera as far as he, or it, could go. The way in which the heritage industry has packaged *Lohengrin* is perhaps not so inappropriate, after all: it has something of the quality of a museum piece, a relic of the defunct religion of the Romantics.

4

Incest in *The Ring*

IN THE EARLY 1910S, AN ANONYMOUS BUT EVIDENTLY PATIENT reviewer, writing in the Berlin theatre journal *Die Schaubühne*, attempted to make clear the family relationships in Wagner's tetralogy:

> Siegfried is the son of his uncle and the nephew of his mother. He is his own cousin, as the nephew and son of his aunt. He is the nephew of his wife, and therefore his own uncle and his own nephew by marriage. He is nephew and uncle in one. He is the son-in-law of his grandfather Wotan, the brother-in-law of his aunt, who is at the same time his mother. Siegmund is the father-in-law of his sister Brünnhilde and the brother-in-law of his son. He is the husband of his sister and the father-in-law of the woman whose father is the father-in-law of his son. Brünnhilde is the daughter-in-law . . .

Chaos reigns in the *Ring* family!

However, we are not dealing here with real family relationships, but with fantasised, fantastical ones. It is these relationships that I would like to explore further. We know that Wagner changed the pattern of family relationships that he found in his sources, the Nordic sagas of the Edda and the courtly epic. He rearranged the family tree, strengthening and multiplying the blood relationships between his characters, to such an extent that the religious scholar Klaus Heinrich could declare that Wagner had transformed the original 'story of the dead' into nothing more than a 'spectacle of incest'.

*

The Ring can be interpreted in numerous ways, and understanding it as a 'spectacle of incest' is one such strategy: a potentially productive one, since incest – or the prohibition of incest – can be seen as an index which demonstrates where 'progression' and 'regression' take place in the narrative. These concepts operate on two interconnected levels: the psychoanalytical, and the anthropological. The psychoanalytical plane is concerned with the complex development of the individual, on his route from childhood to responsible adulthood: it deals with a constant, ahistorical narrative of the psyche. The anthropological plane is concerned with the dynamic process of mankind's progress from nature to culture, from a grey, mythical prehistory to a state of intellectual awareness. Progression and regression can take place on either or both of these planes, and incest in *The Ring*, whether physical or only symbolic, invariably indicates which process is at work. It shows us whether we are witnessing a relapse into an earlier stage, primitive and infantile, or an advance towards humanity, the intellect and light.

Interpretation of these processes is complicated by the fact that the ideas involved in the two 'poles of tension' – nature, myth and infantilism on the one hand, culture, historical awareness and maturity on the other – are themselves ambivalent, Janus-faced. Nature, for example, can imply innocence, instinctive wisdom and energy, and an unselfconscious happiness and beauty. But it can also be barbarous, unruly and menacing, denoting a state of anarchy where murder is legitimate and sexual licence, animal urges and violence prevail. An advanced culture might be expected to resist such a negative manifestation of nature, asserting the values of law and order, meaning and form, art and morality. But culture, too, can turn into a negative image of itself. Overstrained by the continual denial of natural urges, it can become a violator of nature and of humanity. Intuitive values are replaced by rational ones: reflection, inhibition and doubt come to predominate over instinctive wisdom and freedom of action. Adorno's concept of the 'dialectics of enlightenment' helps us to understand this continual interlocking of progressive and regressive values. Relapses within an apparently progressive development and advances within a regressive one are characteristic of the cultural process.

The ambivalence of both nature and culture and their dialectical entanglement in the modern age forms the background to our interpretation of incest. We shall see how Wagner, exponent of the modern in the nineteenth century, gives an 'artistic' account of incest, in contrast to Freud and Lévi-Strauss's later 'scientific' accounts. Freud would have understood Wagner's message, but could scarcely have approved of it, given his own cultural convictions. Lévi-Strauss, on the other hand, praised Wagner for his use of music to rediscover lost mythical structures: as an anthropologist of incest, however, he would have shaken his head over the apparent incest mania in *The Ring*.

At its simplest level, of course, incest is a sexual involvement between blood relatives: it is always concerned with the family, with relationships and their disintegration. However, different cultural portrayals of incest attach different moral values to it. On the one hand, incest is often regarded as the archetype of sin: its curse, as the legends of numerous societies have related, taints entire generations. The story of Oedipus provides the most famous, but certainly not the only example of this link between incest and shame, a link regarded by psychoanalysts of myth as universal. But in some societies incest is portrayed in a positive light, as a mark of superiority. Astrological myths in both East and West testify to this, finding incestuous relationships in the heavens: Zeus and Hera, Isis and Osiris are only the best known of such sibling marriages. The motive of incest can also be found in literary works of all periods, from antiquity through to those modern works in which the 'Wagnerian' idea of incest exerts a direct influence – Thomas Mann's novella *Wälsungenblut*, for example, or less directly, Robert Musil's *The Man without Qualities*, which views love between siblings as an emotional utopia. Incest, when encountered in literature, is always irresistibly fascinating: it simultaneously signifies superiority and criminality.

The association between incest and a 'superior race', an élite, may have its historical origins in the fact that there were sibling marriages in various dynasties among the ancient Egyptians, Persians, Incas and Ptolemies. Although these were exceptional, something of this idea of sibling marriage as a divinely granted prerogative of royalty may have survived in the folk memory. In general, though, the prevailing feeling is that incest should be prohibited: it is regarded as contrary to nature, repulsive, a perversion punished as criminal since biblical times.

Despite this general repulsion, not all types of incest are regarded with equal disgust: different categories have been treated in different ways. A study of myth allows us to identify three 'levels' of incest, graded according to the strength of the taboo associated with them. Relationships between brother and sister are half-tolerated, or excused: the 'sibling complex' is a more recent development in man's evolution than the 'parent complex', as Otto Rank, a disciple of Freud, claims in *The Incest Theme in Literature and Legend*. Rank subdivides the sibling complex into love between siblings of the opposite sex and hatred between siblings of the same sex: the theme of the 'hostile brothers' occurs at least as frequently as that of the 'brother–sister lovers', and sibling incest and fratricide are complementary motives in many myths.

The taboos on sexual relationships between different generations are much stronger, although a father–daughter relationship seems to be slightly more acceptable than one between mother and son. The reason for the slightly weaker taboo on father–daughter relationships may lie in the replacement of ancient matriarchal social structures with more recent patriarchal ones. Such societies have made the situation of a father exploiting his daughter's tendency to become emotionally and even erotically dependent on him a relatively familiar one, both in literature and in real life. By contrast, the mother–son relationship, regarded by Freud as the archetype of incest, carries the heaviest taboo. When writers touch on this situation they frequently change mother and son to stepmother and stepson, so that the age difference can be less extreme, and aesthetic and moral sensibilities – which prefer lovers to be of a similar age – are appeased.

In a sense, one cannot speak at all of incest itself: it exists only as a taboo. In this form, however, it is an integral part of the structure of the bourgeois family, enabling the developing individual to free himself from the core unit. Little more than that is known about the taboo. Scholars disagree on its origin, and no theory is conclusive: neither the biological theory of degeneration, nor the psychological theory of instinctive or acquired abhorrence, nor the political and economic theories, nor even the psychoanalytical one, which can explain why incest is subconsciously desired, but not why it is consciously condemned. All that is certain is that incest is the only universally applicable taboo in human history. Because of this universality, as Lévi-Strauss explains in his *Elementary Structures of*

Kinship, the incest prohibition colours our understanding of nature, of biology and of psychology. A social phenomenon is inscribed as a 'law', part of a system of rules which make up our culture. The incest prohibition, Lévi-Strauss concludes, is 'the fundamental step thanks to which, through which, and, above all, in which the transition from nature to culture is performed'.

The implication of this for *The Ring* is that any transgression of the incest taboo – whether actual or metaphorical – signals a relapse into the anarchy of nature, the prehistoric, mythical state that precedes history and culture. The tetralogy in its entirety presents us with several transformation processes: from the primordial, pre-verbal stage – suggested by the onomatopoeic sounds of the Rhinemaidens, for example – through the higher world of the gods, who are subject to the laws of hierarchy, to the next stage, the Gibichungs, with their culture and politics. Within these stages we can distinguish creatures for whom the concept of incest does *not yet* have meaning – Erda and the Rhinemaidens, who exist in a state prior to reflective consciousness and history – from those for whom incest *no longer* has meaning: Hagen and the Gibichungs, who have lost all links with nature as expressed in their own human feelings and sensual existence. Between these two extremes are those problematic, transitional creatures who are prone to incest: half-mythical and half-historical, half-natural and half-cultured, they perform a balancing act between progressive dynamism and nostalgic regression. Wotan, Brünnhilde and the twin lovers, Siegmund and Sieglinde exemplify this stage, while Siegfried and Alberich share some of its features.

Wotan's ostentatious castle rises beyond the mountain tops: in contrast to Erda, symbol of mythical nature, who lives in the depths, Wotan bestrides the highest cultural stage of his world. But he is also the character who most spectacularly falls. Having violated nature at the outset of his career, his own imperfection stains the culture of which he is part. Like Hamlet, he is 'sicklied o'er with the pale cast of thought': he is plagued by self-doubt and the realisation of his own impotence, condemned to powerlessness amidst all his power. He is too far removed from natural, instinctive knowledge – he has to obtain this from Erda – but he has not yet achieved the political unscrupulousness of the 'cultured' Gibichungs. The 'unfortunate eternal one' is different from the other gods, having passed through stages in his personal history of which they know nothing: 'When young love's / delights waned in me / my spirit longed for power. / Impetuous wishes / roused me to madness ... / and I won the world for myself ... / By treaties I made alliance with / the powers concealing evil ... / Yet from love / I could not let go / Amid my power I longed for love.'

This internal conflict between power and love distinguishes Wotan from his principal rival, Alberich, who is strengthened by the absence of such indecision. Alberich chooses without hesitation to remain alive: as a dwarf, he is crippled within the natural sphere, but he is also crippled culturally, as an early industrial slave-driver. He is linked, through the motive of the hostile brothers, to the pattern of incest: he and Mime are the more sophisticated foils to the brutish giants, Fafner and Fasolt. However, Alberich is of little relevance here, since his character does not develop: his only interest is as the bestial, instinct-driven forerunner of his son, Hagen. The father's enforced renunciation of love is transmuted into vengeance in the son – vengeance not against 'nature', but against 'culture'. Hagen is no longer a cripple, but complete, frighteningly adult.

To return to Wotan, and his desire for love, as well as power: whom then does he love? It is no longer his wife, Fricka. Their dispute about incest – a central scene in the course of the drama – reveals the reason why they cannot understand one another: they represent different stages of cultural development. Wotan regards the Wälsungs' incest as the privilege of an élite: he applauds their disregard for convention. For Fricka, by contrast, love between Siegmund and Sieglinde is nothing short of criminal. She labels what Wagner sees as 'natural necessity' with the worst possible name: blood-shame. And she insists that Wotan should enforce the supreme penalty: death.

Each one of the divine pair clearly has individual interests to protect, but together they personify the multifarious contradictions involved in the 'incest problem'. Fricka, guardian of matrimonial law and opponent of anarchy, symbolises a cultural order whose sole aim is to defend itself against chaos. Restricted by the constraints of her role, like the other gods, she clings to 'the rules', to 'what has always been done': the letter of the law, to her, is immutable. Wotan, on the other hand, represents change: he wishes to achieve cultural progress by absorbing the lessons of nature and changing the law so that it does not break human beings. Ultimately, however, the cultural regressiveness of Fricka, with Hunding as her agent, prevails over Wotan's idea of progress.

Fricka's cultural system may have triumphed in the forest: among the intrigues of the Gibichung court, however, it seems outdated and primitive. Despite all the talk of honour and loyalty, two marriages are actually concluded by means of deception: Siegfried and Gutrune, Gunther and Brünnhilde. These alliances are the result of matrimonial politics: there are no more tales of love, let alone of incest. There is a pair of siblings linked by identical syllables in their names, however, and this again signifies a deeper identity of character between Gunther and Gutrune, who resemble each other in their decadent weakness, and in their dependence on their half-brother, Hagen, who controls and manipulates them. When he berates them for not having married years ago, they are lost in 'silent thought'. The siblings symbolise the negative aspects of 'high culture', a mirror image of the 'good savages', Siegmund and Sieglinde. The court of the Gibichungs represents a culture whose domination of nature is already well advanced: in the source text, the *Nibelungenlied,* people are already pious enough to attend the cathedral. It is a culture, however, which is no longer ready to deal with its own repressions, intrigues and power struggles. Relapses into barbarity are pre-ordained within this society: the murder of Siegfried, who represents a forgotten Nature, satisfies this regressive need.

The sickness of culture, spoken of in the twentieth century by Freud, is prefigured in Wagner. Whereas Freud, sceptical of progress, remains an advocate of the cultural repression of man's 'natural' forces, Wagner, a Romantic and veteran of the 1848 revolutions, seeks different models. Where could he find the longed-for state in which man was neither a slave to nature, nor a violator of it? In Wagner's writings a strangely timeless phrase – the 'purely human' – is used to describe this state. He meant by this the realisation of human qualities, pure and free from the negative aspects of both a crudely natural state and a denatured cultural state. One could see this fictitious utopian point as a moment of transition: where mythical nature has ceased to be and civilisation has not yet begun its destructive work, where a pure essence shines forth.

These moments are marked in *The Ring* by metaphors of light, rays, radiance and laughter – in the music, even more clearly than in the text. They are the few moments of fulfilment which the plot of the tragedy grants to the loving couples. 'What I am, / bright as the day / it came to me' is how Sieglinde describes the awakening of her love for Siegmund – as a kind of self-awakening. Moonlight, or light at least, falls together with love into Hunding's gloomy hut: 'O let me bend / close down to you, / that clearly I might see / the noble light / that breaks forth from your eye / and countenance.' And Siegmund replies: 'In the spring moonlight / you shine brightly; / nobly embraced by your / wavy hair.' The eyes, the place where light enters both body and soul, are frequently referred to: Sieglinde recognises her father in the Wanderer by his gaze, and Hunding learns of his betrayal from the 'shifty worm' shining in the eyes of the siblings. Later, Brünnhilde defends the corrupted Siegfried: let Hagen hide from the gaze of his 'flashing eye – / which even from his lying face / beamed brightly upon me.' 'You laughing joy of my eyes', Wotan calls his daughter, Brünnhilde. And, in parting, he kisses 'that bright pair of eyes ... for that happier man / may their star shine' – but for him, Wotan, it must close in Act Three of *Die Walküre*.

The love scene of Siegfried and Brünnhilde is the point in the drama at which these metaphors become most concentrated. As Siegfried hastens to his bride, the fire represents not a danger but a portent of love to him: 'Ah! Wonderful fire / Radiant brilliance! Radiant and wide open / is the road to me.' When, on the sunlit summit, he loosens Brünnhilde's armour, all nature joins in: 'Shining clouds / in waves form a hem / to the bright heavenly lake; / the radiant sun's / laughing image / shines through waves of clouds!' As with Siegmund and Sieglinde, awakening of love means awakening of the self: only by loving do characters realise their own identity. 'If I am to wake up / I must awaken the maiden,' says Siegfried. 'Only to you was I to waken!' Brünnhilde replies to him, the 'awakener of life', the 'victorious light'. With multiplying metaphors of light, the love scene hastens towards its climax. He: 'The brilliant light of your eyes / I see shining ... Did you not sing to me / that your knowledge / was your love's radiance for me?' He implores her: 'Emerge from the darkness and look: / the day is bright with sunlight!' She yields, overcoming her fear: 'What shines to me now / is Siegfried's star' – her acknowledgement of the moment of fulfilment. Siegfried replies: 'Hail to the light, / that dispels the night! / Hail to the world ... it smiles at me: / gloriously radiant is / Brünnhilde's star!' Then they both sing of 'radiant love' and 'laughing death'.

Three pairs of lovers from whom the essence of the 'purely human' shines forth: Siegmund and Sieglinde, Wotan and Brünnhilde, Brünnhilde and Siegfried. If we consider these lovers dispassionately, bearing in mind their function in the plot, we are struck by the instability of their situations. Contrary to what they themselves might think, the couples are not beyond everything, dependent only on their subjectivity. They have symbolic functions to fulfil: they represent a state of transition. This is why they combine regressive tendencies with progressive ones: their characters are created from ambivalence.

Siegmund and Sieglinde declare themselves in favour of autonomous, human love, rejecting parental–divine authority: they represent the younger generation, progress and emancipation. Sieglinde, however, pays the price: she reflects and realises that she has broken a universal human taboo – she is flooded, *post coitum*, by guilt. Not so Siegmund: in that respect he already prefigures his son. Culturally, the siblings represent a relapse into an atavistic, unregulated nature which acknowledges only its own laws. Wotan's love for his daughter also represents a regression towards quasi-mythical power, since it is a patriarchal, possessive love. However, he aspires to pass to a higher, better stage, and does not want to relinquish love, but he cannot perform this transition himself. As in a relay race, it is accomplished by his daughter. She transforms what he had intended as a patriarchal act of punishment into a gesture of emancipation: by overcoming her fear of love and of human existence, by accepting her own mortality instead of mourning the loss of her divinity, she brings about the transition from a mythical–divine stage to the bright world of human culture. Indeed, she herself becomes the agent of the decline of the old order: by setting fire to the world of her father; she repays Wotan using the same tool which he had once used to keep her in a state of infantile dependence.

Siegfried's case is more complex. For much too long, he remains in a state of nature, of childishness. He is a creature of the forest, a fighter.

Plunged into the world of politics, he does not realise what is going on: he did not even understand the 'lessons' with which Brünnhilde wanted to send him off. Only in the final minutes of his life does he gain a deeper insight into what has happened to him and accept it as his destiny. This breakthrough of awareness rehabilitates him: at the moment of his death he becomes once more the hero whom Wagner – and his music – required.

Pairs of lovers, intimations of the 'purely human', figures of transition. We may recall Lévi-Strauss's idea that the incest taboo marked the point of transition between nature and culture, the link between the two spheres. In Wagner, things are strangely different. This symbolic location is exclusively occupied, not by the incest taboo, but by incest itself, and by pairs of lovers who commit incest – whether actual (Siegmund and Sieglinde), or 'psychic', to use Robert Donington's term (Wotan and Brünnhilde, Brünnhilde and Siegfried).

What can this mean? That incest, for Wagner, is 'true love'? Or that it stands for an ideal of true love – closer to Robert Musil's utopia than to Thomas Mann's sibling caprice? Wagner never offers us a conventional model of marriage that is not somehow in conflict with love. The fact that the original myths did not offer it either is no defence: Wagner altered his sources whenever it suited him to do so. If incest were the model of true love, however – an uncomfortable thought – then the fact that all the incestuous couples come to grief cannot be overlooked. Is this because of their offence against the universal taboo? Wagner's arrangement of the couples allows us to observe the gradations in the strength of the taboo: as we move from sibling complex to parent complex, Wagner employs ever more elaborate techniques of concealment, reflecting the increasing need for repression.

Brother and sister: the same beauty, the same wildness, the same misery. This did not shock even the prudish audiences of Wagner's day. On the contrary: the identity of the two lovers, emphasised by the similarity of their names, undermined the taboo. A sympathetic reaction was demanded and received. The incestuous tie between Wotan and Brünnhilde, father and daughter, is similarly softened. They too appear as different aspects of the same person, embodiments of the philosophical unity between masculine 'will' and feminine 'wish'. Moreover, the sentimentality of the farewell scene masks the true nature of the relationship. It is only Wotan's jealousy, shown when his previously dependent daughter falls in love with a young man, that clearly reveals the 'psychic incest'. Wotan had already complained when Brünnhilde chose to help Siegmund – 'you sweetly enjoyed / blissful pleasure . . . Blissfully you followed / love's power' – and punished her as a result. When another suitor, Siegfried, arrives, Wotan therefore opposes him with the full force of his jealousy. He has no desire to be condemned to impotence and death: he lights the fire around his 'possession' like a flaming chastity-belt. Nevertheless, the young Oedipus kills the old man. (The fact that Siegfried is Wotan's grandson should not debar us from naming him as 'Oedipus', since the grandfather frequently replaces the more problematic figure of the father in myths, and in any case, Siegfried, having taken up the threads of his father's destiny, *is* Siegmund reborn.) He takes revenge, displaced by a generation, against the 'father' who had his own father murdered, and insists on love on his own terms. Wotan's death is symbolised by the breaking of the spear and the stage direction 'disappears in sudden darkness'.

There is another reason for describing Siegfried as Oedipus: it is not merely that he is as ignorant as the hero of Sophocles' tragedy, which Wagner had carefully studied, nor that Siegfried kills his (grand)father Wotan metaphorically and his foster-father Mime in reality. More fundamentally, the relationship between Siegfried and Brünnhilde, the third and most important pair of lovers, attains Oedipal depths, fulfilling all the most strongly repressed fantasies of the infantile psyche. It is because of these very resonances that the Oedipal nature of the relationship is so strongly disguised. The lovers are aunt and nephew rather than mother and son; and the fact that Brünnhilde has slept for twenty years means that she wakes up apparently the same age as the young hero. Both these factors make the love affair seem natural, even normal. The true, archetypal incest of mother and son unconsciously frightened even the fearless Wagner. Indeed, he confessed that he would have preferred to have left Siegfried in the forest solitude, 'under the lime tree'. But something impelled him to resume work on Act Three of *Siegfried* after an interruption of twelve years – 'with dark exalted shudder', as he wrote to King Ludwig in 1869. He would have liked to avoid the issue altogether, but his friend Eduard Devrient, the Karlsruhe *Kapellmeister*, convinced him that it was dramaturgically impossible to show Siegfried and Brünnhilde quarrelling (as Wagner had planned for *Siegfrieds Tod*) without showing a love scene first.

Although Freud himself bypassed Wagner and *The Ring*, thereby neglecting what might have been a goldmine for him, his disciples, Otto Rank and Georg Groddeck, both interested in myths, legends and fairy tales, found it easy enough to decode Act Three of *Siegfried*. Brünnhilde 'is' Siegfried's mother: Brünnhilde knew that Sieglinde was pregnant, she gave the child his name – and did she not already love Siegmund? Sieglinde herself acknowledges this, with feminine solidarity: 'For him whom we loved / I saved the most precious.' The same husband, the same child: the figures of Brünnhilde and Sieglinde merge into one another. It is small wonder that Siegfried cannot tell the two apart. Brünnhilde introduces herself to him, with mysterious whispers, as his mystical, primordial mother: 'I nurtured you, tender one / even before you were fathered / even before you were born, / my shield protected you.' By doing so, she adds to his confusion, failing to give him an explanation of his origins. Her vagueness has a purpose: in order to attain incestuous happiness, she keeps in play the images both of the mother and of the loved woman. She uses a similar strategy to Kundry, but with greater success. Siegfried does not resist: he is no Parsifal. The 'pure fool' was immune to Kundry's vows of vengeance, but Siegfried is impressed by the promises of his 'mother'. Brünnhilde is forced by convention to release the 'son' into the world – but as soon as he inwardly detaches himself from her and takes another woman as his wife, disaster strikes. 'Gutrune is the name of the magic / which robbed me of my husband,' claims Brünnhilde; blinded by jealousy and hurt pride, she wants his death as 'atonement for him and you'. As a result of her attempt to re-establish an ancient, archetypal state of nature, she suffers a sudden moment of regression: she invokes Wotan, whom she had only recently consigned to the scrap-heap of history.

In psychoanalytical terms, Brünnhilde retards the young man's development: she wants to hold him back in an infantile state of Oedipal fulfilment, or else reconquer him for herself. When Wotan's daughter appears at the Gibichung court, Siegfried finds himself caught in a fatal psychological trap – between mother and wife. He must decide between the two, a choice that cannot be made without cruelty: either one of the two women becomes a victim, or else he himself does. Seen from this point of view, his death is a sacrifice, an atonement – but one made for Brünnhilde, too, and not just, as she believes, 'for him and for you' [the Gibichungs]. His guilty guiltlessness lies in the fact that he could not escape the fantasy mother, the *magna mater*, the *phantasmère*. His wife, Gutrune, also fears Brünnhilde's power: she knows that she will be loved only as long as the potion of forgetfulness remains effective, only while the subconscious keeps silent, only while he forgets his 'mother'. With the end of forgetfulness, of repression, awareness returns to the dying Siegfried, along with the decision that his true 'holy bride' is, after all, his first love, his mother.

She, in turn, pays the price for clinging to her incestuous love for her 'son', for their hedonistic relapse into a primeval world where desires roam freely and lawlessly. When they defy the necessary demands of culture, however, these desires become criminal. Perhaps the dialectics of her words from the final scene – 'I had to be / betrayed by the purest / so that a woman became knowing' – can be interpreted as meaning that she understands why Siegfried had to free himself from her – for his own emancipation. But her word is 'knowing', and 'knowing' always belongs to the mythical sphere of Erda. Brünnhilde has learnt that she, too, must make atonement through death. And she celebrates this as a return to the psychologically and historically atavistic unity of incestuous love. Grane, her horse – a symbol of nature – has to accompany her into the fire: an image of elemental power in which bridal bed and deathbed, celebration of incest and atonement for its lustful joy, are united.

Why, one might ask, among the many versions of the conclusion of *The Ring*, is there none in which Brünnhilde appears as the herald of a new humanity to those helplessly standing by? Why did she, the only character qualified, not become a role model, the symbol of a new order? The only answer can be that it is because of her disregard of the incest prohibition. This, as Lévi-Strauss states, 'is the method by which nature overcomes itself ... it is the spark that allows new and more complex structures to arise ... it gives rise to and is itself the emergence of a new order.' Brünnhilde failed to observe the prohibition: she could not and was not permitted to do so. Wagner had his own good, musically effective and, above all, pleasurably incestuous reasons for not allowing her to observe it.

The end of the performance: both the real performance on the stage, which shows us a process of historical transformation, and the composer's parallel intellectual performance, in which he drives and drags his audience through forbidden areas of the infantile psyche, and through a cathartic process of punishment and mourning. Exhausted and stunned, we leave the theatre. If it is true that mythical creations are structured in the same way as our early childhood fantasies, then how could we resist the appeal to our own subconscious? In life, we can have anything except incest; in the real world, we can be anything we like except a fearlessly free hero. All this is possible in legends, fantasy and art. But even there, a cultured person cannot escape censorship: at the level of the word, the plot, *The Ring* as drama, we encounter the cultural, 'progressive' condemnation of exactly that which the music so vigorously celebrates and endorses.

It is the music of *The Ring*, as Ernst Bloch observed, that makes the action so incandescent. It generates such passion that it becomes difficult for culture to prevail over nature, and for the taboo against older and more persistent desires to be enforced. *The Ring* is a fantasy of desires fulfilled through music, a grand narrative of incest performed in numerous disguises, reshapings and mythical transformations. It is an incest fantasy enjoyed by its creator, in and through his music. 'Art begins at the precise point where life ends,' Wagner wrote to Liszt, 'when nothing is there, then we call out in art: I would that.' But art fulfils itself only through form and in form. Wagner's command of form helps him to remain the master of his desires: the structure of his drama allows him to sentence the offender even as he celebrates the offence. Because of the control he exercises, we cultured citizens, despite having been accessories to incest, can go home reassured – almost.

5

The 'Blissful Union': Wotan and Brünnhilde

FROM BEHIND A CLUMP OF ROCKS, A YOUNG GIRL IN ARMOUR bursts upon the stage, jubilant, fierce, childlike – Brünnhilde. Her over-brimming *joie de vivre* is evident from her exuberant cries, leaping from high to low and back again – 'Heiaha! Hojotoho!' Headstrong, angular and jagged, her song is like the mountains all around: it echoes the world of nature that surrounds the Valkyries, the nature that is Brünnhilde's home. There was a similar harmony between the voice and nature back in *Das Rheingold*, when the Rhinemaidens emitted their soft, wavelike, primeval cries. Brünnhilde, like those creatures from the watery depths, leads an untroubled existence, even though it is not the existence of a woman – nor yet of a man, in spite of the fact that she engages in battle. Brünnhilde is at one with herself because she is at ease with her appointed role, and the task that so fulfils her has been assigned to her by Wotan, her father.

It does not occur to her that her mission – luring heroes to their death so that they can reside in Valhalla – is a bloody and ugly one. For her, the justness of her assignments is guaranteed by the fact that her father, whom she loves, commands them. She in turn is his favourite daughter, preferred by him to any of the other 'bad girls' whom he has fathered out of wedlock. In a sense, Brünnhilde is also Wotan's favourite *wife*: he is fond of talking of their 'blissful union'. A man's favourite wife is generally the one who confirms his godhead, rather than challenging it. Brünnhilde is no trouble-maker – unlike Fricka, the wife, with her incessant nagging, or Freia, who refuses to be sold, or Erda, who constantly utters warnings before vanishing into the ground. Brünnhilde rides with Wotan through storms and foul weather, hands him his beer at table and lets herself be kissed by him at all times. Her childlike femininity enchants without offending, her boyish masculinity conceals no Oedipal threats. Wotan's breast can swell with fatherly pride as he summons her into battle to support Siegmund against Hunding. She follows him enthusiastically, though not without teasing him – rather as lovers do – when she catches sight of Fricka approaching in high dudgeon.

The first scene of Act Two of *Die Walküre* conveys an impression of serenity, because authority and obedience are in balance. The daughter is happy being as her father wants her to be, the father is happy because the daughter is his cheerful accomplice, flesh of his flesh, like an extension of his own power. The next encounter between them, however, shows us the same tenderness transposed into a meditative–depressive mood. The stage direction here says: 'Intimately, and anxiously, she puts her hands and head on his knee and in his lap. Wotan looks into her eyes for a long time; then, with profound tenderness, he strokes her hair. As if awaking from profound meditation, he finally begins.' He proceeds to tell her his own story, as if speaking to his own soul: 'I take counsel only with myself / when I speak to you.' The intimacy of this cannot be surpassed. Elsewhere Wotan calls Brünnhilde his 'wish maiden', a phrase which reveals the extent to which his daughter has become the incarnation of his fantasies, as though his unconscious had taken shape in her. Did Brünnhilde perhaps not yet exist outside her father's imagination? Shaken by compassion as she hears of the constraints to which he is subject, she asks in alarm 'O tell me / what is your child to do now?'

Even if we were not in the middle of *The Ring* – in which familiarity with both the Nibelung epic and Wagner's pessimistic dramaturgy tell us that nothing good can last for long – we would realise that such an ideal love is doomed. We are sufficiently well aware of the problems of infantile narcissistic symbiosis within the family circle, and have been ever since Enlightenment called for the independence of the individual and psychoanalysis reinforced its message by demanding maturity. Let us remember Thomas Mann, who coined the phrase 'daughter–adjutant' to describe the role of his favourite daughter Erika, who also acted as his secretary, biographer and guardian of his archive; let us recall Anna Freud, interpreter, successor and 'Antigone' to her eminent father. Brünnhilde belongs to the same breed of 'daughter–adjutant'; the military connotations of the term reflect the element of identification with the masculine role which the daughter undertakes for her father's sake. These masculine associations also suggest the risks involved in such a symbiotic relationship with the father. Daughter–adjutants often lose their own femininity as they renounce their independence, and they frequently end up as childless spinsters, victims of their own devotion. Such women are often depicted as having 'missed out': Ibsen and Schnitzler have both created telling depictions of the fate of this type of woman within bourgeois patriarchal society. The crucial issue for the daughter–adjutant is whether she can detach herself from her father. This is generally not possible without conflict, pain, and the danger of lapsing back into the quasi-incestuous relationship.

Generally speaking, the psychological remedy for such a situation is for the girl to fall in love with a younger, stronger man – ideally a stranger, who removes her from even the temptation of relapse. For Brünnhilde, Siegfried, the young and carefree man of action, is a complete contrast to Wotan, doubter and sceptic. And does not Brünnhilde, freed from the fetters of Wotan, hail Siegfried with a grand gesture that seems to sweep away her father's whole world in favour of sexual love? – 'Farewell, Valhalla's / radiant world! / Fall into dust / your proud castle! / Farewell, sumptuous / splendour of gods! . . . What shines to me now / is Siegfried's star!' Brünnhilde's attachment seems to have been successfully transferred to a young lover, in a classic example of healthy emancipation from a dominant father. But not so fast . . . The Ring does not finish with Siegfried, and a great deal changes before the end really comes.

Most of the conflicts that have been represented on the stage, ever since the days of Aeschylus, are in one way or another clashes of authority. In crude terms, there are only two possible outcomes to such conflicts, after the period of crisis and anarchy has passed: the old order is either consolidated, or replaced by a new one. Conflict between different generations of the same family can be regarded as the archetype of such power struggles between old and new, and Oedipus's parricide forms a basic model for all dramatic conflicts between father and son. Interestingly, however, there is no such clear model for the conflict between father and daughter, perhaps because matters are made more complex by the presence of heterosexual attraction in the relationship, and the tendency of daughters to help and support their father whenever he reveals a weakness. Antigone is perhaps the best archetype of this supportive father–daughter relationship: she selflessly and touchingly accompanied her blinded father, Oedipus, into exile. However, her subsequent behaviour also makes her an archetype of inter-generational conflict, when she rebels against the inhuman, patriarchal authority of her uncle Creon by deciding to give her brother a proper burial. Wagner, significantly, loved and praised the character of Antigone, and Brünnhilde can be regarded as her spiritual kinswoman, though one in whom the neuroses of the nineteenth century have been superimposed. And Brünnhilde's story, too, can be interpreted in terms of emancipation from the older generation by establishing the moral supremacy of the new.

It is love that triggers the first stage of Brünnhilde's emancipation: in this case, for a (half-)brother, Siegmund. Brünnhilde witnesses his uncompromising love for Sieglinde, and this softens the 'cold and hard' heart of the Valkyrie: she refuses her father's command to let Siegmund die and changes her allegiance in order to try and protect him, thereby disobeying her father for the first time in her life. Wagner represents this on stage in a way that makes the alignments of power clear: on the right, high up on the stage, Brünnhilde hovers over Siegmund in a glow of light, protecting him with her shield; to the left, above Hunding, Wotan breaks through the dark clouds. Father and daughter face each other like two ghostly manifestations. The visual presentation makes the severance of their previous complicity clear: their erotically charged symbiotic relationship is about to end.

The prerequisite of this end is a crisis of parental authority itself. Wotan's position of authority has already been challenged: the Ring no longer belongs to him, and he has to worry about his own future. Moreover, he can no longer act according to his own wishes, and he has to punish his daughter for doing what he would like to do. Impotent and forced on to the defensive, his assertions of power are bound to assume a more violent character. In terms of private, family relationships, this means that the two functions of a good father – to provide loving care and to carry out just punishment – no longer operate in tandem, but are severed, acting in opposition to one another. The father becomes Janus-faced, able to turn at will to show a loving or a punishing appearance. Wotan is a textbook case of such a dissociation of authority. As soon as Brünnhilde ventures to contradict him, pointing out that he has always taught her to love Siegmund and that it is therefore unnatural for her suddenly to turn against him, he explodes with wrath: 'Ha, insolent one! Dost thou defy me? . . . Dost thou, child / know my wrath?' His vacillations between fatherly sentimentality and an authoritarian willingness to punish offers her an opportunity to prepare her withdrawal from the role of adjutant, and to find her own destiny and her own lover – but this is a slow, gradual process.

In an example of pathetic fallacy, stormy weather dominates the end of Act Two and the beginning of Act Three of *Die Walküre*: lightning, clouds and driving rain express the ruler's fury at his daughter's insubordination. Fear grips the Valkyrie as she anticipates her punishment, 'Wotan's vengeance'. We are back in the nursery, where we experience the helplessness of a minor at the mercy of parental power: perhaps the familiarity of this scenario is one reason for the popularity of Act Three. We witness the gradual psychological process through which the child becomes emancipated from the parent, and the difficulties involved in detaching oneself from ties of blood. 'Expelled / from the clan of the Eternal ones; / broken is our union: / from my countenance thou art banned!' – Wotan hurls invective at his daughter, scarcely able to do justice in words to the nature of the punishment she deserves. He will plunge her into 'defenceless sleep', abandon her to prostitution, condemn her to a domestic life of shame and disgrace. Brünnhilde breaks down.

The destruction of the father–daughter relationship reaches its negative climax, then the storm quietens down and dusk subsides into night. To the accompaniment of slowly ascending woodwind phrases, Brünnhilde raises herself up again, both physically and psychologically. After all, she was not Wotan's adjutant for nothing. The training in masculine behaviour that this role provided also developed her capability for debate. It is wonderful how she now argues freely against an uncertain and questionable paternal authority, until that authority finally crumbles and Wotan pours out his whole existential misery. She uses the opportunity to suggest to him that he could, without losing face, convert her intended humiliation into a female triumph: by placing her in the circle of fire, she gains the assurance that only the best and strongest man can rescue her, and he gains the consolation that even if she no longer belongs to him, she will not belong to another for some time. The stage is set for the last and most profound love scene between father and daughter: 'Farewell, you bold / you wonderful child!' Almost overloaded with psychologically resonant symbols – the daughter's enclosure in armour, her return to a prenatal state of sleep, the 'bridal fire', the departing god who defies all challengers to his paternal authority – this scene, with its flow of incestuous undertones and exploration of a waning parental authority, has challenged the emotional resources of audiences for more than a century.

One of Wagner's greatest achievements in *The Ring* was the way in which he used family struggles, with which everyone in the audience could identify, to illuminate and explain conflicts of power on a much larger scale. Wotan's self-mutilating destruction of his own capacity for love is made clear through his treatment of his beloved daughter: we understand why he now roams the world as the Wanderer. The ruler deprived of power signifies a time without authority, a transitional period in which the heir can reach maturity. And so he does – but Siegfried, created to be the free, natural man of a future society, paradoxically takes his bearings from the oldest models. Oedipus-like, he shatters the spear of his (grand-)father Wotan, collects the daughter from the rock and begins a radiant love affair with her. Departure for something new and better might now begin.

However, both the lovers are corrupted in the course of their transition to the real, historical world: Siegfried cheats and lies, and Brünnhilde, motivated by affronted love, complies with the plot of Hagen and Gunther to murder Siegfried. There are strange relapses into archaic habits, as when Brünnhilde, helpless in the face of court intrigue, invokes the gods and calls on her father, the old breaker of treaties, as a 'guardian of oaths'. This is where the final stage of *Götterdämmerung* picks up: musically and dramatically it highlights Brünnhilde as the all-knowing, wronged lover, who redeems the ancient curse by flinging the Ring back into the Rhine.

But she is *not* shown as the 'new woman' who might point the way out of corrupt conditions into a more just order. Instead of turning forward towards Utopia, Brünnhilde heads back into myth. Mounting Grane, the mythological steed tying her to her existence as a daughter, virgin and Valkyrie, she leaps on to the pyre to be burnt in love-death. However, the full significance of that regression, of that annulment of her personal emancipation, is only revealed when one understands the meaning of this grandiose auto-da-fé: 'Thus do I set fire / in Valhalla's splendid castle.'

That which she had so ardently wished when Siegfried awakened her from the rock with a kiss – the fall of her father's world – she now turns into action. It is not Alberich who storms and destroys the castle, but Brünnhilde. Having realised the extent of the crime that the father–god committed against her and his other children, she is ready to carry out a colossal act of revenge with her own hands. This revenge, significantly enough, is carried out through the element that caused her own imprisonment – fire. This is doubly significant, for fire was not only the instrument with which Wotan punished her, it was also the substance that ensured that she could be rescued by no one other than Siegfried. This in turn meant that she could never complete the self-emancipation that she had begun with her act of disobedience: for Siegfried, despite appearances, was not the stranger, the other man, who might really have released her from the incestuous ties of her 'blissful union' with her father. To love Siegfried meant an infringement of the incest taboo. Like the other close kinship ties between the characters in *The Ring*, this union was bound to result in guilt – and therefore in punishment. This served the composer's purposes well, for the scenarios that resulted allowed him to unleash his battery of sound effects in a way that made his description of himself as a musical 'plenipotentiary of doom' seem entirely warranted.

The scandalous aspects of the story of *The Ring* are that a father is trying to use his children to prevent his own end, that an old man sweeps young people to death with him, that a ruler makes his descendants pay for his mismanagement. Brünnhilde and her sisters were deliberately conceived as a squadron to ensure their father's victory, while Siegmund and Sieglinde were also created as instruments of the god's will. The cycle plays out the drama of misused and lost children, both on the political and the psychological plane; it is an allegory for the string of disasters triggered when a power-hungry authority refuses to abdicate or to prepare a succession for a different and more just world.

It is a pessimistic end. But the real conclusion of *The Ring* is no longer action, but sound. Hope, if not redemption, can be detected in the music. The motive that comes to dominate the end of the piece has been heard once before in the cycle: Sieglinde sang it in *Die Walküre*, when it expressed her desire to continue living herself, in order to save the life of her unborn child. A child personifies the idea of life in all civilisations: it need not necessarily grow into a Siegfried. This idea – a life saved, and life as a saviour – is the real conclusion of *Götterdämmerung*.

6

The Twice-Solitary Death in *Tristan*

WHY, IN AN AGE OF SEXUAL FREEDOM, IN WHICH THE EROTIC is endlessly represented and analysed in the media, should we be so interested in *Tristan* – this medieval epic of love and suffering, this Celtic legend in a seductive night-dress, which stoked up and satisfied the erotic fantasies of cultured citizens of the Wilhelminian and Victorian eras more powerfully than any other drama? Is there not something adolescent in our continuing fetish for *Tristan*? Does a metaphysically transfigured love-death still have the power to sweep us away, when we have surely become accustomed to much grittier trials of love and death?

Tristan no longer has any 'message' for us, the theatre critic Siegfried Melchinger wrote in 1962. In it, he suggested, Wagner had found a thera-peutic release for his own inner tensions that was necessary if he was to proceed to the 'healthier' *Meistersinger*. In other words, he left us the *beaux restes* of his mid-life crisis, whose most obvious human manifestation was in his infatuation with Mathilde. Tristan and Isolde had to die, so that the composer could live.

Whether or not it is true that *Tristan* has no message, it is interesting to observe that philosophers, poets and critics, whom one might have expected to elucidate its meaning for us, have always, right from the beginning, given us only paraphrases of the work. This began with Nietz-sche's *Fifty Worlds of Strange Delights*, full of that visionary, esoteric, death-haunted Tristanism which was characteristic of the European decadent movement. Then there were Thomas Mann's reflections on 'Tristan's Cosmology of Nostalgia', which he subsequently ironised in his short story named after the opera's hero, and there were Ernst Bloch's whispered words about the 'huge adagio of night'. Even musical scholars who are generally analytical and objective seem to have become infected by a bombastic vagueness where *Tristan* is concerned. Paul Bekker speaks of the 'fundamental will of ascending chromaticism', and Arnold Schoenberg uncharacteristically resorted to the metaphorical plane when considering the *Tristan* chords: 'phenomena of incredible adaptability and non-independence roaming, homeless, among the spheres of keys; spies reconnoitring weaknesses, to exploit them in order to create confusion, deserters for whom surrender of their own personality is an end in itself...'

When a work of art incessantly prompts such verbal paraphrases, we should stop and wonder why. To paraphrase is to circumscribe, it suggests that there is something that cannot be explained simply or directly, that something is being held back and concealed. Why – because the thing concealed might contain something terrifying, or because it is simply incommunicable, unutterable? Without presuming that we can snatch the secret message from *Tristan*, we might try, following the example of King Mark in Act Two, to get closer to that 'deeply mysterious base'.

In terms of both structure and content, *Tristan* is an interplay of opposites – man and woman, night and day, land and sea, reality and illusion, life–love and love–death. On a broader level, too, there is a conflict, as in *Lohengrin*, between the quasi-historical elements of the drama, and its more abstract, timeless aspects. The former are represented by the references to the Middle Ages, courtly customs, honour, and the duty of the vassal, and by the conventional motives of the magic potions and the drama of adultery. The abstract elements of the piece include its emphasis on the psychological condition of slavery to love, the fact that the main part of the action is set 'outside time' in the 'vast realm of the world's night', and the way in which pure emotion becomes a dramatic force in its own right. To use a phrase from Roland Barthes, whose *Fragments d'un discours amoureux* [A Lover's Discourse] will serve us further in this chapter, love forms a 'system of the imaginary'.

The plot is determined by the way in which these contrasts are brought into play. Given these polarised starting points, we might expect the action to be dominated by conflict and clashes of interests. But Wagner prided himself, in this work above all, on his ability to create an art that 'points to mediation and intimate blending of all elements of transition of external moods into one another', as well as on having delicately linked together the two 'pillars' of 'overbrimming life' and 'most devout longing for death'. By contrast with his approach in *Tannhäuser*, his overriding aim here is to provide intermediate stages between the polarities. This aspiration motivates Wagner's distinctive musical approach in this piece: in particular, the method of modulating using chromatic semitonal steps, rather than traditional diatonic cadences. The new approach results in fewer audible contrasts of key and an impression of harmonic continuum. Musically, as well as philosophically, Wagner's aim is to achieve *rapprochement* and conciliation between opposing principles.

But we must beware of imposing too reasonable and democratic an interpretation on the piece. For the action of *Tristan* does not suggest that opposing views can be reconciled through dialogue and mediation: on the contrary, it is full of misunderstandings between characters, both deliberate and inadvertent. The deceptive nature of verbal communication is constantly revealed, and 'lies', 'betrayal', 'illusion' and 'treason' are among the most frequent and most important words in the drama. There is a double meaning to every action and every character. Again, there is an analogy here with Wagner's musical methods, since in this piece (unlike *The Ring*) there are relatively few 'labelled' leitmotifs. Although emotions and ideas are undoubtedly represented, defining them in words is a slippery business. Moreover, motifs suggesting contradictory emotions are constantly combined – the nostalgia motif and the grief motif appear in conjunction from the outset, for example – and this uncertainty of labelling creates a general climate of ambivalence.

Contradiction and paradox pervade the plot, too. Tristan is Tantris; the escort of the bride is the real bridegroom; the physician Isolde is the cause of the disease; the loyal Melot is the enemy; King Mark wants to bring peace but only increases the harvest of death. The dialogue between employers and servants is riddled with mutual incomprehension. Brangäne hears Isolde's wrath but fails to recognise it as love; her wrong potion is the right one, and her warning sounds like a lullaby. Kurwenal fails to understand the truth about Tristan: he believes that some sort of witch-craft or 'love magic' has been at work, and fails to recognise that his master's feverish ravings actually tell the truth, that his sufferings are the result of his own character. 'Treason' – or acting in opposition to one's real wish – is a constant cry: Isolde accuses him of treason against his love when he is acting for Mark, and Mark accuses him of the same crime when he does the opposite.

Deception is at the heart of the whole dramatic machinery: self-deception about love. And even when this first level of misunderstanding is resolved at the end of Act One, the major reversal of the piece is only just beginning: day is overturned by night, and with this comes a paradoxical reversal of the values that have governed the action thus far. Daylight had concealed the truth; darkness brings enlightenment. But the final and cruellest deception of the piece comes at the end, when Tristan dies in Isolde's arms, having ripped off his bandages prematurely. 'Is Isolde cheated, / does she cheat Tristan / out of this only, / eternally brief / last worldly happiness,' Isolde asks in despair – surely they had agreed to die together?

Tristan's breaking of the covenant of simultaneous, symbiotic death reveals a truth that was not properly articulated until after Wagner's time. It took psychoanalysis and modern literature to declare that even in love every person is alone: that love is a projection of the self, a code-name for all sorts of other needs. Although we hold the romantic hope that we can submerge our ego in another person, this is ultimately a pious self-deception – and such self-deception seems to invite catastrophe, as indeed occurs in Act Three of *Tristan*. Surrender of his own personality is an end in itself for Tristan – Schoenberg's 'diagnosis' of the chord holds good for the hero, too. In looking back on his life, Tristan reveals his egotism in death: 'To what destiny chosen / was I then born? / To what fate? / The old tune / tell me again – / to yearn and die, / to die and yearn!' Death is in fact the fulfilment of Tristan's own ego, the destiny to which he had been born. Love seemed to have offered him the chance to keep this forbidden death-wish from himself; but it was ultimately the medium through which that wish was ruthlessly fulfilled.

Tristan exemplifies the modern perception that one cannot escape from oneself. It is in illusion, in love, in madness – as Roland Barthes argues –

that one experiences this 'inability to restrain oneself from being a subject: I am no one else, and this I perceive with terror.' The withdrawal from the megalomaniac fantasy of Act Two, the lovers' joint declaration that 'Even then am I the world', delimits that experience of existential terror in *Tristan*, whose real truth must be concealed, silenced – or paraphrased.

What about Isolde? Does she experience the same existential shock? Had she not, even in Act One, defined their joint addiction to death in love? – 'Chosen for me / lost to me/ ... Doomed head! / Doomed heart!' Isolde – again following Barthes' interpretation – lives a 'catastrophic love', love as an extreme, a psychosis, a trap. Her attitude is that 'I have so violently projected myself into the other that, if he is lost, I can no longer find my way out ... I am lost for ever.'

Wagner's dramaturgy nevertheless reveals certain differences between the lovers' attitudes. Isolde 'follows' Tristan into death, just as she had promised in Act Two; but death was not, for her, the inevitable trajectory of her life. Unlike Tristan, she was not necessarily born for misfortune, only for the radical fulfilment of her passionate desires. In this, the 'wild loving maiden' reveals the uncompromising nature of youth.

The finale belongs to Isolde: musically, it witnesses a resurgence of the sensual world of the love duet from Act Two, which helps to shield the audience from the terrible truth that is known to Tristan. Overwhelmed by the flood of music, the spectator will no doubt reconstruct for himself the utopian unity of the lovers, Tristan and Isolde. Wagner – an old wizard himself when it came to manipulating emotions – has pulled off his last and most spectacular deception of the evening: beneath the glorious cloak of the *Liebestod*, the true tragedy proceeds in silence.

Two worlds, two planes interact in this opera. At one level, as we have discussed, all communication is governed by the principle of deception, and the ambivalence of every verbal utterance is effectively mirrored by the all-pervasive chromaticism of Wagner's music. But there is another level of communication, which exclusively concerns 'the ones dedicated to the night': Tristan and Isolde, now understood separately as man and woman, each with a definite identity and a physical body. Every listener senses that in Act Two they have achieved what they long for, the fulfilment of their love. Is it then possible, after all, that two 'systems of the imaginary' (as Barthes called the illusion of love) can attain congruence – that a relationship can exist, even temporarily, that is not undermined by deception and betrayal?

According to Wagner, *Tristan* is a demonstration of his 'art of resounding silence'. This is of course a logical paradox; normally, something either resounds or it is silent, but here, silence and sound seem to be present simultaneously. It is significant that it is only through paradox that love can realise itself. Inevitably, the merging of opposites cannot last: destruction is inevitable. Fulfilment of love requires the destruction of selfhood: 'Wholly given to ourselves, / to live for love alone... No more Tristan, / nor Isolde!' The 'sweet little word "and" ' – the final rhetorical separation, the final particle of reality which protects the boundaries of the person – is suspended by the lovers' ardour. This is why the promise of total love also contains the promise of death. This is why the most profoundly contradictory experiences can converge into one another: the lovers' bodies grow hot with passion as they become cold with death. The lovers' mystical union, their paradoxical oneness, is described above all in the music of Act Two: gradually the lovers' utterances, increasing in fervour as they diminish in length, are absorbed into this ineffable flow of pure sound.

There are two other bodies of literature that have particularly favoured the linguistic form of the paradox: the writing of the medieval mystics, trying to describe their closeness to God, and the literature of the modern age (Franz Kafka in particular) which has felt obliged to explain its sense of existential remoteness from God. The mystics describe the exaltation of finding a transcendental point of reference; the moderns convey the despair of finding themselves abandoned to their own subjectivity. To the mystic, experience is paradoxical because black and white, light and dark, all coincide in God. To Kafka, on the other hand, the paradox is that all the apparent alternatives in fact lead in the same direction: his world is a blind alley, entirely cut off from the outside.

Like both of these groups, Tristan and Isolde understand their own situation in terms of its paradoxes – and their situation shares something with that of both the mystic and the existentialist. Tristan and Isolde are in fact secularised mystics. Their own experience of love is as ineffable as the mystics' experience of God, but their souls are modern. They pay homage to the religion of the self, like most of Wagner's characters (*Parsifal* is an anachronistic exception) but their attempt at mutual deification leads nowhere. At the end of *Tristan*, all that remains is the deserted island, subjectivity, the twice-solitary death.

7

Folly and Wit in *Die Meistersinger*

OUR CONCEPTION OF *DIE MEISTERSINGER VON NÜRNBERG* IS almost overburdened by visual images: productions tend to leave their remnants in the imagination. Despite the quantity and diversity of productions in recent years, the visual impressions they leave coalesce into a single, slightly imprecise set of images. These images are Old German – think of Dürer and Holbein – with Old Nuremberg as the backdrop. Martin Luther, the spirit of the Reformation, humanism and a certain bourgeois cosiness are there in the background too. Memories of one German in a nightcap beating up another, and of Hans Sachs, the cobbler poet, also tend to rise to the surface when the piece is remembered. But we do not think of the view of medieval Germany presented in *Die Meistersinger* as belonging entirely to the chocolate-box; too many people have made us aware of its political connotations for that. Nietzsche hailed the opera as a 'genuine symbol of the German soul'; Hofmannsthal regarded its national sentiments as the 'perceptible beginnings of German unification, and for the Third Reich, notoriously, it was the opera chosen to rally the Party. Even after the war, when Nuremberg was better known for its rallies than for its singing competitions, it was still regarded as a symbol of traditional German bourgeois values. The persistence of this view defied producers' attempts both to depoliticise, as in 1956, when it was staged in Wieland Wagner's 'New Bayreuth' as an abstract drama of the soul, and to repoliticise, as in Frankfurt in 1993, when the fascist implications of the exhortation to 'Honour your German masters' were clearly suggested. Various productions of *Die Meistersinger*, including that Bayreuth production of 1956, will be discussed in the next chapter, but the present essay is concerned with a particular aspect of the piece itself: the nature of its humour.

It is well known that Wagner planned *Die Meistersinger* as a 'comical play': a kind of 'satyr play' to follow the tragedy of *Tannhäuser*. The word 'comedy' even appears in the subtitle of the second and third prose versions. In 1861, he promised his publisher an 'original, thoroughly cheerful, even hilarious subject', with 'transparent and pithy music of the most cheerful colour'. While composing the piece in 1862, he reported that he was 'sometimes unable to work for laughing and crying', and he wrote to Mathilde Wesendonck that the idea of the piece was that 'people should laugh'. Of course, the clarity of the composer's declared intentions by no means proves that *Die Meistersinger* is witty, or cheerful, or humorous. Many listeners have failed to see the funny side, ever since Wagner complained to Nietzsche's sister Elisabeth that 'Your brother is just like Franz Liszt – he doesn't like my jokes either'. Carl Dahlhaus spoke of a *Meistersinger* humour that could not be trusted, and Adorno called Wagner's humour altogether 'bestial'. Others, such as Dietmar Holland, have argued that the mainspring of the opera's humour is not wit, but *Schadenfreude*: pleasure gained from someone else's discomfiture. By probing the nature of Wagner's 'comedy' – an exception to his usual preference for serious and morbid subjects – we may begin to understand the Janus face of Wagnerian humour.

Much of the comedy of *Die Meistersinger* is derived from conventions that were invented long before Wagner's birth. The composer took some well-known character types and some well-tested situations from the comedies of the eighteenth and early nineteenth centuries: the cranky old man courting a younger woman, a young couple in love, a father who puts obstacles in the way of the lovers by attaching conditions to their marriage, the introduction of a second pair of lovers on a lower social level – and of course, the obligatory happy ending. Admittedly, it is unusual to introduce a second elderly gentleman as a potential suitor, as Wagner does, but this variation on the conventional formula provides additional comic possibilities: thus the two elderly suitors trade insults in the nocturnal second act, unaware that the object of their affections is hidden in the nearby bushes with her preferred choice of husband. The scenario of disguise in *Die Meistersinger* is also in line with comic tradition: here it only involves Magdalene wearing Eva's bonnet to deceive Beckmesser, a rather less sophisticated use of the convention than Mozart and Da Ponte managed in *Figaro*. However, the effectiveness of Wagner's use of the disguise convention lies in the series of repercussions, culminating in a general brawl among nightshirted figures in the St John's Eve darkness – a scene worthy of Feydeau, though with rather less erotic content.

The humour occasioned by errors of judgement in *Die Meistersinger* is not all at this rather farcical level: there is also plenty of the psychological intrigue that is indispensable to comedy. On the morning of the singing contest, for example, Beckmesser stumbles into Sachs' parlour, still dazed and confused from the fighting of the night before. There he finds a manuscript – Walther's poem, transcribed by Sachs. He understandably believes that it is the shoemaker's own effort at writing a 'suitor's song', and he therefore steals it, to eliminate the work of what he perceives as a potential rival. But Sachs enters just in time to discover Beckmesser's theft. Instead of enlightening him about his double error – the mistaken belief that the song is by Sachs, and that Sachs is a serious contender for Eva's hand – he leaves him with his delusion. He has deceived him without actually having to lie: he simply relies on Beckmesser's confused state of mind and his limited artistic judgement. The intrigue succeeds, the trap snaps shut – and Beckmesser is publicly disgraced. In consequence, he disappears from the race and the field is clear for Eva's favourite, Walther.

Tampering with documents, forged letters, communications that fall into the wrong hands – these are all part of the stock-in-trade of comedy. The difference here is that the crucial document is not a love letter, but a song. This change is made in order to reinforce the link between the two strands of action in *Die Meistersinger* – the love story and the artistic conflict. The opera also makes use of the familiar theatrical trick of whipping up the confusion to reach a climax just as the curtain falls. In Act One, there is a cacophonous finale in the singing school, with everyone singing against everyone else. In Act Two, there is the chaos of the brawl;

the words become completely incomprehensible, until the point where buckets of water are emptied over the heads of the hooligans. In Act Three, however, the crowd is represented in a civilised and controlled form: the people sing a great chorus, containing first the Luther chorale, then the hymn to the hero of Nuremberg, Hans Sachs. By now, the function of this figure is no longer comic: he is a representative of order and solemnity.

The paean of praise sung to German art, Nuremberg and Hans Sachs has nothing to do with comic confusion: it signals a change in the genre of the work, from comedy to something akin to *opera seria*. There is nothing inevitable about this last-minute abandonment of the comic muse. In Verdi's *Falstaff*, for example – a piece often compared to *Die Meistersinger* – the ending is of the same character as the rest of the work. The concluding fugue contains the message that all the world is a 'burla' – a trick or joke. The way is left open for more comedy to be written. The ending of *Die Meistersinger*, by contrast, blows away anything comic, witty or cheerful. The chief comedian, Beckmesser, is simply 'lost in the crowd', according to the stage directions. And Wagner was forced to abandon the subtitle 'comedy'. The ending of the piece makes it clear that we are not dealing here with an orthodox comic opera, despite the fact that so many of the conventions of comedy are incorporated within it. It has plenty of humour, yet its overall impact is only ambiguously comic. Let us investigate Wagner's own humour further, in order to try and resolve this paradox.

An anecdote about the piece's genesis may provide some insight into the particular nature of this humour. In 1861, Wagner was in Venice with the Wesendoncks: his former muse, Mathilde, and her husband Otto. On one particular excursion, this curious trio found themselves examining Titian's 'Assumption of the Virgin Mary' with 'an enormous opera glass'. In Wagner's words, this painting had 'an effect of the most exalted kind': he felt his 'old strength all of a sudden revived'. The effect of this experience was sudden and surprising: 'I resolved to execute *Die Meistersinger*.'

There is little obvious similarity between the biblical figures in Titian's painting and the humble folk of Nuremberg; it is not immediately apparent why the sight of this masterpiece should have turned Wagner's thoughts in the direction of Hans Sachs and the libretto he had drafted ten years earlier. The answer to this conundrum perhaps lies in the sense of perspective conveyed by Titian. The Virgin is portrayed with arms outstretched and an expression of ecstasy, carried by angels towards heaven – and away from the bustling world below. On the one hand, the spectator is swept heavenwards with the Virgin; on the other, his gaze takes in the people below, as though observing the throng from a great height. Perhaps this godlike perspective suddenly gave Wagner an idea of the view he should take of the world of the Mastersingers – a view that was peculiarly suitable for a comic opera. This idea resonates with a definition of humour supplied by that other great poet and humorist from Bayreuth, the Romantic writer Jean Paul. He argued that humour was 'the inversion of the exalted': he compared it to a bird who, while turning its tail to the sky, nonetheless flew upwards. The humour of Wagner's Nuremberg derives from the composer's ability to see it from a great height: from this bird's eye (or God's eye) view, the limited and foolish nature of the Mastersingers' preoccupations could be loftily if fondly observed.

The relevance of Jean Paul's idea of humour to *Die Meistersinger* does not stop there. The writer argued that humour must contain the totality of the world represented; it aims at the general, unlike satire, which is concerned with the particular. In *Die Meistersinger*, Wagner makes a conspicuous effort to portray a *whole* world, and this generosity of perspective explains the composer's mild, wholly unsatirical attitude to the ridiculous aspects of that world. His approach is realistic, in stark contrast to his usual preference for a timeless, mythical setting: the place, Nuremberg, and the time, the early sixteenth century, are precisely specified, and this historical milieu is effectively evoked by the slightly archaic and mannered tone of the music. Moreover, the intricate social structures of this society are depicted in fine detail, and the social consequences of characters' economic relationships are revealed. Although this 'realistic' view means that the foolishness of the characters is revealed, Wagner generally takes a lenient view of their foibles. He is a humorist, who cannot deny his kinship with mankind – not a satirist, who regards himself as different from that which he ridicules.

The aspiration to portray the world in general rather than just an aspect of it is also evident from the archetypal quality of most of the principal characters. Many of the names refer to biblical characters who are themselves regarded as representing particular aspects of humanity. Thus Eva is not only Pogner's real-life daughter, but also the biblical Eve about whom Sachs sings. The shoemaker himself may be understood as representing John the Baptist, who is referred to in the opening chorale: Hans is a diminutive of Johannes, his name-day is St John's Day, and in Act Three he symbolically baptises the prize song of Walther. The second pair of lovers in the opera, Magdalene and David, both contain elements of their biblical namesakes, though in the case of the latter he may be understood as a lower-class parody of the biblical figure, with his ruler and piece of chalk on a string. The 'real' King David here is perhaps Walther: after all, Eva sings at the beginning of the biblical David with his sword and sling, just as Master Dürer painted him, and this seems to be the image she attaches to her handsome and valiant knight. Characters also contain elements of figures from the real world who had for some reason assumed an archetypal quality for Wagner. The similarities between Beckmesser and Wagner's nemesis, the critic Hanslick, are well known. Pogner, patron of the arts, is largely based on Otto Wesendonck, Wagner's patron in Zurich. Both Walther and Sachs contain elements of Wagner himself: the rebel artist Walther contains something of the Dresden Wagner, while the conciliatory Sachs is closer to the Wagner of Bayreuth.

The characters of Nuremberg clearly constitute a microcosm through which the wider world can be embraced. Despite its evident limitations, the little world of Nuremberg is drawn with love and kindness. Wagner resists the temptation satirically to debunk its blinkered views, its philistinism, and the pompous self-importance of the craftsmen with their guild rituals. The world of Nuremberg becomes comical only when compared to the larger concept dominating the piece: the idea of art. There is perhaps a hint of self-parody in the fact that Wagner explored lofty aesthetic problems through the medium of these solid bourgeois characters: does one really need gods and heroes to discuss such weighty matters, when bakers, joiners and smiths will do just as well? The Nurembergers are to some extent allied to the composer, because like him, they endeavour to practise their art. But when they reveal their belief that art should be restrained by rules and laws, by guild bureaucracy and the chalking up of mistakes, they unintentionally act in a way that is contrary to the idea of art itself as the nineteenth century understood it, with its ideas of inspiration, natural genius and lofty mission. And in doing so, they become comic.

Humour is not entirely a question of comedy, however. For Wagner, as for Jean Paul, it invariably contained 'the world-despising idea': an element of melancholy which distinguishes true humour from what is merely witty or jocular. Humour often wears a tragic mask, or at least carries it in its hand. In *Die Meistersinger*, this aspect of humour is principally expressed through the character of Sachs. He is a more complex character than is suggested by his initial appearance as the benign and avuncular helper of young lovers. His repressed tensions come to the fore in the erotically charged scene in which he fiddles with the shoe which will not fit Eva; this episode provokes an explosion of pain, fury and sadness about his life as a shoemaker, and what he has had to give up. He was already depressed and melancholy during his nocturnal invocation of Eve in paradise. Now he curses his position as a kind of universal psychiatrist who is himself left empty-handed: 'The cobbler must have skill unending, / patch up what's in need of a mending. / And if he be a poet too, / for that not a moment of peace will he know.'

Sachs' next speech is still more significant for what it tells us of the composer's outlook: following Eva's profession of her daughterly love for him, he refers to the tragedy of Tristan and Isolde in order to articulate his renunciation of her. The orchestral writing immediately assumes a chromatic flavour as Wagner refers to his own previous work, and Sachs declares that 'My child, / of Tristan and Isolde / a grievous tale I know. / Hans Sachs was wise and would not / endure King Marke's woe.' This citation of *Tristan* is, in both content and form, the purest musical expression of humour in the piece. By stepping out of one work and playfully referring to another, Wagner appeals to a public who he knows will understand him. He seems to say to them: 'Look, I've already composed this, it's behind me, so I am sparing myself and you.' This gesture suggests an ability to view his own work with objectivity, as well as a demonstration of triumph over a powerful and destructive emotion. Sachs renounces Eva just as Wagner had renounced Mathilde/Isolde.

This hidden aspect of Sachs' character reveals something of the double-edged quality of the comedy in *Die Meistersinger*. However, Wagner's humour is not simply a matter of leavening the cheerful with the melancholy; if it were, we would be dangerously close to agreeing with Joseph Goebbels, who pressed the cliché about 'that German humour which is said to laugh with one eye and weep with the other' into service in his 1933 hymn of praise to the opera. Humour assumes many different aspects in *Die Meistersinger*: it is not simply a matter of tears and laughter. At least two different types of humour interact and collide in the piece: these may be described as wit and folly*, and an examination of the distinction between the two takes us closer to the heart of the piece than Goebbels was prepared to go.

'Folly, folly, everywhere folly' – thus begins Hans Sachs' famous monologue. Wagner too felt that his life was dominated by folly, as he confessed to his patron King Ludwig while working on the music of Act Three in 1866. Try as he might to escape it, it always caught up with him, even in his Tribschen villa, which he likened to the shoemaker's workshop of Hans Sachs. By Wagner's own admission, then, folly was allowed to take over *Die Meistersinger*: 'even Beckmesser's ludicrous despair receives this magic foil.' The 'folly of love' had been presented by Wagner in *Tristan and Isolde*, the immediate predecessor of *Die Meistersinger*, and the shadow of this particular type of folly falls on the two lovers in the later work. The idea of folly incorporates both error and deception, and magic and the supernatural. But it also suggests the notion of excess, of an antisocial force becoming uncontrollable and all-powerful. Folly, for Wagner, is always an ambivalent concept; it was the demon that haunted him, responsible for many of the prejudices in his ideas and work, yet without it he could not live, and he was never to escape it – not even at Wahnfried.

---

*Nike Wagner follows the example of the libretto itself in using the word 'Wahn' to describe one of the two types of humour at work in *Die Meistersinger*. This rather old-fashioned word has two principal meanings in everyday speech: illusion (or delusion), and madness or mania. The importance of the word to Richard Wagner is shown by the fact that he chose to name his house 'Wahnfried' (see chapter 1). The use made of the word by both Wagners encompasses both of these meanings. Since neither 'illusion' nor 'mania' on its own satisfactorily conveys this, and because it would be confusing to switch from one to the other, the German 'Wahn' is generally translated as 'folly'.

Folly was inescapably linked to his artistic working conditions: it was his heartbeat, the air he breathed.

Wit seems at first sight to be the opposite of folly. It has a sunny, sociable character: unlike folly it does not shy away from the light, but seeks it out. Wit is free and liberating, and the person who practises it sheds a burden from his mind. Of course, Wagner had scarcely built his reputation on the wit of his operas – he had no wish to emulate Rossini – but for once, in *Die Meistersinger*, he tried his hand at it, even if it was only to make some quick and easy money. But what exactly did 'wit' mean for Wagner's era? Jean Paul may again provide a clue: for him, wit was fundamentally a 'comparing force', and its basis lay in the discovery of similarity in the dissimilar. Wagner's original idea of 1851, the seed from which *Die Meistersinger* grew, was just such a comparison – an image of physical and mental mimicry, as the composer related:

> Before I even knew any detail about Sachs and his contemporaries, an idea for an amusing scene came to me during a walk: the cobbler with his hammer on the last, a craftsman-poet, by way of revenge for the Marker's pedantry, decides to teach him a lesson. Everything in my mind focused on the two punch-lines – the Marker holding up the chalk-covered slate and Hans Sachs holding the shoes in the air that he had made by hammering blows as a Marker – both signal failure as a singer.

If wit does indeed result from the discovery of unexpected similarity in heterogeneous spheres, then it must be admitted that Wagner applies this principle superbly in *Die Meistersinger*. Similarity in diversity is high-lighted both at a structural and a local level. The plot is built around the contrasted social levels of the characters, and the fact that the lower level always imitates the higher one, as when David rather grandiosely appoints himself as Walther's teacher in Act One. Similarity in diversity is also found in Wagner's structural device of presenting the same situation twice with different characters and consequences: the marking of mistakes occurs twice, there are two nocturnal serenades, and two episodes of 'prize singing'. At a local level, too, the sophisticated wit used by the Masters, Beckmesser and Sachs in particular, depends heavily on simi-larities, either between two different words or between their meanings. All kinds of verbal parody and caricature are based on imitation, on drawing together two dissimilar objects or ideas for the sake of a moment's amusement. This verbal wit is echoed in the score: Wagner's musical technique, governed by the leitmotif, is well equipped to convey subtle differences and similarities, acts of deception and double meanings. The music supports and emphasises the wit that is already present in the text. For example, Wagner sometimes lends full contrapuntal weight to words that are clearly nonsensical, thus heightening the absurdity; at other times, he expresses irony by setting a phrase or a sentence in such a way that a distorted, sarcastic tone is apparent from the music alone.

If the observation of similarity in heterogeneity is the basis for wit in *Die Meistersinger,* then plentiful opportunities for such comparisons are ensured by the diverse subject matter of the piece: it is not only about poetry and song, words and melodies, but also about the various people who wish to learn to master these arts. These people could be goldsmiths, farriers, bakers, tailors, coppersmiths, spice merchants or, of course, town clerks or shoemakers. These are people whose horizons are represented as limited: if they wish to learn how to make a song, they will tend to express their attempts using analogies drawn from their own trade. Song-making has fairly similar problems to any other craft, as Sachs' apprentice, David, complains to Walther: 'Shoemaker's craft and poet's art / both daily I learn by heart; / first of all the leather smooth I hammer, / consonants and vowels next I stammer; / next must the thread be stiff with wax / then I must learn, it rhymes with Sachs.' Wagner repeatedly draws comic effect from the parallels between poetry and shoemaking – and, in Act Three, from the common ground between shoemaking and love. In the psychologically crucial fourth scene of this act, the 'pained and pale' Eva visits Sachs, worried lest she is unable to marry Walther, the man of her choice. She pretends to Sachs that her shoe does not fit properly: she refuses to tell him where it pinches, but she tries to deceive him by holding it out with her foot still in it. Of course the real shoe does not pinch, only the metaphorical one, as Sachs is perfectly well aware; Walther's entry at the end of the scene and Eva's exclamation, which betrays her love, only confirm this fact.

Wit is sometimes derived, too, from the inversion of the principle: as well as similarity in the dissimilar, Wagner finds difference within apparent identity. The technique of comical repetition with a slight shift of meaning plays an important part in both the verbal and musical texture of *Die Meistersinger*. Repetition is never exact: it is instead a play on the original version which comments on and develops it. The scenes which first inspired Wagner contained such a comical repetition: on the one hand, the Marker's chalk-covered slate, on the other, the cobbler's hammered shoes. This similarity is emphasised by the similarity of words used by Beckmesser and Sachs. In Act One the Marker Beckmesser tells Walther 'On the slate here my work is done.' Sachs makes a mental note of this retort, and in Act Two he himself tells Beckmesser that 'On the shoes here my work is done'. The 'high art' of marking is parodied and mocked by being likened to the humble craft of shoemaking.

Repetition is comical if the words themselves remain unchanged while the environment, or the nature of the person uttering them, is different. The repeated use of the Marker's catchphrase 'Now begin!' ('*Fanget an!*') provides a good example of this. This invitation to start a song becomes comical by being used so many times in the opera, rather like a joke that is only funny by virtue of being repeated so often. The words are first heard as a quotation, when David sings them in order to give Walther a foretaste of what he can expect if he enters a singing contest. Because the words are in ironic quotation marks the first time we hear them, we are conditioned to find them funny even before we first hear them in their proper context, sung by the Marker in the stentorian tones appropriate to the dignity of his office. But the words are unexpectedly picked up by the candidate, Walther, to form the opening phrase of his song: the terrifying call is converted into an appeal to spring and love, and the interval encompassed by the words is now a cheerful fourth rather than the third sung by David and Beckmesser. The phrase also occurs several times in the scene where Sachs takes the role of the Marker while Beckmesser practises his song: on the final occasion, sung over the interval of a fifth, it is clearly ironic, expressing the shoemaker's contempt for the suitor's hopeless cause. It is sung again over the interval of a fifth – but this time seriously – by the guild master, Kothner, when he invites the unfortunate Beckmesser to begin his song. The fact that the rather officious phrase is associated only with Beckmesser seems to confirm its comic intent: when Walther rehearses his song with Sachs, the shoemaker treats him in a less confrontational manner than Beckmesser, and when the knight's turn comes in the real contest, Kothner remains silent. The words 'Now begin!' symbolise the bourgeois pettiness and pedantry that form the Masters' less attractive face, and the absence of the words from Walther's songs confirms that his is the true, inspired art.

The singing contest between Walther and Beckmesser is of course the climax of the piece – and it is also the point at which the principle of varied repetition is most potently employed. The fact that Beckmesser is singing a text stolen from his rival allows the differences between them to emerge more clearly: the comedy comes from the way in which the apparent identity of the two contenders is revealed to be nonsensical. Though the individual words of Beckmesser's version make sense, the way he strings them together produces an absurd effect: so Walther's 'While blossoms rare / made sweet the air, / With beauty glowing / past all knowing, / A garden round me lay' is mangled by Beckmesser into 'With bosom bare, / to greet the air; / With beauty glowing, / faster snowing; / a garden roundelay / wearied my way.' And so the distortion continues, becoming ever more bizarre: Beckmesser's version is a sort of Dadaism *avant la lettre*. Given that Walther's own song could be decried as bombastic, sentimental kitsch, however, it is not entirely clear who is really parodying what. Ernst Bloch made the interesting suggestion that Beckmesser's nonsense verse could be considered as an avant garde parody of the knight's conventional verbosity. Unfortunately, the way in which the plot is finally resolved does not support this appealing conclusion.

If wit is an attribute that characters in *Die Meistersinger* display without being particularly aware of it, then folly, by contrast, is a force to whose potency they constantly attest. The word *Wahn* occurs frequently in the libretto. Sometimes its connotations are relatively harmless, as when Sachs says to Beckmesser 'My friend, you are in serious error' (Mein Freund, Ihr seid im argen Wahn) or 'Believe me, you're mistaken about my wooing' (Doch glaubt, ob der Werbung seid ihr im Wahn). In these cases, *Wahn* simply implies 'mistake', 'error' or 'fallacy'. It has more weighty implications when used in connection with the theory of art. Sachs, unable to offer a rational explanation as to why he liked Walther's trial song so much ('I cannot forget it; nor can I enfold it') at least understands that such art, inspired by youth, love and nature, cannot and should not be imitated. This insight distinguishes him from Beckmesser who is attempting to do just that. Sachs says of Walther that 'If one heard / and madly dared [*wahnbetört*] / that song again to sing / it would bring but scorn and shame.' This central statement on 'madness' or 'folly' as an indispensable component in the creation of art is the lesson Sachs teaches the knight in the shoemaker's parlour. If Freud had been a Wagnerian he would have been delighted: it is just as if Wagner had encountered the passage in Freud's writings where poetry is equated with daydreams, with the infiltration of the deepest desires and images of the unconscious into the conscious mind. Here folly becomes transmuted almost into its opposite. 'My friend,' Sachs says, 'that is the poet's task / To seek in dreams what will come to pass. / In truth the deepest wisdom [*Wahn*] man has known / Has been what dreams have shown. / All verses that our poets write / Are naught but truths that dreams have brought to light.'

Folly and truth are closely related: folly can indeed *be* truth (that is, the opposite of error) but it is a truth that can only be 'thought' within a dream, and is only manifested through art. Art therefore has a taming, domesticating, shape-giving function: it acts as a counterweight and corrective to the terrifying, elemental force of folly.

It is not the only such counterweight that emerges during the course of the piece. Another such force – a centre of gravity, as it were – is identified in the middle of Sachs' 'folly monologue', between his reflections on folly in general, in the 'town and world chronicle', and on folly in particular, in the brawl on St John's Eve. That centre of gravity is the city of Nuremberg: 'With peaceful ways contented / and helpful work in hand, / my Nuremberg lies planted / amidst our fatherland,' the shoemaker muses. The effect of this sentence, insignificant in itself, is musically heightened to a remarkable degree. It is clearly meant to describe the only antidote to that folly, that madness which bears a terrifying face – even though it stems from the same unconscious regions as its good and beautiful brother, the folly of fantasy, the artist's folly. It is the collective folly for which even Sachs can find no precise name and which he therefore describes as the 'old folly' (*alten Wahn*) – not a bad name for the archaic, contradictory forces he finds at work whenever people are struggling 'in aimless frenzied spite'. The person Sachs describes in the grip of such folly is no longer a Nuremberg citizen of the sixteenth century: 'Driven to flight, / he thinks he is hunting; / hears not his own / cry of pain; when he digs into his own flesh / he thinks he is giving himself pleasure.' No, this is a very modern, rather neurotic person, the sadomasochistic pre-fascist citizen of the late nineteenth century. It is against this symbolic figure that Sachs invokes the healing utopia of Nuremberg as the treasure-house of medieval values, as the quintessence of morality, reason and order. It acts in a parallel way to art, which similarly holds a balance between natural urges and the need for censorship, between inspiration and form.

And then Sachs looks back at the preceding night of mayhem, and his own part in it: 'A cobbler in his shop / plucks at the thread of madness [*Wahnes*]: / how soon in alleys and streets / it begins to rage!' His own string-pulling, his toying with the irrational, had unintentionally slipped out of his hands and unleashed an outbreak of primeval collective vio-lence. This is something he is reluctant to believe, and he relapses into poetic explanations: 'A goblin must have helped ... it was the elder-tree'. Of course, neither spirits nor trees were really to blame, but one can understand Sachs' incredulity. It must have seemed scarcely believable, the vile enjoyment with which not only the hooligan apprentices, but also the respectable masters of Act One set about each other: they yelled what they really thought of their neighbours but had always been restrained from saying.

Far from taking the blame for any of this, Sachs proceeds to name himself as the final source of authority through which Nuremberg can be restored to peace and order: 'Now let us see what Sachs can do / so that the folly [*Wahn*] may be turned / and used for nobler work.' If therefore, folly is an integral part of even the most peaceful community, its existence cannot simply be denied; instead, every effort should be made to channel these aggressive urges into a positive course.

A Holy Trinity has therefore been established, through which folly will be tamed and domesticated: art, Nuremberg and Hans Sachs. In keeping with the comic conventions, the mayhem is contained, and the loose ends tied up. The harmonious resolution is symbolised musically by the famous quintet. Everything seems to be in order. Or it would be, were it not for Beckmesser. Much critical attention has been focused on the question of whether Wagner's portrayal of Beckmesser is anti-Semitic, as Adorno famously claimed. This debate has still not been settled, but what is certain is that Beckmesser is made the butt of a cat-and-mouse game which smacks of sadism. And sadism, as we know from social psychology, is inseparable from the syndrome that also produces violent fascism.

It is the fate of Beckmesser that casts the most serious doubt on the opera's claim to be 'comic', despite the fact that the town clerk is first introduced as a comic stock character. The concept of 'fear', for example, is anything but comic, but it occurs frequently in Wagner's directions for Beckmesser, especially during the second and third act – 'extreme fear' during his serenade, 'sweating with fear' at the singing contest. This shows how thin the veneer of comedy is: the fact that the man is a crotchety old pedant and a ridiculous suitor hardly conceals the fact that he is being physically and psychologically destroyed, and that this is the fault of nobody on stage. Beckmesser has the disposition for it from the outset; he is unstable and unsure of himself, and he has a sharply witty and ironic tongue. As Freud pointed out, the conditions that make someone witty are very close to those which produce neurosis. Moreover, this neurosis often manifests itself as a lapse into verbal nonsense: 'a tendency', in Freud's words, 'to seek identical meaning behind identically or similarly sounding words – which results in many errors laughed at by adults'. In Freudian terms, therefore, Beckmesser's humiliation at the contest can be interpreted as a regression into an infantile stage of development. The sense of superiority and *Schadenfreude* which this relapse produces in the onlookers are also infantile urges: Beckmesser's destruction allows the release of urges which are otherwise prohibited in adult life.

One marvels, time and again, at the deviousness of Wagner's subconscious, which allowed him to express his hatred and rejection of his critics by every means possible. Beckmesser's character is constructed so that he himself is responsible for his misfortune, a fact that renders our laughter permissible, if not comfortable.

It is perhaps not surprising that such noble souls as Franz Liszt and Friedrich Nietzsche did not enjoy Wagner's jokes. They may have sensed the ambivalent nature of these jokes, the infantile aggression that lay behind them. After all, they did not experience the subjective pleasure, the relief, the momentary suspension of repression which the composer himself enjoyed. These pleasures sit uncomfortably within the context of comedy, as has already been suggested, and the way in which Wagner indulges them is scarcely witty. However, they do have something in common with the folly whose destructive influence so concerns the citizens of Nuremberg. If, as Sachs argues, such folly is necessary to produce great art, then Wagner himself is the most eloquent proof of this. But while the violence of the folly in Nuremberg has been tamed – by art, civic spirit, and Sachs – the sadistic and destructive aspects of Wagner's own folly remain alive to darken our experience of the opera itself.

8

'No change will come to our Western art': New Bayreuth as waste disposal plant

THE TITLE OF THIS CHAPTER MAY INITIALLY SEEM RATHER puzzling, though the first half is, of course, a misquotation of the famous final words of Hans Sachs from *Die Meistersinger*. When the knight, Walther von Stolzing, expresses his wish to retire into private life rather than become a master, Hans Sachs lectures him on the relationship between politics and art: 'Then may depart / the pomp of Holy Rome, / no change will come / to holy German art,' the shoemaker sings. The poet is transformed into a political prophet, warning of the disruption of the German empire and its contamination by foreigners: holy *German* art is the only defence against these undesirable developments. The alteration of 'German' to the less incriminating 'Western' was proposed by the music critic Hans Heinz Stuckenschmidt on the occasion of Wieland Wagner's provocatively 'abstract' production of the piece in 1956. The suggestion was described as 'amusing' by Stuckenschmidt's fellow critic, Joachim Kaiser, though many in Bayreuth were outraged. As we shall see, however, the apparently bizarre proposal demonstrates the extent to which it was necessary to rethink the implications of *Die Meistersinger* in the immediate aftermath of the war.

During those traumatic years, the term 'waste disposal' acquired a commonly recognised metaphorical meaning. For Germans, it was not only the noxious by-products of the nuclear industry that needed to be safely disposed of: it was also the unpleasant substance of German history itself. In this case, the radioactive material is *Die Meistersinger* itself. This work is a truly radiant one, both in the conventional metaphorical sense – ever since Nietzsche, critics have praised the brilliant and positive C major 'radiance' of this piece, the only one of Wagner's works to have a happy ending – and in this more specialised metaphorical sense of emitting dangerous rays. The ideological rays sent out by the work have been reflected and strengthened by the way in which it was absorbed into Nazi culture: its status as the celebratory opera of the Nuremberg rallies forms a kind of second skin around the work, one which has inevitably affected subsequent interpretations.

No one believes any longer that the conclusion of *Die Meistersinger* is an innocently romantic declaration of the primacy of art over politics. The history of the work's origins show that the ending was connected with the composer's political enthusiasms, and that it may be understood as reflecting Wagner's hopes, repeatedly dashed, for a united Germany. 'It would not have taken much,' Peter Wapnewski complains in his *Wagner Handbook*, 'and the finale could have been spared this jovial national twist.' What it would have taken, in fact, was for Cosima to have kept her own counsel, for it was allegedly she who persuaded the uncertain Wagner to strike the lofty tone of political avowal at the end.

Whatever the truth of this, Wapnewski's comment registers the irritation that many listeners feel about the jingoistic grandiloquence of the ending. This undoubtedly facilitated the Nazi appropriation of the piece. The first post-war commentator to analyse the self-confirmatory function which the conclusion of *Die Meistersinger* was made to serve under the Nazis was the literary critic, Hartmut Zelinsky. The 'Awake' chorus with which the crowd at the *Festwiese* welcomes Sachs was deliberately echoed, Zelinsky claims, by the Nazi slogan, 'Germany awake'. The Nazis were undoubtedly aware of the work's potential to ignite nationalist sentiment. As early as 1924, after all, one audience at a Bayreuth *Meistersinger* spontaneously arose from their seats and intoned the words '*Deutschland über alles*'. At the 1933 festival, Hitler felt it necessary to request those present to refrain from such demonstrations: the 'magnificent expression of the German spirit' in the master's immortal work was enough.

The post-war treatment of this doubly radiant work reveals much about the tensions within those who lived out their youth during the Third Reich, and who were subsequently responsible for the nation's cultural reconstruction. One such person was Wieland Wagner. His interpretations of *Die Meistersinger* – he produced it only twice in Bayreuth, in 1956 and 1963 – betray something of the deep-rooted conflicts and feelings of shame experienced by his generation. But they also reveal the strategies of self-defence and survival that made self-cleansing and rehabilitation possible. After all, life still had to be lived, even in the ruins. But as the ruins were cleared, and culture began to flourish once more, everything that had been repressed gradually re-emerged, but in a strangely distorted form.

It could have been argued that Wieland Wagner was not a suitable candidate to embody the post-Hitler mental state of the country. His privileged birth as the oldest grandson of Richard Wagner and his upbringing as the heir of one of the country's most important assets scarcely made him a typical citizen. Moreover, the fact that Hitler had personally favoured him with exemption from military service made it difficult for him to claim distance from the Third Reich. However, his elitist background did make him the right person to carry out the function later labelled as the 'mourning task'. For him, indeed, such mourning was the only way in which he could deal with his shame and anger at his own blindness. Those who had suffered physically in battle were often spared the wounds of conscience; the torment caused by Wieland's conscience, on the other hand, was only increased by the privileged treatment he had received.

It may seem tendentious to emphasise the coincidence that the location of Wagner's opera was also the city that gave its name to the Nazis' most draconian and notorious race laws. However, we are given ample encouragement to do so by Richard Wilhelm Stock's *Richard Wagner and the City of the Mastersingers*, a sumptuous vellum-bound volume published in 1938 with the support of the Wagner family. Stock notes that 'Richard Wagner's ideological aims have been magnificently fulfilled in the city of his *Meistersinger*, the metropolis of the worldwide struggle against Jewry, where the Führer at the Reich Party Rally of Honour proclaimed the laws for the protection of German blood, the Nuremberg laws.' In this programme of fulfilment, Stock argued, a place was also occupied by 'the young generation around Frau Winifred Wagner'; indeed, in Wieland that generation ' had already borne witness to the will of the blood to master this great inheritance'. Stock is referring to the scenery designs which the twenty-year-old Wieland had made for the Bayreuth production of *Parsifal* in 1937.

After the outbreak of war, Hitler did not exactly order Winifred to continue the festival despite the conflict, but he certainly made it clear that this was his wish. It was once more Winifred's eldest son who obeyed the 'will of the blood': he designed the sets for the only work in the repertoire for 1943 and 1944 – *Die Meistersinger*. The positive spirit of this opera seemed to make it appropriate as cheerful entertainment for the wounded and crippled, the soldiers, nurses and medical orderlies who constituted the new audience for Bayreuth; the intention was that they should return to the service of the nation refreshed by their few hours of pleasure. The secondary and unstated purpose of the wartime festival was to help divert the public's attention from what was really happening. 1943 and 1944 not only witnessed the defeat at Stalingrad, an event whose magnitude and significance had to be disguised from the public, it also saw an intensification of the programme of Jewish deportation.

Thomas Mann's views on German wartime cultural activities were clear. In September 1945, he wrote to Walther von Molo, who was trying to persuade him to return to Germany from the United States:

> It was not permitted, it was impossible to make 'culture' in Germany while all around that which we know about was happening. It meant gilding baseness, adorning criminality. Among the torments we suffered was watching the German spirit and German art continually making themselves available as the shield and outriders of the absolutely hideous. Strange to say, it was not considered that there could be a more honourable occupation than designing Wagner sets for Hitler's Bayreuth.

It was quite clear that Wieland had not had this thought, an oversight that resulted both from his inherited sense of mission and from the psychological balance of his family at the time.

Let us take a closer look at how matters stood in 1943–44. The twenty-six-year-old Wieland was working as a photographer and painter. Given his awareness of the revolution in theatre design that had taken place in late-1920s Berlin, could he not have tried to differentiate his sets for the wartime *Meistersinger* from the emphatically German Nuremberg scenery designed by Benno von Arendt, with its crooked little streets, flags and other historical accoutrements? Given his artistic talents, could he not at least have tried to draw a line between the artistic space inside the Festspielhaus and the Party Rally outside? It must be admitted that he entirely failed to do these things. Contemporary photographs prove the absolute conventionality of his sets. He did not challenge the dictum of Otto Weininger, the Viennese philosopher and ardent Wagnerian, that *Die Meistersinger* expressed 'the essence of Germandom' – a view that Goebbels had parroted in 1933 when, in a broadcast from Bayreuth, he referred to it as 'the most German of German operas'. This essence found its fulfilment in the Nuremberg of Hans Sachs. The designer therefore had nothing to consider – all that was needed was a set that was historically faithful and provided suitable entrances and exits for the performers. Besides, Wagner's stage directions were clearly set out, and any departure from them would be a violation of the work.

There were good reasons for Wieland not to depart from the orthodox view of *Die Meistersinger*, and yet it still seems unsatisfactory that he did not do so. Although it was not yet customary to bend an established theatrical text, to emphasise its historicity or extract topical nuances from it, Wieland was a young man – and from whom, if not the young, could one expect a critical attitude to established conditions? One could at least have expected him to introduce some innovations that might have been interpreted as a resistance to the political appropriation of his grandfather's work.

Instead, what impulses for reform there were came from the older generation. Heinz Tietjen, the artistic director in Bayreuth since Siegfried Wagner's death, introduced a few 'un-German' effects into that wartime *Meistersinger*, such as the revue-style choreography in Act Three, of the kind familiar from the more avant garde theatres of pre-Nazi Berlin. Moreover, Tietjen had regularly employed Emil Preetorius, a stage designer whose aims were 'thoroughgoing simplification' and 'symbolic integrity'. Needless to say, both the education and professional experience of these seasoned men of the theatre were superior to those of Wieland

Wagner, who had grown up in the culturally and ideologically isolated atmosphere of Bayreuth. It was only by applying pressure on his mother, and angrily invoking his hereditary claims, that Wieland had ensured that he, and not Preetorius, was entrusted with the production of *Die Meistersinger*.

Perhaps the dilemma that resulted in the young Wieland following such a conservative artistic and political path may now be more readily understood. The domestic situation at Wahnfried was such that Tietjen had been placed in the role of substitute father: he was not only the chief at the Festspielhaus but also the chief at home, since Winifred had made him the guardian of her children. Wieland nurtured the seeds of Oedipal rebellion against Tietjen. Ironically, this placed the Young Turk on the same side as the old guard: those Wagnerians who, like Wagner's aged daughters, rejected the reign of Winifred, Tietjen and Preetorius as too modern, and who were trying to use the young grandson to rekindle the Grail-guarding spirit of Cosima's era. Rebellion against the existing power structure, and advancement from crown prince to ruler, could only have taken place with the support of Hitler. The Führer would no doubt have understood his protégé's frustrations, and might well have induced the fellow-travelling Tietjen to relinquish his post to Wieland, at least in part. Fortunately, things turned out differently – but only just. In January 1945, when Wieland tried to take up this matter with Hitler in person, it was too late: he could no longer get through to Berlin. However, his awareness of Hitler's status as his protector undoubtedly got the better of his personal aesthetic instincts when it came to the design of *Die Meistersinger*.

'Then it was wartime, but now it is peacetime' – this was the stereotyped response that Allied journalists invariably heard after 1945, whenever they attempted to quiz Germans about their thoughts and emotions. It was the formula that denoted the break with their own history, and relegated what had happened only recently to a symbolically distant past. This reaction is described by Hans Magnus Enzensberger in his *Europe in Ruins*, which also quotes the comments of Alfred Döblin, who observed the ant-like reconstruction work and the revival of cultural life on a post-war tour of the country: 'It will be much easier', Döblin argued, 'to rebuild their towns than to get them to experience what they experienced and to understand how it came about.' Döblin also pointed out the surprising fact that the scale of the destruction did not appear to depress the Germans, but on the contrary provided them with a vigorous stimulus to work.

The activity of Wieland and Wolfgang Wagner in these immediate post-war years was certainly frantic and furious. It was not a time for reflection, but for action: in 1951 the brothers reopened the festival before the astonished eyes of the world. While Wolfgang had thrown himself into the practical activity of rebuilding the theatre, Wieland had devoted himself to the task of artistic reconstruction. His work resulted in a production style that was entirely new to Bayreuth. Under the slogan of 'getting rid of old clutter', Wieland produced a new *Parsifal*, plunged like a mystery play into magical chiaroscuro, and a *Ring* that was almost entirely free from conventional Germanic associations. The basic traits of the New Bayreuth style were found in the reduction of the acting areas to geometrically abstract forms, the choreographic stylisation of choral groups, and the psychological detail with which individual characters were portrayed. But perhaps the most important innovation was in the lighting: the Siemens advertisements in the programme books declared that 'Light is an actor', and its appearance in the new productions was certainly startling. Wieland did away with the 'flat' illumination of the set, which had covered the stage picture like a yellow-brown gravy and made everything uniformly bright and boring. Now Rembrandt-like light and shadow effects were employed; there was magic and mystery, and characters frequently seemed to have been snatched out of the night by the small circle of light that followed them. All the cultural critics agreed that the call for a 'Wagner from within' – sounded by post-war Wagnerians embarrassed by the Nazi appropriation of the composer's work – had been answered here. After some initial opposition from Old Wagnerians and other cultural conservatives, the fame of New Bayreuth soon came to exceed anything dreamed of by other German theatres. The German economic miracle had been accompanied by a Wagner miracle. And the fact that the mess had been sorted out by direct descendants of the composer satisfied the public's fascination with dynasties and its desire for historical continuity after so many ruptures.

What, then, of *Die Meistersinger*? The first post-war production was not directed by Wieland; overburdened by the production of five other works, he was unable to take it on, and probably did not want to in any case. The reason is obvious: it was too closely associated in his mind with the recent Nazi contamination. Nonetheless, as the festival director, he believed that the piece had to be staged: a popular and cheerful foil to *Parsifal* and *The Ring* was needed. But who would be willing to burn his fingers on the former Party Rally opera? Even the title of the work was inescapably associated with Nazism through the Nuremberg connection. At this short distance from the war, however, the stains were not clearly seen, and the question of waste disposal did not even arise. *Die Meistersinger* was publicly claimed as 'the universal property of musical humanity', as Walter Panofsky argued in the 1951 programme book. As for the problematic conclusion, Panofsky dismissed it with a simple gesture. Its national awareness, he argued, reflected nothing more than a perfectly healthy self-assertion. This was an element which 'those national zealots' – he did not use the word Nazi – had simply over-emphasised.

It was in this spirit that Wieland Wagner engaged a tried and tested producer, Rudolf Otto Hartmann of the Munich State Opera, whose 1943 *Meistersinger* under Furtwängler he had liked. He recruited a designer from within the family: the freelance architect, Hans Carl Reissinger, was the uncle of his wife Gertrud and enjoyed a reputation in Bayreuth as a local equivalent of Albert Speer. He had created such buildings as the House of Education and the Ludwig Siebert Hall, and he had been privy to Hitler's grandiose plans to rebuild Wagner's town. The conductor of the production was Herbert von Karajan, who could likewise scarcely be described as a member of the German resistance. The whole production contained nothing that would have upset conventional opinion in the 1940s, but the 1951 public was well satisfied – and the many musical errors were patiently patched up on the tape, according to Walter Legge, head of Columbia Records who produced the recording.

However, this harmless Lortzing-like Meistersinger was clearly out of kilter with the theatrical revolution for which Wieland was striving. It was a survival from the 'German era', a corner of the Augean stables that had not been cleaned out. From a psychological point of view, it was probably not a bad idea to leave the audience this crumb of continuity with the past. As the philosopher Odo Marquand has convincingly argued, at times of crisis, upheaval or drastic modernisation, there is a public need to reach back to something familiar. The 1951 *Meistersinger* was like a well-loved teddy bear to which one could cling in an uncertain present.

In 1956, however, Wieland finally robbed the Bayreuth public of this small comfort, having unwillingly accommodated its old-fashioned Germanness in his modern and clutter-free house. Perhaps it took him those five years to find a way in which he could resuscitate the piece in his own style. He described his method as a 'spiritual solution'. His new *Meistersinger* was no longer set in Nuremberg, a fact that triggered the greatest scandal in the history of the festival. The sacred cow of faithfulness to the work had been slain, and the exclusive identification of the work with the idea of Germany had consequently been destroyed. Where then did his flight from historical memory and his dream of a de-Nazified *Meistersinger* lead the producer?

Beyond time and space, one might reply, into a no man's land of the soul – where ambivalence reigns, where night reaches deep into the day, and where tragedy has narrowly been averted. Hans Sachs was transformed from a Nazi *Kreisleiter* into a psychoanalyst who directed this play of psychological undertones, guiding the erotic urges of Eva and Walther into matrimony and the destructive forces of the citizens into harmless excesses.

The visual references made in this theatre of the soul were diverse and imaginative. St Catherine's Church in Act One was presented in a Gothic style, with naked pictures of Adam and Eve in the Riemenschneider manner hinting at both the Biblical and the erotic subtexts of the work. In Act Two, instead of the familiar streets of half-timbered houses, the audience found itself in a nowhere land of diffuse dream forms: the lighting had an almost synaesthetic quality, as lilac bathed the stage and suggested the scent in the air. Girls performed a somnambulistic dance, figures flitted across the stage, and only evil assumed sharper contours, as the Nuremberg citizens arrived in well-aligned battalions for the brawl scene. However, the aggression of the citizens was offset by the flowing nightshirts which gave the scene a somewhat spectral, dreamlike feel, and the musical form of the fugue in which the scene is constructed was matched by choreographic 'waves of motion'. This was the work of Wieland's wife, Gertrud, a champion of radical choreography whose influence on the aesthetic of New Bayreuth was highly significant.

In Act Three, needless to say, there were no traces of the cobbler's pegs, wire, or thread of previous productions. The set was free and abstract, an airy space with few points of reference, and the fairground with its notorious fascist emblems had disappeared. Instead of the backdrop of the medieval city, there were stylised golden trees of paradise; the drab browns of earlier productions had been replaced with white, yellow and golden hues. And the last traces of folklore were eliminated when, instead of the compact processions of the craft guilds with their banners, a single dancer performed a pantomimic representation of events from the town's history. The Germanness of Hans Sachs' final peroration was negated: he remained standing in the semicircle of the other performers, a refined and elegant figure in simple grey attire.

Who could doubt that Sachs – alias Richard Wagner, alias Wieland Wagner – was concerned only with art: not any particular style or period of art, but art as a mythical, timeless, universal concept? It was no accident that Wieland insisted on securing the Flemish André Cluytens to conduct his 'spiritual' *Meistersinger*. It was evidently important for him to have a conductor who was not steeped in the German Wagner tradition, since he repeatedly implored Cluytens not to conduct 'in a German way': 'Anything but German, you understand?' Wieland's emphasis on the abstract, universal qualities of *Die Meistersinger* was echoed by the formerly orthodox Wagnerian Curt von Westernhagen, who was persuaded by Wieland to contribute an essay to the programme book which noted the affinities between the opera and Greek drama. Given this painstaking 'de-Germanisation' of the piece, was not Stuckenschmidt correct to suggest that a little linguistic cheating at the end of Hans Sachs' speech would have been appropriate?

Wieland's reinvention of his grandfather as a 'Western European' rather than a German chimed well with the political climate of Adenauer's Federal Republic, which placed great emphasis on the shared cultural heritage of Western Europe. This was a principal reason for the colossal success of the production, which remained in the repertoire for an unusually long period. Wieland could be satisfied that his new *Meis-*

tersinger had successfully disposed of the detritus of the Nazi era. Everyone seemed happy, and he had at last proved himself.

When an entirely different *Meistersinger* was staged in Bayreuth in 1963, it seemed as though Wieland had ironically denounced his own aesthetic principles. With the aid of Thomas Schippers, a very young conductor with little experience of Wagner, he now served up not an abstract meta-*Meistersinger*, but its opposite: a robustly specific, historically fixed, firmly localised production. The only element of continuity with 1956 was that this production was also not set in Nuremberg – instead, it was a Shakespearean *Meistersinger*, set in Elizabethan England. The performing space was modelled on the Globe Theatre and remained the same throughout all three acts. Pale boards covered the floor, shades of brown reappeared, and props suggesting the particular milieu were reintroduced: an altar painting, a bower with a seat, massive leather-bound books.

The acting was now down-to-earth and comic. The Masters were nose-picking bumpkins; Sachs was once again an intelligent ruffian, almost a sadist, with no trace of philosophy or kindness; and Pogner, the patron of the arts, patted his money-bag with a vulgarity that made the benefactors of Bayreuth feel personally insulted. Eroticism was no longer suggested, but stated blatantly: Eva was not unlike Lulu and Stolzing was a down-at-heel knight, a kind of Alwa in the garret. Any nervousness about folklore elements had also disappeared in 1963: the crowd was no longer stylised into geometrical shapes, but was allowed to wander freely and dance. And when the Nine Muses made a physical appearance at the *Festwiese*, they were not introduced as a point of identification with the idea of ancient Greece as the cradle of our culture, but as a demonstration of the comical and blinkered way in which *Die Meistersinger* treats humanistic educational values, and a proof that the opera lends itself to being travestied.

The aura of negativity that surrounded the 1963 *Meistersinger* probably had something to do with this 'deconstructive' element. Despite the return to an emphasis on comedy, the public's reaction was one of frustration rather than amusement. After all, Wieland went still further in offending their sensibilities. Hans Sachs's final speech was given an unexpected twist: an intermediate curtain descended towards the end of Act Three, forcing a row of characters forward to the footlights. The words 'Honour your German Masters', and the prediction of the survival of holy German art were hurled out into the auditorium, so that the audience was not quite sure what was happening to them. Perhaps they only sensed the aggression of the gesture, but in reality, it was yet another challenge to traditional preconceptions about the piece.

*

The 1956 production of *Die Meistersinger* had witnessed the removal of the Germanness from the work – in other words, its de-Nazification – and memories of misplaced loyalties and national guilt had been expunged. The equally provocative 1963 production marked the second stage in New Bayreuth's dealings with the past. It was no longer concerned with the philosophical problem of nationalistic Germanness, but with the consequences of Hitlerism for the newly established West German state.

The 1963 programme book defines *Die Meistersinger* as both a satire and a 'play within a play'. These two ideas are clearly interlinked: if satire is a form of distancing, then the idea of presenting the whole as a 'play within a play' is a further step in the same direction. *Die Meistersinger*, it is implied, is Sachs's theatre: in other words, it is a play written by the poet Hans Sachs about himself and his fellow Nurembergers. Although there were precedents for the idea of a 'play within a play' both in antiquity and in Shakespeare, Wieland's use of the idea is more closely aligned with the Brechtian concept of alienation. It should be remembered that Wieland had been deeply impressed with the Berliner Ensemble: indeed, one of the most striking devices in this production, the intermediate curtain, was taken directly from their work. The effect of this curtain is to interrupt the action, to emphasise the theatrical, artificial nature of the experience, and to allow the actor to step out of character in order to make a direct appeal to the audience.

Given the Brechtian connotations of the device, it is not surprising that it, and the production in general, should have irritated its audience. The gesture implied an endorsement of the Marxist view of theatre, and this was a highly provocative position to take – particularly in the middle of the economic miracle and the first wave of consumerism, and particularly in Bayreuth, home of the theatre of total intoxication. With this production, Wieland managed to offend both the conservatives who believed that art should reinforce traditional German values rather than challenging them, and the liberals who favoured art that was formally exquisite and apolitical. Of course, one Brechtian gesture did not mean that Wieland had converted to Marxism and the political theatre, but it is interesting that the programme book from 1963 contains a number of references to political events, including the recent 'Schwabing disturbances' in Munich, suggesting an awareness by the festival that a century-old opera could reflect on current events.

In his youth, Wieland had been an introverted, non-political painter; by his mid-forties, however, he had become a *homo politicus* who kept himself obsessively well informed about public life. Such a man could not have failed to observe that the ideas of 'the old Wagner', as he called his grandfather, were being gradually drawn in to a debate about the precursors of fascism. In 1963, the composer was directly attacked in a book by Ludwig Marcuse entitled *The Memorable Life of Richard Wagner*. Marcuse broke from the consensus that Wagner was an innocent musician whose work was misused during 'the dark period' (a euphemism still in use), and described him as a 'centre of force' through which the German ideology 'penetrated into the nation's blood through a thousand channels'. An abstract of Marcuse's arguments was published in the 1963 *Meistersinger* programme, in which he argued that 'The only German genius who was correctly claimed [by the Nazis] in 1933 was Richard Wagner.'

How was the grandson to react to this new turn of events, to the suggestion of a close, even causal link between Wagner's ideology and National Socialism? Should he ignore the whole issue, or should he give up his own work as a pointless and doomed attempt to cleanse his grandfather's reputation? He did neither, of course, but managed to save his position by choosing a third course – one which enabled him to appear to participate in the debate, without implicating himself in its consequences. He countered Marcuse's arguments by adding a polemic by the Hamburg critic, Walter Abendroth, to the programme book:

Just as sun, moon and stars calmly run their courses, unconcerned whether this person or that may shake his fist at them or try to spit up at them, so the figure and work of Richard Wagner, in the one hundred and fiftieth year of his birth and the eightieth year of his death, stand on the firmament of cultural history in their old lustre, placidly shining down upon all efforts to diminish their radiance.

Thus Abendroth begins his response to Marcuse; the bombastic and grandiloquent style of the opening foreshadows what is to come.

What does this intriguing juxtaposition mean? That Wieland agrees with neither writer and is retreating to the position of ironist and sceptic, or that Faust-like, two contradictory souls inhabit his breast? There is probably some truth in both these suggestions. However, it is also worth noting that given his position, it would have been very difficult for Wieland directly to intervene in the debate. It is difficult to imagine that he would have been particularly sympathetic to Abendroth, given that he was a German nationalist and anti-modernist who had savaged Wieland's first production of *Die Meistersinger*; directors do not tend to forget such treatment in a hurry. It is worth noting, too, the quiet but persistent efforts that Wieland had made to make 'reparations' to the Jewish artistic community, by engaging Jews as conductors or commissioning articles for programme books: Willy Haas, Viktor Valentin Rosenfeld, Ernst Bloch and later Hans Mayer were significant figures during Wieland's regime.

Marcuse's critique of Wagner constitutes the last words in the 1963 *Meistersinger* programme book. However, Wieland adds a final pictorial commentary which, while it does not negate anything that precedes it, gives a defiant twist to the debate. It is a medieval woodcut from the *Nuremberg Chronicle* of 1493, depicting a phoenix rising form the ashes. It was, of course, Wieland's sincerest wish that Wagner's Bayreuth might rise from the ashes of recent history.

Of all the birds in Bayreuth, *Die Meistersinger* was the one that found it hardest to learn how to fly again: because of its German nationalist conclusion, the memory of Hitler's annexation of the piece still stuck to its reputation. The aesthetically sublimated, 'Western' *Meistersinger* of 1956 was an attempt to leave that memory behind. Wieland's second version of 1963 represented the director's attempt satirically to distance himself from the work. In both productions, the negation of all the intrinsically German elements produced a historical shock, which helped to hasten the general directorial trend away from faithfulness to Wagner's texts, and towards experimentation. It was only because of their experimental nature that Wieland's two productions could reflect the ruptures in German self-identity; it was only in this way that Bayreuth could progress beyond the necessary but limited function of waste disposal plant. There was no third *Meistersinger* by Wieland, nor were there any plans for one. After all, for how long can one experiment with squaring a circle, with de-Germanising a German work of art? So long as the shadows of history still fell on the opera, it was probably not possible to present a 'straight' *Meistersinger* in Bayreuth.

But time passes, and the shadows are shortening. After Wieland Wagner's death, the Germanness of *Die Meistersinger* was no longer felt to be a problem. Since then, Germany has been reunited, and very nearly redivided in the process, but while the present speeds towards a global future, the past raises its head with every newly discovered document, every freshly investigated war crime. The theatres of Germany have made their contribution to this process of 'coming to terms with history', by presenting *Meistersinger* productions which make the work's Nazi past ever more explicit: we have had stars of David waved at the *Festwiese* in Frankfurt, and the inclusion of the Brandenburg gate in the final scene in Stuttgart. It is only in Bayreuth that time seems to have stood still. There, in all innocence, we witness a simple celebration of the humanity of the music – colourful, conciliatory, and Western.

9

A Tragedy of Understanding: *Parsifal* and Jewish anti-semitism in *fin de siècle* Vienna

- Wagner is the greatest man since Christ
- The shadow of Ahasuerus hovers unmistakably ... even over his Kundry.
- The real Jew, like the woman, has no ego and hence no proper value.
- Christ was a Jew, but only in order to completely overcome the Jewishness in himself.
- This is what the Aryan owes the Jew – through him he knows what to beware of: Jewishness as a possibility in himself.

THESE SENTENCES, AND MANY MORE LIKE THEM, WERE WRITTEN between 1902 and 1903. They are not to be found in some obscure or forgotten publication, nor even in *Bayreuther Blätter*, but in a book that was a key text, even a cult, for the *fin de siècle* generation. It tapped into the emotional and intellectual currents of its day, and had a radical effect on contemporary thinking. Men as diverse and influential as Kafka, Kraus, Musil, Trakl, Schoenberg, Berg, Strindberg, Kubin and Kokoschka were all impressed or influenced by it. The book was a huge success at the commercial level too: it was translated into numerous languages, including Hebrew, and remained a bestseller well into the 1930s. It was republished in 1980, and the revival of interest this caused provoked Joshua Sobol to write a play about its author. This was premiered in Haifa, produced in various important European theatres, and even turned into a film in Vienna. The author was Otto Weininger:

his book *Geschlecht und Charakter* (Sex and Character) was first published in Vienna in 1903.

The confused sentences quoted above are evidence of the anti-Semitic tendency that spread through Vienna towards the end of the nineteenth century: they also reveal something of the paradoxical trend of *Jewish* anti-Semitism that followed in the wake of Wagner. The Jewish anti-Semite Otto Weininger was correctly described by Roberto Calasso as a 'faithful and clear-eyed chronicler of the phantasms of his culture'. He helps us to understand some of the problems experienced by the Jews who had supposedly been integrated into Christian-bourgeois society. A comparison of *Sex and Character* with Wagner's 'sacred stage festival play' *Parsifal* will show that some of the same phantasms flit between these two manifestations of *fin de siècle* Germanic culture. If we consider the disastrous collision of social, psychological and intellectual factors taking place in that culture, then we see that it was likely, if not inevitable, that the so-called 'assimilated Jews' would be attracted to the promising concepts of German art and culture, with their chiaroscuro of religious experience. (We speak of 'assimilated' rather than 'integrated' Jews here, because the more positive term would conceal the true nature of the problem.) The fantasies and phobias of Wagner and of these Jews coincided to such a degree that in retrospect, we may speak of a tragedy of understanding: the age of psychotic *angst* had arrived.

Weininger was part of a large community of Viennese Jews who were descended from Hungarian and Bohemian immigrants. This group was particularly characterised by its aesthetic, intellectual and scientific interests and achievements. They had become so affluent that they had already achieved economic integration, so they saw academic activity as the field in which the community could achieve further social advancement. The external pressures for adjustment and advancement were accompanied by an inner pressure: family structures throughout *fin de siècle* society were deeply patriarchal, but this was probably intensified within the Jewish community by the traditionally powerful position of the father. Weininger's father, a former goldsmith, was an extreme patriarch, domineering and repressive towards his wife and sons. The traditional model of masculinity with which he was brought up was to leave deep traces in Weininger's work.

The elder Weininger, like many of his contemporaries, was an ardent Wagnerian – so much so that his second son was named Richard in honour of the composer – and like so many Wagnerians, he was also a German nationalist and anti-Semite. Politically and ideologically, therefore, the son's destiny was predetermined. As he was too sensitive to oppose his overbearing father, his only choice was to outdo him: he could try to be an even better person, a better German, a better Wagnerian. It was impossible for him to turn in the opposite direction, to re-embrace Jewish values and culture, since this would have meant a negation of the social advance that his family had painstakingly achieved, as well as an abandonment of the social and intellectual circles in which he now moved. The approach to religion among that avant garde bourgeois Jewish intelligentsia was generally one of adaptation. Most chose to be baptised, as Gustav Mahler and Karl Kraus had done, or they regarded themselves as being 'of no religion', like Arthur Schnitzler and Sigmund Freud. Weininger was unusual in that he converted not to the usual Catholicism, but to the Protestant faith.

Most of the Jews who had moved to Vienna since the 1860s, or who had been born there since that time, no longer felt any deep roots in Jewish culture, nor did they have any desire to return to this identity. They had little or no connection with the orthodox Jewish community, which was mostly based in the city's second district. The problem for the 'assimilated Jews' was that the Christians were also unwilling to make them feel at home in their environment. As a result, many had a rather ambivalent cultural identity, which often manifested itself in a strong attachment to the outward customs of Christianity: Theodor Herzl, though a Zionist, made sure that he had a Christmas tree each year, and Gustav Mahler found it difficult to pass an open church door. Schnitzler, Kraus and Jakob Wassermann were others who identified themselves with this psychological status of 'in-betweenness', and Franz Kafka invented frightening images to describe this state. Such figures may be likened to drowning men who were equally remote from both shores, the Jewish tradition and history on the one hand, and the chimera of full social integration on the other.

In this existential state of inner turmoil and ambivalence, in which many 'assimilated Jews' found themselves, culture alone was left as a basis for faith. Unlike either Judaism or Christianity, it promised a secure identity, which could be celebrated in writing and music. Because of the quasi-religious aura that attached to his work, Richard Wagner undoubtedly filled the void which had been left for many by the absence of gods: through him, culture became both a refuge and a substitute religion.

But the hegemony of Wagnerism was not always inevitable. In the middle of the nineteenth century, in the age of flourishing liberalism, a defence against him was still possible. Ludwig Speidel and Eduard Hanslick, for example, had the critical clear-sightedness necessary to argue against Wagner's ideas, and they were repulsed, above all, by his anti-Semitism. Speidel became particularly vitriolic when confronted with the apparently perverse phenomenon of Jewish Wagnerism: in 1872 he wrote that 'Wagner has treated the Hebrews like mangy dogs, and by way of retribution they run after him, wagging their tails and cheerfully licking his hands.' The point that Speidel overlooked, however, was that the 'Hebrews' were part of that cultured bourgeoisie which was most aware of artistic developments; indeed, they tended as a group to be particularly sensitive to the spirit of the age, which is why they so warmly welcomed Wagner, who so completely symbolised what was modern in the arts. The tide turned inexorably in the composer's favour towards the end of the century, as liberalism became ever weaker in the increasingly unstable Austro-Hungarian empire, and the number of Wagnerians and Wagner associations in Vienna kept growing.

Part of the reason for Wagner's ascendancy was that his work encap-sulated so many of the issues with which the period was concerned: not only the racial problem, but also the 'decadence problem' which was bound to interest the sophisticated younger generation, the issue of money and materialism, which inevitably struck a chord with the sons of capitalists, and the issue of relations between the sexes, which was a crucial concern at the turn of the century. Numerous conflicts of self-definition and identity were articulated in Wagner's music dramas, so it was not surprising that they came to be seen as a panacea for social and psy-chological problems. In the overheated culture of the *fin de siècle,* many saw their route to salvation in the model of redemption offered in Wagner's works – and above all in *Parsifal*.

The mystique attached to Wagner's last work was heightened by the fact that it could only be seen in Bayreuth: until 1913, the Festspielhaus's exclusive right to stage the work was recognised by the law. It was inevitable that a sense of 'pilgrimage' should attach itself to the work. Weininger's own pilgrimage to *Parsifal* was made in 1902, en route for a cultural odyssey to the North which also took in Ibsen and *Peer Gynt*. By this time, he had already received his doctorate in philosophy for the thesis that he was soon to turn into *Sex and Character*, and he had recently converted to Protestantism: the trap was ready to snap shut. He had already expressed the belief that 'After *Parsifal* one should go on a pilgrimage to the end of the earth, and then somehow die away,' but the reality was less poetical. The following year, Weininger committed suicide at the age of twenty-three. His experience of *Parsifal* undoubtedly had a share in his tragic end, even if it was not the immediate cause of his action.

Weininger's visit to *Parsifal* was no road to Damascus: rather, it was a powerful confirmation of what he already sensed, presented in a form which, because of the deliberately archaic effect of the music, penetrated deep into the psyche. If Weininger had until then been a doubter torn apart by internal divisions, then *Parsifal*, as he would have put it, helped him 'overcome his dichotomies'. Now he accomplished the leap into ideology, and drew his ideas together into a system. After his travels, he enlarged his thesis by adding those chapters which were most responsible for both the success and the controversy of his work: 'The Essence of Woman and her Meaning in the Universe', 'Jewry', and 'Woman and Mankind'. The subtitle of his book was *A Fundamental Examination*; it might just as well have been *On Last Things*, the title under which his posthumous aphorisms were published. Both books contain notes and reflections on Wagner and *Parsifal*.

Parsifal is a drama of redemption. According to the religious philosopher Jacob Taubes in his *Western Eschatology*, redemption dramas in many cultures deal with the unclean, unholy intermingling of two spheres: one that is good, light and heavenly and another that is evil, dark and devilish. The intertwining of the two is the precondition necessary for the redemption drama to be set in motion, and their disentanglement is the end to which the drama necessarily moves. In *Parsifal* this disentanglement takes place both on the religious and sexual planes. These two levels have come into contact, which has triggered a fatal mutual dependence. On the one hand, we have the world of the Grail and of salvation, a male domain ruled by a king; on the other we have the world of evil, a female stronghold dominated by Kundry and the flower maidens. However, that world too is ruled by a man: the sorcerer, Klingsor. The two worlds have touched and intermingled, and wounds have been sustained as a result. Amfortas, the king of the Grail, had betrayed the Grail world's laws of chastity by letting himself be seduced by Kundry. As a result, the symbol of his sacred power, his spear, has fallen into the hands of Klingsor, who aspires to rule the Grail community. To prepare himself to seize power, Klingsor has done everything possible to enable him to obey the knightly law of chastity: he has castrated himself – yet another wound.

Klingsor's act proves useful to him also within his own realm: freed from sexual temptation, he has nothing to fear from the seductive woman, Kundry, and this means that he can use her as his sexual assistant. His intention is that she should weaken the chaste male community by carrying sin and guilt into it, thereby speeding its collapse and preparing the ground for Klingsor. In Kundry we again encounter the duality of the world expressed through the internal dichotomy of a human being: she, in a sense, personifies the entire salvation drama. At night she is beautiful and seduces the knights; by day, she atones for her sins by serving the Grail as an ugly woman.

It is between these two worlds that Parsifal, a naive young man from the forests, finds himself. He witnesses Amfortas's sufferings but does not understand them; he falls into the clutches of Klingsor and Kundry but resists sexual temptation by rejecting the seductress. And yet her kiss still has an effect, because it makes him realise the existence of sexuality, sin and guilt. After prolonged journeys in search of the Grail, he eventually returns to the castle carrying the spear, and becomes the king of the Grail himself. The miracle of grace occurs: the cup containing Christ's blood glows with light, Amfortas's wound closes, and Kundry is allowed to die.

The world of the Grail has triumphed over Klingsor's world, and has regenerated itself. Salvation from the impure intermingling of two worlds into the unity of the one good world has been accomplished.

Weininger's *Sex and Character* is a psychological typology of the sexes, culminating in a metaphysics of humanity. Weininger draws an analogy between the polarity of the two sexes and the division of mankind into earthly and spiritual existence, nothingness and the divine – and Judaism and Christianity. In line with these strict divisions, there is an equally strict moral division into good and evil. This quasi-scientific investigation therefore follows the same rules as the redemption drama; for Weininger, any proximity or mingling between the opposed polarities signifies contamination, an unholy, guilty condition. It is not surprising that sexuality is defined as the incarnation of that proximity: intercourse, to Weininger, is the act that again and again produces that unclean state of intermingling.

Logically enough, he condemns that which he holds responsible for this continued need for intercourse; for him, and he is not alone in this, 'woman' is the personification of sexuality. It is through woman that sin and guilt are transferred; it is she who causes the perpetual intermingling of positive and negative polarities. Woman is the element that destroys man, who stands for logic, ethics, consciousness, genius and transcendence. Only the man's chastity, his powers of resistance to this sexual assault, can save his spiritual existence – for Weininger, as for the knights of the Grail. However, since woman's function in this system is to personify sexuality, and since she can never become man, *her* salvation can logically only be defined in terms of her ceasing to exist. To describe this fate, Weininger uses the term *Untergang* [annihilation]: an apocalyptic word also used by Wagner, and one that later became strikingly popular within the discourse of extreme nationalism.

Weininger's model of woman, represented as a hopeless existential paradox, resembles Kundry in every respect. *Parsifal* almost seems to play out the arguments of *Sex and Character* in operatic form – or does *Sex and Character* state the theoretical assumptions from which *Parsifal* proceeds? One could argue that Weininger was more Wagnerian than Wagner: he even 'corrects' Wagner at certain points, as when he argues that Kundry should have died in Act Two at the moment when Parsifal resisted her attempts to seduce him, rather than undergoing the prolonged religious conversion of the last act.

The factor that makes Weininger's book more interesting than the mass of pseudoscientific studies of gender and sexuality published at this time is the idea that he shares with Freud, but which Freud failed to develop any further: the theory of human bisexuality. The psyche of every human being, according to this theory, is always made up of both elements, the male and the female. For Weininger, however, the co-existence is not a happy one. Because of his belief that the feminine, representing the negative, must be exterminated, the masculine ego becomes a site of self-mutilation: the female aspect of man must perish in order that the complete, desexualised man may emerge. The brutal image of Klingsor, who castrated himself with his own hand in order to meet the requirements of salvation, is a vivid dramatisation of Weininger's theory. However, as Weininger argues, Klingsor's action demonstrated his distorted understanding of the spiritual–moral ideal of salvation: 'Klingsor does not wish to attain morality in struggle, but forcibly achieves it through castration. . . the criminal becomes ascetic. . . He fails to sense that he prostitutes the idea of morality by wishing to obtain it ready-made and by desiring it as a possession.'

Parsifal, on the other hand, met Weininger's demands in exact detail. When he was confronted by sexual temptation in the shape of Kundry, he flung her away. At the moment of her kiss, he was assailed by the threat of death, experienced as a sudden shock of knowledge. He does not allow himself to explore the feminine or sexual side of his ego, identifying it with loss of self and denial of the possibility of salvation. The story of his wanderings describes the painful process of inner purification, resulting from his experience of the fall into sin. As a result of his denial of femininity and his deliberate asceticism, his state changes during the drama from the 'foolish purity' described at the start into the genuine purity of the adult. Once he is perfectly masculine, perfectly pure, once he has conquered himself, he is able to redeem others – Amfortas, from his fallen masculinity, and Kundry, from her sinful self. In a sense, Kundry can be seen as nothing more than a dramatic representation of the female aspect of man: she existed only to set in motion the redemption drama, the process of sin and atonement.

Let us recall the argument quoted at the start of this chapter: 'This is what the Aryan owes the Jew – through him he knows what to beware of: Jewishness as a possibility in himself.' The way in which Weininger's analogy operates is obvious. All personalities contain a mixture of Aryan and Jew, as well as of masculine and feminine. Just as the man needs to conquer the feminine/Kundry within himself, in order to become fully male, so the Aryan needs to conquer the Jewish aspect of his own personality in order to become fully Aryan. Though both the analogy and the idea seem absurd to us, they are pursued by Weininger with frightening seriousness. He wants Jewishness to be understood as a psychological quality, not as the product of religious or racial history; the logic of this is that Jews should be subjected to the same stigmatisation and exorcism as women. Although he attempts to present his views in an elevated, philosophical form, Weininger falls into all the familiar misogynistic and anti-Semitic clichés: women and Jews alike are described as changeable, vain, gossipy, mendacious, sentimental, superficial and incapable of sustaining a loving relationship.

Despite all this, there is some psychological truth in Weininger's argument that the anti-Semite and the misogynist are produced by a rejection mechanism: one hates most of all that which is in oneself and which one does not want to be there, one does not hate that which is totally foreign. This applied to Wagner, too, as Weininger realised: 'But even Wagner – the most thorough anti-Semite – cannot be acquitted of an admixture of Jewishness, even in his art.' And he tests this assertion against the responses that Wagner receives from his audience: 'There is no denying that Wagner's music produces the strongest impression both on the Jewish anti-Semite who cannot quite free himself from Jewry and on the anti-Semitic Indo-European who fears becoming addicted to him.' It was because Wagner was not completely German himself that he had been able to express the essence of Germanness so clearly in his *Meistersinger*. For Weininger, achievements in the arts are not sublimations of drives, as in Freud, but the result of defensive reactions against hated parts of one's own ego.

Weininger proceeds to present this fact in a positive way. The Jewish element in Wagner, he argues, had a fermenting effect on him, helping him to identify and affirm the other pole within him: it helped him to struggle through to *Siegfried* and *Parsifal*, and their supreme expression of the Germanic ideal. However, the full meaning of Weininger's speculation only emerges when artistic psychology gives way to Christology. Above the artist stands the founder of religions: 'one even greater than Wagner', he argues, 'first had to overcome the Jewishness in himself before discovering his own mission.' The sum of guilt that might be described as Jewish was concentrated in the figure of Christ; the weight of this guilt meant that the ultimate atonement, death, was required. For Weininger, Christ was the supreme figure because he had most to overcome and because he overcame it 'most completely': he charted the entire course from the negative, Jewish polarity to the positive, Christian one. As a redeemer *from* Jewry, Christ is also the redeemer of Jewry. It is not difficult to imagine the powerful effect that the unearthly final words of *Parsifal* would have had for Weininger when he visited the festival: 'Redemption for the redeemer.'

When Max Kalbeck, the Viennese music critic, attended the premiere of *Parsifal* in 1882, he bitterly observed that the present generation seemed to have no more use for a Christian–Semitic redeemer, but was trying instead to find a Christian–Germanic one: 'Those anti-Semitic gentlemen of the Reich ... have Wagner to thank for this fair-haired Christ.' But to what extent does *Parsifal* depict a conflict between Aryan and Jew? Parsifal himself, a Young Siegfried with noble Nazarene features, is just about recognisable as a fair-haired redeemer, but the role of Jewish antagonist is harder to assign. One would have to guess that the part belongs to Kundry. Characterised by her Ahasuerus-like wanderings through time and space, she has always been present, just like the wandering Jew. 'Archdevil, Hell rose', the conqueror Klingsor calls her, listing a few of her mythical incarnations: 'Herodias you were ... Gundryggia there, Kundry here.' Her wanderings are her 'curse', she complains, and groans; this curse has been upon her ever since she encountered Christ and laughed at his claim to be the Messiah. Part of the curse is the yearning she feels to encounter that redeemer once more.

Wagner ruthlessly exploits the ambiguities between the religious and the sexual here, suggesting that she would find a redeemer in every man who refused himself to her sexually. Amfortas was only half a man, half-

Christ, a precursor. Only the complete man, the other Christ, Parsifal, can offer her atonement and peace: not only through sexual denial, but also through Christian baptism. Paradoxically, though, this very act of conversion confirms the Jewishness of Kundry. The model of redemption that she enacts on stage is exactly the same as that which Wagner offered to the Jews in his notorious 'Judaism in Music'. He decreed in that essay that if the Jew ever wished to reunite with the Aryan people, he should first destroy the Jewishness in himself: 'Reflect that one thing only can be your salvation from the curse resting upon you – the redemption of Ahasuerus, annihilation.' The meaning of the ominous final word (*Untergang* in German) oscillates dangerously between its metaphorical implication – destruction of an undesired element in the self – and its cruder message of destruction of an undesired people. Wagner's apologists have often claimed that he only wished for the end of Jewishness, through baptism and conversion, and not of the Jews themselves – but the debate remains open.

Whatever his meaning here, Wagner undoubtedly saw baptism as the indispensible prerequisite for a Jew who wished to participate in the non-Jewish world, and in particular in its culture. According to Cosima's journal, Hermann Levi, the first conductor of *Parsifal*, should have been baptised and then shared holy communion with the Wagners before being allowed to direct this work – but Levi successfully resisted these demands. Even baptism, though, was not enough, since it was only a formal act. Wagner wanted more: he looked for a guarantee that not only the outward appearance had changed, but also the soul and spirit. In its calls for inner purification, for blood, sweat and tears, 'Judaism in Music', published in 1850, prepared the line of thought from which *Parsifal* would proceed several decades later. In that work, the male – and Aryan – sinners, Amfortas and Parsifal, are given the chance to survive by achieving purity. By contrast, the female sinner – eternal woman and eternal Jew in one – does not successfully reintegrate herself into society. Once she has received baptism from Parsifal on Good Friday, Kundry fades away, 'redeemed' by the sight of the Holy Grail. What else could be left to her? – because she fuses the idea of the feminine and the idea of Jewishness, the path to her salvation is closed forever.

If Wagner had wanted to express his emotionally charged resentment against the Jews in *Parsifal*, then it was an inspired move to present a Jew who was also a woman – moreover, one who was both servant and corruptress, both active and passive. Certain characteristics that were often derogatorily assigned to Jews – reliance on instinct, submissiveness – were ideally suited to portrayal in a feminine form. But despite her wanderings, Kundry is also linked to the historical context of the piece's composition: she symbolises the unhappily assimilated Jew, driven into ambivalence and crises of identity – she may well be the first personification of Jewish self-hate in art. It is a reflection of Wagner's modernity that he not only made manifest the Jewish neurosis, but also linked it with sexual neurosis, and thereby created an image of contemporary man's alienation from nature, society and self.

If Wagner's ideas on these subjects remain fragmentary, contradictory, confused and (most importantly) not easily translated into musical drama, then Weininger, by contrast, is absolutely clear and consistent: women and Jews are the twin essences of evil. While *Parsifal* is a work of art that supports numerous interpretations, Weininger's philosophical system is monolithic and without ambiguity, right to the end. The writer's decision to convert to Protestantism is consistent with his world-view. This is not only because Wagner was a Protestant, but also because the idea of rigorous inner purification of the self found its equivalent in the Protestant ethic of 'overcoming' sin without the help of an intermediary, whether this was the Virgin Mary, Christ or a priest. In a literal sense, Weininger was helpless.

For many of his generation, there may have been a cathartic effect when they were confronted with their spiritualised selves on the stage in *Parsifal*. For a fanatic like Weininger, though, there was no escape. In his desperate lucidity, he only saw the extent of the abyss that prevented a Jew such as himself from becoming a Parsifal. His suicide must be understood as the most radical act of self-purification possible. At the same time, it bears witness to his prophetic sensitivity to the tendencies of his time. Wagner's 'religious' art prompted the young man to practise on himself what the next generation would practise on an entire race: Weininger's action chillingly prefigures the 'purification' of the German race through the elimination of its Jewish elements, baptised or not. But surely even the most self-denying Jew could never have imagined the way in which the drama of 'redemption' would march from the world of art and philosophy into the sphere of life and death.

10

Disquiet about *Parsifal*

PICTURE A TYPICAL PERFORMANCE OF *PARSIFAL*: PERHAPS IT IS Good Friday, and people are dressed in black and affecting a solemn demeanour. The audience luxuriates in the sonorous world of the Grail, and suffers with the chromatic music of Klingsor's agony. After a seemingly unending flow of sound, all is resolved with a flood of reddish light and soft choruses from above proclaiming the happy ending of 'salvation'. Timid applause begins to break out as the audience awakens from that strange state in which *Parsifal* has held it – but is one allowed to clap or not? The singers are bowing, which seems to suggest that one is: Kundry, who has only recently sunk lifeless to the ground, rises to her feet; Amfortas, barely restrained from suicide, stands by the footlights, blood-stained and in rags; Father Titurel has stepped out of his coffin; and even Klingsor appears in his sorcerer's outfit. One might think one was at a vampire opera, were it not for the simpleton turned redeemer, Parsifal himself: fair-haired, gentle, and obviously the hero.

With the costumes and masks, curtain calls and applause, there is no doubt that we are in the theatre. But a moment earlier we had seemed to be in church. This ambiguity lies at the heart of the disquiet that *Parsifal* has always caused: it is a stage play and a sacred drama at the same time – a music drama whose aesthetic autonomy is undeniable, but also a religious work, a Christian passion play. No one is quite sure whether *Parsifal* makes us experience religion as a play, or a play as religion.

Wagner had expressed the hope that it would save the 'core of religion' from the orthodox Christianity of the churches, suggesting that he saw it as something more that a drama *about* religion. Are we to take this aspiration seriously, or is the redemption message of *Parsifal* merely the result of the composer's attempt to express the ultimate in music, and to translate the ineffability of mystical experience into a comprehensible and popular form? Is it a bid to redeem his own work from the chaos and devastation amid which *Götterdämmerung* ended?

The argument as to whether *Parsifal* is religion or art, church or theatre, has simmered ever since its premiere in 1882; even in the post-war era, a period in which the secularisation of society might have made Wagner's use of Christian iconography a less sensitive issue, no settled opinion has been reached. Wagnerians of the old school still insist on its status as religious ceremony: Zdenko von Kraft, for example, remained convinced in 1951 that 'the sacred play was not to be understood in the cheap sense of the word ... it does not wish to be understood ... it is meant to be believed!' Other interpreters, such as Willy Haas and Hans Mayer, have altogether denied the Christianity of *Parsifal*; for Haas, it came 'close to blasphemy', while Mayer spoke of its 'private theology'. Recent musicologists, following Carl Dahlhaus, have often described it as a historical document of nineteenth-century art religion: its piety is not exactly fake, but it is second-hand – piety in quotation marks.

Other interpreters, particularly those who are literary scholars or theologians rather than musical specialists, have preferred to follow the line of Thomas Mann, who argued that Wagner's development from a creator of theatre to a 'brother of the priest' was consistent with the rest of his career. As an artist, Mann argued, Wagner had always dealt in symbols and carried his leitmotifs before him like a monstrance; an 'oratorio of redemption' was a logical conclusion to his output. Christian thinkers, too, have continued to concern themselves with *Parsifal*: Hans Küng, for example, described it as 'true religion'. Whether or not it is true religion – or blasphemy, private theology, quoted piety, decadent religiosity or redemption oratorio – comprehension of *Parsifal* is undeniably dependent on understanding the allusions it makes to Christianity. It is a Passion play, concerned with the suffering represented by the Cross, with guilt and atonement, and with the iconography and rituals of the Church.

There would be little to quarrel with here, were it not for the fact that unease about *Parsifal* persists. No such sentiment is attached to Desdemona's 'Ave Maria' in *Otello*, nor the scene in Münster Cathedral in Meyerbeer's *Le Prophète*, nor Franz Liszt's *Heiligen Elisabeth*, let alone Bach's Passions. There is no intrinsic problem with the use of religious motifs or symbols in the theatre or concert hall; the unease is peculiar to *Parsifal*. Could this be because the particular religiosity of *Parsifal* is qualitatively different to that of the great baroque Passions or of Verdi's church scenes? Is it because the faith depicted in *Parsifal* is no longer naive, but knowing, decadent and neurotic? Friedrich Nietzsche noted that 'religious neurosis' required abstinence: the large amount of discussion here about sexual abstinence and the terrible consequences of its opposite would certainly seem to suggest a neurotic aspect to characters' religiosity. In Freudian terms, religion in *Parsifal* can be seen as a sublimation of needs that have been denied and as a moralisation of worldly torments.

The sin of carnality, committed by Amfortas when he was seduced by the 'arch-devil' Kundry, is the mainspring of the plot in *Parsifal*, since it was this that caused both the Grail community's misery and its need for salvation. The music drama, therefore, is deeply concerned with that which it simultaneously taboos: human sexuality. But sexuality is not merely considered in terms of the body. The libretto symbolically elides Amfortas's wound with those of Christ, which proceeded, of course, from a quite different cause. By this cunning manoeuvre, Wagner transfers sexual suffering into the religious sphere: it becomes a cause for compassion, something that needs redemption. Sexuality is both demonised and turned, in the person of Kundry, into an instrument for gaining domination.

A sexual act is the decisive turning point of *Parsifal*: the moment when Kundry kisses the hero is the moment at which he first understands the guilt of the world. Parsifal's first experience of lust triggers horror and rejection, leading him in the opposite direction, towards purity and abstinence, compassion and salvation. Kundry, meanwhile, shows us the double face of neurotic female sexuality – nymphomania and masochistic self-punishment – with a vividness that makes her one of the most exciting characters in opera. The centrality of sex to *Parsifal* is such that there is ample reason to endorse Thomas Mann's splendid description of the work as a 'sex opera', a precursor of works such as Strauss's *Salome* and Berg's *Lulu*. Hatred of sex is the basis of the religiosity in *Parsifal*, and sex is personified by 'woman' in the customary *fin de siècle* manner: we can therefore see the work as a document of a religious neurosis typical of its time.

This allows us to approach a more precise definition of the disquiet aroused by *Parsifal*. It is not caused by the mixture of sex and the sacred alone, for this is after all an exciting combination, and not one that was peculiar to Wagner. The disturbing effect of the work is not caused by its aspect of 'phantasmagoria' or false appearance, despite Adorno's arguments; nor by Wagner's synthesis of opera and oratorio, or by the overlapping of sacred and profane functions within the drama. Nor is the difficulty caused by the ambiguous meaning of various elements in the plot: the fact that Kundry is both seductress and penitent, that the spear symbolises both salvation and doom, and that the Grail simultaneously gives life and prolongs suffering.

The real problem lies in the way in which the work's carefully constructed ambivalence is abandoned wholesale at the end. Everything is ultimately forced into the unequivocal unity of Christian redemption, blessed by above: this undialectical 'solution' of all conflicts in universal sacred harmony is the cause of our disquiet. It suggests that we have arrived at the end of the world, with only a shadowy and discreet reminder of the horrors overcome and the evil exorcised, in the death of the victim Kundry. The reign of good – without female participation – has begun; the Grail, quintessence of the quest for salvation, has been found and saved, radiant forever. Life stands still, and the flow of time has been replaced by the space of eternity. We are beyond history, in an ultimate state of purity – it is like a euphoric death.

But this is not all. There is also an ideological crusade in *Parsifal*, conducted in the name of the Cross: decisions are made on what may live, what must suffer and what must die. Such crusades are, of course, an important part of the history of early Christianity, motivated by a belief in the need to bring the Judaeo-Christian ideal of salvation to all mankind. However, the crusade in *Parsifal* resonates uncomfortably with contemporary political mythology: ever since the premiere of the piece, listeners have claimed to hear the racist ideas of Wagner and his contemporaries reflected in it.

In aesthetic as well as political terms, the dominance of the Cross over the imagery of *Parsifal* exerts a fundamentally anti-emancipatory effect. It undermines the piece's claims to aesthetic autonomy, and has had the effect of stifling the imagination, associating it forever with the same fixed ideas. The visual uniformity of productions of *Parsifal* has been striking, even after the expiry of Bayreuth's exclusive copyright on the work; its secularisation as an opera among other operas has not helped to rid it of its pseudo-religious garb. If one looks at productions of *Parsifal* since 1914, one invariably encounters the same style, reminiscent of the Oberammergau Passion plays: the same flowing beards and garments, folded hands, liturgical apparatus, blood-red twilight. Mummery has become mummification.

Wieland Wagner was one of those who had tried hard to demystify *Parsifal*, but he confessed shortly before his death in 1966 that he had failed. 'Is Bayreuth, for you, the theatre of mysteries that Wagner dreamed about?' he was asked by Antoine Goléa, a French music critic. 'Sometimes, when I watch the audience during a performance of *Parsifal*, I am inclined to think so,' Wieland replied. His attempts to persuade the public that *Parsifal* was a piece of theatre and nothing but theatre, that it was not a religious ceremony, had, as he admitted, been 'tilting at windmills'. The audience refused to applaud; they wanted their *Parsifal* to remain a 'Christian mystery'. If someone as enlightened and sceptical as Wieland Wagner had been in charge of the Bayreuth Festival and still failed to change public perceptions of *Parsifal*, then was it even possible to salvage the work from what Pierre Boulez has called its 'sickly sweet Christianity', its 'pale ecstasy'? This depends, of course, on having producers who are willing and able to do the necessary and unpopular work of demystification. Wieland attempted this in 1951, but it was only forty years later that another producer continued his work of scraping the Christian glaze from *Parsifal*. If the *Zeitgeist* is like a 'digger', as Jacob Burckhardt has said, then it certainly took its time to dig into *Parsifal*.

Parsifal owes its peculiar treatment not only to its internal qualities, but also to the history of measures that were applied to the work from outside, in order to try and shield it from profanation. The most evident of these measures was the prohibition on staging the work anywhere other than Bayreuth for thirty years after the composer's death. Wagner's widow Cosima attempted to persuade the state to pass a 'Lex *Parsifal*' which would perpetuate this unusual situation, absurdly as it seems to us today, and the argument about this extension raged fiercely at the turn of the century, fuelled by the fact that there was a 'pirate' production at the New York Metropolitan Opera in 1903. Ironically, this production was the inadvertent result of Siegfried Wagner's carelessness. While on a stroll with Ludwig Strecker, director of Schott's publishing house, he gave Strecker permission to bring out a pocket score of the work. Perhaps we can see this as a minor Oedipal rebellion in a life otherwise characterised by complete submission to his fathers commandments.

The 'Lex *Parsifal*' was not ultimately approved by the Reichstag, so from 1914 onwards the piece was in the public domain. Arnold Schoenberg was an influential voice in the debate, arguing for change despite his admiration of Wagner. A style, he wrote, could not emerge if the object on which it was to develop was withdrawn from the influence of life: 'The Bayreuth monopoly is ill suited to produce a style because it guards the tradition. And tradition is the opposite of style, even though the two are often confused with each other.'

The stage set from the original 1882 production, designed by the Russian painter Paul von Joukowsky, was guarded like a relic at Bayreuth and regarded as sacred because 'the master's eye had rested' upon it. Schoenberg realised that the ritual character of the work was being mis-understood: Bayreuth was celebrating the outward ritual of stage designs and directions, sanctifying what was external to *Parsifal* while the work itself became sterile. His arguments anticipated those that would be made by Wieland – though not until forty years later, with a delay in picking up intellectual trends that was typical of Bayreuth. Wieland argued vehe-mently against the view of Wagner that treated him as a historical monu-ment. He had yet to realise the historical irony that would see his own 1951 production embalmed in the name of tradition, thereby perpetuating the sacred character of the work and the 'mystery of Bayreuth', the very things that he had sought to undermine.

The stage set of the original production was used until 1933, having seen service for half a century – an incredibly long period in an art-form as subject to the whims of fashion as theatrical design. Siegfried Wagner and his designer had made some small changes in 1911, though significantly only to Act Two; as Siegfried recorded, when the possibility arose in 1925–26 of 'changing the venerable sets of the Grail scenes', the attempts were quickly abandoned 'because they seemed like sacrilege'. In the era following Siegfried's death in 1930, the question of modernisation of the scenery arose again, this time in response to the wishes expressed by Adolf Hitler, Reichskanzler and close friend of the family. The older Wagnerians grouped quickly to try to forestall this change: Hans von Wolzogen, joined by Toscanini, led a protest in favour of 'the preservation of the original shape of *Parsifal*'. Their petition was first given to the festival management – Winifred Wagner and Heinz Tietjen – and then passed to the Reich government. The protest became a political issue of national importance; it was the state's duty, the conservatives argued, to protect this national shrine. Let other theatres experiment with *Parsifal*; the task of Bayreuth was to preserve it as a 'living, reflecting monument of Wagnerian art'.

Yet it was the state, personified by Hitler, that was in favour of getting rid of the tradition; it needed to do so in order to create its own mythology. Hitler put an end to the dispute by decreeing that modernisation would take place. The production was put in the hands of Heinz Tietjen, artistic director of Bayreuth, but the designer was personally chosen by the Führer. As a youth in Gustav Mahler's Vienna, Hitler had witnessed the revolution in stage design presided over by Alfred Roller. In 1911, he had tried to approach that great artist, but had been too shy to speak to him; now he was a man of power, that weakness could be atoned for and he duly brought the artist to Bayreuth. *Parsifal* was staged using Roller's designs in both 1934 and 1936: the extravagant, showy temple of the original production disappeared in favour of a massive and impressive collection of columns, structured by light and shadow, with no continuous architecture at the top or the rear. The old guard of Wagnerians called it 'an orgy of hell' – which suggests to us that it must have been rather magnificent. But something about the designs of his former idol did not please the Reichskanzler. Moreover, Wieland had been agitating for some time for a chance to establish his own artistic credentials in

Bayreuth. In 1937 his opportunity came, and his *Parsifal* sets replaced those of the Viennese reformer.

At that stage, Wieland's artistic horizons were somewhat limited. He had lived largely in the sheltered and conservative milieu of Bayreuth, and had little understanding of or familiarity with recent developments in scenic design: he did not like the Bayreuth sets of Emil Preetorius, the one innovative designer to whose work he had been exposed. He favoured a conventional approach, and was more concerned with the stage detail – should a tree move to the left or the right? – than with conceptual thought. He sacrificed most of the poetic naivety of the original décor in favour of a prosaic sobriety, but without finding a distinctive style of his own. In consequence, the Nazi press was pleased with his 'unspoiled language' and his lack of recourse to experimental or abstract solutions. But his temple was, in truth, narrow and devoid of poetry, partly because it was closed at the back by a wall; as the custodians of the Grail disparagingly observed, it resembled a thermal hall in a contemporary health spa. There was little that was sacred about it: something of the Nazis' antagonism to Christian mysticism had obviously rubbed off on the young Wieland.

After 1939 the Bayreuth festival effectively became the Strength Through Joy Festival as the Nazi-sponsored movement more or less took control, to the mingled relief and regret of the family. Nonetheless, plans were already being made for a peacetime festival, which would mark the success of the 'great solution' with new productions of both *Tannhäuser* and *Parsifal*. It is clear from a letter written by Wolfgang Wagner in September 1941 that the Führer was still concerned with the issue of *Parsifal*, and that he himself was beginning to experience some disquiet about the sacred elements of the opera. Hitler was increasingly disturbed by the church-like atmosphere of the temple scenes and the ecclesiastical architecture of the knights' hall: future presentations would have to emphasise the elusive and generalised sense of mystery in these scenes, rather than tying them to a particular religion. Wolfgang believed that this solution would only be possible in the reconstructed Festspielhaus – for in 1941, to the delight of the festival directrice and her sons, Hitler had proposed to provide the old half-timbered building with a gigantic encasing structure in the monumental Third Reich architectural style of Albert Speer. Hitler clearly nurtured a dream of a 'desanctified' *Parsifal*, a mystery play of indeterminate location, taking place in a secular temple of Nazism towering over Wagner's town; its text, moreover, would be rewritten according to the orders of Alfred Rosenberg, the National Socialist politician. The attention he devoted to the opera, even in the midst of war, is a clear indication of the disquieting effect it had upon him.

'*Parsifal* always was a thorn in the flesh of the rulers, not only the ecclesiastical ones but also the Nazis. Hitler virtually prohibited *Parsifal*,' Wieland would recall once the war was over. *Parsifal* should therefore have caused *him* no problems, given the radical break that he wanted to make both with the old Bayreuth and with Hitler's Bayreuth. There were no associations with recent German history to be purged, as with *The Ring*, and no embarrassing paeans to Germanness, as in *Die Meistersinger*. The idea that there might be an anti-Semitic programme inside the Christian packaging did not occur to anyone, in spite of the well-known anti-Semitic ideas voiced by Wagner and others at the time of the piece's composition, and the fervidly Aryan accounts of the work regularly presented in the *Bayreuther Blätter*.

Wieland's new production of *Parsifal* was duly chosen to inaugurate the post-war festival. And what did the audience see? At first, almost nothing, because the stage was shrouded in deepest darkness and contained virtually no objects. Gradually, the elliptical disc that formed the scenic basis for all three acts emerged, as did the spectral tree-trunks shot through with oblique rays of light. The temple was reduced to four pillars of light shimmering out of the darkness; at its centre there was a circular structure for the Eucharist, seemingly radiating light from within itself. Klingsor's tower was a projection of a spider's web, with the sorcerer appearing at its centre, and the garden was evoked only by changes in the colours of the lighting. The fields were a mere golden-green background, and bare blocks housed the baptism scene; there were no flowers on the stage. The gestures of the actors were economical, motivated by internal tensions; they moved across the stage and interacted with each other in simple geometrical patterns, in a style that would later be labelled 'oratorio-like' and 'statuesque'. The flower maidens were set in motion in such a phantasmagorical fashion that even Adorno would have fallen for their charms.

The theatre seemed to have reached the limits of self-effacement; there was so little reality, so little action. Instead, there were movements of light in the dark and slowly gliding changes of colour, hints of veiled phantoms and other ghostly figures. It was only in the orchestra that everything was as it was before: Hans Knappertsbusch, a pupil of Hans Richter and relic from the great days of Wagnerian conducting, ensured that the music retained the heavenly splendour and magisterial breadth familiar to pre-war audiences, whatever the disruptions on stage.

The fact that everything was not as it had been was clearly confirmed by the programme book: in a surprising act of *lese-majesté* by the new management, the words 'votive festival drama', Wagner's original description of the work, had quite simply been deleted. As if by way of compensation, there was a reproduction of Wieland's so-called '*Parsifal* Cross': a diagram showing the ideas and characters of the drama arranged in the cross shape. By suggesting that the Cross was now nothing more than a convenient peg on which to hang one's thoughts about the piece, this too contributed to the process of 'desanctification'. The opposed forces of Titurel's 'white magic' and Klingsor's 'black magic' and the parallels between the sinners Amfortas and Kundry are shown on the left–right axis of the cross; the destiny of Parsifal himself is shown as an upward progression along the vertical axis, from the maternal, corporeal principle symbolised by the swan, to the paternal, spiritual principle represented by the dove.

Wieland's production focused not on the external, anecdotal level of the action, but on the inner action, the invisible theatre of the psyche. His *Parsifal* was the developmental drama of a young man's self-discovery, his journey towards a realisation of his masculine, spiritual, divine self. The Christian Cross was replaced by a passion of the psyche, the Christian mystery by the mystery of individuation. The four primal symbols of swan, dove, spear and cup were no longer regarded as Christian, but were treated by Wieland as archetypes deriving from a collective subconscious. The lighting methods that he developed in order to communicate this understanding were based on an analysis of the various leitmotifs as sound symbols. The production thus developed a special homogeneity

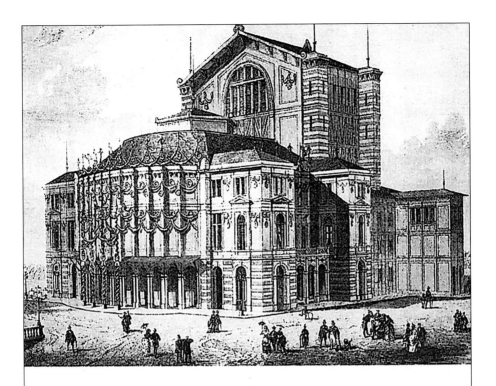

DIE BAYREUTHER FESTSPIELE

sind von Richard Wagner ins Leben gerufen worden und standen seither unter der Leitung von

Richard Wagner
1876-1882

Interimszustand
nach dem Tode Richard Wagners
1883-1884

Cosima Wagner geb. Liszt
1886-1906

Siegfried Wagner
1908-1930

Winifred Wagner
1930-1944

Wieland Wagner
1951-1966

Wolfgang Wagner
1951-

Nach dem Tod Wieland Wagners ist sein Bruder Wolfgang Wagner alleinverantwortlicher Leiter
der Bayreuther Festspiele geworden

The programme for the Bayreuth Festival in 1969, listing the directors since Richard
Wagner founded the festival in 1876.

Richard Wagner

Cosima Liszt

Wahnfried,
1874–1945

The house in
April 1945 after
bomb damage

Wagner's hall at Wahnfried in 1958

The hall today, as it has been since 1976

Franz Liszt, by Jean-Auguste
Dominique Ingres

Marie D'Agoult, by Théodore
Chassériau

The Liszt children: Cosima, Blandine and Daniele, by Friedrich Preller

Eva, Isolde, Siegfried, Daniela and
Blandine with Hans Richter

Winifred and
Siegfried in 1916

Siegfried with his wife and children:
Wolfgang, Verena, Friedelind, Wieland

The 'Wahnfried youngsters' with their guardian Tietjen

Gertrud Reissinger photographed by Wieland

Verena, painted by Wieland

Wolfgang and Wieland
in 1938

Winifred with
Adolf Hitler

20 April 1939, the Festspielhaus decorated for the Führer's birthday

Winifred and Siegfried's
first daughter, Friedelind

Brothers Wolfgang and
Wieland

The outcast: Franz
Wilhelm Beidler

Gertrud and Wieland

Wolfgang and Ellen

Wieland's family: Iris, Daphne, Wolf Siegfried and Nike

Wolfgang's family: Eva, Gottfried and Ellen

The Lafferentz children:
Amélie, Manfred, Winifred
and Wieland with their
aunt Friedelind, their
grandmother Winifred and
their mother Verena

Wieland with
his wife, Gertrud

Wieland with
his lover Anja
Silja, at a
rehearsal for
Lulu in
Stuttgart in
1960

Two different stagings of act III from *Siegfried*: left, in Wieland's production of 1952–59 and right, from Wolfgang's production of 1960–64

The step-sisters: left, Eva and right, Katharina

Eva and her daughter Antoine

Wieland Lafferentz and Verena

Nike and her daughter
Louise

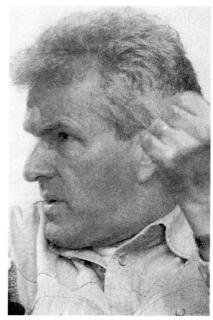

The male heirs: left, Wolf Siegfried in 1982 and right, Gottfried in 1997

The directors of Bayreuth: left,
Wolfgang and right, Gudrun

Daphne Wagner,
one of the new
generation at
Bayreuth

and harmony between its integral components, to which were added movements and gestures co-ordinated with the pulse of the music.

Wieland had derived this archetypal interpretation of the symbols and psychological events in *Parsifal* from his reading of Jung. Predictably enough, he did not discover Jung at home in Bayreuth – despite the anti-Semitic implications of some of Jung's work, it was outlawed by the Nazis as part of the 'Jewish science' of Sigmund Freud – but at Lake Constance, where he fled with his family after Germany's collapse. Even then he only encountered it by accident: Sven Schwed, a paediatrician summoned to the house, turned out to have trained as a psychoanalyst under Jung in Switzerland, and he now passed his knowledge on to Wieland. Incidentally, Schwed was also responsible for Wieland's later reading of Freud, which inspired the changes he made to his production of *Parsifal* in 1963, in the direction of a more overt emphasis on the sexual content of the work.

The theatrical coup of the 1951 production would not have been possible, however, had it not been for another mentor – even though Wieland was later to remove all mention of his former music teacher, Kurt Overhoff, from his biography. This Viennese composer, conductor and intellectual had taught the young Wagner how to read the leitmotifs in his grandfather's works as symbols of the characters' different moods and psychological traits; as a result of Overhoff's teaching, Wieland began to study the scores, in order to derive a production style that was firmly rooted in the works themselves. Overhoff himself wrote a book on *Parsifal* which he dedicated to Wieland, and Wieland's idea of the '*Parsifal* Cross' can be traced back to Overhoff's teaching. However, Overhoff's ideas were expressed in a rather antiquated, unwieldy language; Wieland, on the other hand, soon freed himself from the excessive ballast of Wagner's own philosophical discourse. Indeed, he was famed for helping singers in rehearsals by translating some of his grandfather's more obscure utterances into a witty and journalistic modern German.

Once he took over the festival, Wieland broke abruptly with Overhoff, who had nurtured hopes of a post on the conductor's podium. Wieland wanted more famous conductors for the reopened festival – men such as Knappertsbusch and Karajan – and he did not want to feel dependent on Overhoff, or to risk the danger of his former teacher exploiting him.

Overhoff's early enthusiasm for Nazism provided a convenient pretext for Wieland, who decided that he was unacceptable in the 'de-Nazified' Bayreuth. Overhoff departed on a bitter note, as the ungrateful pupil denied that his former teacher had even influenced him.

The 'dechristianised' 1951 *Parsifal* was anything but an immediate success. Superficial changes caused a disproportionate amount of controversy. There were complaints about the invisibility of the dove, which was hung so high that only Knappertsbusch could see it: he would have refused to conduct had it been banished altogether. There were tears, too, about the absence of green fields, and protests about the darkness. But the public and the press were soon won over. It was acknowledged that a new style had been found, through the incorporation of psychoanalytical archetypes and the reduction of the liturgical elements to a ritualistic play of light and shadow. And this new style prevailed: Wieland's *Parsifal* remained in the repertoire for twenty-three years, with only minor changes, mainly to Act Two. It came to be regarded as the quintessence of New Bayreuth: ironically, therefore, it suffered the same fate as the now-forgotten original production, as style turned into tradition. It is not easy to say whether this situation was brought about by the conservatism of the Bayreuth public, or whether it was the result of an intrinsically 'sacrosanct' quality in the work itself.

Wieland himself soon saw his 1951 production as old hat: he urgently wanted to change it, but was held back by the influence of the legendary Knappertsbusch, as well as by the demands of the public. Wieland the artist had to yield to the responsible festival director who constituted the other part of his persona. It was not until 1966 that he found the collaborator necessary for the *Parsifal* of his dreams, a conductor who would interpret Parsifal as a shadowy drama of time and space, and infuse it with a Debussyan orchestral delicacy. But just as Pierre Boulez had been enticed to Bayreuth, Wieland Wagner died.

From a historical point of view, there were two main factors that contributed to the unprecedented effect of the 1951 *Parsifal*. Stylistically, its tendency towards abstraction and innovative lighting effects, visual symmetries and geometric patterns, pointed back to the radical theatre of the Twenties. But its use of a mythical, archetypal language of symbols and its affirmation of eternally valid human values satisfied the need of the post-war audience, its consciousness damaged by the nation's collapse, to recover a sense of lasting, universal truth. By invoking the timeless essence of Wagner's works, the rebuilders of the festival sought to retrieve the authentic bones of the Wagnerian relic from the ugly brown casket in which the Nazis had placed them. The new spirit of aesthetic purity was perfectly reflected in this deconcretised and dehistoricised *Parsifal*, a concordance that ensured the production's lasting success.

After Wieland had shown the way, many theatres experimented with *Parsifal*: one production interpreted it as an anti-nuclear fable (Rolf Liebermann); another saw it as a family history which revealed the Wagners' covert racism (Wolf Siegfried Wagner); another viewed it as the story of a suffering society in danger of perishing by its own history (Ruth Berghaus). Secularisation had taken root. But it was not until 1991 that a new production genuinely took up what Wieland Wagner had left unfinished. It took place in Hamburg, not Bayreuth, and it was directed not by a Wagner, but by the American Robert Wilson.

While Wieland Wagner had brought the inner action to the stage, Wilson radicalised the piece still further by confining each character to an individual, sealed universe. Withdrawn figures move around the stage, which represents an imaginary space; their movements are slow, in keeping with the spaciousness of the music, but also precise and stylised. They do not communicate with each other, but hold a series of monologues, as if expressing a truth that is intelligible only to them. Amfortas with his lonely outbursts, Kundry with her visions, Gurnemanz with his endless stories, Parsifal in his struggle for self-awareness – each of them is alone with his or her self, in Wagner as in Wilson. It is as though we are witnessing a cultic ritual, but one whose significance is entirely hidden. Wieland's emphasis on just a few symbols is taken still further: here there are no symbols at all, no spear, no dove and no Grail. No lip service is paid to religion, as in Wieland's production. The entire theological fable and all its anecdotal trimmings are gone.

With Wilson, the desanctifying of *Parsifal* has been completed, and so too have the depsychologising and the desexualising. Even the notorious Kundry kiss has disappeared, consigned to the hysterical neuroses of the turn of the century from which it came. The logic of Wieland's lighting innovations is taken still further, and Wilson characterises all the figures and worlds through colour, thus preserving the meaning of the action despite the removal of the religious superstructure. Wilson presents a universal state of suffering which is all the more modern because no one knows its cause; it remains uncomprehended, nameless and unredeemed. This presentation of pure pain could even be justified with reference to Wagner himself, since in a letter written to Mathilde Wesendonck in 1868, during his preliminary work on *Parsifal*, he declared that he wished 'to express the great grief of life' in this work.

Most interpretations of *Parsifal* run the risk of placing themselves in conflict with the hypnotic fascination of the music, but Wilson's production manages to avoid this problem. The separate arts of lighting, colour, movement and space are all encouraged to express themselves, in a way that simultaneously promotes the self-expression of the music. In this autonomous synaesthetic space, the music once more develops its own beauty and power, just as if it were announcing its own redemption from the vagaries of past theatrical practices. Here, it comes into its own and thereby once more provides the long-desired metaphysical effect. The finality of the conclusion seems to have been abolished.

Perhaps it is appropriate for one of Germany's most distinguished living composers to have the last word. When asked his opinion of *Parsifal* in 1982, Wolfgang Rihm observed that:

> Its position between opera and cultic performance ... offers great future potential for music theatre. Absolute music and dramatic music are no longer opposites. There is something new, a third way, a Utopia to be heard – it is a language of sound which seems to flow with time itself. The question of – and hence the search for – states of music which are 'real' in this way suddenly occurred to me when (at the age of fifteen) I was shaken by *Parsifal* ... There is no getting away.

There is indeed no need to get away from *Parsifal*, if it is considered as a 'state of music', as a 'language of sound' which speaks symbolically of human suffering.

PART TWO

The Theatre of the Wagners

11

Wieland Wagner: a 'negative' life

RICHARD WAGNER'S GRANDSON HAS A SECURE PLACE IN THE history of theatrical and intellectual life in Germany since the end of the Second World War. The real man tends to disappear behind that public figure: in some ways, this is as it should be. The externals of his life can be summarised in headlines. Wieland Wagner was born in Bayreuth in 1917 and attended school there. Except for a few years at university in Munich, he lived and worked in his home town. It was there, too, that his terminal illness took hold. He could be seen at Wahnfried, or walking to the newspaper kiosk by the railway station, or around the Festspielhaus. He was easily identifiable by his 'Wagner nose'; only strangers mistook him for his brother, Wolfgang. As a Wagner, he felt at home in Wagner's town, even though the sausage industry was almost the only aspect of civic culture in which he took any interest. This mixture of closeness and distance, of rootedness and isolation, endowed him with a certain aura. Those who were close to him feared his explosions of anger; those who were mere acquaintances appreciated his ironic courtesy. His premature death at the age of forty-nine only served to intensify the mystique that surrounded him.

After his death, Wieland was mourned as the man whose fresh interpretations of Wagner's works had brought new splendour and excitement to the town; as the director who had held the Wagner empire together through determination, wit and intellect; as the living guarantee that tastelessness would never be inflicted on the stage of Bayreuth, and mediocrity only rarely; as the man who restored a measure of national pride in the German theatre. After all, he was the 'genius grandson', the creator of the modern 'director's opera', a valuable German cultural export, whose unlikely achievement was to make Munich seem pallid by comparison with Bayreuth. More importantly still, he had made the world forget Hitler's Wagner by replacing him with Wieland's Wagner: he had abolished both the old, tradition-bound Bayreuth, and the wartime 'Aryan citadel' Bayreuth, in favour of his own 'New Bayreuth'. Without doubt, Wieland Wagner fully discharged the task imposed on him by his personal and historical position. He both cleansed and saved the work of Wagner, and the new West Germany duly recognised his merit.

Wieland's importance to the history and culture of his era is defined and documented by his achievements on the stage of the Festspielhaus. But theatrical productions, by their very nature, provide only fragile evidence of their producer's distinction. Even if his last and best productions had been kept in the repertoire a little longer, as they should have been, the wheel of history would still have passed over them. Ten years after Wieland's corporeal death, his stylistic death took place. The mystical, empty spaces for reflection which characterised his productions were superseded by the historicising detail that preoccupied his successors. Any producer and designer who succeeds in embracing the theatrical moment inevitably becomes a victim of history.

Wieland Wagner's character will be better understood if one traces his career at a more abstract level of intellectual history. From the surface Wieland whom we remember, we can extract a symbolic one. This Wieland demonstrates that there is truth in the arguments of a certain strand of German philosophy, when it claims that the spiritual development of a 'subject', his ontology, obeys the same laws as objective historical processes – and that the individual's developing consciousness reflects, in microcosm, the course of the great states of the world.

Herbert Marcuse has stated, interpreting Hegel, that 'The concept of man is his history, as it is understood by philosophy.' The individual, according to this view, develops in a complex way, caught between the conflicting demands of the 'spirit of the family' on one hand, and the

'general will' or 'common weal' on the other. This approach to understanding an individual life will allow us to free our understanding of
Wieland's career from the ephemera of theatrical and social history; it
will help us to explore the shadowy space that lies behind the mere stage
prop of his body.

Wieland's work so shaped and transformed the post-war generation's
understanding of Wagner, that his opinions and tastes became the yard-
stick for the theatrical world of his day. Anyone else who produced Wagner
was measured against and compared with Wieland. It should be said,
though, that if Wieland captured the flavour of a historical moment in
his interpretations of Wagner, then this was not his deliberate intention.
He was not at all concerned with realising 'the spirit of history' in his
productions: he was interested solely in himself. The changes in his style
clearly reflected phases in his self-realisation, and not any external reality.
There was a clear stylistic development from the void, the darkness and
the pure line of his early productions, to the visual symbols, the subtle
differentiations of design and the complex lighting effects that characterised his later work. It is as though his personality first had to sweep
everything away, and could only then shape itself and become aware of
its own autonomy. Needless to say, the private ownership of the Bayreuth
theatre made this personal odyssey a much more realistic proposition
than it would have been had Wieland been confined to the state-funded
or municipal repertory theatres. This explains why other producers
appeared to limp rather half-heartedly in Wieland's wake; but then how,
in any case, could a concept based on someone else's subjective mental
processes be copied?

Following the Hegelian interpretation, it may be said that because
Wieland not only experienced but also created history, he was himself a
personification of the 'spirit of history': history sought and found in him
an agent of its self-realisation. But anyone familiar with Hegel knows
that the process through which the spirit passes into history or into an
individual consciousness is not a straightforward one. Negative phases
always have to be surmounted before positive advances can take place:
the force of negativity is the motor of spiritual development, as the
individual negates the given conditions then transforms them into his

own conscious work. Through its negativity, the unquiet consciousness *en route* to self-realisation produces continually new dissonances from temporary consonances, until it arrives at the truth of its existence.

Wieland Wagner's negativity was an essential aspect of his nature, one that ran through all his activities like a coloured thread. In normal life, this is usually translated into psychological terms as a tendency towards depression and destructive behaviour. These tendencies were not entirely absent in Wieland's case: even as a child, he was sullen and bad-tempered, troublesome to his mother and a tyrant to his younger brother. The environment in which he grew up and his position as one of a number of siblings may have dictated that this could not have been otherwise. But such a literal understanding of negativity tells us nothing of the productive uses to which it was put in his work: we need once more to delve beneath the surface.

Hegel describes 'action' as the expression of negativity, identical with negative movement. Without action, through which the individual makes the world into a world of his own creation, he would remain an 'unreal shadow': condemned to float perpetually between alien elements without ever arriving at himself, spellbound between the archaic laws imposed on him by the 'blood of the family', and the contradictory 'moral' demands of society and the state. To escape from the former and satisfy the latter, even though both suppress the spirit of individuality: this is the task of becoming aware of oneself, a task that is inevitably self-contradictory. For any action always implies a 'separation'. The individual's loyalty to one of the two systems of law invariably means a violation of the other. This classic double-bind produces 'guilt' and a sense of 'fate' for the individual. In the ancient tragedies – to which Hegel refers in his discussion of the rights of the family and the rights of the state – only death can expunge the guilt acquired through the emancipation of self-awareness. In death, the individual gains the paradoxical dimension of 'universal individuality'.

The negative elements of Wieland Wagner's life, accordingly, were sited in the struggle between the 'spirit of the family' and the 'common weal'. The child had been fettered by family expectations ever since his birth: his destiny was to assume the throne of the family empire. But then, confusingly, his father's will declared him only an equal co-regent with his siblings. At this point, Wieland rejected his mission and tried to become a painter and photographer – a first negation of the family laws. His relationship with the state, on the other hand, was at that time one of unthinking alignment with Hitler's Germany. After the war, however, when the extent of the Nazis' perversion of the 'common weal' was revealed, this near-fatal act of consonance gave way to a new dissonance – and from that point onwards he viewed the German state with a fundamental mistrust. From this dissonance, he developed a new consonance with the realm of the family. He finally identified himself with his inheritance and accepted the artistic directorship of the festival, with the help of his brother Wolfgang.

It was not always self-evident that Wieland would take this 'action'; after all, there were plenty of reasons for self-doubt. From a position of negativity, however, he developed energy and courage, even though he had had little training in the theatre, and was often regarded as a dilettante. He decided to make his wife his closest collaborator: this dependence on the family is significant from our point of view, connoting a desire for reassurance through the familiar substance. Family spirit, in itself passive, was thereby transformed into an active element, and New Bayreuth was created with a series of novel productions. However, the tradition-bound post-war public perceived the negation of the familiar by the family enterprise as an arbitrary act of desecration. Wieland was condemned for having betrayed his grandfather, as though the negative force unleashed by the grandson's uncluttering of the stage could have destroyed the Master himself. Wieland was rehabilitated by the developing spirit of the age; eventually the public cheered, the Adenauer state was satisfied, and the iconoclast became the icon. Much as Wieland enjoyed his public acclaim, it did not exhaust the negative aspects of his intellect: he was merely driven into subtler forms of negation.

These acts of negation were first directed, in a new strategy of self-opposition, against his own stage, whose empty depth he now furnished with symbols in order to achieve a flexibly articulated space; at times, as in his second *Meistersinger*, he even turned to realism. As a social protest, his negativity was unleashed against the bourgeois institution of marriage; he gave free rein to his anarchic erotic drives elsewhere. As an artistic protest, negativity was finally directed against the family theatre itself, as he decided he was no longer willing to share control of the Festspielhaus with his brother. He wanted to break out of Bayreuth, believing that the 'blood of the family' was choking and stifling him, so he applied, unsuccessfully, for the Intendant's post in Berlin. He also wanted to break free from the work of his grandfather, which had become routine to him: he produced other operas in other theatres, particularly Verdi, Strauss and Berg. Over the years, this need for an ever more unconstrained realisation of his self as a negation of his own familiar substance reached almost suicidal proportions. At the same time, the demands made by his decision to move away from the private theatre of Bayreuth towards work in the state-funded theatre were draining his mental energy; he feared the possibility of surrender to public authority, which would have left his imagination stultified. He still aspired to carry out acts of negation – he provocatively engaged the arch-modernist Pierre Boulez as an 'anti-conductor' for *Parsifal* in Bayreuth – but at this point his strength gave way, and Wieland died. Cancer had attacked his lung, robbing him of his breath, and a tumour blocked his heart; the bodily sources of his creativity, emotion and air, were destroyed.

It is a mistake to think that tragic death no longer exists in our secularised world: Wieland's pathway to self-emancipation was also a road to self-encumbrance and self-dissolution. It should come as no surprise that Wieland felt a great kinship for the ancient Greeks; the laws of their drama were to overtake his life.

Now, consigned to the soil of Bayreuth, Wieland belongs neither to the 'underground power' of the family, nor to the 'common weal'. He made sacrifices to both, but did not become the victim of either. The force of his negativity saved him both from remaining an 'unreal shadow', and from sacrificing his individuality and vitality to the demands of the general public. It may seem to us that his life was unfinished and tragic, and that there was a premature and abrupt transition from the 'becoming' of an unquiet consciousness to the 'being' of a quiet death. In a philosophical sense, however, this does not mean that his self-realisation had not been completed to a very high degree: he had succeeded, after all, in attaching his name to a moment in intellectual history.

12

'To us, he wasn't the Führer at all' – the enigma of Winifred Wagner

WE COULD, IF WE WANTED, tell her story rather like this:

In 1930, following the death of her husband, a young woman of thirty-three found herself in charge of a summer theatre festival. And not just any festival, but one which was described in 1932 by the influential journal *Deutsche Rundschau* as 'a national shrine of worldwide importance' and a 'unique incarnation of the German spirit.' The woman's name was Winifred, and she did not seem at all presumptuous or domineering. To the surprise of the German musical public, and especially those closely connected with the Wagner family, she invited two men from outside the family circle to join her management team: Heinz Tietjen, the General Intendant of the Prussian State Theatre, and the conductor Wilhelm Furtwängler. The cosmopolitan music critic Hans Heinz Stuckenschmidt suggested that these appointments could be regarded as a welcome gesture of liberalism: 'Tietjen, although personally neutral so far, is an exponent of a democratic arts policy and a servant of the progressive Prussian Ministry of Culture. This decision by the management of the Bayreuth Festival, which has been flirting with the Nazis ever more conspicuously in recent years, could signify a new direction.'

Tietjen, born in Tangier and an open-minded man of the theatre, was indeed responsible for the modern experiments with Wagner at the Kroll Opera in Berlin, and Furtwängler was praised by Stuckenschmidt as an 'internationally recognised master' and 'the most suitable of the younger conductors'. Winifred, likewise, seemed eminently suited to the position she had attained. Born in England in 1897, she was brought up from her tenth year in the Berlin home of Karl Klindworth, a pianist, disciple of Liszt and editor of piano editions of Wagner's works. At the age of eighteen, she moved from this Wagner-saturated atmosphere into Wahnfried, where she found herself under the tutelage as much of her mother-in-law Cosima as of her new husband Siegfried. Despite the knowledge she had gained, she was still very young when her husband died and would therefore, the modernisers hoped, be open to innovations.

It would not be easy to convince the public, even with the help of a new direction. As Stuckenschmidt observed, the young – even, strangely, the Hitler Youth – had less interest in Wagner than ever before: 'They feel uneasy with his emotional style, they scarcely understand his language. How can they be won over?' It was still more difficult, strangely enough, to win over the orthodox Wagnerians. For both political and artistic reasons, the old guard opposed the new director and her team. This opposition was expressed on the one hand through laments about the loss of the authority conveyed by Siegfried Wagner and the 'old atmosphere': the 'depersonalisation' and 'factualisation' of Bayreuth were casually deplored, whatever those phrases meant. On the other hand, there were complaints about the lack of harmony among the artists. It was true that Toscanini had departed in a state of fury and did not return in 1933, and Furtwängler left the management before the festival had even begun. His place was taken by Emil Preetorius, a renowned designer and friend of Thomas Mann, the writer who had been in disgrace with the family ever since he made a speech about Wagner that they perceived as excessively critical. The principles guiding the work of the Tietjen–Preetorius alliance were decidedly progressive, in line with the general theatrical tendencies of the 1920s: 'Our efforts are aimed at detaching the production, the stage set and the costumes of Wagner's works from the traditional sphere of historicism and naturalism, and at penetrating to its core substance, the musical drama.'

That was all very well, but the Old Wagnerians linked their aesthetic prejudices with their political ones to oppose the new regime: they disliked Tietjen because his roster of conductors at the State Opera still included men like Klemperer and Kleiber, which made the house a 'bastion of German anti-spirit'. Tietjen himself was described by the leading Wagnerian Paul Pretzsch as the 'former drawing-room communist who was again appointing racially suspect collaborators to leading posts in the festival operation.' The attacks, however, did not only come from within Germany. Adolf Zinsstag, the president of the Swiss Richard Wagner Association, protested vociferously in 1933 against 'subversive Jewish poison' finding its way onto the festival stage in the shape of Preetorius's abstract Valkyrie rock. And in the following year, when the festival management wanted to redesign the sets of *Parsifal* which had remained unchanged since the first night, the same gentleman accused it of 'incomprehensibly and disastrously contradicting the intellectual rebirth and moral elevation of the German people since National Socialism's rise to power.' The general complaint was that 'Frau Wagner thinks only of innovation', as the Rostock philologist Walther Golther put it in 1933. Innovation was regarded as synonymous with modernism, political liberalism and a disrespect for tradition. A new era of liberalism did indeed seem to have dawned in Bayreuth since the death of Siegfried, and the modern attitudes were personified by the young Winifred just as much as by her artistic directors.

The new management of the festival opposed the Old Wagnerians insofar as they desired innovation. It seemed logical, therefore, that Winifred must have been opposed to the Nazis, because the Old Wagnerians invariably belonged to that German nationalist conservative camp which drifted over to National Socialism in the early 1920s once the problems of the Weimar Republic began. Had not Winifred's husband forbidden the singing of German Nationalist songs as early as 1924? And there were no swastikas inside the Festspielhaus as there were in other theatres, and all proposals to incorporate Nazi insignia into the sets of *The Ring* were rejected. If little jokes were practised from time to time, such as the inclusion in the chorus of *Götterdämmerung* of lookalikes of Goering and Goebbels, then that was surely harmless enough. Winifred also courageously opposed the plan to hold a Reich Youth Rally in the Festspielhaus. At a time when all cultural associations were supposed to be attached to a party organisation, she fought to preserve the complete independence of the Richard Wagner Association of German Women. She 'democratised' the festival by admitting the hitherto detested media, and she even had a press gallery built in the auditorium for them. She also opened up the festival to academic research, instituting a German Richard Wagner Research Centre in 1938, where the contents of the family archives were made available to researchers for the first time.

It is true that Winifred had joined the Nazi Party in 1926, but that was only because Hitler had particularly requested it. And she only received the Party Gold Badge because her membership number was 29,349, and everyone with a number under 100,000 was granted this honour. She certainly did not receive the award for any special service to the Party, as was falsely assumed. She never held any post or performed any task for the Party, nor did she make any donations to Party funds. Nor did she ever join the Reich Theatre Chamber. And as for the charge that she sent paper to the exiled Hitler, she could even joke about that herself, many years later: 'Heavens above, now people are accusing me of having supplied the paper for *Mein Kampf*. As if I were responsible for *Mein Kampf* having been written. It doesn't matter what you did, you are always attacked for something.'

Any unprejudiced examination of Winifred's period of control in Bayreuth (1933–44) is forced to conclude that she did nothing more and nothing less than to ensure the financial and artistic survival of the festival. The means used were as honourable as they could be: after all, a private theatre could only function with subsidies from the state. What good fortune that the head of the state was a passionate Wagnerian! The Bayreuth Festival had not regained economic stability since its reopening in 1924, and the political climate in Germany was not one that made it easy to attract foreign visitors. Additional problems were caused by the public opposition to the new management. It was just as well, really, that the young woman had a private line of communication to the Reichskanzler! In June 1933, she made a hasty trip to see him in Berlin, as he had promised his support for the festival. After that, the Reich's cultural fund provided about 55,000 marks each year to subsidise new productions. This was a trivial sum, relatively speaking: over twice that amount was given to support operettas, and on one occasion Hitler had contributed 350,000 marks to promote Mozart. If there was the occasional extra subsidy in the form of state-purchased tickets, then this was just a personal kindness from the art-loving new Reichskanzler, to help the festival get back on its feet. And Hitler's personal gifts to Winifred were trifling: just an ivory sewing-case one year and a small pendant in the shape of a triple swastika the next, and a leather vanity case which her son Wieland later sold on, and then that new Mercedes for Christmas in 1938.

At the outbreak of war, Winifred intended to close down the Festspielhaus, as had been done in 1914. But when the head of state demanded that performances should continue, when he arranged for the staff to be exempted from military service and ensured that the tickets would be sold, when he provided an audience and had it brought in free of charge through the Strength Through Joy organisation, then was this not wonderful and altogether in keeping with the socialist ideals of the founder of the house? And did not the wartime festivals, with their cheerful *Meistersinger*, provide the wounded and crippled with a much-needed uplifting of the spirits?

What, then, might the young Frau Wagner's attitudes have been to politics, and more particularly, to the Jewish question? She only once tried to meddle in politics, on the occasion when she hoped to arrange a meeting between Hitler and the British Ambassador, Sir Neville Henderson, in her box at the Festspielhaus in July 1939. The attempt was in vain: Hitler would never discuss politics with her, and just kept talking about Wagner, casting problems, relations between artists, and stagecraft. It is doubtful whether her belief that Rudolf Hess had gone to Britain to convey the Führer's secret wish for an agreement was founded on intimate conversations with Hitler. And she could not understand why, in the final years of the war, Hitler only wanted to hear *Götterdämmerung*.

She was entirely unaware of conditions in the concentration camps, because the press did not report them and released prisoners were forced to keep silent. When former inmates asked her to help them she did so unselfishly, but without taking any interest in the reasons for their detention. The only time she was kept fully informed was when the singer Max Lorenz, her indispensable Siegfried, was arrested on a charge of homosexuality; an embarrassing trial could only be avoided with Hitler's help. Winifred was always willing to use her hotline to the top for the benefit of others: she often brought Jewish doctors or other acquaintances back to Bayreuth from the concentration camps. She had more than thirty letters from Jews thanking her for the services she had rendered in this way. And whenever Jewish artists were contracted to Bayreuth she tried to keep them on wherever possible – one example being the conductor Franz von Hoesslin, who was deemed to be related to Jews by marriage. After 1943, however, Hitler asked her not to address her petitions to him directly, as they were being intercepted by Martin Bormann; she therefore sent subsequent requests on behalf of the victims of persecution through his physician, Dr Brand. Naturally, the humane director of Bayreuth knew that Hitler himself was innocent as far as the Jews were concerned: she would insist that it was that Julius Streicher, whom 'none of us liked', that was pulling the strings. To spare her feelings, Hitler would not bring Streicher with him when he visited Wahnfried; she was grateful, as always, for his consideration.

It is perfectly possible to present the relationship between Winifred Wagner and the Third Reich in that way. None of the facts presented is untrue and indeed, many more instances of Winifred's personal innocence and integrity could have been given. Do we have to revise our notions of what guilt is? Did not Faust become involved with Mephistopheles, and nonetheless save his soul? Was not Winifred in some sense part of the resistance? She certainly thought so, writing in 1947 that 'I believe that I can rather claim to have passively resisted all the violent measures of the Party.' That, too, is not incorrect. She employed Jews for longer than any other institution, because she had not joined the Reich Theatre Chamber, and her staff included at least as many members of the Social Democratic Party as of the National Socialist Party. And the Nazi Party itself had always been regarded as rather vulgar at Wahnfried. All she had really liked about Nazism was the enthusiasm of its beginnings and the fact that it took the unemployed off the streets. She had only favoured a kind of 'noble' or 'superior' National Socialism – and this kind of National Socialism, as she was to remind people as late as 1947, was entirely in keeping with the spirit of her father-in-law's work, which 'reflected more emphatically than anything a Christian attitude, genuine morality and good manners'.

When asked by Furtwängler, after the war, how she was able to tolerate having those 'buckets of filth' thrown at her, Winifred appeared unmoved:

'I told him that basically it does not bother me at all, it does not touch me inwardly ... simply because I did not feel in any way guilty of an offence or a crime ... so the buckets just ran off me.' She was, in a way, immune from criticism where Nazism was concerned: 'After all, I had nothing to do with it personally.'

This self-image, typical of the escapist reductionism of the German post-war consciousness, has been reaffirmed at every event at which Winifred has been commemorated at the Bayreuth Festival, including one occasion as recent as 1997. In one sense this is appalling – but it is scarcely surprising, given that the festival is headed by Winifred's son, who was himself one of Hitler's soldiers. It is telling that he dismissed her notorious declaration of 1976 – 'If Hitler came through this door today, I'd be just as glad, just as happy, to see him here, to have him here, as ever' – as old woman's babble, rather than being alarmed by it. Like his mother, Wolfgang was blinded by the effects of his personal acquaintance with Hitler, which prevented him from seeing the reality of what had happened, let alone beginning the process of mourning for it.

The truth of one story about a person's life can only be measured by being compared with another story of the same kind. It would be easy to build up a monstrous weight of evidence against Winifred – easy, but irrelevant, since her 'false consciousness' of her own actions was not touched even by the most watertight of arguments. The only way to counteract Winifred's defence is by using Winifred's own words.

Two things are important here: what she leaves unspoken, and the way in which events are reflected in her language. It is difficult to tell whether her silences are preserved for tactical reasons, or whether it is because there are certain things that she cannot talk about, or does not wish to talk about. However, the unconscious aspect of her discourse, her linguistic behaviour, betrays her in every case, exposing the immaculate self-portrait that she presented at the de-Nazification tribunal as a gigantic edifice of lies. But even this seems strange – or pathological – because Winifred was not really capable of lying, dissembling or scheming. On the contrary, she was always proud of her honesty and her direct and uncomplicated manner. This is why this English-born woman was the only self-confessed National Socialist whom Klaus Mann could find, when he was travelling through Germany after the war. Her share of the guilt can only be gleaned from her words, and not from her good or bad actions. The consciousness which reveals itself in her language ultimately aligns the former director of the Bayreuth Festival with those women with whom she initially appears to have little in common: the wives of SS men who lived with their husbands close to the concentration camps, who had inmates working for them and yet were themselves innocent, and who were hardly known to the public because they rarely stood trial. After the war, these SS wives showed no more remorse than Winifred. But did they not also belong to an elite, albeit of a different kind? And was there not a perverse similarity between this elite and the Grail community of Bayreuth, which was guarded by the far from ailing Winifred?

It is only when Winifred is at her wit's end, when she can no longer express herself, when her language abandons her and her self-righteous assertiveness breaks down, that we can give her further assistance. As in the final scene of Part II of Goethe's *Faust*, when the angels approach to take the blind Faust away from Mephistopheles, his old adversary who is digging his grave – it is only when Winifred is finally silenced that her soul can be released from its assignation with the devil.

A few examples:

'I am basically a totally unpolitical person and I was astonished when the de-Nazification tribunal accused me of political involvement. I said that I hadn't been involved in politics, and they all laughed … but I *wasn't* involved in politics!'* That qualification that she uses so often – 'basically' – betrays her discomfort at her own statement. In fact, she had been politically involved at least since 1923, when she first made the acquaintance of the fervent young Hitler, who came to Bayreuth as a speaker on 'German Day' and whom she did not want to let out of her sight from that moment on. Following his arrest during the events in Munich that November, she wrote him an open letter expressing her support for his 'constructive work': 'With his fervent love of the father-land', the twenty-six-year-old wrote, he was 'sacrificing his life for the

---

*Winifred Wagner's statements are quoted from the 1976 film, *Winifred Wagner*, the typescript of which was kindly placed at the author's disposal by the director, Hans Jürgen Syberberg.

idea of a purified, united, nationalist Greater Germany', by trying to open the workers' eyes to Marxism, the internal enemy, and striving to turn people into brothers and to eradicate class hatred.' So this was not politics? And her donations to help the families of the arrested *putschists* were not politically motivated? Her husband's complaints that she was forever running off to Party meetings were well known, even when he appeared to be supporting her by saying that 'My wife is working like a lioness for Hitler.' Her conspicuous interest in politics was noticed by everybody in the generally unpolitical house of Wahnfried.

The same political acumen – however coloured by right-wing nationalism – enabled her to know exactly when she needed to defend herself against politics. This is shown by her own accounts of how she kept the theatre free from Party control. But she herself was constantly and directly involved in politics; her understanding may have been that of an amateur, but it was certainly there.

Was not the war politically motivated, for example? On the one hand, she observed that she and her 'noble National Socialists' were not 'war fanatics', but on the other, she was willing to condone the war: 'Any reasonable person must surely realise that with the large number of enemies surrounding Germany ... this small country was not viable in the long run, so a catastrophe was bound to come sooner or later.' And did she not admit that her own daughter, Friedelind, had emigrated for political reasons? By describing her as a 'traitor to her country', she seemed to do so. And when the visitors to the wartime festivals told her about their 'terrible experiences in the munitions factories' or on the front, did it not occur to her that Bayreuth was being politically exploited? And how had the people she helped from the concentration camps got there in the first place? Did she never ask herself these simple questions? Politics was everywhere in Bayreuth, the Party was everywhere, men in uniform came to lunch, her children climbed onto the laps of Party comrades, and on the Führer's fiftieth birthday the Festspielhaus was smothered in swastikas. Can one swim in the water and claim that one did not get wet? How could this disturbance of perception be explained? Could her elevated position as 'Frau Wagner' have deluded her into thinking that she stood above politics and was concerned solely with art?

Winifred's real views tended to spill out only indirectly, and on surprising occasions. On the occasion when Toscanini refused to conduct at Bayreuth in 1933 because of his opposition to fascism, Winifred's reaction was symptomatic. Her anger at having been let down brought out elements in her language which revealed her deep-rooted anti-Semitism, even though the initial incident had nothing directly to do with the Jews. She gave a rambling account of the incident to Hans Jürgen Syberberg during her 1976 television interview:

> You know, when Toscanini was to conduct here, the Jews of New York worked on him to such an extent, urging him not to come here, that in the end he gave in; they told him that if he stayed in New York and didn't go to Bayreuth, he'd get blank cheques for his conducting in New York – he could write his own cheques in that case. That's how it was. I mean that, basically, the New York Jews – as you know the entire musical life in New York … simply takes place in Jewish circles. Wherever you look – and these people worked on him, quite certainly!

Her 'quite certainly', like her 'basically', is a sign that she is unsure of her ground, but this momentary hesitation is defeated by the defiance of her beliefs. Needless to say, she had the traditional defence of the anti-Semite ready and waiting – 'We had heaps of Jewish friends' – unaware of how transparent this rhetorical strategy now seemed.

We now come to the central issue, which is Winifred's ability to divide and separate the world into two independent areas. It is because of this ability that she is able to define herself as an 'unpolitical person'. There were always parts of her mind which had 'nothing to do with each other'. She accepted these divisions passively, never reflecting on them. On the one hand, there was the private world of Wahnfried, and the person of Adolf Hitler was totally absorbed into this inner world, this great 'WE'. (Winifred always spoke in the 'We' form.) On the other hand, there was the outside world, the 'non-WE', the world of politics, the petty affairs of the Party, and probably the Jewish question too, and whatever else there was that was 'not noble' about National Socialism. This 'non-WE' was even permitted to include part of the beloved Führer: his 'dark sides', as Winifred put it. Of course, Winifred was not alone in her ability to distinguish between Hitler as a person and the Nazi Party, as though separating good from evil: this friend–foe pattern is a basic part of the mass psychology of fascism. Nonetheless, the setting of Wahnfried lends it a particular and fatal note: we watch with fascination as the sober, unsentimental, pragmatic Englishwoman, Winifred, moves over into the realm of fantasy.

Let us once more take her at her word. As she saw it, 'enemies all round' were ranged against Germany after 1918. Her perceptions were similar in 1931 and 1933, when she saw her own little dominion at the Bayreuth festival under threat: 'powers of darkness' were 'ceaselessly at work' all around her. 'Supremely tragic situation', the Wahnfried secretary Liselotte Schmidt recorded, 'in that Bayreuth had never been attacked from so many sides as in the Third Reich. We stand in icy solitude.' Germany and Bayreuth clearly blend into one in Winifred's perception. And this perception is confirmed by the heroic Hitler, since he 'saves' both from the 'powers of darkness' – Germany from the Bolsheviks and Bayreuth from the Old Wagnerians. And now Germany and Bayreuth are like islands: nothing can affect them. This is why Winifred is not involved in politics, because politics does not reach through to 'US' on our little art island. Winifred had developed the ability simply to deny anything that might upset her own pattern of perceptions. Anything that might blacken the integrity of the person of Adolf Hitler, for example, did not exist for her. Like Eva Braun, for example – one had scarcely known of her existence, and she had not even been publicly photographed with the Führer, Winifred tendentiously argued. Of Winifred herself, by contrast, there were many pictures with the Führer. But of course, the leader of the Germans could not have married her, an Englishwoman. This is why he had always insisted that she should remain unmarried, so that she could continue to be 'a queen – yes, a queen'. She was not like that 'fanatical Englishwoman', Unity Mitford, who had 'glued' herself to Hitler and had therefore been punningly dubbed the '*Mitfahrt*' [hitch-hiker] by the 'whole entourage'.

Winifred realised instinctively that her real rival was the Party, and not any other woman. She could hardly deny the Party its existence – she was too realistic for that – but she could choose to ignore it. 'My National Socialism was really only connected with the person of Adolf Hitler. All the rest was less interesting to me.' Ignoring something is also a form of psychological defence. Winifred's lines of communication with Hitler were always direct, intimate, unique, going far above the heads of the 'small Party fry'. He was exceptional, she was exceptional. For Winifred, the whole constellation, Wahnfried–Wagner–Germany–I–He, constituted one large exception to the rules. This understanding was epitomised by the monstrous claim that 'I altogether exempt Adolf Hitler from the whole of society' – a claim that nonetheless has a certain validity, though in the opposite sense to that which Winifred intended.

Every madness has its own logic, and the disjunctions, aberrations and narcissistic identifications demonstrated by Winifred are no exception. If we try to enter Winifred's imaginary domain, we realise that although she undoubtedly had a fantasy image of Hitler as a unique saviour, the political aspect of this fantasy was quite insignificant. Winifred's personal history provides the key to this understanding. She had not forgotten the humiliations that she had received from her arrogant new relations when she moved into Wahnfried, an eighteen-year-old Cinderella. Only her husband had been able to protect her, but he died in 1930 and left her alone. But not quite alone, because by then she had acquired a much more powerful protector. It was like a fairy tale: just as she had stood by him in his time of need, persecuted as the leader of an illegal part, so he now looked after her as her Lohengrin and Chancellor. He saved the festival by bringing money and prestige, and he loved Wahnfried and her children unreservedly. This is why Winifred said that 'I will always remember him with gratitude, because he literally tended the flowerbeds here in Bayreuth and helped me in every way.' Winifred handled her situation better than the hapless Elsa in *Lohengrin*, who had to know exactly *who* her protector was, and therefore provoked the catastrophe. Winifred, by contrast, brushed off anything that might cause her eyes to be opened, and was therefore able to maintain her image of Hitler as an unblemished saviour, resolutely and blindly. Anything that contradicted that was twisted until it fitted her own image of how things were. The Jews? – that was Streicher. The murder of Röhm? – that was the others. The bombing of London? – that was the military, they forced Hitler into it. As for the fact that as late as 1944 he could still hear 'the rush of the wings of the goddess of victory', that was the fault of Dr Morell and the many injections he prescribed.

'I am able entirely to separate the Hitler I know from all that he is nowadays accused of,' Winifred declared. If she had not been able to do so, it would have destroyed the basis of her own life, since she claimed loyalty as her greatest virtue. 'I am basically a madly loyal person, so if I have once formed an attachment to someone, then it endures through thick and thin. I mean, supposing Gottfried [her grandson] were to leave here and, let us say, slaughter some girl and bury her, etc., etc., that would not affect my relationship with him at all.'

To understand in full the bizarre division in the mind of this 'normal' and 'charming' person, we must look back even further. At the age of two, the little English girl Winifred became an orphan; until her tenth year she was passed around between various orphanages. There were no positive role models in that primal disorder and anarchy: she had to be her own anchor. From an early age, she had been obliged to wear emotional armour, to protect and insulate her person. And then Germany became her sanctuary. Both in the home of Klindworth and then at Wahnfried, the only 'life-belt' offered to her was a romantically German Wagnerism, characterised by defensiveness against the outside world and a super-cilious elitism within the family network. She fused these values with her own: her ideal of loyalty was brilliantly confirmed by the Wagnerian concept of *Nibelungentreue*.

For Winifred, Hitler was the only person who had matched up to this ideal: 'He had this Austrian delicacy of the heart and this warmth ... I knew him for twenty-two years and was never disappointed by him as a human being.' Other 'saviours' had proved to have feet of clay: Heinz Tietjen abandoned her after the war and sacrificed their joint achievements in Bayreuth to pursue his own ends, and Wieland disappointed her with his disloyalty towards his former patron, 'Uncle Wolf'. For her, loyalty superseded all other virtues, so she found it incomprehensible that others did not think the same way.

Winifred's descriptions of Hitler display the helpless and sentimental characteristics of a forbidden love, one that could not be articulated in a more conventional way. Nonetheless, the erotic enchantment rings through. Hitler undoubtedly flirted with her: in the inner world of Wahn-fried they would address each other using the familiar 'du' form, while in the outside world of the Festspielhaus, he would kiss her hand and address her as 'Gnädige Frau'. Since she had previously only been permitted the roles of virtuous wife, mother and employer, she now enjoyed both his public appreciation of her as an attractive woman, and the secrecy that surrounded their private relationship. 'And everything that is dark about him, I know that exists, but for me it doesn't exist, because I don't know that part ... That will perhaps remain incomprehensible for ever, you must leave it to a psychoanalyst to explain my relationship with Hitler ... And I think if it remains a mystery to anybody who may listen, then let it remain one, in God's name. I can't explain it to myself, I don't know if you can understand that.'

Winifred simply did not know. Her carefully protected and compartmentalised world allowed her no perspective from which she could talk about it. And in the words of Wittgenstein's description of the mystical, 'whereof one cannot speak, thereof one must remain silent.' Winifred too must remain silent about that which she cannot talk about. In her relationship with Hitler she found herself in dimensions – mystical, religious, amorous, devotional – which were otherwise alien to her. This is why she no longer understood herself. But at that very moment, when she found herself divested of her defiant self-assurance and lost in the speechless abyss of her own enigma, she was, in the words of *Faust*, both condemned and redeemed. Love is probably the only theology in which God and the Devil become one.

13

The Wagner Family and its Home

The genius can only remedy the drawback of coming from a family by making sure that he doesn't leave one behind him.

Karl Kraus

A LIVING FAMILY, LIKE A ROYAL COURT OR A STATE, IS NEVER entirely stable: it is always a whirlwind of competing and changing forces. Once it reaches the graveyard, by contrast, peace and order reign. Out there in the world of the living, we find plots and intrigues, pleasures and suffering, love and estrangement, but here in the cemetery we see the guilty and their victims, the bad and the good, the powerful, the rebels and the drop-outs quietly arranged alongside each other, or sharing the same tomb: everyone loves them and appreciates their merits. The cemetery is a museum of lives. Nonetheless, our culture dictates that we attempt to avoid or postpone our arrival at this ultimate destination, to outwit the biological certainty of death by leaving footprints or monuments that will endure: *he said … he made … he painted …* Anything that is prematurely removed from life, buried before its time, continues to exist as something unfulfilled in the minds of the living, haunting their desires and suffering: that which 'survives itself', on the other hand, scarcely arouses grief or regret. These variations of longevity or endurance can be explained both historically and physiologically. The unpredictable reactions of a physical organism – the varying effects that genius or stupidity, good health or sickness can have on a constitution – are super-imposed upon the historical picture, so that in retrospect it seems that some mysterious logic, or at least a 'natural' law has dictated the outcome: things happened because they had to happen that way.

Accepting that a single change in the wind could have changed all the events of history, and that the dice actually cast represent the reality but not all the possibilities, we will try to trace here the development of a dynasty, from its combative beginnings to its final stagnation and burial. The inner history of the Haus Wahnfried and the attitudes of its inhabitants will always also reflect history in general. This is guaranteed by the link that joins Wagner's work and the institution of Bayreuth to the political culture of Germany. Just as the entrails of sacrificial animals allowed ancient soothsayers to foretell the destiny of the state, so the dissection of the Wagner family will allow us to understand something of the state of Germany in their time.

Wagner's need to root his life in a particular physical location is eloquently expressed in a letter of 1871 to King Ludwig II of Bavaria:

> I need to know at long last where I belong, where my permanent residence is and where I can care for my family like a bourgeois. I have had to sacrifice many years of my life to the savage workings of chance, I cannot call any property my own and I live in the world like a refugee ... I have to live in a place where I can feel assured of finding an appropriate sphere of activity. This must be in the heart of Germany.

A few years later, we can see that the harvest has been brought in by the refugee composer. The permanent residence is here: a villa in its own grounds, adjoining the garden of the Margrave of Bayreuth, almost entirely a present from his 'noble benefactor' and 'gracious friend' King Ludwig. And on the green hill, enthroned over the town, stands the theatre where his works were to be performed: a gift from the town fathers, its upkeep subsidised by his own fervent supporters. Wagner had risen to a glorious position at the head of a dynasty, a situation of power unprecedented for an artist. It is little wonder that having experienced this transformation, the Wagners condescendingly declined the offer of ennoblement for their family: Cosima's refusal to take a 'von' before her surname was surely not a throwback to her husband's earlier socialist attitudes, but an assertion that the composer's own achievements had brought more glory to his family than state acknowledgement could ever do. Wagner's lack of interest in the trappings of aristocratic status did not trouble the aristocracy themselves: they believed in the truth of the old proverb about the cobbler sticking to his last, and the Kaiser was heard to remark that a *Siegfried* by Wagner was better than a 'Siegfried *von* Wagner'. As for his family, civil recognition – an honorary degree of the University of Berlin was awarded to Cosima in 1910 – should be enough.

In any case, as a Wagner one automatically enjoyed a position within the artistic elite – and the social elite, too, since the hysterical Wagnerism of turn-of-the-century Europe had brought prosperity to the family. Bayreuth was the principal beneficiary of this mania, since it alone was capable of staging the *Ring* cycle, whose demands exceeded what the court theatres could offer, and it was also the only theatre permitted to stage *Parsifal*, the Wagnerian Holy of Holies. In 1913, however, the flow of royalties from the works – the basis of the family income – began to dry up, a situation that became increasingly parlous over the next few decades. As the Berlin journalist Maximilian Harden remarked, the 'genius pension', which had comfortably featherbedded the family's existence, was at an end. The hyper-inflation of 1921–22 ended Richard Wagner's hopes that his son would never have to work for money. The family once more became vulnerable to 'the savage workings of chance' to which the founder himself had been exposed as a political refugee. The extent of this vulnerability was tempered, however, by the family's substantial assets, both artistic and material. The life of the Wagners as a bourgeois family, of which Richard Wagner had humbly dreamed in 1871, could finally begin.

We do not need a sociologist to define the bourgois family: this small social unit is clearly recognisable by its careful handling of the economic constraints of the moments, and its concern to safeguard, even to increase, the legacy that will be passed down to its descendants. In these respects, the Wagners were no different to any other family whose principal concern is the prudent management of their business. It is inevitable that the division of the profits will not always be conducted fairly or amicably: the dynamics of family histories have always been marked by the residue of an economic and psychological 'wolf principle', and by the suffering which the operation of that principle has caused. The roles of the sexes, too, are largely prescribed by the patriarchal culture of which the bourgeois family is part: its head is the father. (Wagner, the early socialist, demonstrated his bitter awareness of the connections between capitalism and the masculine principle in *The Ring*.) The fact that female rulers appear in the Wagner genealogy does not contradict the basic pattern, but rather confirms it: only women who assume 'masculine' characteristics stand a chance of prevailing within this male-dominated bourgeois tradition, and the behaviour of Cosima and Winifred bears this out.

Within a framework of sociological determination, however, each family possesses its own characteristics and its own rules of engagement. The family is also subject to the chance elements of birth and death: because it is founded on the principle of deference to the eldest male member, a case of exceptional longevity can skew the family's development, meaning that the necessary waves of change beat in vain against an ancient rock. Difficulties can also arise when structural changes in society mean that the family must amend its rigid rules and bend to the demands of democracy. What happens when there are two pretenders of equal merit to the throne, or only female contenders? What happens when the younger sons are no longer happy to be consigned into the army or the legal professions, and the daughters no longer wish to attend finishing school?

There are two factors in particular that set the Wagner family apart. Both are closely linked to the character of Wagner's work, and both continue to affect the family subconscious: they are the demand that each family member should submit to his or her cultural mission, and the psychology that results from the shared musical heritage. The first of these factors is perhaps the more obvious to the outsider. The nature of the festival enterprise places both economic and artistic demands upon the family: each generation is required to produce at least one member with artistic vision. This irrational union of dynastic and artistic principles – which was Cosima's doing, since Wagner himself left no last will and testament and did not appoint an heir – has had curious and, in human terms, disastrous effects ever since the composer's death. It has greatly intensified the psychopathological tensions which exist, to an extent, in any family network. Genealogy has become a frantic search for artistic genius: each newly born Wagner is expected to have not only the right physiognomy – the Wagner nose! – but also a conspicuous artistic talent. The family itself is in thrall to this absurd principle just as much as the general public which, impressed by the spectacle of the illustrious union of the Liszt and Wagner families, assumed that a continuous string of artistically talented descendants would follow. Childhood in the family is overshadowed by the weight of this expectation: it reaches deep into the relations between parents and children, brothers and sisters. Even courtship and marriage can be governed by the hegemony of the artistic principle. Every member of the family has probably suffered the silly question 'But are you actually musical?' Misguided faith in hereditary genius has brought about both the rise and fall of the Wagner family, its astonishing achievements as well as its self-destruction.

The influence of Wagner's music upon the mentalities of his descendants and the occupants of Wahnfried is no less important, even if it is in the background. Immersed from an early age in Wagner's musical style, colours and gestures, accustomed from an early age to the relaxed modes of behaviour produced by the 'universal eroticism' of Wagner's work, to use Thomas Mann's phrase – the family's collective subconscious is quite different from what one might find in the families of Prussian aristocrats, nationalist industrialists or Protestant parsons, for example. When it came to sexual scandal and the breaking of taboos, the family had enough role models in the amorous bravura pieces of the Romantic era: the younger generations followed the examples of the founding couples of the dynasty – Liszt and Marie d'Agoult, Richard and Cosima – in producing a positive swarm of illegitimate children, illicit unions and broken marriages.

Unfortunately, other aspects of Liszt's world-view, such as his respect for human diversity, do not seem to have been passed on. He once told Cosima and her sister that just because they were quite pretty and had some talent, this did not entitle them to any attention from the world: 'the one and only thing that will give you this right is if you give everyone you encounter the necessary respect for their individuality, without distinction of person, or country, or rank.' Cosima claimed to have preached her father's message to her own children, but it does not seem to have had much effect. Indeed, the Wagner family has in general demonstrated the exact opposite of Liszt's tolerant, inclusive attitude to the world. The sectarian principle of dividing outside forces into 'friend and foe' – which aided Wagner's initial conquest of the world by forcing musicians to declare themselves for or against him – has become the cultural norm within the family network. It leads to a state of partial blindness in which only the Wagnerian can be accepted and assimilated, while anything which is alien and cannot be dissolved in the Wagnerian 'primal broth' must be rejected; there are marked similarities between this approach to the world and the mentality of fascism. The traces of this Wagnerian manner can be seen clearly in the behaviour of individual family members: self-glorifying egos permit themselves astonishing liberties in word and deed, solidarities become antagonisms, and conflicts broaden into vendettas. The rejection and expulsion of weaker members of the family, particularly women, becomes preferable to an attempt at integration, and the selfish gesture, the divisive action and the polarisation of enemies are accepted strategies of survival.

The voices of reason and tolerance are quiet. The Wahnfried drama has followed other, more spectacular models. *The Ring*, for example: the family story also features multi-generational quarrelling about how their hoard of treasure is to be governed. There is a *Rheingold* stage here, too: the period which Richard Wagner himself spent at Wahnfried, from the inauguration of the festivals in 1874 until his death in 1883, is a mythical pre-history which continually resurfaces in family stories. There is a *Walküre* period: the era of the widow, Cosima, who was in control of the festival until 1906, but lived on to a great age, like Erda, not dying until 1930. This was followed by the *Siegfried* period: despite his dissimilarities with his heroic namesake, Richard and Cosima's son guided the destiny of the family and the festival until he died in the same year as his mother. After him the reign passed to his widow, Winifred – a Brünnhilde though without the shining armour – who presided over the festival until its political *Götterdämmerung* in 1944. Here the family story outgrows the four-part framework of the original: there are two more episodes to be told. The first of these concerns the period during which Winifred's sons,

Wieland and Wolfgang, reconstructed the festival after the war, like Fasolt and Fafner building a new Valhalla. The second episode is the era of Wolfgang, who has presided alone since Wieland's death in 1966. Here, a pause has arrived, for the time being: everyone is waiting for a new Young Siegfried to continue the drama.

But because the setting of this family drama is Haus Wahnfried, and because a good stage set prepares the audience for the actors who will make their entrance, we should let the walls of the house speak first. The story of the changes to the villa is a commentary on the events themselves. In contrast to the Festspielhaus, which is like a static monument transcending history – never destroyed, only renewed and extended – Wahnfried physically experienced all the blows of internal and external history. It is a visible testimony of changing times.

In 1871, while searching for a suitable location for the future festival theatre in Bayreuth, Richard Wagner discovered an 'attractive meadowland site', with a natural enclosure of wild roses and hawthorn, bounded at the rear by the tall ash avenues of the margravial court garden. The Festspielhaus was originally intended to be situated quite close to this plot, on what is now the Schützenplatz. However, the ground there proved too damp for building, and construction of the theatre was moved to a hill overlooking the town. Wagner was still attracted to the original plot, however, and he decided to build a residence there according to his own plans. He attached particular importance to a long avenue of chestnut trees which would form a solemn approach to the house, and to outbuildings on either side of the house which would screen it from the road. Orchards and vegetable gardens would be planted on each side of the chestnut avenue, and hedges rather than walls would hide them from the road. The more intimate garden behind the house was also conceived as a park, with a central fountain, circular paths, and the future family vault half-hidden on the central axis of the property. Because this garden adjoined the public park, an illusion of boundless greenery and of a unified open space was created.

The name of the house evolved gradually. Wagner originally claimed that he would call it 'Ärgersheim' (Annoyance House), having suffered the seemingly endless delays and construction problems familiar to all who build their own homes. That idea was short-lived however, and a further suggestion was recorded by Cosima in her diary: 'Moonlight, stepping out on the balcony with R., we catch sight of the vault, and he calls the house "Zum letzten Glück" (Last Happiness).' A few days later it is called 'Wahnfriedheim', soon abridged to Wahnfried. An inscription above the entrance of the house, to the left of the name, explains its derivation: 'Hier wo mein Wähnen Frieden fand' (Here where my foolish fancies found peace). The couplet is completed by the words to the right: 'Sei dieses Haus von mir benannt' (Let this house be named by me). The panel over the entrance was decorated by a home-made mythological graffito, instead of the planned sundial. The classical ornamental columns originally planned for the wings were scrapped at a late stage, like many of the decorative elements of the Festspielhaus. As Wagner declared with his customary grandiosity, 'we have something that greatly surprises all the world, because of its novelty and originality in omitting all external ornament.' Both Wagner's home and his theatre were indeed remarkable for their abstinence from that early patrician decorative excess which was much to the composer's personal taste, but while the lack of ornament in the Festspielhaus is successful in helping the listener to concentrate on Wagner's music, the stark, windowless central block of Wahnfried rather suggests a mausoleum.

The family moved in on 28 April 1874, and the composer could at least convince himself that he had now found peace. Contemporaries describe the moment in May when, on his sixty-first birthday, he stepped out on the balcony to listen to the serenade from the infantry band in the court garden. Despite the rather raucous performances of his *Kaisermarsch* and the Pilgrims' Chorus from *Tannhäuser*, this was a moment of symbolic calm in the composer's life: he experienced it almost as a suspension of history. Dream and reality, theatre and life had at last merged after decades of struggle and hardship. 'Performances, concerts, travel, all of them torment; here, in the sheltering house, let him bear what comes, and then let me depart this world with him,' Cosima wrote. But peace was not to be found there. It became a place of artistic struggle: *Götterdämmerung* was to be completed and *Parsifal* composed at Wahnfried. It also became a family home, noisy with children's shouts, parties and concerts, the scene of weddings and lyings-in-state. Wagner himself no longer enjoyed much of his 'sheltering house'. He felt the need, time and again, to escape to the south, and he died far from Wahnfried, in a Venetian palazzo.

After Wagner's death in 1883, time was made to stand still at Wahnfried until the early 1930s. Nothing, Cosima decreed, was to be changed, internally or externally, in any of the rooms that the master had occupied; nothing was to be moved, no furniture, picture, or even book – nothing, except the couch on which he died, which she moved into her own bedroom. Wahnfried became a living museum. Visitors from throughout the world streamed through the lobby with its Steinway and busts of Richard and Cosima by Gustav Kietz, and the hall with its library of books from throughout Europe and Lenbach paintings on the wall. Many were given a brief audience in Cosima's lilac salon, full of family portraits. One day in 1913, disaster struck this grand display with its many pianos and plaster gilt-and-silk interiors: Wagner's spectacles, until then lying on his desk, disappeared into the pocket of a thief.

In the spacious nursery overlooking the garden on the first floor, the children from both Cosima's marriages grew up together. Later, the children of Siegfried and Winifred would work, play and sleep in the same rooms. Little changed for decades at Wahnfried. Even the new cottages slipped harmoniously into the picture: one for Siegfried to compose in, added in 1892 on the left of the main building, and one for a gardener. The only really visible change came during the First World War, when the meadowland in front of the house reluctantly gave way to the planting of potatoes.

Real structural change did not come about until 1932, in a way that rather shadowed the political changes taking place in Germany. The extension of Siegfried's 'composing cottage' was purportedly undertaken for the conductor, Toscanini, but its real beneficiary was the festival's most important visitor, Adolf Hitler, who frequently stayed there with his staff. A wing of grey marine chalk was added on the garden side of the cottage, with a roof terrace and an ornamental basin with a rather petty-bourgeois stone sculpture of a fish. The building was also extended towards the road, furnished with a flat roof and a ribbed facing on the exterior walls, as if to demonstrate that official favour had now passed from the Bauhaus style to crude classicism. The architect of these changes was Hans Carl Reissinger, the uncle of Wieland's future wife, who was enticed to Bayreuth by Winifred from his post as city architect of Düsseldorf. The spirit of the age could be seen in the internal fittings of the reconstructed 'cottage', the stone facings of the fireplaces and the corner columns which featured stylised versions of the occupiers' zodiac signs. Wood panelling on the walls and concealed ceiling lights implied a businesslike atmosphere, but the reproduction Chippendale and Sheraton furniture suggested the ostentatious philistine comfort of the embassy room. There were wrought iron lamps, Nibelung symbols on parchment and chairs in the Nordic-Germanic style cultivated by the Nazis and beloved of the young mistress of Bayreuth. On his arrival, the Führer probably scarcely noticed the difference from his private rooms at the Old Reich Chancellery or his Berghof home. On the surface, the cool interiors favoured by Winifred formed a contrast to the rich, plush furnishings of the old Wahnfried; in reality, they were merely manifestations of Nazi modernism, which was only a continuation by other means of the highly decorative style of the late nineteenth century. The sandstone wall screening the front garden from the road was a final visual legacy of Winifred's period of control: something had to be done to discourage the growing curiosity of the public, particularly during important state visits.

Early in 1945, Bayreuth was bombed. While the Festspielhaus remained intact – the rumours were that it was deliberately reprieved by culture-conscious Americans – Wahnfried was devastated by a bomb landing in the hall. Wagner's grand piano was blown out by the blast, heraldic decorations presented by other towns associated with Wagner dangled in tatters from the walls, Cosima's precious Japanese kimonos were burnt, and the wrecked roof hung over the former nursery like Wotan's slouch hat over his missing eye. While the garden facade of the house was in ruins, the front was undamaged: Wahnfried had become an empty shell. Only the extended 'cottage' – now known as the 'Führer block' – remained unscathed. Its air-raid shelter saved the lives of those few family members who had not already taken refuge in the Wagners' timber holiday home on Lake Constance: Winifred, her daughter-in-law, Ellen, and the children's nurse. Wieland and his brother-in-law had survived the raid under a bridge in Bayreuth; returning to Wahnfried from the road, they were able for a moment to convince themselves that the house had been spared.

During the next few years, the worst of the damage was patched up. Discussions about the difficulty of obtaining roofing felt dominate the correspondence between Wolfgang and Wieland during that period, which has become notorious both for the brothers' energy and for their amoral behaviour. Wolfgang, working amid the rubble, took charge of the tasks of rebuilding and of protecting the family archive, already removed from the house, from the approaching Americans. Wieland, trapped with his family in the French zone on Lake Constance, was mainly concerned with planting potatoes and obtaining food from the peasants, but he was also using political skills and bribery to prepare for the possible resumption of the festival. In 1949, he and his wife returned home, as Germans were doing everywhere, to work in a barely habitable room, the former office of his mother, known as the 'command post'; the couple lived in a minute studio in the garden. This was a period of family unity, though, because Wolfgang was living next door in the gardener's cottage. The shortage of coal brought the family together around the same stove: to rise from the ruins was their common objective.

It was not long, however, before the brothers and their families separated, Wolfgang declining Wieland's offer to share Wahnfried with him. Wieland and his family moved there alone, while Wolfgang obtained a villa directly next to the Festspielhaus a few years later, arguing with typical shrewdness that a property of one's own was more secure than a mere share in the family home.

One advantage of the poverty of the post-war years was that it led to architectural choices that were much simpler, clearer and more honest than those of the Nazi era. Little attempt was made to disguise the fact that Wahnfried had suffered during the war: the semicircular hole that had been left after the destruction of the projection on the garden side of the house, that had once housed the library and the nursery, was left as it was. It was not until the years of increasing prosperity that the crater was densely filled with wild, tall plants, giving the impression, at least to childish eyes, of a remote tropical island. The garden, too, had a new simplicity imposed upon it: the circular fountain and the elegant promenades were dispensed with, leaving a large open meadow, with trees remaining only around the family tomb. A similarly austere approach was taken to the interior. Lenbach's portraits of a disgruntled Schopenhauer and a silvery Cosima, at first restored only superficially, continued to hang there for a while; the stained leather armchairs still stood under a standard lamp with a pleated paper shade, with the dark-veneered radiogram underneath. Meals were still hoisted from the basement kitchen using the ancient dumb waiter. The latest clutch of children was given a new nursery with four railed cots, on the upper floor of the surviving wing.

These provisional arrangements for both house and garden gave way, towards the end of the fifties, to a transformation in line with the new owners' taste. The guiding principle now was not nostalgia, but concepts developed by the pre-war modernist movement with its demands for transparency, light and space. Just as the New Bayreuth style had revolutionised the appearance of the festival stage, so these changes swept away the last remnants of deference to the past from the restored Wahnfried. The new mistress of the house, Wieland's wife Gertrud, converted the row of tall rooms which had been created in the empty shell into one airy room, suitable for a variety of uses: not only a family living room, it was also a music room, study and salon. The remaining family portraits disappeared into a broom cupboard, including a valuable drawing of Liszt by Ingres. Tapestries and carpets required no disposal: they had mercifully been reduced to cinders. Had it not been for the bomb damage, all attempts to change the appearance of Wahnfried would probably have foundered under the weight of family bric-à-brac preserved in the name of heritage: thanks to the war, modernisation became possible.

German style of this period was not all high modernism, however. Much was borrowed, in this time of economic miracle, from the American middle classes; something was salvaged, too, from that pious German bourgeois nationalism that characterised the late nineteenth century. The Wahnfried of the transition years did not escape this double contamination, despite the good taste and modernising zeal of Gertrud: while the garden was decked out with a swimming-pool, terrace and Hollywood-style swing hammock, the salon still housed a screen of parchment representing equestrian figures in the Spanish style. The antique sofa was re-covered with a modest floral fabric and the new record-player was discreetly hidden in an old carved-wood chest. There were also two relics symbolising the founding period of Wahnfried: Richard Wagner's fine glasses in their old lilac case, and the wooden feet which served as a model for his shoemaker. These artefacts, metaphorical reminders of the mission entrusted to him, did not leave Wieland's desk until they were stolen by some young thieves, never to be recovered.

If the nineteenth century was not quite swept away by Wieland and Gertrud, then there was indisputably a calculated and specific rejection of certain parts of the twentieth. Turning Wahnfried into a modern residence with a slightly Mediterranean feel enabled Wieland Wagner to proclaim his distance from his mother, Winifred, who still lived next door in the 'Führer block'. After the war she had, in a rather coquettish gesture of self-banishment, retreated to a chalet in the Fichtelbirge mountains which she named 'Exil'. On her return, however, she soon began to take tea with her old Nazi friends – Edda Goering and Ilse Hess among them – in a garden that was then, naturally, shared with the inhabitants of the main house. In order not to have to see or hear his unrepentant mother's visitors, and also, if subconsciously, to settle some Oedipal scores, Wieland had a curved wall built across the garden. From Winifred's point of view, this dividing wall – a personal forerunner of the Berlin Wall – must have seemed brutal, a boycott set in stone.

Even this symbolic gesture of resistance, however, had to yield to the forces of history. Wieland died in 1966, and his family lost its right to remain in the official residence of the festival director. Growing opposition to the Wagnerian tradition, increased discomfort about the family's relationship with the leaders of the Third Reich, and the younger generation's desire to develop their own lives outside Wahnfried meant that the house for a while lay untended and mouldering. It was only the centenary of the first Bayreuth Festival in 1976 that brought about the public interest necessary to salvage the house. Both the Ancient Monuments Department of the federal state and the town of Bayreuth became involved: thanks to their work, Wahnfried was restored to something like its original appearance. The library opened once more into the garden, Wagner's books were placed behind glass, and the nursery received its curved balcony back. Winifred drifted around, reminiscing about her youth and giving vent to her recollections of Old Wahnfried. The entrance lobby was painted in Pompeian red once more, the busts of the founders reclaimed their old places, and the former private rooms were filled with

Wagneriana. Wahnfried became a museum – and the same fate befell the 'Führer Block', now tactfully renamed the 'Siegfried Wagner House'. It now houses the Wagner archive, and the curious 'Nazi fireplace room' is now occupied by a few office chairs facing a video player on which films of Wagner's works are shown.

As a result of the conversion of the Bayreuth Festival and its assets into a foundation, the house now belongs to the town of Bayreuth. Bureaucrats have dictated not only the aesthetic reconstruction of Wahnfried itself, but also the appearance of its surroundings. An unintelligent submission to the constraints of practicality has ruined the chestnut avenue leading to the house: several of the trees were removed in order to make room for cars and tour buses, and the visual effect so carefully calculated by Wagner has been destroyed.

This, then, is what Wagner's Wahnfried looks like today. Where there was velvet, there is now polyester; silk has been replaced by nylon. Where music played and guests were received, there are now loudspeakers. Visitors flood through the house once more, but none of the many Wagner descendants is there to receive them. The world of Wagner is now stage-managed, stuffed, a museum piece. Wagner is history, and an admission fee must be paid in order to view his relics. Even the grandchildren have to pay in order to enter their parental home; so too do the great-grandchildren, who are rarely even recognised by the receptionists. Yet it is quiet at Wahnfried: there is a profound calm. Surely this is not the peace that Wagner had in mind when he named his house; surely the golden letters were never supposed to adorn the entrance to a graveyard?

14

1874–1930: the first generation at Wahnfried

LET US STEP FORWARD FROM THE STAGE SET OF HISTORY, FROM THE drama of walls and rooms, to confront the lives of the players themselves. Of course, one can never be sure how 'things really were', during this great four-generation saga that takes us from Old Wahnfried through Hitler's Germany through New Bayreuth and on to the museum era. Nonetheless, the elements that consciously and unconsciously repeat themselves between different generations give us a secure framework from which to start. These include physical features: a notorious 'Wagner nose' and the Cosima hairstyles, the root-like hands and the hammer toes, the blue eyes and the curled little fingers, the soft flesh and the weak hearts. There are also the personality types that reappear down the generations, like musical motives transposed into different keys: the iron mother, the rejected sister, the daddy's girl, the mummy's boy and the childless aunt. There is also the prematurely dying father and the long-lived mother, and the old man who marries a young wife and enjoys the happiness of a second family.

The way in which these characteristics play themselves out varies, of course, according to the individual. Nonetheless, the family connections are strong enough to create the sense of a deep identity across the ages, a sense that, in the words of Hofmannsthal, '. . . in lives centuries old I share / and kinsmen laid in coffins long ago / are yet as close to me as my own hair, / are no less one with me than my own hair.' These continuities create the family's history. This Wahnfried history is inescapably chained to the history of the festival and must move with the vicissitudes of that history as the lining of a coat follows the cloth: the festival's highs, lows, and, indeed, periods where nothing much seems to happen are all experienced within the family too. The chain of events also goes beyond Bayreuth: the destiny of the festival is itself determined by the greater destiny of world history, and the interruptions to the festival caused by the two World Wars imposed similar periods of hiatus in the history of the family.

It was blissful to be alive at the dawn of Wahnfried; and to be young there was very heaven. The villa, gardens, even the Festspielhaus were playgrounds, and in addition to this, there was the exquisite thrill of being like a king in the small town, of being stared at, of receiving an 'artist's discount' in the shops. Animals were part of those early days, perhaps not wolves or dragons, but certainly dogs: the Newfoundlands left behind by Richard Wagner were given personal tombstones in the garden, while in Winifred's day, schnauzers chased around. Siegfried kept a horse and a large number of chickens, and at one stage a lonely sheep grazed the Wahnfried meadow, while swans in the neighbouring Hofgarten provided a touch of *Lohengrin*. These idyllic conditions were enjoyed by three successive generations of children, and the degree of freedom afforded increased as tutors and finishing schools gave way to Bayreuth grammar schools and Bavarian boarding schools, and the curriculum taught became broader, less dogmatically Wagnerian.

The early years of the first generation of Wagner children are little more than a *tableau vivant* for us: they emerge from the dark, like figures in a child's pop-up book. Life seems to have been very theatrical, judging by the diaries and memoirs of contemporaries, which describe the children dressing up in bearskins and suits of armour, playing with drinking horns and spears, reciting verses and making music to the applause of their parents, organising games of charades, processions and plays on the children's stage. There were also social events and concerts to be attended in elegant costumes, and visits to Italy. These first Wahnfried children were still rehearsing plays even as adults, particularly at Christmas, when they all congregated to perform European classics or home-made farces, or to have fun with the puppet theatre which the French writer Judith Gautier had presented to her beloved Master. These young people were invariably surrounded, too, by squadrons of servants, gardeners and tutors, who serviced their quasi-aristocratic lifestyle.

Wagner the father was unconventional and anarchic, fun-loving and always ready for pranks: he once entertained his children by dancing to Beethoven 'in the most adroit and charming manner'. Cosima, by contrast, was more serious, and after Wagner's death she took the children's education firmly into her own hands. While they were young she taught them herself with a syllabus that reflected her own strict ethical and religious convictions, but which also included instruction in classical humanism as taught in the best schools. The education of the girls was later directed along a more conventional route, with the aim of preparing them for charitable work and for their future roles as 'helpers' to a husband or ageing mother, while the main focus of the family's pedagogic attention was focused on Siegfried. Nearly everything that could be done wrong was done wrong, as far as Siegfried's upbringing was concerned. He was an isolated child in his old-fashioned tailored suits: he was only permitted playmates whom Cosima had approved, and his development was constantly scrutinised. From the start, any manifestation of talent, however minute, was observed, recorded and analysed, whether he had struck a few notes on the piano or scrawled a few doodles with his pencil. His parents endlessly debated his education: Wagner originally intended to set up a special school in Bayreuth with Siegfried as one of only seven pupils, but in the end a private tutor was deemed adequate and finally, at the age of fourteen, he was allowed to attend a Bayreuth grammar school.

Occasionally, the citizens of Bayreuth saw little Siegfried walking in the Hofgarten with his grandfather, for the cast at Wahnfried had been augmented, on special occasions, by the aged Franz Liszt – who drank cognac, moved around like a ghost and liked nothing better than to play whist in the evenings. He stayed at the house during the first festival in 1876, whose deficit he offered to meet from his own pocket; he was seen again at the family dining table in 1882 for the première of *Parsifal*; he appeared again in 1883 for the first festival after Wagner's death, but then did not return until 1886, having moved to a private house nearby after some family disputes. Family peace had been disturbed: whereas Wagner, in spite of all his public expressions of gratitude to his friend and patron, was always a little irritated by Liszt's fervent Catholicism, Cosima harboured a more deep-rooted resentment against her father. This came to the fore after Wagner's death: she refused to see him when he came to Bayreuth in 1884 to promote Wagner's cause, though she had no scruples about using him when the need arose. In fact, Liszt, now resident in Weimar, had long complained of being treated as 'Wagner's poodle' when he came to Bayreuth, and he resented being expected, despite his age and infirmity, to advertise his presence by waving to the audience from the family box after the fall of the curtain. But his grumpiness, however justified, was an inadequate defence when family arguments blew up. In 1886, for example, when his granddaughter Daniela was due to marry the art historian Henry Thode in Bayreuth, his presence was summarily demanded. The 'slave' – as he described himself to his companion, the Princess Carolyne von Sayn-Wittgenstein – obeyed his daughter, as he knew the alternative would be another long period of silence between them, as had happened from 1868 when she declared her allegiance to Wagner and moved to Tribschen.

As with any family conflict, apparently extreme reactions can often be explained by examining the subject's childhood. If Siegfried's compliant nature was shaped by his parents' overprotective approach to his upbringing, then Cosima's combative character was the product of quite different treatment: emotional neglect on the one hand and excessive severity on the other. Born illegitimately, like her own children by Wagner, she was troubled by uncertainty about her name and status until the age of seven, when her father finally acknowledged her. She was later to describe herself as 'come into this world strangely disinherited', and her insecurity was compounded by being shunted between a number of different addresses. It probably suited her mother, Marie d'Agoult, that Liszt kept her children away from her and, albeit indirectly, assumed responsibility for them. She had worked diligently, since the scandal of her involvement with the virtuoso, to regain her place in the intellectual salons of Paris: she was beginning a new career as a writer and historian and was later to enjoy success under the pseudonym of Daniel Stern. For the teenage children, however, every visit to the salon or library of the 'grande dame' made a deep impression. Unlike Liszt, who discarded the role of Romantic revolutionary in favour of 'throne and altar', the comtesse, perhaps under the influence of the revolutionary poet Georg Herwegh, declared herself in favour of the ideals of democracy and the Republic. With her 'Essai sur la liberté' of 1847, she entered history as a pioneer of the feminist movement, though she managed to do so without sacrificing anything of her elegant appearance or her *faubourg* lifestyle.

There was at least some sort of stability for Cosima and her two siblings at this time, since they spent most of their time in Paris in the home of Liszt's warm-hearted mother. Unfortunately, this was not to last. Liszt, undoubtedly influenced by the Princess von Sayn-Wittgenstein – who was jealous, domineering, conservative and ultra-Catholic – removed the children from their 'low-born grandmother' and forced them into the custody of two elderly St Petersburg governesses, who drilled them on how to behave in good society. Apart from learning foreign languages, which were a matter of course, and the worship of their father, which was a matter of duty, they were taught to converse in clichés and witty aperçus. Liszt himself was not particularly impressed by such education in general dilettantism and salon culture, to which he had been introduced by the children's mother. But the emotional chill of this upbringing 'in the spirit of the restoration' was a formative influence on Cosima. The Liszt children were united in their hatred of their governesses, and learnt to be hypocritical as a form of self-defence; this strategy was also used against their father, whose attempts to become closer to them were unfortunately limited to moralistic preaching. Questions about the future of Cosima and her beautiful elder sister, Blandine, received the conventional response from Liszt: marriage, what else? Though he was happy for the girls to be musically educated, he derisively dismissed their mother's wish that Cosima should become a professional pianist.

The next step in the girls' education, controlled by Liszt from Weimar, was to remove them definitively from their mother and to send them to Berlin, into the house of the von Bülows: his former pupil and secretary, Hans, and his somewhat insensitive mother, Franziska. Liszt's mother wrote to her son in despair at this brutal action: 'But dear child, to put these children into a fourth pair of hands, into a foreign country, where they do not know anybody, can surely not be a matter of indifference to them … and I fear that one or the other may fall sick.' The daughters survived, however, and were instructed in music by Hans: in accordance with Liszt's wishes, they were trained as 'good propagandists for the music of the future'. Blandine soon re-entered her mother's world of Parisian high society, fulfilling the family's aristocratic ambitions by marrying Emile Ollivier, the foreign minister of Napoleon III. The more troublesome but more intelligent Cosima, though, clung with mysterious obstinacy to the world of music. After two years' wait, she married her piano teacher, Hans von Bülow – against the wishes of both their mothers, but with her father's approval.

Bülow was a superb pianist and possibly the best conductor of his day, but he was a difficult person to live with: unbalanced, depressive and choleric, with a biting sarcasm. It is difficult to see why the seventeen-year-old 'Cosimette' was so fascinated with 'pauvre Hans', as Blandine called him. Was it a means of escape from the perpetual guardianship of elderly ladies, or did his erratic brilliance appeal to that fanatical side of her nature that was to emerge fully in later life? From Bülow's point of view, there was reason to think that he was marrying the daughter for the sake of the father. The composer Peter Cornelius, who belonged to Liszt's closest circle in Weimar, wrote that 'Bülow's marriage to Cosima was a sacrifice of friendship he made to his master, Liszt, to give a brilliant and honourable name to the natural child and, hence, profound reassurance to the father. That is what he aimed at – it was an act of gratitude.' There is also an account by Cosima of the events of that time which is frightening in its detachment: 'How it happened that we got married I still do not know,' she wrote in a letter to her then-adult daughter Daniela. Although the young Frau von Bülow tried hard to establish a salon in the chill of Berlin, and to support her husband in all things, it was not a happy marriage. The family story that she had to apologise to her overworked husband for the 'disturbances' caused by her pregnancies does not seem entirely implausible. Following the premature death of both her siblings, which exacerbated her sense of deracination, her relationship with her father improved: she visited and looked after him several times in the Altenburg and earned his increasing respect. Despite this, they never really became close, though much of the reason for this must have stemmed from the inner distance that Liszt maintained from everybody: his 'etiquette', his 'mask for the world'.

It must have seemed incomprehensible to Cosima that, when she left Hans von Bülow for Richard Wagner, following exactly the same pattern as her parents – adultery, elopement with an artist, illegitimate children – she was rejected by, of all people, her father, the one-time charmer and libertine. By switching her allegiance to Wagner, who was only two years younger than her father, she repaired the damage done by her upbringing: the trauma of separation, the absence of the father, the sense of never feeling 'at home'. 'Reading old letters of my father', she noted in her diary thirty years later, 'shows me again that I had neither a father nor a mother. R. was everything to me, he alone loved me.' Having been diverted by an unsuitable marriage to a 'brother figure' – Bülow was Liszt's pupil and the composer confessed to loving him like a son – Cosima then found the 'good father' in Wagner. Indeed, he was a 'super-father', for was he not undoubtedly a greater composer than her papa? Had not Liszt (and Bülow) been his loyal followers, thereby acknowledging his musical superiority? Marrying Wagner was like a psychological revenge against her father: Wagner, for Cosima, supplanted Liszt at both an artistic and an emotional level. He was now all that she needed. In one sense, Cosima's devotion to her husband can ironically be seen as an act of filial obedience, the inheritance of a mission: just as Liszt had at one stage used his celebrity to rescue the young and unknown Wagner, so his daughter saved the elderly, restless and exhausted composer, making his daily life comfortable and nurturing an intimate bond of marital solidarity. On the other hand, her absolute tie to Wagner is perhaps better understood as a reaction against the confusion and pain of her early life. And her bond with the ebullient Wagner was anything but a replica of her childhood relationship with the distant Liszt.

Cosima's years of devoted marriage to her husband, who was twenty-four years older than her, can be seen as a rehearsal for the widowhood which she knew was likely to occupy the greater part of her life: in the event, she lived for forty-seven more years after his death in 1883. The fact that the Bayreuth Festival continued to grow and prosper in this period was due in large part to her dedication, her talents – along with the financial and administrative genius of Adolf von Gross – and her resistance to those who tried to construe Wagner's lack of a will as a vote of no confidence in his wife. Even her father's death in Bayreuth on 31 July 1886 was a matter of relatively little importance to her, compared with the smooth running of the festival. Mourning was not permitted to interrupt the festival, and there were no musical tributes paid to the man lying in state in the hall of Wahnfried: only a brief requiem mass after the funeral, when instead of performing any of Liszt's own music, Cosima instructed Anton Bruckner to improvise on the 'faith theme' from *Parsifal*. Cosima's lack of concern to commemorate his death no doubt reflected the fact that he had long been dead to her, but, more than this, it showed that Wagner was still the only person of any significance in her life. The acknowledgement of anyone else was merely a nod to social convention: although Liszt's musical output had been a fundamental part of Cosima's education, and although Siegfried would time and again orchestrate and conduct his grandfather's works, the family in general had a fairly low opinion of his musical importance. They would marginalise him in death, as Cosima had already done in life, and frequently ridiculed him as 'the abbé'. Visitors to the town cemetery, as the Wagner vault began to fill, would be led unknowingly past the Romanesque chapel that commemorated Liszt.

The 'French branch' of Cosima's family, the descendants of Blandine who lived in Paris, were treated in a similarly perfunctory way. They occasionally came to attend the festival, but they were never integrated into the Wahnfried family. Political motives were at work here, too: the half-French Cosima's loathing of the French, rooted in the unhappy events of her childhood, had manifested itself for a long time in a virulent German nationalism. This hatred of France as the 'traditional enemy' was continued and amplified in the next generation – the generation of National Socialism – and even after the war, the neighbouring country was treated with a wary reserve. It is only in the fourth generation of Wagners that the French threads have been picked up again, with French liaisons established, French marriages made and half-French children born.

Let us return, though, to the first generation of Wahnfried youngsters. Once the young gods had grown up, the shadows of Nibelheim began to fall upon the cloudy heights: shadows of envy, jealousy, frustration and the thirst for power. The lives of the children, the daughters in particular, revealed the damage caused by their parents: the abuse was less obvious than that of the previous generation, to be sure, but the family pattern of a repressive, doctrinaire and authoritarian upbringing was nonetheless perpetuated. Cosima and Richard were both indelibly marked by their own painful experiences: their failed first marriages and the difficulties caused by their liaison, which could only be legitimated after the death of his wife on Wagner's side and a painful divorce on Cosima's. Wahnfried, for them, signified consolidation, order, the establishment and defence of a jointly fulfilling artistic life. For the family, there was 'nothing but Wahnfried' – and the subsidiary branches of Wahnfried that had resulted from the children's marriages – as Cosima recorded. This helped to foster a strong sense of family among the children, just as, in the previous generation, the shared feeling of having been abandoned created a strong bond between Cosima and her siblings. United in the 'Wagner mission' – often seen as synonymous with the 'German mission' – this family consciousness began to acquire a rather clannish aspect. Whoever was not with the Wagners was against them, and whoever was against them was a renegade, an enemy of culture, a traitor to the German spirit. Submission to the cause was expected: in the outside world, this attitude was expressed in the assumption that musicians would be happy to serve the Master's every instruction, without fee if at all possible; in the family, this meant that members were expected to submit to Cosima's dynastic plans by making suitable marriages. Cosima ran Wahnfried like a royal court, and as in a royal family, the idea that a member could have individual aspirations was scarcely thinkable. Ironically, this pattern echoed the aristocratic lifestyle with which the detested Princess Sayn-Wittgenstein had surrounded Cosima's father at the Altenburg: there, too, visitors and friends were remoulded into disciples and propagandists, and were expected to serve the cause of Liszt's 'New German' music.

Wahnfried, like any royal court, placed quite different expectations on its male and female children. Siegfried's musical education, after leaving grammar school, was artfully entrusted to various faithful Wagnerians: Engelbert Humperdinck became his composition teacher, and he was surrounded by loyal followers of his father wherever he travelled, in Frankfurt, Berlin and London. The protégé was passed on from hand to Wagnerian hand, until the point where he 'freely' decided that he wished to assume the role in Bayreuth for which his name and paternity had always destined him. The fate of Cosima's daughters, Daniela, Blandine,

Isolde and Eva, was similarly circumscribed but rather less interesting: they had a choice between making a suitable marriage within their own social class, and graciously agreeing to care for their ageing mother. Either way, they were expected to remain aloof from any direct involvement in the festival. There was only room for one 'mistress of Bayreuth': Cosima herself had escaped the limitations of a female role and experienced the masculine intoxication of artistic power, but she prevented any such transformation from taking place in her daughters' lives, by denying them the knowledge and experience that would equip them to play a part in the festival. At the end of their lives, the then elderly sisters would be marginalised once more, by Winifred, another wife who had assumed the masculine role. As Daniela recorded in 1934, they were dismissed as 'the aunts', and 'totally excluded from any participation, however passive, in festival matters.' Even their financial security was in question: they were forced into a humiliating plea to Richard Strauss, a friend from their youth and now President of the Reich Chamber of Music, that he should use his best offices to ensure that the honorary royalties granted to their mother during the years of inflation could now be transferred to them.

Daniela, the eldest daughter of Cosima's marriage to Bülow, was deliberately trained to care for her own father: Cosima used her to bear the burden of the guilt which she still felt about 'pauvre Hans', even decades after her divorce. Her diaries tell time and again of her entreaties to Daniela to write to her father. The child obediently assumed the role prescribed for her, and tried to lighten her mother's emotional burden by looking after the 'fervently loved father'. In February 1894, when he was sent to recover from illness in Egypt, it was she who, in tears, carried the dying man onto his ship in Trieste. Her preoccupation with von Bülow at least had the peripheral benefit of helping her to fulfil her talents as a pianist, one who would still be giving recitals in Bayreuth in later life. But she also had a second father, and in this relationship, too, she was fettered by her mother's expectations. Although she was renowned for her vivacity and her critical intelligence, she was also completely absorbed in the Wagnerian world: she collected the Master's sayings for a calendar, she matched her mother's ethical devotion to the preservation of the tradition, and even her choice of husband was conditioned by her sense of an obligation to extend the Wagner empire.

At the age of twenty-four, Daniela had become engaged to a stage mechanic and stage manager, Fritz Brandt, who had assumed the technical arrangements for the première of *Parsifal* and whose father had created the technical equipment for the first festival. But this Wagnerian background was not enough to satisfy Cosima, and like her sister Eva, Daniela was forced to subordinate her own happiness to her mother's dynastic ambitions. When she did eventually get married, two years later, it was not to Brandt but to Henry Thode, a Dresden-born art historian and committed Wagnerian intellectual. Thode, who later became a close friend of Siegfried, had been the director of the Städel Museum in Frankfurt, then a professor in Heidelberg, but his real passion was for Wagner: he was a contributor to *Bayreuther Blätter* and, as Cosima reported to King Ludwig, a 'man who sees the world as we do'. His breathless comments on the marriage, written in the grandiloquent style all too characteristic of the Wagnerians of this period, suggest that he really married the daughter out of enthusiasm for the mother:

> To become a member of a family such as this one is the greatest happiness
> that can befall a person – it quite simply is the house of one of the greatest
> geniuses who ever walked this earth and, with the incomparable greatness
> and vastness of the views, it stands high, high above all everyday life. Even
> this, though, is not worth another glance in comparison to the contact that
> the house offers with this most magnificent of all women.

This, needless to say, was Cosima, not Daniela. The newlywed Thodes maintained a house in Frankfurt, which was occasionally visited by the young Richard Strauss when he was in town for concerts, and where Siegfried lodged during his years at university – he described it as a 'miniature Wahnfried', and portraits of Cosima adorned the walls there too. The ideological outlook was certainly similar to that of Wahnfried: the Thodes' views were arrogant, nationalist, anti-French and anti-Semitic.

The marriage was unhappy, reportedly unconsummated, and it finally broke up when Thode was drawn towards the more alluring arms of Isadora Duncan, whom he had met when she came to Bayreuth in 1904 to choreograph the 'Bacchanal' in *Tannhäuser*. Daniela withdrew, snail-like, into the world of Wahnfried, and together with Eva, she cared for the ageing Cosima. Siegfried eventually encouraged her to take a more active role at Bayreuth: from 1912 onwards, she was entrusted with the administration of the costume department, a task for which she felt qualified owing to her marriage to an art historian. She maintained this role until 1933, the year in which she took joint control with Heinz Tietjen of the production of *Parsifal*: her friend Richard Strauss was the conductor. She increasingly sought to compensate herself for her lack of children, and she did so with great talent. As 'Aunt Lulu', with her two differently coloured eyes, one blue and the other brown, she enjoyed great popularity with the next generation of Wahnfried children: her nonchalant attitude to education was a refreshing contrast to the prevailing orthodoxy. On the reopening of the festival in 1924, she had miniature versions of the *Ring* costumes made for Siegfried's children, complete with helmets, spears and breastplates. This symbolic act encapsulated her two guiding principles in life: her commitment to the younger generation and her roots in the Bayreuth tradition. She was similarly generous to her Italian nephews and nieces, the children of her sister Blandine, but her favourite was the young Wieland, whom she used to take for carriage rides around Bayreuth with his girlfriend, Gertrud. Her affection was challenged, however, in 1937, when she found Wieland's new stage sets for *Parsifal* difficult to accept: they may seem conventional to us today, but from her perspective, conditioned by memories of the première, a tree no longer looked like a tree, and Gurnemanz's hut no longer stood where it used to. She had been loyal all her life 'to the Master's work, to the work of my mother and brother', but young Wieland's designs represented a break with tradition that she found difficult to accept.

The Nibelung watchword of 'loyalty' was also to become the slogan of the woman whom Daniela detested: her young sister-in-law, Winifred, who entered Wahnfried in 1915 and stole her brother from her. Since the disappointment of her own marriage, Daniela had made Siegfried the principal object of her affections; being a strong character herself, she knew how to handle him. It was probably inevitable, therefore, that she would find herself in conflict with Winifred: this young woman who, with the innocent pertness she had acquired in Berlin, claimed a place in the strange and increasingly ageing drawing-room at Wahnfried; and who irrevocably consolidated that place by presenting child after child, year after year, to Siegfried, until then a 'confirmed bachelor'. Daniela experienced a mixture of fury and helplessness in the face of this rival. Wartime provided a convenient excuse for retreat as she went to Jena as a Red Cross nurse; it would be many years before she returned.

If Daniela had sacrificed her own independence to the interests of her mother and family, then the same was probably true to an even greater extent of her half-sister, Eva. The youngest of Cosima's four daughters, she was never permitted to be anything other than her mother's 'secretary', servant and helper. Her prickly, waspish character – her nieces and nephews called her the 'pin-cushion' – must at least in part have been the result of such treatment. Cosima had ambitious marriage plans for Eva, hoping that she would ensnare the fiery and talented Richard Strauss, which would have been a spectacular *coup*, since it would have secured his services for Bayreuth and Wagner in perpetuity. Strauss smelt a rat, however, and hurriedly departed with the temperamental singer, Pauline de Ahna. Like Daniela, Eva was forced to accept a second choice. The substitute produced by Cosima was an Englishman, Houston Stewart Chamberlain: a long-standing correspondent and confidant of Cosima, a fervent Wagnerian and philosopher of the Aryan race – with the benefit of hindsight, he was ideally placed to provide the crucial link between the Wagner family and the Nazis.

The marriage between Chamberlain and Eva took place in 1908, and the couple were given a house next to Wahnfried as a wedding present from Cosima. Eva was forty-one: her husband, who was twelve years older, was soon to develop the progressive paralysis that left him dependent on her care. Chamberlain became another example of the Wagner family's curious tendency to absorb foreigners who ultimately became more papal than the Pope, more German than the Germans considered it proper to be. Whereas Wagner himself had leavened his German nationalism with some criticism of his fellow countrymen, the French Cosima, the English Winifred, and now Chamberlain did not dare to voice such complaints. For Eva, the marriage at least prevented her from being seen as an old maid; for Chamberlain, his alliance to 'the daughter of the master of all masters' was one that brought him status and prestige. It entitled him to claim connections going far beyond the Wagner family: he wrote to Kaiser

Wilhelm II, for example, that 'the exalted mother, in the goodness of her heart, has given this union her blessing. I have the feeling that this marriage is bringing me closer to Your Majesty both in space and in spirit.' Chamberlain was still closer, in space and spirit, to that Wagnerian who visited him and Eva on 'German Day' in 1923, and who called formally the next day on Siegfried, Winifred and the four children. Although she was a less militant nationalist than her mother Cosima and sister-in-law Winifred, it was nonetheless Eva's destiny to be the conduit through which Wahnfried first welcomed Adolf Hitler.

But we must return to 1914 – a year of crisis for the Wagners as for Europe. Although the celebrations of the centenary of Wagner's birth the previous year had shown Bayreuth to be in good financial and organisational shape, there were clouds on the horizon. *Parsifal* was no longer the exclusive property of the Festspielhaus and, with Siegfried in his mid-forties and unmarried, it seemed that there would be no successor to the throne. Cosima, who had first-hand experience of the problems of intestacy, drew up her own will. Unsurprisingly – though with considerable legal difficulty, because of his illegitimate birth – Siegfried was made the sole heir of all the physical assets of the estate, the daughters receiving only a fifth share each of their mother's personal capital. This preferential treatment inevitably created resentment and divisiveness among the siblings. It is salutary, though, to look ahead to 1929, when Siegfried and his wife produced a joint will that gave all their children equal shares in the property, as reversionary heirs of his mother: we find that this democratic solution had no more success than the previous generation's application of the principle of male succession, in avoiding unrest and ensuring co-operation in the running of the festival. Siegfried's solution can be seen as an attempt to atone for the injustice meted out in the previous generation, just as Cosima was motivated by the desire to avoid a repetition of the problems caused by her husband's intestacy. The wheel came full circle in 1966, when Wieland died intestate, opening the door to still more family acrimony and resentment, proving the truth of a family adage: 'whatever you do, you can't get it right.'

Cosima's strictly dynastic settlement implied the virtual disinheritance of her daughters, a situation to which they were bound to react in one way or another: either by accepting it passively, using cunning to try and improve it, or withdrawing in offence. Between them, the four daughters demonstrated all three reactions. Acceptance and perseverance were Daniela's choice. As the eldest, she had probably been most intensively exposed to Cosima's ideas on parenthood and succession, so she came to terms with the circumstances and accepted her mother's will. In addition, she was probably too fond of her brother to wish to challenge his supremacy.

Withdrawal was the option chosen by Blandine, the second von Bülow daughter, who had never been so much of a problem for her mother in any case. Named after her aunt in France, she was regarded as the most beautiful and elegant of all the sisters. Even during Wagner's lifetime, she had entered the aristocratic circles for which her mother had prepared her. In 1881, she married the Italian Count Biagio Gravina, moving with him to Florence where she bore him four children. Blandine soon cultivated an ironic distance from the affairs of Wahnfried: she seems to have been the only sister more or less to escape 'The Little Curse that is Everyone's Fate' (*Flüchlein, das Jeder mitbekam* – the title of an opera by Siegfried). The young Richard Strauss, after visiting her home in Ramacca in 1893, described it as 'Little Wahnfried under an Italian sky'. Her son Gilberto, a conductor who looked like a cross between Franz Liszt and Pinocchio, made the opposite journey to his mother: he sought his Grail in Bayreuth where he was content to earn a living by performing the most varied tasks, from singing coach to curtain signaller. Adhering to the conventions of the 'Italian branch' of the family, he largely avoided Wahnfried: he was seen almost everywhere else in Bayreuth in his stylish bowtie, playing the flute, conducting the works of his grandfather and uncle, but never at the villa. The only thing that came to sadden the ageing Gil was hearing the uneducated members of the fourth Wagner generation making disrespectful remarks behind the stage. Decades later another Italian branch of the family was to be founded by one of the members of this generation: Wolfgang's son, Gottfried, who after a failed first marriage, found the climate of Italy more conducive to family harmony.

Unlike the Bülow children, Wagner's natural daughters, Isolde and Eva fully participated in the power struggle. Their methods were different, however: Isolde was willing to stand up to Cosima, while Eva tended to rely on cunning. It was understandable that she should find it difficult to speak up for herself: her home life with her husband and her position as her mother's secretary meant that she had to remain in Bayreuth, and she had no standing or contacts outside the Wagner circle with which to buttress any act of protest. She had little option but to try and pull strings from the inside, seeking, by intrigue and manoeuvre, to gain privileges otherwise denied. These strategies, aided by her loyal and influential husband, were generally successful.

If the losers in the battle of succession had little room for manoeuvre, then life was little easier for the nominal victor. Siegfried, the only son of the family, had been burdened since birth by the high expectations of his parents; he had been hailed on his arrival as the 'surgeon' of their pains and therefore nicknamed 'Helferich' (little helper), while the name they chose for public consumption scarcely suggested that they would be content with modest achievements. He now found himself in an ambiguous and restricted position: expected wholly to serve his parents, but also to be wholly his own person. He dealt with an impossible situation remarkably well. He was weighed down by the excessive love of his mother and the equally burdensome pressure to be the Master's successor, and his natural disposition, moreover, was mild and conciliatory. Nonetheless, he accepted his predestined role with good grace, after only a brief excursion into architecture, and the tour of world- and self-discovery then customary for a young man from a distinguished family. From 1892, he devoted himself to the Festspielhaus, fulfilling his father's decree that he should preserve his works for the world. If it was, as Claude Debussy sceptically observed, 'not quite so simple as taking over a draper's shop', then this was perhaps something that Siegfried himself never quite realised.

He cheerfully fulfilled all the demands that the world – or rather his mother – placed upon him. He conducted the works of his father with appropriate devotion, and accepted 1906 without argument as the date at which sole management of the festival would be handed over to him. He was jovially disposed towards everybody, never really leaving the 'cloudy heights' of his childhood: even as a man in his fifties he still ran joyfully to meet his Mama and obeyed her to the letter. His outward appearance, always dressed in an elegant cream suit with a hint of the Prussian equestrian, marked him as a decadent of the 1900s – but he was never idle. His life was invariably filled with work, particularly during his efforts to restart the festival after the First World War. At the same time, he bravely continued to compose his own operas, undeterred by the scathing reactions of the likes of Richard Strauss ('Classicist simpleton!') and Karl Kraus ('Such a fellow never inherits the talent, but always the nose!') In fact, Siegfried's profile conveyed only a delicate echo of his father's aquiline features, and his fairy-tale operas, likewise, create a much cheerier and more playful impression than his father's sombre and warlike works. Where there was ambivalence and dichotomy in his father's work, here it is resolved in sunny good humour.

It seemed scarcely possible that Siegfried could have accepted his family destiny with such cheerful equanimity, and with such a complete absence of resistance. His rebellion, such as it was, came in the form of a complex sex life. He indulged his homosexual orientations with surprising freedom, and kept them even from his family with a remarkable degree of success. Even Cosima only discovered the secret because of the activities of blackmailers, who made demands that time and again had to be settled by Adolf von Gross, the family's financial administrator. Somehow, though, the news reached members of the press: most damagingly, Maximilian Harden, editor of *Zukunft* and whistleblower on homosexual scandals at the court of Kaiser Wilhelm II. He now had the power to ruin the Wagners as he had ruined Count Philipp von Eulenberg. Wahnfried, expecting to remain without an heir – after all, Siegfried would be forty-five in 1914 – had to act. It did so by offering to transform its entire assets – the house, the archive, the Festspielhaus – into a 'Wahnfried Foundation for the German Nation'. This seemingly generous offer succeeded in taking the wind out of the sails of the blackmailers and critics. The Chamberlain family was only too pleased to support this proposal, seeing it as a means of improving their impoverished position, or at least of reducing the rest of the family to the same level as themselves. The Chamberlains were concerned lest the scandal around Siegfried should improve the position of Isolde, Siegfried's once-favourite sister, who was rapidly becoming a controversial figure at Wahnfried: they were desperate to deny Isolde and her family what had already been denied to them.

Isolde was a rebellious, unstable, reportedly extravagant character. In 1900, after Cosima had stamped out an early love affair because the man concerned was not in her social class, she married the Swiss conductor, Franz Beidler, who had been engaged for the past four years as a musical assistant at the Festspielhaus. Although their wedding took place at Wahnfried with all due ceremony, Beidler – who was beginning to make a name for himself outside Bayreuth as a conductor of Wagner – never felt at home in the Wagner family. It is indicative that, unlike Henry Thode for example, he does not feature in any photographs of the extended family. The young couple settled near Bayreuth in the picturesque little château of Colmdorf, but relative distance did not secure family harmony. Cosima did not take to Beidler: although she attributed their disagreements to his difficult nature, the underlying problem was probably the rivalry between Siegfried and his brother-in-law, the two gentleman conductors of the family. Beidler detested the uncritical adulation which Siegfried and his work received, both in the family and in the press. In the eyes of the public, he felt, he had been eclipsed by Siegfried. This offended his ambitious nature: he believed that he deserved at least artistic equality with his brother-in-law.

Despite the tension with the family, Beidler's career at Bayreuth was making what, for anyone else, would be considered good progress: in 1904 he shared the conducting of *The Ring* with Hans Richter and in 1906 he shared *Parsifal* with Karl Muck. He wanted more, though, and when he pressed Cosima for additional conducting assignments, the matriarch chose to regard this as blackmail, and took the opportunity to dispense with his services altogether. This effectively meant the end of his career. Although the old family friend Hans Richter helped to get him a conducting post in Manchester (for which Siegfried profusely thanked 'Mama's benefactor') he gave up conducting soon afterwards and became a businessman. The lesson of his downfall was clear: no other family member would be allowed to claim a position alongside Siegfried, and any attempt to use family connections to gain artistic power would be ruthlessly suppressed. Cosima's fear of the threat represented by Isolde was heightened by the fact that she had given birth to a son in 1901: Cosima was afraid of the possibility that any male descendant of Richard Wagner might emerge as a challenger to her beloved Siegfried. The resultant treatment of Isolde and her family revealed the cruellest aspects of Cosima's obsession with dynastic power.

In 1913–14, the frictions between the Beidlers and Cosima came to a head, with tragic consequences for Isolde. Under pressure from her affronted husband, Isolde drove Cosima into a suicidal lawsuit, suing her for denied identity. No one could emerge victorious from this, and it resulted in Isolde's complete estrangement from her family. The financial and legal jargon in which the claim had to be clothed was so complex that its basis was not properly understood, but this did not discourage the world's press from taking a keen interest in the story: they revelled in the family's sexual and legal chaos, as they had done half a century before when Cosima was caught between the rival claims of Bülow and Wagner. The journal *Simplissimus* published a cartoon representing Isolde as Sieglinde, with a slightly altered version of Siegmund's words from *Die Walküre* underneath: 'I cannot call myself a Wagner; I do not want to be a Bülow; a Beidler, alas, I must remain.'

The case was a complex one. Although Isolde was publicly known as Wagner's daughter she, like all Cosima's daughters, bore the surname of von Bülow, and she had accepted her share of the conductor's inheritance under this name. Isolde received only a modest alllowance from Cosima, and she felt that she was excessively dependent on her mother's fragile good will; this, together with the insecurity caused by the expiry of Wagner's copyrights and the publication of Cosima's will, prompted her now to demand her rightful share of Richard Wagner's estate. Had Cosima granted this, however, it would have meant a legal acknowledgement that Isolde was Wagner's daughter. This she was unwilling to give, fearing the threat that a legitimate male descendant of Wagner might pose to her only son. She preferred to stick to the lie that Isolde was the daughter of Bülow: she was happier to present herself as immoral, by implying that she had been having sexual relations simultaneously with Bülow and Wagner, than to change her ideas about family order. She was only saved from having to commit perjury in the court by an arcane presumption that was part of Bavarian law at the time, that while a marriage was valid, the wife's sexual intercourse would be considered to be 'exclusive'.

From this moment onwards, Cosima decreed, in true Old Testament style, that Isolde's name should never be mentioned at Wahnfried. None of the other members of the family was willing or able to challenge this ruling: Siegfried also opposed Isolde, for understandable reasons, but so too did the Chamberlain family, who selfishly believed that Eva would profit from being regarded as Wagner's only daughter, if Isolde's paternity was denied. In their efforts to suppress Isolde's claims, the Wahnfried clan benefited from external distractions; the outbreak of war meant that the world suddenly had more important concerns than inheritance quarrels within the family of a dead composer. The rejected Wagner daughter, meanwhile, suffered further misfortunes. She was humiliated by the fact that her husband fathered a number of illegitimate children with other women. She died of tuberculosis on Davos in 1919, aged only fifty-four. She was initially buried in Munich, but her remains were subsequently transferred – humiliation beyond the grave – to the cemetery where her former husband lay with his second wife. Cosima did not even learn of the death of her once-favourite daughter until ten years after the event. Isolde's expulsion, meanwhile, had repercussions into the next generation: in 1925, Eva banished her sister's son, Franz Wilhelm Beidler, from Bayreuth. Whether this was because that proud German nationalist knew that the younger Beidler had become involved with the Social Democrats in Berlin, or whether it was because she had become intoxicated with power, it is difficult to say; the latter explanation could also account for her decision, after her mother's death, to burn the entire body of correspondence between Richard and Cosima.

The Festspielhaus closed its wooden doors for the next ten years, and the idea of a foundation was dropped again as a Wahnfried welcomed Siegfried's four children and prepared for the next upturn in the Wagners' fortunes. The family power struggles, however, had caused much suffering. The Swiss branch of the family was defeated beyond recovery. As Franz Wilhelm Beidler was later to remark, the birth in 1917 of Wieland, Siegfried's son and Wagner's second grandson, had cost him his 'uniqueness and succession to the Bayreuth throne'. Alienated from his father, whom he blamed for his mother's misfortunes, the young Beidler studied law and, after graduation, joined the Prussian Ministry of Education. A self-proclaimed 'left-wing socialist', he openly rejected National Socialism; this stance, together with his marriage to Ellen A. Gottschalk, the daughter of a Jewish physician, cost him his job in 1933. Since he was half-Swiss, exile in Switzerland seemed the obvious course of action:

he complained in a letter, shortly after his dismissal, that 'nationally unreliable, Marx-infected and Jew-related as I am, and of course will remain, there is no place for me any longer in our dear homeland.'

The fact that the long tentacles of Wahnfried stretched out to hurt him even in his new home is merely one more in that house's long list of unpunished crimes. This time, the Wagner museum in Tribschen was the conduit of Wahnfried's vengeance. Beidler had applied to rent the vacant upper floor of the museum, which relied financially on loans from the Wagner family, but its president refused him: he explained that 'the circumstance of distancing yourself from Wahnfried and from the "new regime" in Bayreuth would ... inevitably result in ill feeling if Lucerne were to let you have the floor.' One advantage of the situation, however, was the chance it offered Beidler to renew his longstanding friendship with Thomas Mann, who was also in exile in Zurich. Beidler read to Mann from a book he was writing at that time: a biography of his grandmother, Cosima, in which he applied his left-wing principles to family history by accusing her of deliberately distorting Wagner's revolutionary message. By this choice of subject, Beidler – who became Secretary of the Swiss Writer's Union in 1943 – demonstrated the hold that Wahnfried still had on him: he frequently described himself as 'Richard Wagner's lost grandson'.

After the collapse of Germany in 1945, when no one knew what to do about the compromised Wagners and their festival, a chance seemed open for Beidler to retrieve his lost – or rather stolen – identity. He was invited by the new Social Democratic mayor of Bayreuth to consider the future of the festival. Deeply moved by the offer, he immediately drafted a proposal. The centrepiece of his plan was the removal of Winifred and her children from their inherited positions of power, and their replacement by an international committee. Once again, however, members of the Wahnfried clan responded effectively to the Beidler threat, acting quickly to entrench their own position and to quash the pretender's hopes. Naturally enough, Wieland and Wolfgang did not even take Beidler's proposals seriously – to do so would have meant acknowledging the illegitimacy of their own position – and they did not find it difficult to thwart him. They had the bonus of the Wagner name, which proved a considerable advantage when securing positions in the post-war carve-up, and they had no intention of letting their position be undermined by 'Willi', as Beidler is sneeringly described in their letters to each other. Both 'Willi' – who never came to any of the brothers' post-war productions because he had decided 'not to forget' – and his descendants were subsequently excluded from any participation in the affairs of Bayreuth.

The instruments of Beidler's exclusion were themselves the product of a veritable miracle that had taken place in Wahnfried. It is true that their father, Siegfried, had neither split an anvil in two nor entered a ring of fire – as he himself joked, in a self-deprecating denial of the character implied by his name – but the fathering of four young Wagners between 1917 and 1920 must have seemed almost as improbable at the time. Not that Siegfried's fertility was in question: he had already fathered a son on a Bayreuth pastor's wife in 1901, a boy named Walter Aign, who was integrated into the festival as a musical assistant between 1924 and 1931, and again from 1951 to 1957 – remarkably, without any family conflict and without the public learning of his paternity. Nonetheless, Siegfried resisted his family's pleas to produce a legitimate son and heir for many years. When he did act, however, he did so decisively, helped by the fact that he was by now one of the most eligible bachelors in Germany, and by the popularity with women that he owed to his wit and good manners.

Siegfried's marriage had been delayed in part because he had an exacting and rather unusual set of requirements for any potential partner. He had long declared that he could only marry a woman who was 'quite poor' and 'without family'. This somewhat odd statement – running quite counter to the usual principles of matrimonial politics – can only be explained in psychological terms: Siegfried's security clearly depended on finding a mate who stood socially below him, who would not cross swords with his beloved mother, and who made no demands of her own. She would need to be someone to whom serving Siegfried would be everything; moreover, she had to be someone who would not be worried by his homosexual peccadilloes. It is fairly clear, too, that this dream of a poor wife also betrayed Siegfried's need to remain within his personal fairy tale, not to awaken from that enchanted world which he himself brought to life in his operas. Most of the women he met – singers, musicians, aristocrats, bluestockings – would by definition fail to meet these requirements. Instead, he brought home a schoolgirl of seventeen:

tall and slim, with a rather severe, masculine beauty, ignorant of worldly matters but deeply affected by Wagner's music. In Winifred, Siegfried had found his Cinderella: the glass slipper of Wahnfried fitted her perfectly.

Winifred Williams matched Siegfried's improbable requirements in her conspicuous lack of both family and means. She was born in Hastings and spent her early years in a rather Dickensian English orphanage: distant relatives rescued her from there at the age of nine, because of her poor health, and she was brought to Berlin. There, she was accepted into the house of Karl Klindworth who, at the age of seventy-eight and with a wife scarcely any younger, made the remarkable commitment to adopt and bring up the young Winifred. Klindworth was a pianist who had been taught by Liszt, a conductor, and a convinced anti-Semite; he was also a committed Wagnerian who had arranged Wagner's scores for piano, who maintained an amicable correspondence with Cosima and who came to Bayreuth every year for the dress rehearsals. In 1914 he took his adopted daughter, whom he had nicknamed 'Senta', to Bayreuth for the first time; the family was greeted by Cosima, they talked to her daughters, and Siegfried took the girl to have tea with him between the acts. After the outbreak of war, when Siegfried was conducting benefit concerts in Berlin, he took the opportunity to renew the acquaintance; in 1915, he asked for her hand in marriage, and the wedding took place in September of the same year. Before this took place, however, Winifred had to be naturalised as a German citizen – not an easy bureaucratic feat in wartime.

The father marrying the daughter: the psychological pattern of Siegfried's parents was unconsciously repeated, and the result was just as successful. In Winifred, Siegfried acquired an utterly devoted pupil and assistant, and the elderly Cosima gained someone who was willing both to care for and to read to her. Marriage made little difference to Siegfried's lifestyle: he continued his work uninterrupted in his bachelor cottage, and he did not even have to give up his sexual practices. Not that Winifred was physically unattractive to him: her very inexperience somewhat rejuvenated the old roué, who felt happy and secure with her. She consolidated her position in the family in the best way possible by bearing him a child every year. Each arrival further marginalised Siegfried's sisters: they were pushed aside, silenced, robbed of all power. The young mother ruled the roost at Wahnfried: during the next ten years, it was only the increasingly frail Cosima and the conciliatory manner of Siegfried that prevented the outbreak of open warfare between the envious 'aunts' and the flinty woman who had ensconced herself as the 'saviour of the dynasty'.

Winifred's first child, Wieland, was born in January 1917. The event was a dramatic one: as if sharing his mother's fears that she might not be able to continue the male line of Wagners, the baby emerged blue and almost dead, refusing to cry. Soon he became strong, however, and Wahnfried was once again lit by the sunshine of an assured succession: the atmosphere recalled those distant days in June 1869, when Siegfried himself arrived while his father was composing the love scenes from the work that bore his name. Although no such creative efforts accompanied Wieland's birth, the occasion was marked symbolically by Cosima, who came down from her apartment for the first time in many years and played a few bars on the grand piano which had stood closed since Wagner's death.

At the age of one, the heir was dressed in an embroidered white shirt and laced bootees, to be photographed for the sake of posterity on his grandmother's lap; Cosima, wrapped in an exquisite kimono, is pictured turning her now-dull gaze towards a future that she would not be able to witness. The baby's face shows, in an almost uncanny way, the features of the mature Wieland: that strange sarcastic, spoiled, depressive look that his family and collaborators would come to fear. Wieland would certainly not be a happy child. Though he was good-looking, with a head of fair curls, he was invariably grumpy and dissatisfied; no doubt upset by the rapidly increasing crowd of siblings and the consequent withdrawal of his mother's attentions. His happiness meant little to the family, however, by comparison with the mere fact of his existence: the sight of Cosima with Wieland meant that the chain of the generations had once more been established. Siegfried, like his father, composed a piece of music to commemorate the event: *Wahnfried Idyll*, for voice and piano, was his rather more modest offering.

The next child was Friedelind, the third was Wolfgang and the fourth was Verena. Balance between the sexes had been restored and Cosima's description of Wahnfried as 'our convent' now only reflected its self-imposed intellectual insularity. The children knew and cared little of that: Wahnfried witnessed a second wave of 'magical childhood', as Friedelind would testify later. They were not adversely affected by the cramped conditions, although post-war heating problems had made it necessary for nine family members, including the Italian branch, temporarily to share Siegfried's small out-building. Winifred was a progressive mother, breastfeeding all the children and allowing them the maximum possible freedom. Siegfried, though rarely seen by the children, shared her relaxed attitude: he wanted to raise them by love, not severity. His non-authoritarian attitude may have implied some criticism of his strict mother, but it was more significantly a product of his own character and the fact that he had never had to fight for anything in life.

The children's life was shared by Emma Baer, their devoted nanny from Franconia, who devoted her whole life to the family and later looked after Wieland's children. There were also cooks, governesses, domestic servants and tutors. Many of the visitors to Wahnfried and Wagner's tomb regarded the tribe of siblings as cheeky, ill-mannered and unruly: especially Friedelind, whose impertinent tongue and disobedient nature caused particular problems. At least this generation of Wahnfried children – chasing their dogs, kicking footballs, running around barefoot – emerged from the nest with more vivacity than their predecessors. Unlike Cosima's daughters, they suffered no debilitating insecurity about their Wagnerian identity: their paternity was clear enough from their 'Wagner noses'. Their schooling was less constrained and traditional than that of the previous generation: the early education available in their own house (the Wahnfried library, the travel souvenirs and art treasures in their father's composing cottage) was soon backed up by the classical education of the grammar school and by piano lessons, particularly for Wieland.

Even from the early years, though, parental injustice covertly corrupted the childhood paradise. Winifred adored her first-born above all (and Wieland was pampered all his life by the nanny); Siegfried's favourite was Friedelind (her name was of his own invention, taken from his opera *The Smith of Marienburg*). These parental preferences sowed the seeds of sibling rivalries to come – and all too soon the change from cheerful gang to lawless horde took place.

It was eventually possible to restart the festival in 1924, thanks to hard work from the family and generous financial support from the public.

The significance of the re-opening went far beyond the world of opera: the press described the 1924 festival as 'a consolidation festival for the German spirit' and 'the German redemption festival'. Although the history of Bayreuth should have prepared him for it, Siegfried had not fully understood the extent to which aesthetics had changed into ideology, and art had become politics. The Festspielhaus now had a clear political function: it was being used for German nationalist demonstrations and as an illegal meeting place for the prohibited new National Socialist Party. Wahnfried, too, engaged in politics: its inmates unanimously agreed to assume the honorary presidency of the newly established 'Bayreuth League of Youth', whose manifesto declared an aspiration towards 'the closest unity ... between Bayreuth and National Socialism.'

Siegfried's political metamorphosis was not untypical for an aesthete of his generation: Gabriele d'Annunzio, the poet, proto-Fascist, and friend of Siegfried's sister Daniela, is a comparable example. The real driving force behind the politicisation of Wahnfried, however, was Winifred, who was becoming increasingly active and independent in her political involvement. The Wahnfried family had never had much sympathy for the Weimar Republic, seeing it as weak and chaotic: they agreed on the need for a 'strong man to take charge'. The recollections of Erich Ebenmayer, a close friend of Winifred, ring true: 'Anyone who came into any contact during those years with the spirit of the Haus Wahnfried must have been shocked by the narrowness of its political horizon, which would have been more appropriate to a farmhouse in distant Pomerania than to the descendants of Richard Wagner.'

Adolf Hitler burst like a comet into this narrow world in October 1923: dishevelled, haggard and preoccupied, rather like a Flying Dutchman walking respectfully through Wahnfried's sacred halls. This appearance clearly triggered a response in Winifred, who immediately reverted to her childhood role as Senta. The redeeming role of the woman, inculcated in her by Wagnerian ideology, seemed to find its fulfilment here. As Hitler would redeem Germany, so she would redeem him. It is often claimed that it was maternal instinct that instantly and warmly bound the young woman to this leader of an illegal party – but this seems unlikely. The real motivation for her feelings is hinted at in the diaries of Joseph Goebbels, describing a dinner party at Wahnfried in 1926: 'She put her sorrows to me,' he recorded, 'Siegfried is so limp.'

There are thousands of testimonies during the Third Reich to the female fantasies excited by Hitler, despite the fact that he looked more like a barber's assistant or travelling salesman than a 'young Siegfried'. One such fantasy was played out at Wahnfried: since decorum and the political role of Bayreuth prohibited sexual fulfilment of the fantasy, the desires aroused were sublimated into a heroically idealised 'loyalty' and 'unbreakable friendship'. The fact that Winifred still raved about Hitler's blue eyes fifty years after meeting him, and her boast that she would have loved to welcome him as a dear friend if only he could have stepped through her door again, clearly reveals her fixation on Hitler's person: a fixation that went beyond all critical reason and political judgement, but which obeyed the rules of an archaic desire for submission. Even the children were aware of her feelings: the precocious Friedelind was reported to have told a visitor, curious about the rumours of a possible marriage that had been circulating since the mid-1920s, that 'My mother would like to, but Uncle Wolf wouldn't.' Winifred herself remained unaware of her desires, but at the age of twenty-seven, sizzling with an erotic energy that was mainly channelled into eating – 'Winnie, don't stuff yourself so', Siegfried would constantly remind the corpulent woman – she was old enough to desire the whip-cracking authority of the dominating man. She no longer wanted the benign papa: rather the strong Führer. There may also have been other aspects of Hitler that appealed to her extravagant sense of solidarity. Was not he a 'lone wolf', like her? Had he not also come from nowhere, in need of salvation as she had been? She perceived in Hitler an end to such social exclusion: this Cinderella, whose acceptance at the Wahnfried court had surely not been without its social humiliations, openly declared her admiration for Hitler's success in 'removing the downright unbridgeable class hatred in Germany'. Now that she herself was firmly established in the Wagner dynasty, how could she not extend the hand of friendship to him? This Sieglinde had sensed the presence of her Siegmund.

If the naive Siegfried did not fully comprehend his wife's obsession with Hitler's person, then he nonetheless shared her sympathy for his political mission. By chance, the couple witnessed the unsuccessful

Munich coup of November 1923 at close range, and this heightened Winifred's revolutionary zeal. She gave an eyewitness account to the small local Nazi party, and in a letter she extolled 'the moral strength and purity of this man, to whom the Haus Wahnfried will remain loyal not only in days of fortune but also in days of need.' The following year, as soon as the first festival and her representative duties as the new Frau Wagner were over, she was packing gift parcels for the poor internee in Landsberg – parcels which included enough paper for him to write *Mein Kampf.* In 1925, upon his release, Hitler expressed the desire to visit his friends in Bayreuth, to which the police responded that they would, in that event, occupy Wahnfried. Siegfried was momentarily alerted to reality, and his wife was forced to cancel the visit. However, her passion could no longer be restrained. She openly displayed her political sympathies by visiting Munich for the re-foundation of the Party, and soon afterwards Hitler spent a night at Wahnfried for the first time. He visited the festival that summer, also for the first time – and just as, two years previously, he had promised to bring *Parsifal* back to the dishonoured Bayreuth, he now promised not to cause any more difficulties for his hosts, and to return again only as the leader of the nation. This did not come to pass until 1933, when the Flying Dutchman emerged as a radiant Lohengrin, and Senta was transformed into a jubilant Elsa as her dreams became reality.

During the intervening eight years, Hitler nevertheless repeatedly visited Wahnfried, as Bayreuth was favourably situated along the 'marching route' from Munich to Berlin. Winifred was enraptured, while her husband was becoming increasingly annoyed by her constant involvement in Party affairs. 'She is destroying everything I have built up', he remarked, remembering his father's hatred of party politics – a hatred hypocritically unaffected by his continual involvement. Siegfried tried to keep his Bayreuth non-political: the hopeless, belated gesture of one who had lived life as an aesthetic fairy tale. For Winifred, the attraction of her political activities was only increased by the opportunity they offered to free herself from her guardianship of the ageing Wahnfried court, where she had always been regarded as a fledgling. Moreover, she regarded the Nazis' ideological jargon as a living application of those heroic and idealistic concepts with which she had been brought up in the Klindworths' home, concepts which until then had seemed relevant only to Wagnerian drama, not to life. Fanatical commitment to the new Germany seemed the best outlet for her energies, artificially channelled until now into domestic and secretarial work.

Hitler became an honorary member of the Wahnfried household: Winifred involved him in its affairs as much as his commitments would allow, she offered the persecuted man home and hearth, she good-humouredly taught him some table manners, and she gave him some of the comforts of family life by allowing him to befriend her children. To them he was an affectionate but mysterious figure, constantly arriving and departing in larger and larger cars: a man who had stories to tell from the great outside world. It is not surprising that the children were unaware of the real nature of their mysterious visitor: conversation in Wahnfried was almost always about art. Their mother's enthusiasm for the strange 'Uncle Wolf' – the name was at once a cover and a term of endearment – legitimated their feelings for him: she presented him to them in a way that was bound to make them love him more than their mostly absent father. The six-year-old Wieland is reported to have declared that he would rather have 'Uncle Wolf' as his father and his father as his uncle. He was not to know that only seven years later, an alteration in family relationships of almost this magnitude would be brought about by his father's sudden death.

15

1930–51: the deaths of Cosima and Siegfried to the post-war festival

IN 1930 A DISASTROUS DOUBLE BLOW WAS DEALT TO THE OEDIPAL tranquillity of Wahnfried. In early April Cosima died, followed in early August by Siegfried. Wagner's widow had at least survived to the great age of ninety-two: warned by a heart attack, she had retired to the upstairs apartment at the beginning of the century, handing over the reins to her son and living for decades as a shadowy, remote, ancestral figure. Siegfried, by contrast, had been cut off in his prime at the age of sixty-one. His chain-smoking had put a constant strain on his weak heart, and the stress caused by rehearsals for his new production of *Tannhäuser* was probably an additional factor. It scarcely needed Sigmund Freud – whose new science had been ignored by mother and son like most other manifestations of the contemporary spirit – to infer a symbolic unity between the two departed spirits from this coincidence of deaths. Their love-death was almost too accurate a confirmation of the theories of psychoanalysis. For those who were allowed to read them, it was all to be found in Cosima's diaries. These recorded how Wagner, at Siegfried's birth, was working on the love scenes in Act Three of Siegfried; and how he said to Cosima, still confined, that it was a wonderful coincidence that his jubilation theme ('She is everything to me') perfectly joined with the 'Hail to the mother who bore me' motif, 'so that this jubilation rings out in the orchestra continually until the moment Siegfried himself joins in.' Siegfried had indeed always joined in: he had always concurred with his Wagnerian destiny, demonstrating a loyalty in real life that was the prerogative of the female characters on stage.

Those attending the ceremonies commemorating the two deaths would have been able to tell a lot about the differences between the status and the personality of the two deceased. For Cosima, the black carriage and the funeral procession filed past the theatre to mark her part in its history, before returning to Wahnfried where she was buried to the accompaniment of the Pilgrims' Chorus from *Tannhäuser* and extracts from *Parsifal*. She was laid to rest in the second and last place, long reserved for her, in Richard Wagner's tomb in the Wahnfried garden. To Siegfried, by contrast, fell the honour of inaugurating his family's plot in the municipal cemetery, his name inscribed on a simple cruciform gravestone in the laconic style of the thirties. A concert was held in the Festspielhaus to commemorate him, presided over by two rival conductors, as if two epochs were shaking hands: Arturo Toscanini, newly arrived in Bayreuth, took charge of the *Siegfried Idyll*, while Cosima's old friend Karl Muck, like a 'mummy' on the podium according to one eyewitness, led the 'Funeral March' from *Götterdämmerung*, that tribute to another Siegfried who was not permitted to be a free man. These paternal musical representations of his birth and death were leavened with a reminder that Siegfried had his own, albeit modest, musical genius: Karl Elmendorff presented extracts from his works, whose titles, *Friedensengel* ('The Angel of Peace') and *Glaube* ('Faith') were as guilelessly benign as the character of their creator. In another coincidence that seems almost too appropriate, 1930 also saw the death of Franz Beidler, Cosima's banished son-in-law and Siegfried's old antagonist. This went virtually unnoticed by the Wahnfried family, and it was only Beidler's son Franz Wilhelm who, as he sarcastically commented, 'did not get out of his mourning clothes that year'.

Siegfried's children, then aged between nine and thirteen, did not witness their father's death because they were still on holiday, and they were not allowed to attend his funeral. The death in itself was probably not felt too deeply by any of them, with the possible exception of Friedelind, his favourite, who was summoned home from England but was prevented from visiting his sickbed. The problems stemmed more from the resultant lack of father-figure: a particular difficulty for Wieland, since it both increased the natural high-handedness of the first-born, and drove him into a deep and troublesome fixation on his mother. A repetition of the mother-son alliance from the previous generation was taking shape; this one still more dangerous because the mother was young and modern, a driver and chain-smoker with a loud and coarse laugh, and someone who inspired confidence and increasingly radiated authority. The plump boy had said to his schoolfriend Gertrud with the round freckled face that 'I'll never marry you; I'll only marry a woman who is as beautiful as my mother!' And what did he do, having earned his first wages by photographing artists, the Festspielhaus and (by special permission) the Führer? He emptied his bank account and bought his mother a new car – the American Ford V-8 – because he thought her German Mercedes too slow for her.

The teenaged Friedelind, always in an unhappy state of rivalry with her mother, chose the other way out, giving her heart to a substitute father: Toscanini, who had been brought to Bayreuth and therefore 'sanctified' by her father. Besides, 'Mausi' had already been almost rejected by Wahnfried as a threat to family peace, which prepared the ground for her politically motivated emigration later in life. From 1930, when she was twelve, she had been sent to boarding schools in both England and Germany, because Winifried could not deal with a child who seemed to make permanent revolution her watchword. She only returned home for Christmas and the Bayreuth Festival. Her early experiences of alienation from Wahnfried and from the 'primal horde of the family' were undoubtedly painful for her; at the same time, though, they gave her the detachment which later enabled her to see political affairs in a clearer light than the rest of the family.

Overshadowed by the two 'big ones' – who were arming themselves against the adult world with an obesity which was scarcely helped by the prodigious quantities of Knackwurst at Winifred's table – the younger siblings flourished, happily spared from any maternal interference. They seem to have been less complicated personalities, and as if to provide a visual reminder of this difference, they also remained slim. 'Wolfi' spent his childhood engaged in practical hobbies such as wrought-iron work; he was easy-going and cheerful, entertaining the family at table with his wit. While he was making schoolboy friendships which laid the foundations of his empire – many of his schoolmates were later to be found on the Festspielhaus staff – his elder brother was more interested in the girls. He still mocked them at the moment, and threw footballs at them, but he knew what pretty legs were, and Gertrud, who first came to the house as Friedelind's friend, certainly had those. Before long, the two fourteen-year-olds became inseparable: Gertrud became the patient object of his photographic and artistic activities, and hung out with the Wahnfried gang at school, in the garden and at the skating rink. All this left only one role for Verena, the youngest: the pampered pet with a ribbon in her hair. She grew up into a pretty, capricious girl, whose delicate Wagner nose and un-German elegance charmed the Führer and his assistants; Hitler was happy to accept the pleasant impertinence of his 'Nickerl' during the long evenings at the Wahnfried hearth.

After two generations of children at Wahnfried, we can already see the cyclical pattern of family history emerging. If we compare 1883 to 1930, it is not so much the outward circumstances as the inner relationships that are similar: the father of the family dead, a young widow, a group of children still under age, and the future direction of the festival an unanswered question. The forces of orthodoxy appear on the battlefield, siding with the deceased Wagner and against the widow. They use either her 'foreignness' or her supposed lack of leadership qualities as a pretext, but their real concern is that the slightest deviation from traditional practice represents treason against Wagner's work. After Siegfried's death, it was the aunts who joined battle, beating the drum against the hated usurper. They enlisted the help of the town of Bayreuth, which offered Winifred alternative accommodation so that they could turn Wahnfried into a museum. The patriarchal system was striking the blows that are customary after a burial, a phenomenon that Wieland's widow would also experience following his death. Winifred, at least, was protected by the terms of Siegfried's legacy, which secured the immediate future. In point of fact, though, Winifred was not entirely content with the will, despite having countersigned it. She would have preferred to see the *Erbhof* laws of the Third Reich prevail, passing the whole estate to her eldest son, rather than having it partitioned among the four children. And she complained bitterly about the provision made by Siegfried, perhaps warned by her enthusiasm for Hitler, that in the event of her remarriage she would have to renounce the estate in full: Winifred, anxious to emulate Cosima, had no intention of doing this.

Winifred had certain advantages over Cosima: whereas her mother-in-law had taken over Bayreuth at a stage when consolidation was needed, the time was now ripe to modernise. Winifred seized that opportunity effectively. She did not make the mistake of overestimating her own abilities, so from 1933 she entrusted the overall artistic direction to the man whom Siegfried had recommended: Heinz Tietjen, who since 1925 had been the Generalintendant of the Prussian state theatres in Berlin, a post which included control of both the Kroll Opera and the Berlin State Opera. His track record as an Intendant, as well as his dual abilities as a producer and a conductor, made him the ideal candidate for the Bayreuth post; the director of the Festspielhaus had always been someone with varied artistic abilities, poet-composer or conductor-producer. (Wieland was trained to acquire a similarly Renaissance-like combination of skills; though his visual abilities were recognised at an early stage, he still received training as a conductor and tested himself with a *Dutchman* in Heidelberg.) Tietjen, moreover, seemed to be receptive to contemporary movements in the arts, even if he was not exactly a radical: he presided over moderate innovation at Bayreuth, and encouraged the changes in visual style initiated by the designer Emil Preetorius. Tietjen's political stance was hard to determine, thanks to his adroitness: his enemies in Bayreuth condemned him as a 'one-time drawing room Communist', and he was not a Nazi party member and was said to dislike Hitler – but on the other hand he enjoyed the patronage of Hermann Goering. In any case, contacts with the state were sufficiently guaranteed by Winifred's friendship with the Reichskanzler, which resulted in generous financial support. The modern-minded Winifred also improved Bayreuth's public relations, showing that she had learned from the Reich's use of propaganda as a tool of demagogy. She initiated the publication of the correspondence between Richard Wagner and King Ludwig, and she made the festival far more open to the press.

Hitler was a less frequent visitor to Wahnfried now that he had ascended to the starry firmament of power: he descended only to attend festival performances. His place was to some extent taken by Tietjen, who had moved in to the house. 'In no time', Friedelind recalled, 'Tietjen had my mother in his pocket.' Once again, we see the apparently authoritarian Winifred striking a pose of masochistic obedience. All the Wahnfried children remember her almost slave-like relationship with Tietjen. Time and again, whenever there was any disagreement with him, she would sit in tears at the breakfast table. Tietjen's outward physical charms were no more obvious than those of Hitler: he was a short, almost inconspicuous intellectual, with an appearance of grave seriousness and an unctuous tone of voice. Nonetheless, he was known as a charmer of women and as a man with exquisitely refined skills of diplomacy; he was far superior in this respect to the rather clumsy Winifred. Her devoted simplicity was no match for the Tartuffe-like Tietjen, who forestalled her with promises of marriage while tormenting her with other 'affairs'. She clung to him and made him the guardian of her children. After the war, when his political survival was at stake, she loyally testified to his anti-Nazi tendencies, incapable of revenge even though he had let her down by marrying another woman.

From 1933, when he took up his post at the Festspielhaus, Tietjen became the new master of Wahnfried. Once again, the children were offered a substitute father – but this time, they were too old to be so easily led. The negative aspects of Winifred's educational philosophy of letting them grow up 'like savages' were now apparent. The older they grew, the more militantly they reacted against Winifred's rather belated application of the iron fist. In 1935–36 Friedelind, who had spent most of her adolescence either abroad at school or in hospitals or sanatoria because of her obesity, was despatched at her mother's command to attend a year's course at a domestic science school. This somewhat implausible attempt to tame the rebel was followed by a period of training at the Berlin Opera. Verena, meanwhile, had graduated from the Luisenstift near Dresden and decided to study medicine: a rare demonstration of independence. Winifred's main attentions, though, were focused on the two boys, who needed to be prepared for the tasks that awaited them.

The educational horizons of Wahnfried were now much more limited than those of the founders of the family, who had viewed life, and in particular the arts, from the broad perspective offered by having lived in many parts of Europe. This generation was mostly confined to the pleasures common among middle-class families in Nazi Germany: visits to Jena, Weimar and Eisenach, trips to performances of Wagner operas in small towns, Schiller and Kleist in the evening, read aloud by Winifred. Little music was permitted other than that of Wagner's domestic deities: a little Beethoven, a little Weber in *Freischütz* vein. Entire genres, such as chamber music, were disapproved of – the ideology of the 'total work of art' had seen to that. In the visual arts, the family knew of little other than the *Jugendstil* painter Franz Stassen, a friend of Siegfried's, a few remants of nineteenth-century realism, and the styles approved by the Reich. Wieland was taught painting by Ferdinand Staeger, an academic traditionalist and 'war artist' with symbolist tendencies, popular in the Third Reich but forgotten today. Wieland had been impressed by Staeger's giant paintings in Bayreuth's Siebert Hall (the Nazi name for the Margraves' riding school).

Whichever way the children turned, they seemed to find Nazis. Their nanny, Emma, was a fanatical Party member, as was a girl named Liselotte Schmidt who had been engaged by Winifred as an after-school coach. Otto Strobel, the director of the Wagner archive who tried to guide the young Wieland, was a committed Nazi Wagnerian, and Wieland's music teacher, Kurt Overhoff, had been an idealistic follower of the movement in its early days.

In 1937, when their artistic mentor Franz Stassen guided Wieland and Gertrud round the now-notorious exhibition of 'Degenerate Art', they were silent and confused: neither knew any better than to accept the condemnations presented to them. Gertrud's family was little more enlightened than Wieland's: although her mother, Luise, bravely maintained her friendships with Jews, her father, Adolf Reissinger, an eminent scientist and mathematician, invariably wore the Nazi Party badge and refused to hide it even when the victorious Allies entered Bayreuth. In 1937, Gertrud had enrolled as a student at the Günther-Schule, the best modern dance school in Munich, where Carl Orff was then teaching. Here, too, there was little respite from politics. Dorothee Günther's girl pupils danced before Goebbels at the Ministry of Propaganda, Günther students danced the 'Olympic Dance' in Berlin in 1936, and were subsequently even sent on political missions to the Occupied Territories. Gertrud, though, was politically unaware and was enjoying her dancing:

she graduated with a diploma from the Reich Theatre Chamber in 1940 and was preparing to make use of her new-found artistic skills in contributing to Wieland's first theatrical efforts.

Within this dull, enclosed and Nazified environment, Heinz Tietjen, the diminutive man of the world, must have been like a breath of fresh air, and the youngsters initially reacted to him positively. But they soon sensed the danger he posed to their mother: Wieland in particular felt that Tietjen was 'treating her badly', though the director was perhaps just reacting against her possessiveness. Tietjen manipulated the situation by deliberately breaking up the siblings' united front, playing them off against each other. One day, he would build up Friedelind's position by letting her help him off-stage; another day he would court Verena's favours. Sometimes he would portray Wolfgang as the man of the future; at others, he seemed to be favouring Wieland, as when he used him as his stage designer for the 1937 production of *Parsifal* and the wartime *Meistersinger*. The collaboration did not dampen Wieland's hostility, however. While Wolfgang proved more pliable, Wieland became increasingly antagonistic to what he perceived as the power bloc of Winifred and Tietjen. Unlike his father Siegfried, who had been a 'happy Oedipus', Wieland was a doubly unhappy one: his 'dream father' was away in the Reich Chancellery preparing for world war, and his 'house father' was monopolising his mother's attentions at home.

In 1936, Wieland left the town's classical grammar school, crowning his achievements by giving a graduation speech in fluent ancient Greek. A Mercedes awaited him outside Wahnfried, a gift from 'Uncle Wolf'. He went through national service and a few tests of his abilities as a designer, on *Parsifal* and some of his father's operas, which did not prove his talents to be anything out of the ordinary. But his antagonism to Tietjen had now reached the point of being a palace revolution: he accused the director of having deliberately refused him a musical education, in order to keep him dependent and therefore to safeguard his own unfettered power. Tietjen's response to this was to draw up an educational programme that would last eight to ten years, based at the State Opera, during which he would teach Wieland everything that a future director of Bayreuth would need to know, from the assistant stage manager's role upwards. Wieland, probably correctly, saw this as an elaborate ploy to keep him away from

Bayreuth, and quite apart from his hatred of Tietjen, the programme was much too protracted. He therefore cut himself off from all connections with the Festspielhaus, and moved to a studio in Munich to begin a serious study of painting.

Wieland felt freer there, at least in terms of family relationships. He worked at his easel day and night, leaving only reluctantly and in response to the pestering of Gertrud, whose dance school was just around the corner. 'No one's ever become famous from walking,' he would tell her, though the joke perhaps revealed more of his inner stress than he intended. The outbreak of war created a new and difficult situation for him: as the heir of Bayreuth, Hitler had personally granted him exemption from active service, but this privilege carried with it the obligation that he would study music in order to prepare for the future management of the festival. He could no longer devote himself to painting, and Hitler could claim the credit for having brought the apostate back into the fold. The training programme that was proposed for him now had the merit of being completely different to Tietjen's. The new course was drawn up by the Viennese-born Kurt Overhoff, who left his post as general director of music in Heidelberg – at the Führer's command, Tietjen hinted – in order to become Wieland's private tutor. During the next ten years, Wieland was trained by Overhoff to study Wagner's scores in the minutest detail, in order to divine their symbolic and psychological meaning. This process may have proved trying at times, but it provided Wieland with a solid basis from which to begin the visual expression of musical ideas, the very skill for which his productions later became famous. Moreover, Overhoff persuaded the young man to abandon his 'false obsession with tradition', which had made him criticise the expressionist approach of Tietjen and Preetorius on the grounds of its 'disloyalty' to Wagner – his perspective then was almost the same as his Aunt Daniela's. Of course, Overhoff's work was not entirely selfless: he hoped to secure a position in Bayreuth once his protégé had assumed control. Meanwhile, in a manoeuvre worthy of a Shakespearean history play, Heinz Tietjen was overseeing the education of Wolfgang – albeit in a more telescoped form than he had planned for Wieland – building up the younger brother's reputation as 'his man'.

Tietjen liked to speak in a stage whisper of the 'disastrous conflict of brothers', whose repercussions were to shape the next era of Bayreuth's history. The conflict began to emerge during those war years, in which the two brothers were each out for their own ends, each pursuing the same goal. Though they had only recently been sufficiently happy with each other's company to make a joint educational trip to Italy – they were in Rome at the same time as Hitler who 'was extremely sorry [they] didn't contact him', according to Winifred – a Cain and Abel pattern now began to emerge.

The war affected the brothers' lives and ambitions in different ways. Wieland, Hitler's protégé, initially seemed to have all the advantages. He was building up his career: in 1943–44 he had created stage sets for a *Ring* cycle performed in both Nuremberg and Altenburg, where Overhoff had conducted, as well as for a production of Weber's *Freischütz*. Wolfgang, on the other hand, was called up in 1939 and took part in the campaign against Poland. Decades later, his memoirs, *Acts*, betrayed his bitterness over this life-and-death discrimination, which made him bitterly aware of his 'second-rateness'. But he was fortunate in misfortune, and was sent back with a wounded hand to the Charité Hospital in Berlin, where he was treated by the famous Professor Sauerbruch. The Supreme War Lord had the opportunity to compensate Wolfgang for the injustice done to him: he made frequent visits to his sickbed and discharged him from the Wehrmacht.

Wolfgang was now in a position to catch up with Wieland's lead: indeed, he had an advantage, since he was able to gain experience in Bayreuth itself, where the Führer had decreed that wartime festivals should take place from 1940. The Nazi-sponsored 'Strength Through Joy' (*Kraft durch Freude*) organisation relieved Winifred of any financial worries and provided an audience, albeit a less elegant one than usual. Over the next four years, Bayreuth was thus responsible for the artistic education of the troops in the hinterland. Even as late as 1945, Tietjen offered to stage a spectacle of acting and singing if the Führer so wished.

Wolfgang's star continued to shine. In accordance with the training programme that Wieland had rejected, he was engaged by Tietjen at the Berlin State Opera, and in the eyes of both Winifred and his guardian, he was the 'sensible little one'. It was suggested to him that the conclusion of his training should coincide with the completion of the reconstruction of the Festspielhaus, which was itself part of the Reich's ambitious plans to reshape Bayreuth into a *Gauforum*, a regional centre. After this, it was proposed, Wolfgang and Wieland could take over the running of the festival and could inaugurate the 'peacetime festival' with *Tannhäuser*. However, Wolfgang made the error of taking seriously his brother's claims to have renounced his directorial ambitions in favour of becoming a painter: he therefore offered Wieland, with apparent generosity, the chance once again to build the sets when he, Wolfgang, was in charge. 'Mama and Heinz view me as the more gifted of us,' he wrote to his brother in Munich. Wieland was furious and retaliated by requesting Wolfgang to leave the artistic direction to him. This Wolfgang indignantly refused to do. There was no obvious resolution to the crisis; it is difficult not to think of the scene where Alberich and Mime quarrel about the treasure outside the *Neidhöhle*.

At the Berlin State Opera, Wolfgang was discharging his duties skilfully, eagerly and with an admirable lack of pretension. He had learnt about the theatre from the bottom up, thereby, in his view, earning the right to a lifetime in that profession. His personal life was also progressing satisfactorily. Through Gertrud, who was then a member of Tietjen's ballet group, he met a pretty dancer, Ellen Drexel. His description of her attractions clearly reveals that he was not looking for a dominating female along the lines of his mother or elder sister: 'Unlike any of the available or attention-seeking ladies within my family's ambience, Ellen Drexel was very reserved and inconspicuous.' He felt some pressure to make a move, since women had always been more interested in his gentler and more sensitive brother. This was clear from Winifred's rather transparent attempts to play matrimonial politics at Wahnfried: she kept inviting young blondes, racially 'correct' in appearance and from good families, probably in the hope of detaching Wieland from his childhood sweet-heart, the brown-haired Gertrud. Though this did not happen, Wieland was nonetheless more successful than his brother when such temptations were presented before them, as Wolfgang laconically admitted, with what became a family catchphrase: 'The one has two and the other has none.' In Ellen, at least he had 'one', and he married her in 1943. Two years earlier, Wieland had entered – or had been entered – into matrimony; he hated the institution, and only submitted because of an ultimatum from his mother. He grumpily took Gertrud off to the registry office in Nussdorf, a holiday centre on Lake Constance. There was no question of a honeymoon: the new husband went back to his easel and his bride, no less disappointed than her mother-in-law by this unconventional disregard for a central event in her life, soon departed for a more cheerful Italy where she took a course of language studies.

There was another wedding at Bayreuth in 1943, the same year as Wolfgang's, and this occasion, too, did not pass without certain strange family neuroses coming to the fore. Winifred sat sobbing in her armchair throughout the ceremony: the vivacious Verena had chosen an 'old man' the same age as her mother, and one, moreover, with a failed marriage behind him. It was little consolation to Winifred that the tall man from Kiel, Bodo Lafferentz, had come to Bayreuth in his capacity as a leader of the 'Strength Through Joy' tour group. Verena, who could have chosen almost anyone, had revealed her inner needs by her choice: the familiar theme of fatherlessness reappeared and was resolved by an incestuous 'father-daughter' type of marriage. A by-product of her decision was that she, the youngest, was now in a stronger position within the family. Bodo was a husband of some consequence: he had an impressive appearance and a powerful voice, he had played an important part in the development of the Volkswagen company, and his Nazi credentials were impeccable. Moreover, because Winifred was dependent on his purchase of festival tickets for 'Strength Through Joy', her position had been symbolically weakened. Verena became pregnant almost immediately, and as a result gave up her medical studies. Her daughter, Amélie, was born in 1944, and was swiftly followed by two sons and two more daughters. The consequences of this only became clear later. Verena's husband was extremely jealous of her past and attempted to confine her to a domestic role, thereby preventing her from taking any part in her Bayreuth inheritance, let alone from resuming her medical career. The frustrations of this were compounded by the fact that the couple lived in the back of beyond, in Nussdorf where Wieland had unwillingly married. Verena's psychological condition could be guessed at from apparently minor symptoms such as the changes in her voice: she had previously had a rich and powerful lower voice, but after her marriage she only ever spoke softly. She did not break her marriage, but her marriage broke her.

If the pretty and charming youngest child had suffered the fate of a Chrysothemis – 'I am a woman and I want a woman's fate' as that character said in *Elektra* – then the more headstrong and resilient Frie-delind continued to act out the title role, rebellious and childless. She could not forget her father's death, the crucial caesura in her life: all the rest had been struggle against her iron-willed mother. She was always intrigued by politics – as a young girl she wore a silver swastika round her neck and enjoyed visiting the Reich Chancellery – but opposition to her mother soon led her into society whose perspectives were broader than those of Wahnfried. Her closest friend and protector was the singer Frida Leider, who was married to a Jew, and she had other Jewish friends; added to these connections was her intense sympathy for the under-privileged and persecuted, which formed a strange antidote to her native 'Wagner pride'. After making an appearance at the 1938 festival, she emi-grated to Switzerland and thence to America the following year, with the assistance of her friend Toscanini. This daughter solved the problem of her fatherlessness in a different way to Verena, by shifting the psychological conflict into the political sphere.

She made a meagre living for herself in New York through journalistic work and lectures; she also involved herself in several Wagner-related projects which turned out to be lost causes. Whenever she attacked Nazi Germany on the radio or in the press – and she did this often – she invariably also attacked Winifred. An evil mother and an evil motherland had become the same thing for Friedelind. The whole tragedy of a fruitless search for a mother-figure, the story of love repudiated and answered by aggression, emerges clearly in Friedelind's memoirs when she mentions the rare and brief moments when her mother needed her, when she turned towards her for a few seconds. Just as Isolde foundered against the rock of Cosima's dynastic determination, so Friedelind's life was ruined by the personal and political inflexibility of Winifred. It is said, often in disbelief, that Winifred, sent to Zurich in 1940 on Himmler's behalf to retrieve Friedelind for Nazi Germany, threatened her daughter that she would be 'extirpated and exterminated' if she did not return. Sadly, it is entirely possible that that woman would have used those words at that time. Wolfgang and Wieland, too, felt that Friedelind was a disgrace to the family and a traitor to her country. She in turn was consoled by thoughts of her grandfather, with whom she identified as a fellow 'rebel against injustice', and who had also sought asylum in Zurich.

The Friedelind affair resulted in a slight cooling of the cordial relations between Hitler and Winifred. Nonetheless, a senior SS officer in the Reich Ministry of Public Enlightenment and Propaganda reassured the anxious mother in 1942 that her daughter was not necessarily 'rotten to the core', and that 'if she was brought back under German influence' she would be able to find her way home. In the event, it was thirteen years before the now Americanised Friedelind returned to Bayreuth. With her Hollywood-blonde hair and scarlet lips, she posed for the press with her discredited mother in a 'demonstration of unity': a bizarre and belated application for readmission to the family.

Total war had been declared in the spring of 1943, and the extermination machines in the East were running at full speed. Wahnfried, ana-chronistically, seemed to be in a state of truce. That summer, *Die Meis-tersinger* was performed with stage sets by Wieland, with Wolfgang assisting Tietjen with the direction, and with Wilhelm Furtwängler and Hermann Abendroth conducting. In the early summer of the following year, however, the first results of the two brothers' training programmes, as well as their shared family devotion, could be clearly seen: each deliv-ered a Siegfried Wagner production to his respective theatre, to mark the seventy-fifth anniversary of their father's birth. An Old Franconian knightly play from Wolfgang in Berlin, a Grimm fairy tale from Wieland in Altenberg – both end in harmony and appeal to man's goodness and peaceable nature, while the world outside slowly collapses.

The 'inner consciousness' of the Wagners, by now thoroughly impreg-nated with fascism, managed to avoid taking notice of that outside world for a while longer, and Bayreuth enjoyed its last wartime festival in 1944, with *Die Meistersinger* again the principal attraction. It had to be some-thing cheerful because, as Winifred observed to the Führer as early as 1942, Tristan's cries of anguish in Act Three would be too much for many of the wounded or bereaved members of the audience to bear. Art had to be prevented from opening its audiences' eyes to life.

Shortly after that festival, as the likely outcome of the war became clear even to those who had resisted seeing it for so long, Wieland and Gertrud made a final visit to Hitler, prompted this time by Wieland's concerns about the physical survival of Wagner's work. He was hoping to retrieve the original scores of several operas (*Die Feen, Das Liebesverbot, Rienzi, Das Rheingold* and *Die Walküre*) that had been given to the Führer as a fiftieth birthday present by the Central Association of German Industrialists. Wieland was hoping to take them from Berlin to a safer home in Bayreuth. The couple were invited to a 'luncheon' which took place shortly before midnight, where Hitler had his arm in a sling after the assassination attempt of 20 July. They put their request to him, but Hitler assured them that everything was quite safe in his bunker: the scores have been missing ever since.

In August 1944, the theatres in Germany closed down. The men of the family – Wolfgang, Wieland and their brother-in-law, Bodo Lafferentz – were enlisted in Bayreuth to work in 'enterprises of importance to the war effort'. Wolfgang, as a technical assistant in the municipal building department, built emergency accommodation and dug trenches; Wieland was employed in a secret military research organisation managed by Bodo, whose administrative skills were highly prized. Finally, though, reality caught up with Wieland: he became friendly with a slave labourer working next to him, who was able to tell him one or two things about the true nature of the Third Reich. Wieland's 'silence' began at that time – a silence that seemed to become part of his nature, and which his family frequently complained about. A tendency towards self-hatred seemed to emerge at about the same time: 'You know that I don't like myself?' he once said to his wife, when he cut himself shaving. It seems likely that these negative feelings resulted from the disillusionment of this period, and from his guilt at his terrible error of political judgement.

In the first days of April 1945, American bombs started to fall on Bayreuth and partially destroyed Wahnfried, anticipating the arrival of ground troops by a few days. They gave the signal that every man should now look after his own, and this the Wagners certainly did. Wieland and Bodo extracted the manuscript score of *Tristan* from the family treasures and struggled through to their families in Nussdorf in a methane-fuelled car. Wolfgang remained in Bayreuth and triumphantly demonstrated his practical abilities. In a series of operations, he shipped the entire stash of family valuables – paintings, busts and archives – past the last Wehrmacht and SS patrols, and past the first Americans, taking them from an interim depository to their resting-place in Oberwarmensteinach. There, on 14 April – the day that Bayreuth was occupied – his first child, Eva, was born by candlelight. Eva's grandmother, Winifred, was only just dissuaded from following Sieglinde's example, and rushing out with the baby into the forest to seek protection from the approaching fury – not of Wotan, but of the Americans. Shortly afterwards Wolfgang, sifting through the rubble of Wahnfried, found Wagner's missing spectacles in the debris. Would he have tried them on, in order to understand that the narrow view through Wagner's glasses might be connected to the destruction all around? Was he not standing in the ruined hall of the Gibichungs? This was probably not the moment for such thoughts – but even as an old man, the blinkered Wolfgang claimed that 'we had no reason to put on sackcloth and ashes or to beat our breasts in repentance ... we did not have to seek any justification for what we did or failed to do.'

In the timber chalet at Nussdorf, close to the bank of Lake Constance, the families of Verena and Wieland huddled together. There was already a Lafferentz child, Amélie, and Verena was pregnant again. Gertrud had given birth twice: to Iris in 1942 while the family was still in Bayreuth, and to Wolf Siegfried in 1943. She too was expecting another child. In order to help cope with this household, Gertrud's sisters in Munich were called over to help: first the lively and efficient Elfried, and later on also the practical Lilo, who ceaselessly made puppets for the children. Supplies of tea, oat flakes, bacon and hosiery arrived for the family from New York: a little from Friedelind, but more from Maria 'Mitzi' Dernburg, an old family friend from Siegfried's day. She was a beautiful, cultivated Viennese, whom Wieland described as his 'artistic wet-nurse' because she had always brought some light into the 'total desert' of Wahnfried with her interesting art books.

Shortly before the feared French occupation, a brief episode occurred that might be seen as either funny or embarrassing – certainly as foolish. Bodo, the natural administrator, had secured a boat in which the families might escape across the lake to Switzerland; there, it was said, a family of Swiss Wagnerians would certainly help them. They left the house at night in a farm cart, not bothering to lock the doors because they believed they would never return. In the middle of the lake, however, they were stopped by patrol boats, rifles at the ready. Waving the *Tristan* score above their heads, Wieland and Bodo protested their good intentions, but to no avail – they were forced to turn back. Meanwhile, their neighbours had not been idle: they had stolen what was worth stealing and worse, had left a clothes rack full of Nazi uniforms. These life-threatening items were discovered and disposed of only hours before the French troops entered the house.

In May, when the radio reported the apocalyptic downfall of Hitler and his Reich, no one said a word. The daily routine continued, potatoes were planted and baby clothes knitted. When words became necessary once again, when the Germans were to be interrogated by the Allies, judged, de-Nazified, punished and re-educated, only Winifred could think of a solution that might have prevented the great disaster. In an interview with Associated Press, shortly before her tribunal hearing in 1947, she declared, pragmatically as ever: 'I often said to [Hitler] in a reproachful tone that his bachelor existence was not the right thing for him. If he'd had a home and a sensible wife there would have been no war.' It is obviously in her thoughts that this sensible wife should really have been her, since she had always been loyal and honest.

Ironically, the period between the collapse of the Third Reich and the reopening of the festival six years later was probably the happiest time that the Wagner family had ever known. The Festspielhaus, that nest of discord, had been confiscated, and Wahnfried was destroyed. The family, cemented together by their common culpability and especially that of the 'iron mother', had been stripped of its power. Now, at last, Winifred's four children stood solidly behind her: even Friedelind in New York did not wish her book of memoirs to be used as incriminating evidence, and Wieland completely failed to understand what his poor mother was being accused of. 'Surely you never did anyone any harm?' he wrote to her at the time. Wieland was now also getting on better with Wolfgang, who kept him informed of events in Bayreuth, the 'theatre of war'; indeed, he wrote in a letter to Mitzi that they were now as close as in the old days, 'before that trouble-maker from Berlin drove us ... apart'. There was still not much news from Friedelind. At first she sent parcels of provisions, in exchange for the *Tristan* sets which her brother sent her to use in a planned lecture tour. Nothing was said about Wieland's many fine oil paintings, mostly portraits, which she was supposed to have exchanged in America for food for the family; she probably sold them to keep herself solvent, just as she had done with the jewellery entrusted to her by the mother of Gottfried von Einem, her ex-fiancé, to keep it safe from the Nazis.

The self-awareness of the family undoubtedly developed during those days of Nibelung-like tragedy. Even when they returned to Bayreuth, they were impoverished, like all Germans, and they had no accommodation of their own. The 'Führer block', which had escaped the bombing, was occupied by the American Counter-Intelligence Corps. The family's response was to discover a new solidarity and unity. Gertrud, in a letter to Mitzi in 1948, sketched a genre picture of a poor but happy life with Wieland at the ruined house: 'Quite cosy. One grand piano, above it papa's picture, one sofa, one working desk and one round iron stove – that's all. True, all round there's rubble and dust, but we don't mind. Each noon I make Wieland's coffee on the iron stove and that makes us forget everyday matters a little. If, moreover, one can plan the festival and play *Parsifal* on the grand piano, one can be downright happy.'

At this stage, however, the so-called de-Nazification proceedings had not yet been completed. Bodo was in an internment camp in Freiburg and was being cleared by the testimonies of his former employees. Wolfgang profited from the fact that Hitler's interest and sympathy had always been focused on Wieland: he was quick to realise the strategic advantages of his 'third rank' among the siblings, which now allowed him to be a 'normal citizen'. His contacts with important figures of the Reich such as Hans Frank, the Governor-General of Poland, could scarcely be held against him, and nor could his personal views. It is true that when he heard his sister-in-law Gertrud express sympathy for 'those poor Poles' after their country's occupation, he had brutally and sneeringly mocked her for it – but what secular court would condemn him for that? Or for his slogan, brought back from military service: 'There's no such thing as emotions'? Wolfgang had learned how to wear the armour that was necessary to protect him in peacetime.

Things were more difficult for Wieland. He was said to have joined the Nazi Party at Hitler's personal request. Although no documentary evidence of this was ever produced, he had undoubtedly accepted presents from the Führer and had been seen as his protégé. The photos of Hitler that he had taken and sold were also uncomfortable evidence for him, scarcely suggesting resistance. Nor was he helped by his introverted, passive nature, which he shared with many 'non-political' artists in the Third Reich. Although Gertrud, as a teenager, had accused him of being a 'bad Nazi' because of his lack of interest in the Party, he was now dependent for exoneration on the testimony of others: Franz von Hoesslin, the conductor (himself politically tarnished), and the slave labourer to whom he had talked in the armaments factory. He was branded a 'beneficiary of Adolf Hitler' by Kurt Overhoff, his old teacher – himself an unrepentant Nazi from the outset – but the hearing eventually classified him as a 'fellow traveller'. Unlike his more practical brother, who had simply been an obedient soldier and could now roll up his sleeves and get back to work, Wieland struggled with the psychological trauma of being part of a generation that had sold itself to the Nazis. A photograph of the two brothers in front of their destroyed childhood home reveals this difference of psychological make-up: Wolfgang the 'doer' is cheerful, a pipe in his hand; Wieland the 'thinker' looks reflective. Their different responses to the situation are encapsulated in Goethe's words: 'The active person is always without a conscience; no one but the observer has a conscience.'

In the eyes of the public, however, the mother was much guiltier than the sons. Winifred, now fifty, had to answer to the court for her political 'marriage' to Hitler. Defiant, and dressed in a hairshirt style reminiscent of Mother Courage, she presented herself to the tribunals in Bayreuth in 1947. She was defended by Fritz Meyer, a prominent local politician and lawyer who had himself been classified as a 'fellow traveller': Meyer's plea veered off into such a sympathetic portrait of the 'revolutionary' Hitler that he had to be called to order. Winifred herself escaped being classified as an activist only after several appeal procedures; this would have meant compulsory labour, a ban on practising any profession, and a considerable loss of property. She was, however, accused of having remained silent when the Scholl siblings, the pianist Karlrobert Kreiten and a Munich music critic were murdered, and therefore classified as a 'Category Three lesser incriminated'. In her favour, it was acknowledged that she had helped people on many occasions. The testimony of the Jewish pianist Alice Ripper was crucial here: she had stated in an affadivit in 1946 that Winifred's 'energetic help' and 'noble human character and attitude' had not only saved her own life, but had also saved 'a large number of people from certain death'. Eventually, the judges found her to be culpable principally in 'having thrown the weight of one of the most famous names in cultural history into the balance in Hitler's favour'.

For Winifred, the main punishment was probably that she was forced to hand over the direction of the festival to her two sons, who were regarded as 'not incriminated'. The judges made this the condition under which the festival could continue under family management: Winifred eventually surrendered in January 1949, an act that completed her 'de-Nazification'. The court also banned her from speaking in public about Nazism; this 'muzzle', as she described it, effectively silenced her for almost thirty years. It was not until the centenary of the Bayreuth Festival in 1976 that this Pandora opened her box once again. Once she was seated in front of a television camera as a representative of 'the old days', she poured out her heart and declared her continuing personal loyalty to Adolf Hitler. At the age of almost eighty, she had scored one last point over her family, who had, ever since the end of the war, worked for a democratic Bayreuth purged of all fascist associations. She portrayed herself once more as Mother Courage, somehow likeable because of her very inflexibility. Her personality, if not her views, impressed the nation. Yet if the public was surprised, they should not have been: twenty years earlier, Wieland had claimed to the press of a now solidly established West Germany that his mother still believed in the 'final victory', but his comments seemed so outrageous that they were mistaken for a joke.

The years between 1945 and 1949, before the festival was finally handed over to the next generation, were ones in which everything was at stake for the family. Its inheritance and mission, its identity and possessions had never before been so endangered as in that interim period. Germany was seeking to come to terms with what it had done and to reorient itself; this process threatened the Wagners, like many other German families.

For the first time in many years, the family was forced to submit to the views of outside authorities. The Festspielhaus had been sequestrated and placed in trusteeship, first of the Americans, then of the town of Bayreuth. The new mayor of Bayreuth, Oskar Meyer, believed that 'the last twenty years of Bayreuth history must be deleted and expunged' because the Wagner family had abused its mission. The Bavarian government, too, supported the separation of Richard Wagner's work from his family, at least until early 1949. Various plans emerged during this period, all designed to prevent the re-emergence of the 'Wagner–German' ideology that had disfigured the house in the pre-war years. Ideas were floated of using the Festspielhaus as a place where the work of composers persecuted by the Nazis could be performed, or as a theatre for contemporary opera, or indeed as a 'German Salzburg' with a varied musical programme. All of these plans, however, would have required the nationalisation of the Wagner family assets, since the terms of Siegfried's will specifically ruled out any diversification of the musical repertoire. However, the civic authorities in Bayreuth opposed these plans for nationalisation, conscious that this would mean the town, as well as the Wagners, surrendering much of its existing power to the Bavarian authorities in Munich. A compromise was sought – in the shape of politically uncompromised Wagners.

This was the hour for the expelled Wagners – Franz Wilhelm Beidler in Zurich and Friedelind Wagner in New York – to come forward. In 1946, the mayor of Bayreuth issued an appeal to both of them to hold themselves in readiness to take over the festival. It will always remain a mystery that Friedelind failed to seize this historic opportunity, especially as she had written to the town that 'All my life I knew that one day I would have to undertake the burden of continuing the festival.' It is probable that Wolfgang, who had maintained close contacts with the civic authorities, had worked to prevent this competition from his sister. This can be the only explanation of his strategically defeatist attitude in 1947, when he declared that 'our family' was 'incapable' of resuming control of the festival. Perhaps Friedelind had also miscalculated: engrossed in the establishment of her own opera company, she did not believe that economic conditions would allow the Bayreuth festival to be re-established for another ten years. This was to underestimate the efforts of her brothers and the authorities. Later, Friedelind – using moral reasons to disguise what was probably an attack of cold feet – stated that she had not wanted to kick her Nazi family while they were down. However, her reluctance was probably also motivated by the realisation that, if she pushed herself forward, this would mean open and permanent hostility between herself and the united brothers, not to mention her mother. To be a pariah in Bayreuth would probably be even worse than foreign exile.

Beidler, on the other hand, responded enthusiastically to the town's appeal by submitting an extremely democratic proposal to establish a Richard Wagner Foundation. The Wagner family did not figure in this plan: they were to be expropriated. The Foundation would be administrated by a Board of Management with Thomas Mann (representing the 'positive Wagner tradition') as its honorary president: membership of this Board would include the mayor of Bayreuth as president, Beidler himself as secretary-general, and official delegates from UNESCO, the military and civic authorities of Bavaria, the future German Federal Republic, and Switzerland. A separate artistic committee would determine the programme of the festival: this would include both management experts and prominent figures from theatre and the visual arts, as well as from music (Schoenberg, Hindemith, Honegger and Karl Amadeus Hartmann were mentioned as possibilities).

This proposal, which in retrospect seems like the road to salvation, was brushed off very easily at the time by Wolfgang. Friedelind's restraint, too – as late as 1949 the Bavarian minister of culture wished her to play a major part in the festival – was greeted by him with a sneer. The Wahnfried brothers knew that the real threat to their position would come not from the victorious Allies or the Jewish councillors returning to Bayreuth, but from family and erstwhile colleagues. The most dangerous of these figures was Heinz Tietjen, whose correspondence with his old colleague Emil Preetorius reflected his continuing fury with 'that arsehole Wieland', and who made every effort to prevent the Wagner brothers from taking his old position.

Wolfgang's efforts to maintain the family's control of the festival were obvious, but Wieland was no less busy behind the scenes, despite being trapped in the French zone of occupation. He was making extensive enquiries about possible singers and conductors for the main festival, and was even toying with the idea of a 'Bayreuth abroad' in Monte Carlo, an enterprise in which all the family would have equal shares. Moreover, he was using his enforced leisure at Lake Constance to develop his theoretical understanding: to 'ponder with Gertrud on artistic problems', as he wrote to Mitzi, and to read some of the studies of psychoanalysis and art history whose circulation had been prohibited in the Nazi years.

The interests of the dynasty eventually coincided with political expediency. The adversarial Oskar Meyer's term as mayor of Bayreuth was expiring and Hans Rollwagen, who succeeded him in 1948, was favourably disposed towards the family. The Social Democrats had successfully run for office on the town council with the slogan that the house of Wagner and the town of Bayreuth belonged together, and the government of Bavaria, sensing that the tide was running against nationalisation, decided to relent. Winifred's resignation allowed the Festspielhaus to be released from its trusteeship, and the road was clear for the 'Wahnfried boys' – even though these boys, now in their mid-thirties, were immature and unsuited to high office in the eyes of their opponents, especially those in the Ministry of Education in Munich. The brothers were defiant, though: Wieland wanted to show the world that Wagner had not been a Nazi – to disprove Thomas Mann's argument that there was certainly 'a lot of Hitler in Wagner' – and Wolfgang was throwing himself with great verve into the administrative preparations.

The means he resorted to were not always entirely proper. In the early days of the return to family control, there were severe liquidity problems, and the man brought in to ease them – Gerhard Rossbach, a former Freikorps member now employed by an insurance company – had a rather shady reputation. Soon, though, a 'Society of Friends of Bayreuth' was set up from patrons in business and industry, and this provided the substantial financial support necessary. Once the Bavarian state and the broadcasting companies had pledged further subsidies, the problem was solved. The political climate of Adenauer's Germany was also conducive to the success of the festival, since the absence of a sense of guilt or desire for recrimination meant that the brothers did not need to be unduly restrained in their choice of artists. The festival was reinaugurated with a performance of Beethoven's Ninth Symphony conducted by Wilhelm Furtwängler, who like many of the other artists involved had been active during the Third Reich. There was a feeling that the resources that remained within Germany had to be used: complete ideological purity was a luxury that could not be afforded. 'The body of the German nation is bleeding from grave and deep wounds ... the only thing that remains intact is the German soul', the industrialist Moritz Klönne told the Society of Friends on the occasion of a Festspielhaus concert conducted by Herbert von Karajan, whose reputation was at least as suspect as that of Furtwängler. To that 'German soul' belonged, above all, the music of Wagner, the one thing that 'no one can take from us'.

The festival accepted the return of former Nazis as a matter of course: Heinrich Sesselmann, who had been the Festspielhaus accountant, now became head of personnel and financial administrator; Paul Eberhard returned to his old post as lighting expert. As Klönne lamented in his speech, it was only 'our revered Frau Winifred' who was legally prevented from involving herself with affairs in Bayreuth; nonetheless, Klönne continued, she would continue to be revered as 'the representative of this house, in which she so often appeared as mistress'. Indeed, the festival seemed to be more concerned with not offending former Nazis than with not employing them. As late as 1953, the chairman of the patrons, the Düsseldorf consul Franz Hilger, rejected with alarm the proposal that Thomas Mann should be invited to give a lecture during the festival: this 'highly controversial person' would be 'explosive', and there was no need to undergo that risk. Hilger was probably thinking about Mann's Munich lecture of 1933 – Wagnerians including the Bayreuth conductor Hans Knappertsbusch had signed a protest complaining about the 'derogatory image of Wagner' that it presented – or about his broadcasts from the USA with their criticisms of Hitler.

A visible symbol of the ideological continuity of Bayreuth is provided by the huge Wagner bust by Arno Breker, former court sculptor of the Third Reich, which was presented to Wolfgang and Wieland by the Society of Friends and displayed in the Festspielhaus park. Although German museums later rejected his work on ideological grounds, Breker continued his involvement with the festival until the late seventies; Liszt and his daughter Cosima were among those whom Breker turned into massive, fearsome heads. Only one person seemed to be genuinely happy with this late flowering of fascist aesthetics: the indefatigable Winifred, who sat for the sculptor in 1977. Her head was never displayed at the Festspielhaus, but was tactfully confined to the foyer of the Bayreuth Municipal Hall.

16

1951–66: the reign of the brothers

THE REOPENING OF THE FESTIVAL IN THE SUMMER OF 1951 attracted great international interest – to the delight of the festival management, who had issued a brochure entitled 'the world-wide discussion about Bayreuth', in the hope that the festival itself would spark just that. Much of the excitement was undoubtedly caused by Wieland's innovative ideas about styles of acting and scenery. This is not to say that everything in the festival was new and radical, contrary to the impression given by much of the media coverage. There was a very conventional production of *Die Meistersinger*, intended to pacify the traditionalists, and presided over by two veterans: Hans Carl Reissinger, Winifred's architect and Gertrud's uncle, was the designer, and Rudolf Otto Hartmann from the Munich State Opera the producer. Moreover, the presence of star conductors such as Herbert von Karajan, Hans Knappertsbusch and Joseph Keilberth ensured that musical standards were at least up to the high standards of the pre-war years. But Wieland's productions of *Parsifal* and *The Ring* offended the sensibilities of the traditional Wagnerians, to a degree scarcely imaginable today. The productions left them with no visual reminders of the pieces they thought they knew: they were confronted with emptiness and darkness, with just a few abstract topographical hints as to what was happening on the stage. The outrage was fierce. Old Wagnerians formed a 'Club for the Faithful Rendition of Richard Wagner's Works'; the management feared a financial deficit, for a time, as tickets were returned. As the first few festivals continued, however, the changes began to be accepted, and the long-postponed 'world-wide discussion' began to take place in both Europe and America. Bayreuth opened its doors to the press, to international celebrities, to trade unions and students. The new leaders of politics and industry were also present in force. The only conspicuous absentee was Federal President Theodor Heuss, but his reasons were aesthetic rather than political: he explained to the disgruntled festival management that he had always disliked being redeemed by Wagner.

It was not difficult to guess the political affiliations of those who protested most vehemently against the 'de-Wagnerisation of Wagner': these arguments were largely a rearguard action from unrepentant Nazis, and it was this very fact that made them easy for the festival to counter. Nothing seemed as dated as the Third Reich, during that period of post-war regeneration. Any argument coming from that quarter had little credibility, and the sporadic reservations that had been voiced from outside Germany soon began to die away. It was clever of the new masters to forestall discussion by displaying a poster indicating that they were well aware of the political dangers involved: 'In the interests of a smooth operation of the festival we request visitors kindly to refrain from conversations and discussions of a political nature on the Festspielhaus hill.' Tellingly, the poster added that well-known quotation from *Die Meistersinger*: 'It is art that matters here'. The same quotation had been used by Siegfried Wagner in the precarious political situation of 1925, to prevent the audience from singing the German national anthem after the opera's conclusion, as had happened the previous year. The guileless request to keep art and politics separate had not changed the course of events on that occasion, any more than Hitler's similar request in 1933. But now, in the strangely depoliticised context of post-war Germany, art that was non-political – even opposed to politics – was in the ascendancy.

Wagner would probably never again seem so free from ideology as during this short period of new beginnings, when his music seemed as liberated as the German people themselves wanted to be: there was no more talk of guilt. The exceptional, almost euphoric climate of co-operation was partly responsible; so too was the material poverty of the post-war years, which created a sense of the community binding together. The minimalism and restraint of Wieland's stage designs, though stemming from purely aesthetic choices, nevertheless seemed to fit with the mood of the times. The austerity on stage matched that visible in German towns, through whose empty spaces the wind whistled.

There are occasional periods in history where it suddenly seems possible that an artistic Utopia can be achieved; this experience often follows cataclysmic political change, as it did for the Russian avant-garde of the 1920s. Such periods only ever last for a short time, and post-war Bayreuth – now generally described as 'New Bayreuth' – was no exception to this. It only lasted nine years in its true form, the length of time it took Wieland to produce the Wagner repertoire on the green hill. After this, the style of the productions and the understanding of the works changed irrevocably.

The inner pathos of the new beginning was revealed in a brief scene during which family history seemed once more to be standing still and drawing breath. Shortly before the house lights went down for the first post-war performance – Wieland's production of *Parsifal* – the eldest Wagner grandchild unexpectedly stepped in front of the curtain to express what this moment meant to him. His improvised address was not recorded or transcribed, but everyone present remembers that it was very moving in its almost dreamlike quality. Along with its 'thanks' and 'beginning' and 'history', it gave a brief but penetrating insight into the tormented soul of a man burdened by his historical mission. It was as though this was the moment towards which Wieland had been moving ever since his birth: his reticence was now finally burst open by the abundance of hope and fear, triumph and remorse. It was one of those rare moments that transcends time – in which history seems briefly able to look itself in the face – as those present were instinctively aware. The rest was left to the music.

Wolfgang, too, had every reason to be satisfied. By 1953, the financial difficulties had been overcome, tickets were selling well, and the control of the two brothers had been accepted both by the festival's benefactors in Munich and the international media. The spirit of experiment allowed New Bayreuth to lead an aesthetic and ideological renaissance – 'director's opera' really began here – and it also made a significant contribution to the economy of the new West Germany. The family had proved strong enough to resist the attempts to dissolve it in 'the fluidity of the state'. After the long era of feudalism, Wahnfried was now ready to launch itself as a democratic enterprise.

The problems caused by the joint reign of the brothers were slower to emerge than the advantages, and for a long time the public was entirely unaware that any tension existed. In private, though, no sooner had family solidarity been restored in the face of external crisis than a slow process of division and dissociation began once again. It was not only the disagreements between the brothers; there were also family divisions between the sexes. It was as though the gods held the family's fate in a balance: as material success was piled into one side of the scales, private contentment was taken from the other.

To begin with, all went well. The rapid expansion of the family heralded a welcome diversification of interests. Wieland's family had increased with the birth of another two children: Nike, born in 1945 and described by her father as 'superfluous', and Daphne, born in 1946 and intended to be a boy. The family had moved into the patched-up Wahnfried in 1949; Wolfgang, invited to do the same, vehemently declared that 'No one will get me into that house again!' He preferred the small gardener's cottage next to the main building, despite the fact that his daughter Eva had been followed in 1947 by a son, Gottfried. In 1955, to everyone's surprise, he purchased a villa of his own, beautifully situated in a park next to the Festspielhaus; it had previously been owned by the festival's administrative director, Wilhelm Schuler. Verena's large family remained on Lake Constance because Bodo had business interests in the region: Amélie had been succeeded by Manfred (1945), Winifred (1947), Wieland (1949) and a little Verena (1952). They tended to see the Bayreuth branches of the family mainly during the festival. No one seemed to know what had become of the sidelined 'Swiss branch', although news must have reached Winifred of the birth of another Wagner great-grandchild: Franz Wilhelm Beidler's daughter Dagny Ricarda, born in 1942. Following the premature death of her mother in Berlin, she was brought up in Zurich by her father, who remarried soon afterwards. Dagny was a complete stranger to the Bayreuth families, and did not even visit the town until she was twenty-two.

*

If discord was already threatening the adults' fragile truce, then the youngest generation of Wagners was blissfully oblivious to this. Once again, Wahnfried provided a magical environment for childhood adventures – for the third and last time in its history. As in the original group of Wagner children, there was a single son surrounded by a swarm of sisters. Once again, Christmas and birthdays were extravagantly celebrated; large dogs scampered through the spacious rooms; the Festspielhaus, with its lighting gantries and stage traps, its musty costumes and its paint store reeking of turpentine, became once more the most exciting playground in the world. Wieland's quartet – Iris, Wolf Siegfried, Nike and Daphne – were often joined by their uncle's two fair-haired children, and the Wahnfried garden, complete with swing and sandpit under the tall trees, was enjoyed by them all. The peace was only occasionally disturbed, when little Gottfried furiously kicked the window-pane of the basement kitchen. The 1945 generation, Eva and Nike, trotted together down Richard Wagner Street to the elementary school where they were in the same class; the youngest of each branch of the family, Daphne and Gottfried, pursued their childish sexual explorations together in the dim light between the tall twin doors of the house. Soon, however, Wolfgang's children had to move into their splendid new villa, and the doors of Wahnfried closed behind them. Nearly forty years later, Wolfgang was still pleased with himself for having pulled off that coup, for having separated his family from Wieland's: 'Frederick the Great had his "Sans Souci" and I at last had my "Sans Famille",' he proudly recalled.

This move to the 'Villa Drexel' – as Wieland contemptuously called it, after his sister-in-law's maiden name – brought the rapprochement between the two families to an end. The fact that Wolfgang's children had already been offically forbidden to play with Wieland's, on the grounds that they would only learn 'bad words' from them, meant that relations could scarcely have been described as cordial in any case. The disobedient Gottfried was severely punished for disregarding this ban: to this day, he remembers the pain of being smacked by his father's crippled hand, which probably hit all the harder for having lost all sensation in a war injury. The children were driven still further apart by being sent to different boarding schools, and by Wolfgang's unwillingness to let his children play in the Festspielhaus. While Wieland's children were in and out of rehearsals and performances, witnessing all the triumphs and disasters, Eva and Gottfried were rarely seen there. Gottfried recalls now that there was a particular ban on watching Uncle Wieland at work; though he occasionally sneaked in for Wieland's rehearsals, this always ran a particular risk of punishment. None of this was known at Wahnfried, so no one could put in a good word for him.

Contact with the Lafferentzes was also rare, although Wieland's family had been on close terms with them before the move back to the restored Wahnfried. Despite the infrequency of meetings, a hard-to-define bond united these two branches of the family. Was this because little Amélie received her first language lesson from Wolf Siegfried, or 'Wummi' as he was known in the family? Or because Iris learnt to swim in Lake Constance? Or because the little trousers knitted by Grandma were constantly shuttling between the two families? Or because Nike used to clamber up on the knees of the huge Bodo Lafferentz, and Wummi's first toy car rattled over the cobbles of Nussdorf? Because Lake Constance created shared memories, despite being mostly veiled by mist? The oatmeal porridge and roast potatoes of the immediate post-war years had certainly created a shared warmth between the two families. For the children, this warmth was idyllic: it was a 'pre-political' era for them, with no sense of responsibilities to come, even if it was 'post-political' for their parents.

But now the Americans were occupying the former 'Führer block': they caused great excitement among the children, and gave them their first taste of chocolate. There were also occasional visits to Grandma's chalet, 'Exil', in Oberwarmensteinach, where, like a shadow from the distant past, Herr Tietjen would turn up to join her walks. (Tietjen was actually invited back to the Festspielhaus in 1959 by his old Oedipal enemy, Wieland, to conduct a production of *Lohengrin*.) Soon afterwards came the first potted chicken and the Mercedes at the door: the economic miracle, assisted by the re-opening of the festival, had swept into Bayreuth. The Wahnfried children were drawn into the town's modest world of jazz cellars, of ponytails, petticoats and ice-cream parlours, and of those grammar schools where they encountered social envy for the first time: 'You think you're something special, don't you, just because your name is Wagner?'

In point of fact, the Wagner great-grandchildren *were* 'something special' in the small-town mentality of Bayreuth – that was ensured by the festival itself. They would meet their Lake Constance relations in the darkness of the family box – the girls in their piqué dresses, the boys in their smart dark suits, surrounded by their parents in festive attire, the ladies mostly wearing off-the-shoulder gowns with an obligatory tulle stole, the gentlemen always the same in their dinner jackets. During the intervals the generations separated: Winifred held court in a small room in the royal block; Wieland and Gertrud rushed to the singers' dressing rooms to apportion praise and blame, if they were not receiving visitors in their primitive offices; and the children raced around the building, meeting either over Franconian grilled sausages in the canteen or over ices and Coca-Cola in the Festspielhaus restaurant, whose rustic appearance was half-heartedly concealed by folds of material on the walls. The only absentees from the first nights were Wolfgang's children and gazelle-like wife, Ellen. Gottfried later complained that they were always packed off on holiday when the hustle and bustle began, and Ellen was always described in the family as 'shy'. One never knew exactly what was happening: was Wolfgang trying to shield his family from the kind of gossip of which his mother was so fond?

While preparing to re-open the festival, the brothers had agreed that Wieland would assume responsibility for artistic matters – direction, stage sets and costumes – while Wolfgang would attend to the vast range of practical matters that had to be dealt with. This division of labour had advantages for both brothers: Wieland was able to realise his artistic ambitions without apparent hindrance, while Wolfgang could watch how things were developing from his familiar position in his brother's shadow. Had he been in charge of the artistic direction, he certainly would not have risked the theatrical scandals with which his brother instantly polarised the public, seeming, at least temporarily, to jeopardise the whole enterprise. From the outside, their co-operation seemed entirely harmonious. The complementary nature of their talents appealed to the public and it was obvious that, despite being so dissimilar, they liked one another. Wolfgang tended to orient himself to fit in with his more difficult elder brother, as he had done on their now legendary pre-war trip to Italy. They enjoyed the game of avoiding discussing awkward matters in public: 'Why don't you talk this over with my brother?' became a familiar refrain.

The perception that they complemented each other well was enhanced by their similar 'Wagner features'. Even though Wieland was a little flabby and penguin-like, with his feet turned inwards, and Wolfgang was smart, slim and athletic, press photographers frequently confused the two: Wolfgang's picture was captioned as Wieland, and vice versa. These everyday mistakes revealed the collective desire to see the brothers as having one heart and one soul, one nature split into two earthly forms, like the heavenly pair of twins amongst the stars. Bayreuth had a new family myth, to displace the discredited matriarchs: Wagner's grandsons were seen as latter-day versions of those other twins linked by alliterative names, Romulus and Remus.

The progress from one stage of the myth to the next was marked by the sacrifice of Winifred: the need to purge had been satisfied. However, Winifred's removal from power – resignation would be too elegant a word for this enforced departure – only solved the issue as far as the outside world was concerned, by removing what was politically offensive. Numerous internal family problems still had to be settled. How, for example, was Siegfried's widow to live in future? It was agreed that a tenancy relationship would be established between the generations of the family. Winifred, whose legal ownership of all the Wagner assets was still inalienable, would rent the Festspielhaus to her children in return for maintenance payments. This would simultaneously ensure her financial independence, and preserve her domestic supremacy. This seemed straightforward enough, until the question was asked: which children? Under the terms of her husband's will, all four children had equal rights, a view of the situation confirmed by a meeting of sponsors in 1949. The tenancy agreement, however, was concluded only with the two sons, which seemed to be a clear breach of the will's intentions. Winifred, trained to think in masculine terms, had not thought it necessary even to inform Verena or Friedelind. The bitterness of the former at her mother's betrayal is clear from her complaint that 'no notice whatever is taken of us and it does not even remotely occur to anyone that, along with our love for the Bayreuth business, we also have rights, which it is your duty to defend.'

We have heard similar complaints from the daughters of Cosima: now, as then, they were made to little effect. The sisters had lost out because the brothers had clearly been part of the conspiracy, and because the agreement, concluded behind the women's backs, was already in force. Siegfried's will had simply been ignored. Wolfgang defended the brothers' action by pointing to the right of the stronger: they had the 'best prerequisites', and had shown the 'greatest application and zeal' to keep the festival in family hands. The familiar pattern had repeated itself: first of all the daughters are sent to finishing school, then it is found, to everyone's surprise and regret, that they lack 'the best prerequisites' for a career in the theatre. The sons, whose gifts are equally unproven, are the beneficiaries of biological and social custom: there is an automatic assumption of male hegemony. Even the most cursory look back at the female contribution to the festival should have convinced the family of the error of this policy. Both Cosima and Winifred had presided successfully over the festival for many years. The former had admittedly received a musical education which surpassed that of most men of her day, but Winifred had no more 'prerequisites' for running the festival than her daughters: although her educators had credited her with a good mind and some commercial talent, she was sent to domestic science school rather than anything more academically challenging. Like Cosima, whose severely classical hairstyle she imitated, Winifred denied her daughters the chance to realise their talents as she herself had done. With one swift blow, she severed the thread of life that connected them to Bayreuth.

The family dispute did not end there, though. The sisters were merely the immediate victims of the carve-up between the mother and her sons – others were soon to follow. The resumption of the festival was a catalyst for renewed hostilities between the brothers, suspended since the war. The conflict, probably inevitable anyway, was significantly worsened by the behaviour of Winifred. Deprived of her potential husbands, she now found her own 'masculine' strength constantly yielding in the face of male demands. She made crucial mistakes in the treatment of her two strong sons: the self-willed, impressive one whom she found difficult to handle, and the adroit, efficient one who had inherited her business acumen but whose shrewdness vastly surpassed her own. The elder son demanded sole artistic control, a right which his experience should already have earned him, but the younger son held firm for an equal share.

Having already gone down the dubious path of ignoring Siegfried's will, Winifred could have followed this policy to the bitter end; but instead, she preferred to create a façade of justice, and endowed the two men with equal rights and responsibilities. This decision, sure to lead to conflict, was based on the questionable and belated application of maternal sentiment: Wolfgang would help his brother, Wieland needed him, one must treat one's children equally. In preliminary talks between the brothers, Wieland had tried to convince Wolfgang that joint control was an unworkable nonsense. He asked him to leave the artistic side of the business to him, but this only ended in acrimony. One cannot really blame Wolfgang, however, for not backing down gracefully: he was desperate to escape his childhood role, not to be regarded as the perpetual Number Two. He was too arrogant to foresee that, whatever their official status, employees such as Paul Eberhard would regularly approach Wieland with the complaint 'Herr Wagner, your kid brother … '; and that the history of New Bayreuth would mercilessly label him as what he really was – a highly efficient organiser and an untalented stage director.

Winifred, too, was utterly blind to these inevitable consequences. With a single signature, she unknowingly condemned her sons to perpetual conflict: henceforth, they would act out the roles of Alberich and Mime, of Fafner and Fasolt.

The brothers' first two years in charge of the festival were marked by a change in its ethos – from temple to workshop. Despite the outward conflicts, the festival itself ran in a co-operative and productive fashion. Wieland's artistic assurance was growing fast: he was increasingly convinced that he was on the right road. Ironically, it was at this point that he had to surrender his sole artistic control, since 1953 was the year in which it was Wolfgang's turn to stage one of their grandfather's works: he made his festival debut with *Lohengrin*. Wieland made one last effort to free himself from his brother's threatening shadow when, despite the presence of Gertrud's sister, he gave full vent to his bitterness and anger.

Wieland's violence could not be explained by overwork alone. He was an artistic perfectionist: frequently unhappy with the discrepancy between his ideas and the reality on stage, or with the impossibility of obtaining a particular shading of colours with the primitive lighting equipment available. He often unleashed his fury on his staff, sacking employees for trivial offences; on one occasion he furiously overturned his crammed desk because there was no carbon paper. Festival staff started to use the term 'festival corpses' to describe those who had fallen foul of his temper. There were 'kitchen corpses', too. Woe betide the domestic staff if something went wrong with a meal: plates would fly through the air and doors would slam. One day, when Wieland marched down the chestnut avenue back to the Festspielhaus after such a scene, the Silesian cook shook her head, hands on her hips, and declared – feminist before her time – 'Better no man than one like that!'

Wolfgang had no intention of becoming a 'festival corpse', however. He stuck to his course and delivered *Lohengrin* and other festival productions, undeterred by his brother's moods. But his bitterness increased: he tried to understand the reasons for the lack of recognition for his own work, and for the relentlessly competitive relationship with his brother. He found that reason in Gertrud, his sister-in-law; she was now the element in the family constellation that disturbed him most deeply. There had been no problem with the young girl who had always been part of the Wahnfried crowd of youngsters, and who looked up shyly to Frau Winifred; indeed, during their time together at the Berlin State Opera, and again on holidays in Nussdorf, a real camaraderie had developed between them. Gertrud, who had long come to regard the Wagners as her own family, was spontaneous and creative, affected by sudden enthusiasms and sensitivities, but always uncompromising in aesthetic matters. Everyone in the Wagner family seemed to get on well with her, and Winifred – mindful of her husband's history – had been pleased that her relationship with the schoolboy Wieland had forestalled any chance of homosexual tendencies emerging.

Unlike the Wagner daughters, however, Gertrud had pursued her own artistic training with determination. Her passion was for dance and choreography: she helped Wieland with these aspects of his first productions in Altenburg and Nuremberg, and later they pondered together over ideas for Bayreuth. It was an unusually fruitful partnership between complementary creative talents. Wieland's primary talent was for design: 'In my case the musical gifts have shifted to the visual,' he remarked to Gertrud during his period of score study with Overhoff, and it was indeed his interpretation of the action in terms of colours and shapes, light and darkness, that was the most significant aspect of his theatrical style. Gertrud, for her part, was responsible for the movement of the body in space: she passed on to her husband the results of her training in the expressive dance movement of the twenties. It was from her that he learnt to direct movement on the stage – as Wolfgang accurately observed, she 'activated' his productions.

She also 'activated' the ponderous and melancholy Wieland himself. Their children were familiar with the scene: Wagner's music would be playing on records – while Wieland was sitting in an armchair with the piano score, Gertrud would be lying down, striding around, leaping and twisting through the room until she had found the right solution for an acting problem. In life, too, it was Gertrud who initiated movement: unlike Wieland, she was not weighed down by family history. She was the 'engine' in their relationship, driving Wieland onwards into a break with tradition, into open waters. 'We'll manage it,' was her attitude – to which Wieland generally replied 'And I put my head on the line for it.'

It was this artistic marriage, rather than any personal objection to Gertrud, that troubled Wolfgang in the 1940s; it got in the way of the fraternal union of which he had been dreaming. Surely it was he who had been chosen to be his brother's confidant: only with him would Wieland succeed. These worries, of course, could never be precisely articulated, but they undoubtedly caused problems for the festival management. One thing on which the brothers had always agreed was their vow that 'The womenfolk will stay out of our business!' This determination was obviously motivated in part by a deep-seated and general misogyny, but it was also the product of a specific desire to avoid the interference of that ambitious, domineering type of woman in which the Wagner family seemed to specialise: first Cosima, then Winifred, then their sister Friedelind. Did Wieland realise that, for Wolfgang, Gertrud was becoming precisely that sort of woman, ambitious to make her own mark on the festival?

Wieland always involved her as a matter of course in his work at the Festspielhaus, and from the second season onwards she was listed in the programme book as the choreographer. Her precise contribution to the productions, both artistic and financial, always remained concealed under Wieland's name – he, too, had his ego to maintain – but on the occasions where the operas gave her an opportunity to put on an individual show, she was sensationally successful. In the 1954 *Tannhäuser*, the rhythmic sexuality of her 'Bacchanal' shocked the audiences: her penitent pilgrims dragged themselves asynchronously across the stage, and the guests at the singers' contest entered the hall of the Wartburg with movements somehow gliding above the music. The flower maidens in *Parsifal* were created again and again: at one time floating impressionistically, at another solid and plant-like. The fugal brawl in several productions of *Die Meistersinger*, the electrifying sailors with their foursquare dance in the 1959 *Flying Dutchman*, and the procession of women to the Minster in the 1958 *Lohengrin* all bore her unique stamp. She rehearsed countless individual ensemble and solo scenes, and found new choreographic sequences to accompany each new interpretation of a piece. In contrast to her husband's predominantly symmetrical approach to direction and design, she loved to make use of diagonal lines, and frequently emphasised movements on unstressed beats of the bar to achieve a kind of 'choreographic syncopation'.

It was the presence of Gertrud that made the oath of blood-brother-hood hard to put into practice. To make matters worse, her behaviour at the Festspielhaus was frequently not very tactful or considerate. Her mind was totally focused on her work: she was aware of her capabilities and of Wieland's need for her, perhaps that he was even somewhat dependent on her aesthetic judgement. Her position in the court of Wahnfried had entirely displaced any loyalty to her own family, and she had perhaps become slightly haughty as a result. Because she had been involved with the Wagners for so long, she regarded Wolfgang as her 'kid brother' too. It was understandable that he – not to mention the excluded sisters whom she had entirely displaced from Wahnfried – should view her influential position with dismay. But none of them could do anything to undermine Gertrud, unless Wieland himself was a party to the plot. Given the nature of their working relationship, this was unlikely. It was not only in Bayreuth that they worked together: Gertrud had also assisted on Wieland's foreign productions of works as diverse as Wagner's *Rienzi*, Gluck's *Orfeo*, Beethoven's *Fidelio*, Orff's *Antigone* and *Comoedia de Christi Resurrectione*,

Bizet's *Carmen*, Verdi's *Aida* and *Otello*, and Strauss's *Salome* and *Elektra*. Wieland's work could not be imagined without her: the attack, if attempted at all, had to come through her private life.

Despite the strength of their artistic collaboration, the marriage between this difficult man and this impulsive woman had never been an easy one. The equilibrium between them had recently been under particular strain, because of the resumption of their joint work at the festival and the domestic problems at Wahnfried. Both partners knew that they were in a rut, and that they had to free themselves from it in order to develop further as individuals. Only emancipation from Gertrud could enhance Wieland's self-esteem; Gertrud, for her part, needed to escape from the oppression which her marriage entailed, and on which she blamed her numerous mysterious allergies. For Wieland, marriage had never precluded erotic escapades: these resulted not only from his consistent rejection of the bourgeois model of marriage, but also from a belief that a man – an artist in particular – had a natural right to exercise sexual privileges. It is also possible that his wife's change of role to that of mother had become a problem for him, as it does for many husbands: in his eyes, a woman who was a lover should not breastfeed children or spend time knitting. Whenever he found Gertrud engaged in either of these activities he would viciously criticise and mock her. The fact that this caused the young mother's milk to dry up – particularly inconvenient during wartime – is evidence of her hypersensitive nature and tendency to react psychosomatically, as well as of her dependence on Wieland. He solved the problem by finding himself other, less complicated partners. The fact that he found them near to home testifies, almost touchingly, to his inner guilt about the liberties he was taking: he frequently excused himself by claiming that 'I'm not taking anything away from you.' Gertrud had long refused to see the evidence of her husband's double and triple life. She preferred to assume the best and it took a Feydeauesque *in flagrante* incident to convince her otherwise. Her attitude to marriage was in any case quite different: to her, it was a sacred part of her life, deeply rooted in her emotions and in the law. It did not matter, though, how often she challenged her husband, like an angry Fricka; it made no difference to his actions. Her numerous vague ailments were her only form of escape from this situation.

Wieland would argue that erotic emancipation from their 'childish' marriage was necessary for her, too, and he would frequently urge her in that direction. 'You need another man,' he would tell her frequently, booking hotels for her in Rome or Munich, taking her to the railway station and driving her into the arms of prominent artists – only a mixed pleasure for this woman who still felt so strongly tied to him. She required the help of a psychoanalyst in order to fortify herself sufficiently to allow her to continue her roles at the festival and at Wahnfried. The children noticed this change in her, towards the end of the 1950s: 'Mama has become cheeky,' they would say. Everyone concerned realised that it was really Wieland who needed psychoanalysis, but he refused to contemplate the possible change of lifestyle that this might entail. He willingly accepted the jokes about the fact that it was his wife who appeared to be breaking out: after all, he was using her search for her individuality to buy his own freedom. Gertrud would later see her relationship with Wieland as a 'struggle for love', as a sincere attempt to preserve this exceptional partnership. It was true that he would never really let her down: he protected her as though he was perpetually grateful to her, and he showered her with gifts, from Italian designer clothes to a house on the island of Sylt which he only afforded by going into debt. Though he was constantly intimidated by her moral puritanism, and vexed by her theatrical perfectionism, he was always aware of Gertrud's value to him: from an artistic point of view, he was always aware that he had a valuable horse in his stable.

'Now at last one can live with you!' she exclaimed towards the end of this process of mutual emancipation. But the irony of fate decreed otherwise. 'I break out in order to be able to live' was Wieland's slogan. This applied to art and politics as well as life: to his aggressive abandonment of the museum curator's approach to music drama, and his denunciation of his mother's fascism, as well as his new romantic liaison. This latest breach of the marriage contract could no longer be concealed from the public, for this time Wieland found a woman who – to put it in vulgar terms – was probably his type at last. With her slim, flat-chested, almost masculine figure, and her red hair and long legs; with her artistic malleability, not to mention the 'sweet bird of youth' which arrived with her on the festival hill, the singer Anja Silja was almost designed to create a mid-life crisis for Wieland. The girl, proclaimed as a child prodigy, had auditioned at Bayreuth a number of times, but Wieland had always avoided being present on these occasions. But when the Viennese singer Leonie Rysanek cancelled her engagement as Senta for the 1960 production of *The Flying Dutchman*, Wolfgang Sawallisch, the conductor of the production, urged Wieland to hear Anja for himself. She was engaged on the spot: after all, she matched to perfection Wieland's dream of a new, slimmed-down type of Wagnerian singer. Besides, with her childlike appearance on the stage, and her ability convincingly to convey the experiences of somnambulism and ecstasy, she fitted his idea of Senta to perfection. Gertrud was equally enthusiastic about her, and would remain so when, two years later, she rehearsed the 'Dance of the Seven Veils' with her in Stuttgart: a dance which Anja performed as probably no Salome ever had.

The liaison between Wieland and Anja lasted until his death six years later. From her first appearance in Bayreuth onwards, she almost invariably sang under Wieland's direction – both in Bayreuth (Elsa, Venus, Eva, Freia) and outside (Salome, Isolde, Brünnhilde, Elektra, Desdemona, Leonore, Lulu, Marie). A new working partnership had been born, one which naturally enough soon excluded Gertrud. It kept the gossip columns busy: there was something titillatingly anarchistic and anti-bourgeois about the couple – something of Professor Higgins and Eliza, something of Tristan and Isolde, something of Doctor Schön and Lulu. It polarised the theatrical world, and tore the family apart. There was no more talk of artistic comradeship at the Festspielhaus: everyone was busy taking sides. Anyone who was against Anja – who had a cheeky Berlin tongue and whose singing, with a tendency towards shrillness, was open to criticism – risked being sacked by the autocratic Wieland. The director surrounded himself with an Anja clique, whose motives were not always entirely noble and selfless. Hostile fronts also formed within the family. To Winifred, the redhead was simply 'the whore from the Kurfürstendamm', a remark which completed her estrangement from Wieland. Wolfgang probably had similar views, but was careful not to voice them in the vicinity of the touchy Wieland, whose fame was growing with every new production.

Gertrud had been robbed of everything by this rival in the bedroom and on the stage. She tried every possible strategy: she cried and fought, she clung on to him and pushed him away, she burnt the love letters of their youth and took to travelling, she sought consolation in building plans and she threw his money out of the window. Nothing helped. The children meanwhile, now grown into immature teenagers and living in various student rooms in Tübingen, Berlin, Munich and Vienna, were caught up in the vortex of events, faced with the unattractive choice of isolating their father or causing pain to their mother. 'Believe me, Anja is not very different from you,' he once told his daughters, who were only a few years younger than the singer, seeking understanding and help. He did not want to be regarded as a pariah, just because he had had to 'break out' to live his life. The children were instinctively aware that their father's pain over the family break-up was deep and unresolvable, unlike their mother's, because he had brought it on himself, like a guilty–innocent Wotan. But despite this understanding, they could not connect with him. He was almost always away on productions with Anja – in Stuttgart, Brussels, Cologne, Geneva, Naples, Copenhagen, Paris, Milan, Rome, Frankfurt, Hamburg. When he was there to talk, discussions were almost always abandoned with mutual recrimination, or reduced to businesslike exchanges. The children eventually wrote to their father to ask him to end the terrible state of affairs with a clean divorce.

Anja's attempts to move into Wahnfried and the house on the island of Sylt were clear enough; Wieland had not been able to prevent them, any more than he could avoid becoming a victim of her artistic temperament. If he did not obey her, and insisted on sticking to his wife and children, she would blackmail him by refusing to sing – ideally on the opening night of a new production. Anja did not understand that, having come from a marriage, he did not want to marry again: to do so would have falsified the whole meaning of their affair for him. This was the motive behind his rejection of divorce, which he communicated to his family soon after his children had suggested this final solution.

A final solution nevertheless came – but not in the way anticipated. In the summer of 1966, Wieland developed an illness which was originally diagnosed as a tumour on the heart, but which was later found to be masking the cancer of the lung which must have long been rooted in this body. Just as, in a symbolic sense, his life was breathless – caught between the demands of two women, struggling with financial insecurity and fraternal rivalry, and desperately pursuing a frantic schedule in which he lived in fear of self-repetition – now he had no breath left in reality. Death only rarely reflects the problems of life so closely: it was appropriate that it was Wieland's breath that was cut off, now he was struggling to give voice to his conflicting emotions, and that his heart should have been struck, at a time when he was torn between the too-many people whom he wanted to love and who loved him. 'Believe me, children, I am content to die,' he told his daughters when they visited him in hospital. Happily, this is disproved by the fact that even on his sickbed, Wieland was planning new productions, including a *Don Giovanni* which he hoped to realise with his new-found spiritual brother, the conductor Pierre Boulez.

The official tributes to Wieland concentrated on his role in the continuation and revival of the festival: he was presented above all as a Wagner, as the successor of Richard and Siegfried. The funeral ceremonies emphasised the Wagner tradition rather than the ways in which Wieland had broken away from this tradition; they followed the same lines as the commemorations of Siegfried and Cosima on the green hill. The organiser selected herself: Gertrud, the widow, reclaimed the exclusive matrimonial rights that she had had to share for so long. No one contested her authority to determine what was appropriate: Wolfgang had wanted to hold a memorial ceremony during the following year's festival, but he gave in to the wishes of his sister-in-law who wanted the commemoration to form part of the burial ceremony. She chose the orators, who included the philosopher Ernst Bloch, and the conductor, Pierre Boulez, as well as the place, backstage at the Festspielhaus. Wolfgang arranged to assemble the festival orchestra, all of whom agreed to return, and hung the wreaths on the back of the iron curtain so that they formed a huge floral wall. Family disagreements emerged only over the protocol of dealing with Wieland's body. His four children insisted that they should spend time, alone and in silence, with their father's coffin at Wahnfried, where it had been transferred from Munich. Winifred complained bitterly that she should be part of this occasion, but remained excluded: it was only at the public ceremony that she was allowed to pay her last respects to her son. By contrast with his mother's belligerent attitude, Wolfgang was diplomacy personified, slipping graciously back into the role of assistant, the position he had occupied in the days when the brothers got on better.

The joint directorship of the festival had not in fact functioned properly for many years, even if Wieland's funeral was not the appropriate occasion to say so. Since 1953, when Wolfgang first began to establish himself as a director on the festival stage, Wieland had found it virtually impossible to collaborate with him. Matters were made worse by the terms on which the festival had to function, which virtually enshrined the competition between the brothers. Because the repertoire from which the festival could choose was very limited, the same works had to be continually represented. This meant that each brother, sooner or later, would have presented each work, which meant that critical comparisons were bound to be made between their interpretations – the Wagnerian merry-go-round soon turned into a rather nightmarish roller-coaster for the brothers. The most significant works had been grabbed by Wieland in the first two years of the reopened festival: *The Ring* and *Parsifal* in 1951, *Tristan* in 1952. Wolfgang made his debut with *Lohengrin* in 1953, followed by Wieland's *Tannhäuser* in 1954, Wolfgang's *The Flying Dutchman* in 1955, Wieland's *Die Meistersinger* in 1956 and Wolfgang's *Tristan* in 1957. In 1958 Wieland produced *Lohengrin* and in 1959 he produced a *Dutchman*; the reason for the change in the sequence was that Wolfgang was working on a new *Ring* for 1960. By 1960, then, both brothers had almost completed the canon of Wagner's mature works, though Wolfgang had still not produced *Tannhäuser, Die Meistersinger* or *Parsifal*.

The differences between the brothers were clear from every public statement they made: whereas Wieland, in one of his numerous self-justificatory letters to the outraged Society of Friends of Bayreuth, described himself as a person 'who is always deadly serious about art', Wolfgang at the same time confessed that 'I just look for a middle way. I am not a radical.' One can only imagine what co-operation between such dissimilar temperaments must have been like: two bulls under a single yoke, one furiously pulling, the other comfortably chewing the cud! It was inevitable that the cart would get stuck, quite apart from the injuries the bulls would cause each other. This is why Wieland, in tandem with his erotic 'breaking out', attempted to stage a professional one: in 1960, he applied for the post of Intendant at the German Opera in Berlin. Away from Bayreuth, outside the stultifying enforced co-operation with his brother, he would be released from the Wagner straitjacket, and able to test his creative powers on the likes of Verdi, Strauss, and Berg. But while other roads to freedom opened for him, the road to Berlin was blocked: the job went to a rival, Gustav Rudolf Sellner.

Wieland remained chained to Bayreuth and his brother. But perhaps his mission there was not yet at an end. In contrast to what Wolfgang was later to assert in his memoirs – that Wieland's creative powers were 'exhausted' by this stage – he brought about an exciting second phase of New Bayreuth. Abstractionist tendencies remained, but they were accompanied by an increased interest in visual symbols which brought out new aspects of the works: his 1962 *Tristan* emphasised the sexual imagery of the piece; his 1963 *Meistersinger* was like a boorishly comic piece of Shakespeare; and his 1965 *Ring* powerfully expressed the political force of the work, with a stage design dominated by walls and grilles whose significance was entirely lost on his contemporaries.

Wieland Wagner's influence as a director, a costume designer, a set designer and a lighting director was overwhelming, as his obituaries testified. Most revealed shock at his premature death. 'Nothing makes sense any more,' lamented the composer and music critic Wolf Rosenberg, who had championed Wieland, especially among those Jewish musicians who still harboured reservations about Bayreuth. In view of his fame and artistic reputation, it is surprising that he did not become more relaxed: indeed, his irritability seemed only to increase with the years. Most of the time, he was able to display an exquisite courtesy and patience, even (especially) towards the declared opponents of his theatrical style. One thing, however, proved impossible to cope with and progressively robbed him of his strength: the shadow attached to his heels, the demon who sucked the blood from his veins in the full light of day, the sprite he had crushed a hundred times and who always returned to his feet – his brother.

'Wieland and Wolfgang, Wolfgang and Wieland. A fraternal wrestling match about the status of New Bayreuth' was the headline of the 1960 festival survey by Johannes Jacobi, the conservative critic of *Die Zeit*. Without realising the deeper meaning of his words, Jacobi put his finger on the pulse of what was happening: 'Wolfgang exploits the opportunity of every successor for smoothing out the excesses of the first attempts. Thus he bent the flat "Wieland disc" into a shallow bowl . . . meaning that it can revolve and be dismantled.' Someone else picked on the same point with greater perspicacity. The aged Viktor Valentin Rosenfeld, refugee from Freud's Vienna, psychoanalyst and musicologist, emerged, pale with excitement, from the première of Wolfgang's *Ring*. Rushing over to Gertrud he almost screamed 'But this is murder. He has murdered his brother. Wolfgang has taken Wieland's disc and broken it in pieces!'

The circular 'disc' had become a visual symbol of Wieland's Bayreuth, just as Preetorius's slate-grey rock had been for Tietjen's regime. The disc – also known as the 'hot plate' or 'Wieland's plate' – was a fundamental element of Wieland's set designs. It gave expression to his symmetrical, centralised thinking about the dramas, and allowed the expansion or contraction of psychological space to be powerfully externalised. Although Wolfgang had shyly and half-heartedly copied his brother's stylistic peculiarity in his earlier productions, he now prepared to inflict a heavier blow – quite innocently, and yet with the helpless defiance of one from whom too much is expected. Wieland had demanded that he take over the *Ring* at much too late a date, and Wolfgang had to defend himself against this aggressive act. With a great deal of trouble, he persuaded his brother to grant him an extra year's preparation. He could not know that he was the indirect victim of his sister-in-law, Gertrud, who had criticised Wieland's *Ring* as having 'got old' and thus provoked him into destructive self-recrimination. Wolfgang mobilised his forces by having his own *Ring*-disc built, with the aid of a huge steel structure: *his* disc could be divided into several segments which, by being moved against one another, created new spaces for action. The circular shape always remained visible, though often in a distorted form. It was a massive feat of stage technology, demanding a huge quantity of steel, power and human strength; Wolfgang's subconscious was not squeamish when it came to dismembering his brother's achievement. Wolfgang moreover made use of his new technological fetish: a mechanically controlled xenon light which permitted impressive large-scale projections, as if he wished to destroy the subtle gradations characteristic of Wieland's lighting designs. Festival commentaries reported that the structure, which had grown from a symbolic disc into a complex, multi-purpose construction, revealed itself as an 'oversized and vicious monster', which provided a 'theatre of its own' at nearly every performance when its technology went haywire.

The comedy stemming from Wolfgang's hubristic idea does not conceal the fact that this was the climax of a family drama: a spiritual fratricide conducted in the full glare of the public gaze, and legitimated by the terms of the family's legal agreements.

The copying, bending and breaking of the *Ring*-disc was the most visible aspect of Wolfgang's rebellion against his inner dependence on Wieland, but this symbolic murder had been preceded by many years during which the elder brother's intellectual property had been appropriated and exploited. In order fully to understand this psycho-drama, one would have to imagine Picasso having a close relative, also a painter, who was sufficiently gifted to use, copy, and assimilate to his own requirements the style and pictorial inventions of the original Picasso, without the authentic artist being able to claim any copyright on his ideas. Just as it is not difficult to imitate Picasso, so it was not difficult to imitate Wieland Wagner. In this case, moreover, there was another change in the transition from original to copy, one that can only be judged as a misunderstanding on Wolfgang's part. Wieland's disc was not an object but a spiritual symbol, the image of an idea. Wolfgang, on the other hand, treated it as a material object that could be dissected and reassembled at will. This objectification deprived the symbol of its mystical function, reducing it to an earthly artefact, to its practical application. When, more than twenty years later, he commended Wieland's disc as 'ideal' theatrically and even more so financially – no storage costs, no labour costs and extremely cheap considering it provided the major part of the scenery for four operas – he himself testified to his misconception.

Because 'New Bayreuth' had become a general label for anything abstract, the general public was unable to perceive this crucial difference. Wolfgang similarly mistreated Wieland's trademark 'empty space'. Wieland's empty stage was a framework for slow, statuesque movements – the work of Gertrud – and was the visual expression of an 'overall choreography', a system of tensions. By contrast, Wolfgang's empty stage – in his *Tristan* for example – was filled according to operatic convention, and thus produced yawning boredom. (One of Wolfgang's stage directions to Theo Adam, his 1963 Wotan, rather cruelly found its way into the press. When the singer asked how, given his noble role, the director wished him to cross the large area of the stage, Wolfgang gave a rather unilluminating reply: 'Somewhat like a god, Herr Adam, somewhat like a god.')

Wolfgang got away with his protracted exploitation of his brother's artistic ego, his parasitical appropriation of his ideas, only because the perceptions of the public were blunted by the simplistic formula: two brothers, one Bayreuth! Who troubled with the fine distinctions between the two? Was it not wonderful that the outward features of the new Wagner performances resembled one another? It was only the closest circle who realised the family tragedy contained in this very similarity. Moreover, nature itself probably assisted the public misconception. Of course the two brothers' productions resembled each other. Had Wolfgang's work been radically different, the brothers' personal relationship would have been easier. But the strategy of assimilation, which aimed at creating a composite identity and expecting the public not to discern any differences, was a crushing and annihilating process for the brother whose work was imitated and falsified.

After Wieland himself had been buried, Wolfgang realised that he would not be able to bury the 'Wieland myth' – even his own existence would remind the world of his brother – so he adopted a different and highly effective strategy. He identified himself with his dead brother, to the point where their work could not be distinguished. The photographs of their stage sets, which now hang alongside each other in the Wahnfried museum, are indeed as alike as peas in a pod. Who could convince an unsuspecting visitor that in reality, these productions were as different as the brothers themselves? Nor are visitors likely to notice the other aspects that are different. Wieland's idea of Bayreuth as a 'workshop', for example, was originally directed against the Old Wagnerians and Nazi Bayreuth. Wolfgang has never detached himself from the word, but he has dragged the faded label into a present in which the reality of the festival no longer matches that definition.

Wolfgang 'became Wieland', too, by seeming to follow the pattern of his private life, his break away from marriage and family. The blamelessly uxorious and domesticated Wolfgang surprised the public in 1976 – the centenary of the festival, when the eyes of the world were on Bayreuth – by turning up with a new wife. Whereas Wieland's 'spring awakening' foundered on his own self-doubt and guilt, Wolfgang carried his through with characteristic practicality and determination. He actually divorced his wife, Ellen, and brusquely removed the children from their parental home. And while Wieland had more or less stumbled into his affair, Wolfgang's coup had been carefully prepared and was, moreover, given a political seal of approval: the Mayor of Bayreuth, Hans Walter Wild, was a witness at the wedding. His new wife – who bore the appropriately Wagnerian name of Gudrun – had worked in the Festspielhaus press office since 1965 and had risen to the grade of personal assistant. Born into the family of a research chemist in 1944 in Allenstein, East Prussia, Fraulein Armann had been married to the theatre scholar Dietrich Mack: a protégé of Wolfgang and the co-editor of Cosima's diaries. The story that Mack handed over his wife to his friend Wolfgang in exchange for the directorship of the newly founded Theatre Research Institute in Thurgau was probably only a piece of cruel gossip.

In spite of all his freedom of action, not even Wolfgang entirely escaped the secret constraints of the family subconscious. His choice of wife followed the pattern set by his grandfather and father. (And had not Wieland's second choice of partner also followed this father–daughter model?) Once again, an older man had married a woman from a younger generation: at thirty-six, Gudrun was twenty years younger than her new husband. As a servant and assistant of her husband, she assumed the same tasks that had been undertaken by Winifred in a previous era. With the birth of Wolfgang's daughter Katharina two years later, he continued the series of generational displacements that had begun with Cosima's first Wagner children. The new great-grandchild, in age more like a great-great-grandchild, could have been the child of his own children.

If Wolfgang had sought, consciously or not, to imitate the external contours of Wieland's private life, then the differences between their 'second choices' – Anja the singer and lover, Gudrun the secretary and wife – reveals once more their opposed personalities. Gudrun's talents and occupation seem to suggest a subconscious return by Wolfgang to the image of his mother; at any rate, the contrast with his gentle and easily dominated first wife, Ellen, is conspicuous, and in matters of succession Gudrun is sometimes regarded as the latest 'exalted lady'. Anja Silja, on the other hand, seemed at the time to be used by Wieland as the antidote – the exorcism – of his close ties with his mother.

Sometimes, however, the passage of time can shed a different light on these matters. A quarter of a century after Wieland's death, having in the mean time married the conductor Christoph von Dohnanyi and borne him three children, Anja Silja looked back on her career following a performance in Vienna. Alone, spotlit in the dark, she spoke frankly and calmly of her youth in Bayreuth, and of her life with Wieland, who had shaped her as an artist and whom she still regarded as a major influence. (To the delight of those present she once got the names wrong, referring to Wieland as Christoph.) She was unchanged by the years, except that she now seemed markedly more in control of her life. Had the older generations of the Wagner family been among the audience, they would have witnessed an alarming metamorphosis. The mature Anja seemed to have been transformed into a young Winifred: the same unsentimental and nonchalant style of speech, with a slight Berlin tinge to the accent; the same slightly masculine appearance, sturdy despite her slimness, tall, and with determined gestures and movements. What was the leitmotif of Wieland's production, with their tendency towards the archetypical? 'Return to the mothers.'

The history of the festival since 1953 is in part a history of gradual assimilation, of the incorporation of the image of one brother into the plans of the other. This fusion of the two brothers' identities is what Wolfgang had intended; his success demonstrates that history can, at times, be controlled and managed. The first-born, so confined even during his lifetime that he could not resist the tide of incorporation, was all the more helpless after his death. In 1991, twenty-five years after Wieland's death, Wolfgang described his relationship with him as one of love. In a certain mythical sense this was actually the truth. Because the threat represented by Wieland had been swallowed up and incorporated, Wolfgang was now free to love him again, as he had during his childhood and youth. But perhaps the truth is more complex still: when one identifies oneself with a beloved 'other', one becomes able to love oneself. As his 1994 memoirs reveal, Wolfgang has fallen in love with himself: vanity has finally consumed him.

17

1966–80: Wolfgang and the next generation

IN THE MIDST OF THE IMBROGLIO, A THIRD GENERATION OF 'Wahnfried youngsters' was growing up, creating its own patterns of family relationships. The closeness in age between the four children of Wieland and Gertrud ensured a close bond between them, but also intensified that family battle which is the inevitable result of parental aspirations and preferences. The different roles assumed in such conflicts mean that brother and sister can have quite a different perspective on the same childhood: one can remember it as blissful, the other as traumatic. Each position in the family brings its own point of view: the first-born is mercilessly ejected from a short-lived position of supremacy; those in the middle slide comfortably into the protection of the group; while the youngest experiences both privilege and suppression. These variations of experience are further inflected by differences of gender. The son, particularly the eldest, is pressurised by the expectation that he will fulfil a special role, that he will further the family's dynastic mission, while the daughters have a little more room for manoeuvre.

After a wonderful early childhood provided by liberal, artistic parents, the lives of the young Wagners were rather derailed by the destruction of their domestic stability. Although the constant presence of their Reissinger aunts provided a certain measure of consistency during their parents' frequent absences, the obvious crises in both the work and the marriage of Wieland and Gertrud inevitably affected the children's lives.

The children reacted to the resultant lack of family leadership, initially at least, with the time-honoured strategy of looking for a good time. All control was soon lost. Wolf Siegfried took ample advantage of the family wine cellars for his early alcoholic experiments. When reproached for this by Winifred, he argued that 'My father does what he feels like, so why shouldn't I?' Wahnfried now became known among the pupils of the local grammar schools for the wildness of the teenagers' parties, where precocious drunkenness and promiscuity were routine – to the horror of Emma, the faithful family nanny. The traditional solution was adopted and they were all packed off, though in this case it was not to the draconian regime of a boarding school, but to the luxurious country estate of Max Wiskott, an old family friend. There, the four Wagners were brought up just as liberally as at home: whereas Wolfgang's children were sent to the stricter Bavarian institutions, the education of the Wahnfried children was always more influenced by the pleasure principle than the reality principle. Wieland's half-hearted attempts to force his daughters to acquire secretarial skills, for example, failed before they had even started.

'The past', as it was euphemistically known, played little part in the children's education, either at boarding school, where the textbooks only covered German history until the First World War, or at home. It was not that Wahnfried maintained a deliberate silence on the subject – but life was dominated by the daily problems of a large and busy household, and questions about the Nazi years were not exactly encouraged, even though the extended family included two former devotees of the Party, Emma and Winifred. The former now managed the kitchen and cellar with exemplary discipline; the latter lived next door but was always present at birthday, Christmas and New Year's Eve dinners. Wieland's sarcastic treatment probably restrained her from expressing some of her more fervent views on such family occasions. Adolf Hitler himself never cropped up in family conversation, unless something trivial released the genie, as when Nike, aged about five, said that her cuddly bunny was 'Adolf Hitler's champion' – causing much amusement and many significant glances among the grown-ups. The children were aware, though, that their father's productions had swept aside 'all that Nazi business' and that they could therefore consider themselves as having been born 'on the good side'. That was all they needed to know, for now.

There were hints that the events of the past were all too present in Wieland's mind, even if he rarely spoke of them directly. Occasionally, in his sceptical way, he would disparage Adenauer's government, observing that 'the old Nazis were back at the helm'. In a tomboyish phase, Nike used to whittle spears from willow wands, and when she asked her father what she should call these favourite missiles, Wieland suggested 'V2' – the name of Hitler's secret weapon against Britain. Phrases such as 'all the way into the gas chamber' or 'it's good enough for shooting' peppered his conversation. And his sketch-pad would sometimes reveal absent-minded drawings of women who resembled the Aryan ideal, with their blonde hair, chiselled profiles and athletic physiques. In bed at night, Wieland would read all the newspapers he could get his hands on – *Der Spiegel* was his favourite: when one of the children enjoyed the occasional privilege of sleeping in his room, they would sometimes be frightened by the sight of a headline or photograph alluding to the horrors of recent history. Wieland's bookshelf – with volumes by Oswald Spengler and Gregor von Rezzori next to an edition of Wagner's letters – provided another reminder of the events that were never mentioned.

Gertrud, on the other hand, never seemed to consider the past at all; she was too busy running the big house and knocking the new staff into shape. The children liked the delightful smell of her dressing-room with its double-kidney dressing table: Gertrud's life to them seemed somehow cheerful and fragrant, with a vitality that contrasted with their father's more laconic, melancholy temperament. The Nazi past, though recent in chronological terms, was psychologically remote, seeming to belong to their grandmother rather than their parents. The children were aware of Winifred's former associations, even if they didn't know the details. On one occasion in the early sixties, the Bayreuth schools were taken to see Erwin Leiser's documentary film, *Mein Kampf.* Young Wolf Siegfried craftily took his grandmother's arm and asked her whether she wouldn't like to come and see it with him. The expected reply came promptly: 'I'm not going to see that. It's all lies, anyway. Nothing but propaganda.' Their grandmother's willing identification with the Nazi era somehow defined it for the children, placing it on the other side of a mythical boundary. Those stories came from the mists of prehistory, they happened as long ago as grandmother was old – and besides, had not their father put everything right again?

It was not just Nazism that seemed remote and irrelevant: the family also seemed to have renounced that domestic ideology – a combination of imperialist Wagnerism and German cultural nationalism – that had infected Wahnfried long before Nazism took root. Although Wieland was forever reading philosophical studies of his grandfather's work, in search of suitable quotations for his programme books, one never had the impression that he was really a Wagnerian. On the contrary, Richard Wagner seemed to represent the family burden – servitude and oppression. The whole atmosphere of Bayreuth weighed heavily on Wieland, but on the Frisian island of Sylt, a fresh wind blew. The family holiday home proved an effective anti-depressant for Wieland, and became a second home for the family: the only reminder of the woes of Bayreuth came from the way the sea buffeted the island as in *The Flying Dutchman*.

The cult of Wagner as a purely German artist, who had nothing to do with and nothing to say to the rest of the world, was firmly rejected by Wieland and Gertrud – they treated it with irony and contempt, like all fundamentalist forms of Wagnerism. They saw Wagner in his context, and passed this view on to their children: he was a European artist, one among many, rather than a timeless, godlike figure. Whereas Wahnfried had previously educated its children in the self-perpetuating and philistine view that only Wagner's art mattered, the children's eyes were now opened to a wide range of European art – Picasso, Paul Klee, Henry Moore – and literature – Thomas Mann, Bertolt Brecht, Jean Anouilh, Paul Claudel, Jean Giraudoux. They were also encouraged to develop their own artistic and musical interests, and their parents displayed discreet pleasure at the piano playing of their daughters and the artistic creations of their son. Their formative cultural experiences, apart from the continual diet of Wagner at home, included Fritz Kortner's productions in Munich and those of the Brecht Theatre in East Berlin, an occasional Klemperer concert, and, of course, their father's productions, which they were always allowed to go and see. Despite their liberal upbringing, however, the children made a conservative choice of university courses, as though only so much deviation from the family tradition could be tolerated in the space of one generation.

Wolf Siegfried began by studying architecture, but then switched to stage direction and theatre; Iris and Nike studied literature and music; Daphne attended drama school. The academic choices of most of the other great-grandchildren also remained within the humanities and fine arts. Although Eva was pushed towards management studies, her brother Gottfried studied musicology; of Verena's five children, the older son Manfred trained as a town planner, and the younger, Wieland, as a conductor; of the daughters, Amélie studied history and theatre studies, Winifred began with modern languages then decided to become a painter, and the youngest, Verena, studied art history. By and large, the fourth generation – many instantly recognisable as Wagners, with some distant physiognomical echoes of Franz Liszt, too – moved to the big cities: Bayreuth, when all was said and done, was somewhat provincial. The stage was set for the clash between inherited values and individual development to take its course.

In 1964, during the long withdrawal of the Bayreuth great-grandchildren from their family homes, another great-grandaughter was making the opposite journey: Dagny Ricarda, from the ostracised Swiss branch of the family, made her first Bayreuth appearance in the very den of the lioness, Winifred. Given the events that had passed between the two branches of the family, this obviously could not have taken place without some delicate negotiations to prepare the way. Of the numerous visitors to Wahnfried who also maintained contact with Franz Wilhelm Beidler, Dagny's father, Curt von Westernhagen was the chosen intermediary. An eminent Wagner scholar, conservative and politically somewhat tainted, he was probably the right person to remind his old friend Winifred of the existence of a further Wagner descendant. Winifred immediately let Westernhagen know that she was ready to receive Dagny; the great-granddaughter in turn arranged a rendez-vous in Bayreuth without her father's knowledge. When he did find out, Beidler's somewhat ironic comment was that he did not wish to 'stand in the way of her happiness'. The anti-fascist Beidler could not conceal his bitterness when he did eventually renew contact with the friend of Hitler – his first words on the telephone were 'After a thousand years ...', an obvious dig at the unrealised ambitions of the Third Reich. Contact between Beidler and the

Bayreuth family unsurprisingly remained superficial, but Dagny became a frequent guest at the Siegfried Wagner House. Despite the fact that she was studying English language and literature, she certainly did not converse in English with the aged Winifred, who had considered herself as German for so long that she had almost forgotten her native tongue.

While in Bayreuth, Dagny also got to know her Aunt Friedelind, the family member whom everyone said resembled Dagny's grandmother, Isolde. Friedelind, who had herself experienced the bitterness of rejection and emigration, took Dagny to her heart. She was aware of the historic injustice done to the Beidler family, and she also undoubtedly enjoyed defying the complacent Wahnfried establishment by championing the newcomer. Through Dagny, Beidler also renewed contact with Friedelind: they had in common not only their shared expulsion from Bayreuth, but also their leftist political views. Neither of the dispossessed was ultimately successful in their attempts to re-establish themselves at Bayreuth, and Friedelind eventually retreated to Switzerland herself. Rather ironically, since Wagner himself had found asylum there during his revolutionary days, Switzerland seemed to have become a sanctuary for any Wagner who dared to express left wing, democratic, or anti-Nazi views.

1966 – and Wieland's death – formed a crucial break in history: both for the festival and for the family. The festival was of course solidly established and widely celebrated by then, and with the permanent sell-out of tickets it seemed paradoxical to talk of a crisis. Yet there was a sense that its purpose was wavering, that it was in transition: Wolfgang initially found it hard to justify himself to the press, and Friedelind and Gertrud did not disguise their objections to his regime. By common consent, New Bayreuth was at an end: the revolution brought about by Wieland was being quietly consigned to history. This is illustrated by two small but symbolic gestures. In 1967 a rather undistinguished street, linking the Richard-Wagner-Strasse with the new Hohenzollernring, was named Wieland-Wagner-Strasse; the following year, a bronze bust of Wieland was placed in Bayreuth's mini-Valhalla, the foyer of the Municipal Hall. By commemorating the past, the festival neutralised it: if Wieland's ideas could be successfully portrayed as part of the festival's heritage, then they would no longer pose a threat.

The employees of the festival soon rallied round the new regime: with the exception of Anja Silja, who declared that she never wanted to perform in Bayreuth again and who stuck to that decision, all the same singers continued to work at the Festspielhaus, and even the most devoted women from Wieland's private office soon transferred their allegiance to Wolfgang. The Society of Friends, too, proved loyal: they had long forgotten the incident of 1961, when Consul Franz Hilger, the most important of the patrons, had written to Wieland requesting him to dismiss Wolfgang since even the most tolerant of the Friends could not bear to sit through his *Ring*. Times had changed: by 1967 Hilger himself had accepted Wolfgang's control, since he responded to a plea from Iris that her father's stage designs should be given to Gertrud by declaring that 'Fräulein Wagner, Wolfgang is now the boss and we want our Bayreuth.' Political expediency had won the day, a verdict that was confirmed later that year when Konrad Pöhner, Bavarian finance minister and chairman of the Board, succeeded in persuading the Friends to pass a unanimous vote of confidence in Wolfgang.

This was no time for sentimentality, either at Wahnfried or the Festspielhaus. Little sensitivity was shown to the immediate family of the deceased director. In 1967, for example, when Wieland's children wanted to hold a reception at Wahnfried for the artists who had worked on a revival of his production of *Götterdämmerung*, Wolfgang refused permission on the grounds that a fee would now have to be paid for the use of the premises. Wieland's artistic progeny fared little better. Although Hans Peter Lehmann, Wieland's assistant during his final years, kept his productions going for a few years, they soon disappeared from the repertoire: his celebrated *Ring*, for example, disappeared after a mere four years. Many of his close collaborators were instantly dismissed, his stage sets were demolished, letters and drawings disappeared, and his pencilled notes were erased from the production books. As *Der Spiegel* reported, 'even the rubber breasts from his sexually charged productions went back into the store'. Wolfgang was quoted as saying that 'The round things must go – my brother must have been a breast fetishist.' An officiously bureaucratic approach began to prevail: the theatre personnel had to sign an undertaking that they would reveal nothing of what went on in the Festspielhaus, and even the family and their friends now had to sign themselves in if they wished to be admitted to performances. In a similar spirit, the offices were reorganised for the sake of greater efficiency: they were divided and soundproofed, so that soon nothing remained that would recall the past. The clear-out extended to the old wickerwork seats from the Festspielhaus auditorium, which were replaced in 1968; the new wooden seats were no more comfortable, but at least eighty-three additional spaces were created to boost the box-office takings. More than twenty years later, nostalgic buyers were happily snapping up the old seats at the Bayreuth flea-market. One piece of bureaucracy, dating from this period, has had more long-term consequences: the decision to exclude musical historians from the theatre archives, or at least severely to restrict their access. Strangely enough, biographers of Wieland such as the Englishman Geoffrey Skelton seemed to be treated with particular harshness. The Bayreuth Institute often complains that there is still no scholarly history of the Festspielhaus, but it is difficult to see how this can happen if the conditions for researchers are made so difficult.

The death of one brother brought about the rebirth of the other – a paradox encapsulated in the macabre story that, when Wolfgang was visiting Wieland in the university clinic in Munich where he was dying, a drunk kept embracing him and would not stop singing 'Happy Birthday'. Wolfgang's second birth gave him unfettered personal power over the affairs of the Festspielhaus, and a tenure of office that would have been unthinkable for any normal theatre manager. Over the first ten years he consolidated his position as Intendant; over the next ten, by which time he was already of pensionable age, he enhanced his personal financial position, finding a combination of determination, political skills and gift of the gab that is clearly an irresistible recipe for worldly success. His countless decorations – innumerable medals and honours, and, in 1994, an honorary degree from the University of Bayreuth – are a visible representation of the social position he has acquired from his period of control.

Wolfgang was realistic enough to understand that one man could not take sole control over the artistic programme of the theatre. From 1969, therefore, he began to invite directors who were not family members to work in Bayreuth – a pragmatic and artistically necessary move. The first outsider was the conservative August Everding, who was entrusted with

The Flying Dutchman; in 1972, Götz Friedrich from East Berlin produced his 'socialist' *Tannhäuser*. But Wolfgang himself continued to take the lion's share of the productions: six out of seven in 1975, for example. It was not until 1976, the festival's centenary, that the introduction of outside directors had a really significant impact. That year's production of *The Ring*, conducted by Pierre Boulez and directed by Patrice Chéreau, not only accomplished the break with New Bayreuth, now well past its sell-by date: it was also a dynamic and enlightening piece of theatre in its own right. Nostalgia for the Wieland era had finally been displaced by a new, lively and highly involved approach to Wagner direction. Even Wieland's family breathed a sigh of relief that the deceased was at last allowed to rest in peace, after years of having the corpses of his productions raked over by a festival direction which had no ideas of its own.

If the 1976 *Ring* was a historic break with Wieland's production style, then closer inspection reveals that the late director had still had some part in its making. The transformations of 1976 would probably never have come about had it not been for Pierre Boulez – the conductor whom Wieland befriended in the last year of his life, and whom he brought to Bayreuth on the recommendation of the composer Karl Amadeus Hartmann. Boulez helped Wolfgang out of a tricky situation during the planning for the vital centenary year. Wolfgang's original choice as director, Peter Stein from the Berliner Schaubühne, had reacted to the 'fascist landscape' of Bayreuth by planning a provocative act of deconstruction: he wanted to remove the cover from the orchestra pit, which would have changed the entire acoustic structure of the famously refined 'Bayreuth sound'. This was unacceptable to Wolfgang, but he could think of no suitable alternative as director. It was Boulez who came to his assistance – or rather his sister Jeanne, an enthusiastic theatregoer who suggested the name of Patrice Chéreau. Wolfgang clutched at the name like a straw, even though neither he nor Boulez had seen Chéreau's work. But Wolfgang was soon able to claim the credit for Chéreau's theatrical triumph – one which finally, and fortuitously, safeguarded his own position as festival Intendant. The freedom of the town of Bayreuth, bestowed on him that year, was a symbolic recognition of the new phase in his directorship: having spent ten years establishing himself, his position was now unchallenged.

*

Wolfgang's successful rise to a position of autonomy was accompanied, perhaps inevitably, by the undermining of the position of Wieland's family – and less predictably, by the hopeless struggle of his own children to safeguard their own inheritance. Consolidation of his rule went hand in hand with his family's loss of home; the new springtime of his second marriage was accompanied by his children's enforced and wintry farewell to Bayreuth. The only branch of the family to be unaffected by the change of director was the Lafferentzes on Lake Constance: Verena's family had long been excluded from the Festspielhaus by Winifred. But Wieland's family were swiftly expelled from Bayreuth – as Winifred put it, no more sympathetic for having been orphaned herself, 'when the forester dies, the forester's children just have to move out.' For the next ten years, the forester's children and their mother were hardly ever seen on the green hill. For the children at least, the chance to acquire a greater knowledge of the world was some compensation for the loss of Wahnfried, but their brutal uprooting nevertheless left them with painful psychological scars, whose consequences emerged only later in their lives. Their banishment was effected as suddenly and efficiently as if a stage trap had swallowed them up, and the world into which they fell was different indeed: the daughters entered the underground world of the late sixties, with its communes, student movements and Marxist-Leninist groups, while the son followed his aunt's example by making for America.

The only person who really benefited from that first phase of Wolfgang's rise was his daughter, Eva. Like her father, she was a practical type rather than an intellectual; like her namesake and great-aunt, Eva Chamberlain, she was blonde, attractive and self-assured. She had just finished training as a kindergarten nurse, but she was now catapulted by her father into the festival management. While her less favoured brother, Gottfried, continued to struggle through his musical training, Eva was installed by her father in various key positions in the musical world. These included a post with Robert Schulz, a prominent operatic agent in Munich, and a spell with Unitel, an operatic film company belonging to the media mogul, Leo Kirch.

But Wolfgang's first attempt to secure the continuity of his family's power ended in catastrophe in 1976, when his remarriage triggered a classically Oedipal crisis. It was inevitable that there would be conflict and rupture between Eva and Gudrun, the two women at his side, particularly as neither of them was exactly bashful. One would have to become a victim – and it was Eva who was kicked out of the Festspielhaus with a brutality incomprehensible to outsiders. From now on, she would hear from her father only in the form of brief, bureaucratic memos; and his wrath would extend, Wotan-like, into the next generation. Eva's son, Antoine, who was born in 1982, would be given no chance to make his grandfather's acquaintance, even though Eva brought him back, year after year, to the dress rehearsals at Bayreuth – whether in a spirit of humility or defiance it is difficult to say. She was by no means unsuccessful after her departure from Bayreuth: she occupied posts at Covent Garden and at the Bastille Opera in Paris; she worked as a 'singers' scout' for many of the world's great opera houses; she would win a kind and talented husband in Yves Pasquier, a French film agent; and she surrounded herself with rich and famous friends. Yet the pain of her expulsion from the Wagner paradise, inflicted by a father from whom she could not psychologically distance herself, has never diminished. The ancient family motif of the rejected daughter – Isolde, Friedelind – has surfaced again with Eva, though events have been orchestrated slightly differently in her case: this time it was the father who blew the sinister horn that was once sounded by the mothers.

Eva was only the last in a series of victims of Wolfgang's rise to power. Like an elephant who never forgets an insult, Wolfgang never forgot that masculine bond that he made with his brother, which he believed Wieland had broken: the oath that the 'womenfolk' would be kept out of the affairs of the Festspielhaus. With typical efficiency, Wolfgang eliminated the threat posed by each of the Wagner women: Winifred, Friedelind, Gertrud.

Winifred herself provided Wolfgang with the ammunition necessary to destroy her influence, when her expression of continuing adoration for Hitler was captured on film. In one blow, she undermined all the patient work of her sons, who had tried for thirty years to make symbolic reparation for past misdemeanours, and to establish the democratic credentials of Bayreuth. Hans Jürgen Syberberg's documentary had been authorised in advance by Wolfgang: he had handed her the loaded revolver. Once the outrage erupted, Wolfgang tried to play down her comments by describing them as 'old woman's waffle', but he nonetheless took them seriously enough to ban her from the Festspielhaus. A cartoon showed the old lady with a lapdog bearing Hitler's face, being rebuked by Wolfgang in policeman's uniform and denied entry to the theatre. The issue hit a nerve: the question of whether members of the older generation were 'really' Nazis, or merely fellow travellers, was one whose relevance went beyond the Wagner family.

Winifred's face in the film is like a weathered old monument; beneath the moss, we can glimpse the truth from another age, that 'past that will not pass'. In that same year, Winifred's views gained endorsement from a surprising quarter: Cosima, whose diaries were published at last in 1976. Though the insights they offer into Wagner's working practices are interesting – 'R is working' is a frequent refrain – the real impact of these jottings lay in their revelation of Cosima's anti-Semitism. The public had been aware of this in general terms, but the details were still shocking. Perhaps we should be grateful to Cosima and Winifred, the two ancient female custodians of the Grail. After years of silence about the political associations of Bayreuth, these two first-hand testimonies had once again moved the issue into the spotlight. It was particularly apt that this took place in the centenary year: it made the event less of a bland celebration than it would otherwise have been, and meant that it was observed with a political realism that is usually lacking on these occasions.

The implications of Winifred's testimony were enormous, but her immediate threat to the festival was fairly easy for Wolfgang to marginalise. Friedelind was a more complex case. Wolfgang had never felt comfortable in the presence of his 'big sister': sharp-tongued, alert, anti-authoritarian and unwilling to accept compromises with the truth, her Americanised speech patterns now made her seem even more of an outsider in provincial Bayreuth. His recollection of her one and only attempt to direct an opera – *Lohengrin* at Bielefeld in 1968 – certainly suggests that there is unpleasant and unfinished business between them: 'The woman did her first production at the age my brother died, at forty-nine and three quarters. If she waits as long for her second production, until she's ninety-nine and a half, that will be fine. But in the mean time, she should drop the habit of claiming that I, her brother, make nothing but shit.' Wolfgang had always regarded 'the woman' as a Wieland follower, and now, at this critical moment, she gave him a political stab in the back. She publicly linked the Festspielhaus with a series of NPD (National Democratic Party) successes in Bayreuth, and accused the festival of having reverted to a reactionary – if not neo-Nazi – political stance.

The moment had come for Wolfgang to take his revenge, and to send this perpetual emigrant abroad once more. He had already effectively removed her from Bayreuth once, in 1967, when he banned her from running her 'masterclasses' at the Festspielhaus. Friedelind had organised the classes since 1959 as part of an international academy for opera students, in order that they should benefit from attending rehearsals and performances in Wagner's own theatre: they had provided an important foundation for the careers of many singers. Wolfgang's excuse for banning them was that Friedelind had failed to run them 'realistically': by eliminating her pedagogical work, he also eliminated her main justification for being in Bayreuth, which was undoubtedly his intention. The rest of the family was fond of disparaging Friedelind – Winifred spoke of her as a family 'black sheep' who had 'never quite made it' in professional terms – but her failure to establish herself undoubtedly owed as much to the problems deliberately created by her family, as to any personal shortcomings. Friedelind was unable to resume her educational work until 1972, when she set up a project in Eaglescliff, near Stockton-on-Tees in the industrial north-east of England. This work continued until 1982, when the Thatcher government's cuts in public sector funding forced her to abandon her attempts to bring cultural renewal to this area: once again a 'wicked mother' figure was the cause of her downfall.

When Friedelind tried once more to settle in Bayreuth – how often had she attempted this already? – she was once again forced out by quarrels with Wolfgang, and barracking in the streets from right-wing activists. She soon left Bayreuth again, and took up residence in Switzerland – the promised land of so many European refugees – where she lived until her death in 1991. She probably spent her happiest years there, fulfilling her 'passion for the underdogs' by engaging in charitable works. It is touching, in one sense, that she also spent much of this time conducting research into her mother's origins – she found a lot of information about Winifred's Danish relations – but it is also frightening evidence of the psychological hold which that ruthless woman could exert, even from beyond the grave.

Wolfgang never had any problems with his younger sister, the adaptable Verena: she was never one of the domineering womenfolk, and did not queer his pitch, at least not in public. On the occasion of the sharing out of Winifred's estate, her two youngest children – now in their mid-seventies and white-haired – sat together, hunched over photographs of their younger days on the festival hill. There was plenty of 'Do you remember ...?' and 'Wasn't that ...?' – much of it directed at those Nazi dignitaries who had once formed a guard of honour for Hitler at Bayreuth.

Winifred, Friedelind – the third in the trio of problematic womenfolk with whom Wolfgang had to deal was Gertrud, his brother's widow. In the immediate aftermath of Wieland's death, Wolfgang's relationship with the family was reasonably cordial: indeed, Wolfgang even once whispered to Daphne, Wieland's youngest daughter, that 'I'll always be there for you!' The initial relationship with the widowed Gertrud was also harmonious, as Wolfgang submitted to her every wish in relation to her husband's funeral. However, matters soon deteriorated. Gertrud was the first of the 'womenfolk' to be removed from the Festspielhaus by Wolfgang. She did not go without a fight: she appeared on television to tell the world of how she had been 'cheated', and she claimed that because of her long collaboration with him, she was the only person capable of preserving and continuing the spirit of Wieland's productions.

To Wolfgang, this must have sounded like a declaration of war, and it was a war that he knew he could win, thanks to the substantial power that was now on his side. Although Gertrud carried out the productions that Wieland had been contracted to direct outside Bayreuth – *Salome* in Geneva in 1966, *The Flying Dutchman* in Vienna in 1965 – her position was an untenable one, because she was known only as Wieland's widow and not as his collaborator. Though the world knew everything about the creative partnership of Wieland and Anja Silja, very few people appreciated the contribution that Gertrud had made to Wieland's productions: her claims to be able to continue his work were therefore regarded as impertinent. She was suffering for her husband's sins of omission, in never having made any written record of her work. All that she had in evidence was a handwritten dedication, in Walter Panofsky's illustrated book of 1964 on Wieland's productions, where he had written in his round hand that 'This really should be a book about you – without you there would be no picture + no concept!!!'

This was not enough to help her, and nor was anything else. Meanwhile Winifred, worried about Gertrud's share of Wieland's inheritance, was busily plotting her exclusion. She planted the false rumour that Wieland and Gertrud had divorced, and shamelessly addressed her letters to 'Gertrud Reissinger'. The family's final weapon was blackmail: Wolfgang let it be known that, if she continued to produce Wagner's work, either at Bayreuth or elsewhere, he would discontinue her allowance. Gertrud, with no means of earning her own living and with her children at the beginning of an expensive period of professional training, was financially dependent on Wolfgang and the festival – thanks to the brothers' partnership agreement of 1962, which had set down that in the event of one brother's death, the surviving brother would support the widow.

In view of her insolvency, there could be no question of Gertrud resisting Wolfgang and attempting to maintain her position at Wahnfried. She withdrew to her holiday home on Sylt – the end of the world, as it seemed to her. Wieland had made her a present of the large property at Keitum as a joint retirement home; he was probably also anxious to provide some independent security for her. 'Children, if I drown in the North Sea, the house is yours,' he would joke with typical black humour, alluding to the life insurance which he believed would cover the money borrowed for the house. But his confidence was ill-founded. His life insurance had for a long time been insufficient to cover his debts. The house on Sylt therefore had to be sold, bit by bit. Gertrud, symbolically, was left in the last part. Prematurely and forcibly retired, the decades she spent there seemed to be endless; it was only in the summer, with the family's visits, that the house was brought to life. Gertrud's position was desperate: she had been cut off from her life-blood, the Bayreuth festivals; her work was not in demand because no one realised it was hers; she had been ostracised by the extended Wagner family in which she had been integrated since her teenage years – what options remained open?

She tried twice to escape to Munich, the city of her dancing days, where she dreamed up new theatrical projects, refusing to accept that excluded women in their mid-sixties had no chance of obtaining new work. She returned time and again to her solitude at Keitum. An offer of a production did come her way on one occasion – *Fidelio* in Copenhagen, in 1979 – but she discovered that it was not easy to impose original ideas at a repertory theatre. Work in the public arena seemed closed to her, but her other survival technique was more promising. The woman whose life had been dominated by dance and physical movement began to read, to reflect, to analyse. Ironically, her principal subject-matter was the life and ideas of the original author of her troubles: she eventually became so familiar with his life that she just called him 'Richard', as though he were a lodger in her house. But she also read Thomas Mann, Adorno, von Weizsäcker, Goethe, as well as *Der Spiegel* – owned by her good friend Rudolf Augstein – and finally feminist literature. But the wound of Bayreuth was always open, and new salt was rubbed into it with every new book about Wagner, every piece of news from the Festspielhaus. Her self-exploration through Wagner seemed to go round in endless circles. Her grown-up children, visiting during university vacations, were not necessarily thrilled when their mother thrust her latest insights into Wotan's behaviour at them over breakfast. Isolation had meant that Gertrud's ceaseless dialogue with the dead developed into a kind of Wagner disease – or perhaps it was an advanced stage of that notorious Wagnerian 'inner consciousness' that had taken possession of her from her first visits to Wahnfried at the age of fourteen. External events certainly seem to corroborate the idea of an obsession. After the sale of the house at Sylt had finally saved her from the fate of being buried alive there, Gertrud once more moved to Munich, to be near her devoted youngest daughter, Daphne, who was an actress in one of the city's main theatres. The address of her new home must have been irresistible to her: the Meistersinger-Strasse in the Cosima Park.

Her last trip took her to Aix-en-Provence, in pursuit of a *Don Giovanni* which she was destined never to see. Struck by an illness that obviously required some attention, she was admitted to a clinic in the town. Three days later, on the evening of 11 July 1998, she died alone in her room.

On the condition that the local press were not informed, Gertrud's four children obtained permission from their all-powerful uncle to honour their mother with a necessarily intimate funeral ceremony at

Wahnfried, and to re-open Wieland's tomb so that Gertrud could be laid to rest there. The only words spoken at the ceremony, which made those present cry, have not been recorded – the speaker, Gertrud's grand-daughter Louise, threw her notes for the oration into the open tomb, along with her flowers. So the final truth about Gertrud is guarded by Gertrud herself, safe from the prying of biographers.

In this panorama of troubled Wagner women, we must not overlook one whose fate was similar, but perhaps even more painful than Gertrud's – this is Wolfgang's first wife, Ellen. Although her son, Gottfried, believes that she experienced such 'total identification with the Bayreuth Festival' that she scarcely found time for her role as mother, she nonetheless missed her crucial opportunity at the festival: when Wolfgang became its sole ruler, she failed to fill the position of First Lady. Perhaps she found it difficult to trample over her strong-willed daughter, Eva, who seemed destined to fill that role, with the help of her father and grandmother. Ellen's isolation from the outside world, always apparent, certainly increased in the decade after 1966. And then, in the centenary year of 1976, the blow was struck – like her sister-in-law and former dancing colleague at Tietjen's Opera Unter den Linden in Berlin, she was deprived at one stroke of husband, home and status in Bayreuth. Her divorce after thirty-three years of marriage was a traumatic experience: her Munich lawyer called her a 'broken woman', and various attempted suicides were kept from the public.

The inequality between the two parties could easily serve as a textbook study of the horrors of bourgeois marriage. Wolfgang, the 'guilty party', had the power, the money, the legal backing, and a new partner; for Ellen, at nearly sixty, there was only a modest sum of compensation, an enforced dependency on her children, and the prospect of a life which could only ever be a shadow of her earlier existence. Immediately after her divorce in 1976 – carried out, according to Gottfried, with speed and brutality – the humbled woman was appropriated by Winifred to be a 'lady's com-panion' in the Siegfried Wagner House, where she had been married. Winifred argued, with characteristic unsentimentality, that 'if things remain like this, then this solution is more agreeable to me than if I had to get used to a paid employee, because at eighty living entirely alone in a large house would hardly be practicable in the long run'. Soon, however, her 'new life' forced Ellen into the care of psychiatrists, and she had several spells in hospital. She drifted between Wiesbaden, where she had relations, and Bayreuth, where she tried to settle down again, with a mixture of masochism and hope. In the end, she decided in favour of the more welcoming Wiesbaden, where she lives in very modest circumstances, supported by her daughter. She has always refused to blame her husband for the breakdown of their marriage: still trapped in patriarchal dependence, she assigns all the blame to 'the other woman'.

1976 was a momentous year for the Wagner family: it saw the centenary of the festival, the divorce and remarriage of its chief, the banishment of his daughter, the publication of Cosima's diaries and Winifred's profession of loyalty to Hitler. As if that were not enough, there was another event that was crucial in both historical and psychological terms: the opening of Wahnfried as a museum.

This was yet another change in the family's relationship to its material assets, a relationship that has always been somewhat peculiar. The principal value of the assets has always in any case been aesthetic. The Festspielhaus, the villa, the 12,000 square metres of grounds, the archive, the Wahnfried treasures with the library, the busts, the paintings and the souvenirs – these were suited to quiet enjoyment and historical appreciation, rather than quick conversion into liquid form. As with the gold in the Rhine, any attempt to convert the assets into material profit seemed to be doomed. But occasional incidents had threatened the integrity of the estate, and exposed the family to the transient nature of material possessions. One notorious occasion was in 1965, when Winifred, who was the owner of all the treasures under the terms of her husband's will, discovered that her heirloom, a silver-paint portrait of Franz Liszt painted by Dominique Ingres in 1839, was being offered for sale in the catalogue of a reputable Munich auctioneer. The search for the thief ended almost as soon as it had begun. Wieland's son Wolf Siegfried, then a somewhat unruly youth, had got into the Wahnfried broom cupboard where all sorts of ancestral portraits were stacked, thanks to his father's iconoclastic attitude to family history. The apprentice thief had hoped for nothing more than some old junk with which to eke out his pocket money – he innocently chose the best-known and most valuable piece in the collection. Having got its hands on it, the auction house was reluctant to give up the chance of a sizeable profit; the furious grandmother was also determined, and threatened legal action to get her Liszt back. The festival management was concerned, above all, to avoid a scandal, and so the picture had to be bought back at auction by a front man.

This expensive prank was one of the incidents that made the family's control of its hoard of treasure seem a little more fragile. A chronic shortage of money had led to minor forays into the treasure on more than one occasion. Wummi's action was only one incident in a history of dubious dealings that began with the founder of the dynasty, who may have set his critique of capitalist materialism to music, but was otherwise rather free in his financial attitudes and apt to confuse loans with gifts. The expropriation of family property gained pace with Wagner's daughter Eva, though in her case it was motivated by the need for psychological compensation for a perceived damage to her prospects. Eva took illicit possession of Cosima's diaries, intended for her brother Siegfried: she then passed them over to the town of Bayreuth, in return for a lifetime annuity and a promise that they would not be opened until thirty years after her own death, which eventually took place in 1942.

The family history of larceny continued with Friedelind, who caused great embarrassment when it turned out that some jewellery entrusted to her for safekeeping by the Baroness von Einem could not be found after the war. Decades later her son, the composer Gottfried von Einem, complained that the festival had never made the agreed reparations – one of Richard Wagner's draft scores – and his relationship with the festival continued to be dominated by anger over this incident. Financial matters also soured relations between Wolfgang and Wieland when they assumed control over the festival. Their characters were different in this as in every other area: Wieland was known as a spendthrift, Wolfgang was a careful realist. And while Wieland concerned himself with the artistic development of Bayreuth, Wolfgang tightened his grip on the festival finances. Infuriated by the way in which his brother had arrogated financial control to himself, and by the increasing secrecy with which he conducted financial dealings, Wieland progressively incurred debts which it was then up to his brother to settle.

The underlying problem for the family has been the mismatch between its expensive tastes and the more modest fiscal reality; this tendency has contributed to the difficulties of every family member, with the sole exception of Wolfgang. Each generation has felt an obligation to cut a certain figure in society, but has not generally had the income to support it. This began with Franz Liszt's daughters, who viewed themselves as aristocrats – they inherited their mother's 'grande dame' feudal awareness, and felt superior to the bourgeoisie because of their 'fantastic, legendary' father – but were in reality penniless. This trait has continued right through to the fourth generation, with Wieland's children. Despatched to their places of study with a modest monthly cheque, but imbued with pride in their origins and under pressure to mix at a certain level of society, they were bound to find themselves resorting to small deceits: borrowed evening dresses, the occasional realisation of family assets. They were not the only family members to carry out such petty crimes, most of which were conducted with considerably more skill and forethought than Wummi's Ingres escapade, but the family chronicles keep a discreet silence on this subject. Time and again, scores, letters and other heirlooms crop up in strange places, and there is no way of discovering how they have come to be in the hands of their present owners.

The gap between financial perception and reality has affected other aspects of the family's history. The heads of the family have always been irrationally regarded as rich by the outside world, but they have generally been dependent on the approval of the festival board for the granting of modest fees – modest, at any rate, in relation to the lifestyle of Wieland's large family. Winifred's personal subsistence was guaranteed by the lease of the Festspielhaus to her sons, but towards the end of her life she became increasingly concerned about the family's financial future. Since the post-war reopening, the festival had been reliant on public and private sub-sidies, unable to break even from the sale of tickets alone. To restore Wahnfried would have required several million marks, which simply were not there. Shaken by the incident with Wolf Siegfried, Winifred was worried about how best to safeguard her inheritance. The state, too, was alarmed by the disputes that had grown within the family since the death of Wieland, and which seemed to jeopardise the position of the festival director, whom they supported with large amounts of public money.

Wieland himself had come to realise that a family-run theatre on the scale of Bayreuth was an economic anachronism that could not continue indefinitely. The idea of transforming the family assets into a public foundation clearly had much to recommend it – as it had done in 1913 when the idea had first been floated. The private ownership of Bayreuth was only safeguarded in 1924 thanks to donations from outside the family, and the threat of nationalisation was only narrowly averted in 1945. Sooner or later, private ownership and management would have to be abandoned.

But how would this take place? The terms of Siegfried's will forbade the selling of the Festspielhaus. Family propriety prevented the sale of Wahnfried from being contemplated; after all, it was Richard Wagner's tomb. The archive alone was theoretically worth millions, but any hope of achieving a realistic market value would founder against the law that prohibited significant German cultural assets from being exported: the state could be the only bidder. Negotiations with possible buyers – the town of Bayreuth, the representatives of Upper Franconia, Bavaria and the Federal Republic – thus dragged on over the years, until the family accepted the (much too low) price of two and a half million marks, in return for a contract that (in the words of the mayor of Bayreuth) 'changed everything without much being changed'.

In 1973 the newly established Richard Wagner Foundation took over the powers that had previously belonged to Winifred. The Foundation would not control the festival itself, but would contract it out to an entrepreneur: needless to say, this was Wolfgang, who simply continued in his old post, though he was technically no longer a part-owner. The appointment of a future festival director would be in the hands of a Foundation Council on which there would be twenty-four votes: five representing both the Federal Republic and the Land of Bavaria, three from the town of Bayreuth, two from the district of Upper Franconia, the Bavarian Land foundation and the Society of Friends, and one from the Upper Franconian foundation. Finally, each of Siegfried Wagner's heirs was granted a vote: while Winifred was alive, this meant that the family had five votes, Wieland's being cast in proxy by his children. After her death, they were reduced to four. The Wagner descendants were granted the right to propose a successor: in the seemingly unlikely event of them being able to agree on a single candidate from among themselves, he or she would be officially regarded as having precedence over a candidate from outside, though the success of the family choice would not be guaranteed. The powers of a once-mighty dynasty had been reduced to this modest clause, an achievement for which Wolfgang had had to fight hard. (He had not yet created his second family, and at this time he had no desire to see the festival directorship remain in the family's hands.) His son recorded that 'the last of the Wagners' (as Wolfgang once described himself) regarded this clause as the 'greatest coup of his life'.

A separate arrangement was made for the sale of the Wahnfried estate, one which cunningly circumvented the ethical obligation not to sell the villa itself. The outbuilding, the Siegfried Wagner House, was acquired for six hundred thousand marks, along with the land on which the villa stood; the catch was that the investor was obliged to restore the villa to its original state. 'Nostalgia for Wahnfried' was the headline in the Bavarian papers in May 1973, when the completion of negotiations was reported. 'Don't you feel a touch of nostalgia, Herr Wagner, when you see Wahnfried, where you spent your youth, becoming a museum?' the Bayreuth journalist Werner Meyer asked Wolfgang on that occasion. 'There's no cause for emotions,' replied Wolfgang. 'What must be, must be.'

Perhaps not everyone shared this view. Even though there was an audible sigh of relief when Richard Wagner's hoard of Rhine gold was finally shared among the descendants, the psychological effects were much more complex. The Bayreuth sale meant that a part of one's self had been sold. Henceforth, any family member attending the festival would merely be a 'visitor'; any element of identification had gone. The transformation of Wahnfried into a museum represented an external disentangling of the family's affairs, accompanied by an inner sense of alienation and expulsion. The request of Wieland's children to preserve at least the upper floor of Wahnfried as a flat for the family fell on deaf ears, even though it was also supported by their grandmother. Future festivals therefore featured the bizarre spectacle of dispossessed Wagners seeking shelter with friends, relations, or in hotels.

There were more subtle effects of the sale of Wahnfried, too. The old understanding of the 'branches' of the family slowly disappeared, since without a principal home and family seat, the 'core family' could not be defined. Without this, the concept of a branch was meaningless; without

Wahnfried as their central focus, the branches became a diaspora, alienated and remote from its ancestral home. This sense of alienation created much misery within the family, even if individual clans were now materially better off. The misery resides deep in the soul, half suppressed, released only in occasional surges of emotion. When the family now travels to Bayreuth from Berlin, Munich, Keitum, Hamburg, Vienna, Paris or Milan, its reunion generates that vague feeling of unease familiar to everyone who has returned to their place of birth after a long absence – that bitter taste of returning to where home used to be, but is no longer.

It is perhaps significant that among the partners of the fourth generation of Wagners, there are numerous foreigners, exiles, outsiders and eccentrics. Far fewer of this generation have taken 'neighbours' or other Germans as husbands or wives: it is as if family members have tried to find an echo for their inner sense of estrangement in the gratifying otherness of their partners. Perhaps we should rejoice in the fact that the clannishness and narrow nationalism of preceding generations seem to have been banished. Of this fourth generation, Eva married a Frenchman; Gottfried, after a first marriage to an Austrian, married again to an Italian; Nike had a child by a Frenchman and married a Swiss; Daphne had a brief marriage with a Viennese; Winifred, Verena's second daughter, married a Frenchman and lies in Canada; her younger brother Wieland married an Austrian. It is only Wolf Siegfried, whose short marriage ended in divorce, and three of Verena's children who have married fellow Germans. This new cosmopolitanism was, in terms of family history, a throwback to the Franz Liszt years, and indeed to the European Wagner of the pre-Bayreuth years.

The other noticeable trend in this generation is the drastic reduction in the number of children, which is much more exaggerated than general social trends would suggest. The only great-grandchild with more than one child is Winifred, who has two; Eva, Gottfried, Nike, Amélie, Manfred, Wieland and Wolf Siegfried all have a single child. Could this reflect an unconscious rejection of the traditional family structure? It would scarcely be surprising if this generation had felt a collective loss of faith in the cohesiveness of the large family, given the experiences it has had.

18

1980–90: after the death of Winifred

THE CONVERSION OF THE FAMILY ASSETS INTO A FOUNDATION HAD successfully softened the blow of the 'day of judgement' that Wolfgang had always warned of: the day when Winifred Wagner would die and the family quarrels about the inheritance would erupt in earnest. These problems had now been largely defused with the fundamental restructuring of the estate – but as the mayor of Bayreuth observed, outwardly nothing seemed to have changed. The festival continued smoothly, under the same management as before, into the 1980s; old Winifred could be seen drifting around the Siegfried Wagner House just as before, wearing a silk blouson dress and smoking a cigarette out of the corner of her mouth, even though she was now living there only by the grace of the town of Bayreuth. The final four years of her life, after her scandalous return into the limelight in 1976, were increasingly lonely. She eventually died at the age of 83 in March 1980, at a clinic in Überlingen on Lake Constance, having spent her final days with her daughter Verena at Nussdorf.

Many of her grandchildren visited her for a last farewell: some had not seen each other for decades, and registered the greying hair with astonishment. Which of them was most affected by the death of this controversial woman? Which of them could love their mother or grandmother despite the grievous mistakes she had made both in her public and private life? Love is perhaps not quite the right word to describe the tangled complex of strong emotions that the descendants felt for Win-ifred. Her two eldest children, Wieland and Friedelind, had undoubtedly been deeply marked by her: the strength of their early dependence was matched by the pain of their later detachment. For her two younger children, the ties were probably less binding. She was never really a problem for Wolfgang. He recalls her in a very relaxed way in his memoirs, in striking contrast to the tone he uses to describe the rest of the family.

Of the eleven grandchildren – increased to a round dozen with the birth of Wolfgang's daughter by his second marriage in 1978 – Iris, Eva and Amélie, the eldest of each clan, perhaps had the strongest childhood bonds with her. The grandchildren who had the most time alone with her, Verena's children in particular, retained a strong attachment: they perhaps remembered how she patiently read to them when they were sick as children, and they certainly felt affection for her as the mother of their own much-loved father or mother. Winifred's affection for Iris, her eldest grandchild, was perhaps the strongest: she used to call out for her 'Isilein' when the child was playing in the Wahnfried garden. Iris returned her feelings until, later in life, the undisguised ambivalence of Wieland's attitude to his mother caused his own children to regard her as something of a monster. One can only imagine Winifred's emotions when, on her eightieth birthday, her favourite grandchild sent her a telegram reading 'Normally the dragons die BEFORE Siegfried...'

Amélie, who was often known as the 'D'Agoult' by Wieland's children because of her noble, carved features, dedicated herself to her grand-mother: she accompanied her on voyages to the Mediterranean and, using her abilities as a historian, planned to make her life the subject of an essay. Amélie's brother, named Wieland after his uncle, maintains to this day that Winifred had been 'sensational' as a grandmother. Eva, too, was close to Winifred, whom she increasingly came to resemble in her proud outward demeanour and her managerial talents. Other grandchildren, such as Manfred, Nike and Daphne, felt by contrast that they had been little more than numbers to her: they perceived her brusque manner as coldness. Gottfried was later to describe her as merely an 'unscrupulous businesswoman', though this one-sided assessment should be understood in the context of Gottfried's self-appointed role as the destroyer of the family's history of anti-Semitism.

Winifred's body was transferred to Wahnfried, and she lay in state in the restored hall where, sixty-five years earlier, she had arrived as a bride. Her face looked somehow ageless: her features had regained a strange youthfulness in death, just as Wieland's had done. The whispering relations circled the coffin in the gloom, witnessing the strange spectacle of the archetypal German sinner, now raised to the status of legend. The tributes were generous: her last benefactor, Hans Jürgen Syberberg, referred to her as a 'Shakespearean figure in the myth of the twentieth century'; the mayor of Bayreuth called her a 'great personality' at her memorial service on the rehearsal stage behind the Festspielhaus. Some of the tributes ingeniously managed to turn her disgrace into a virtue, by giving her credit for saving the artistic integrity of the festival from the grip of the Third Reich; this she was only able to do, of course, because of her personal intimacy with Hitler. The Society of Friends went still further by praising her for never having been 'cowardly in voicing her opinion'; this was certainly true, as the assembled family silently agreed. Perhaps more generous reflections were present too: her descendants may have thought about the historical conditions that had conspired to turn loyalty into a vice, or considered that it is difficult for personal warmth to be given by one who has never received it herself.

The 'saviour of the family' was finally interred in the family tomb at the municipal cemetery, fifty years after her husband Siegfried and fourteen years after her son Wieland. 'At least we meet again at funerals' was the bitter remark circulating among the family. A small bundle of papers, her correspondence with Adolf Hitler, was said to have been seen for the last time at a meeting of the clans in her house to discuss the inheritance. But anything else of importance to her had long been hidden away. Much of it was sent to Amélie, who has since, like a second Eva Chamberlain, kept a mysterious cupboard to which no one else has access – not even the Supreme Master of the festival.

'What? Will the line stretch out to the crack of doom?' The English journalist Bernard Levin quoted Shakespeare in an article of 1991, expressing distaste for the continuing procession of the Wagner family, with its apparently never-ending succession of vile individuals, stemming from the vilest of them all, Richard Wagner. But this most recent phase of family history has in fact been strangely uneventful: although the line has stretched out, with thirteen great-grandchildren in the fourth generation, no fundamentally new patterns of behaviour have revealed themselves. In this protracted family twilight, as in the final part of the *Ring* cycle, no new motifs are presented, and it is only the 'father and son' motif that is even presented in a different key. Other than that, novelty can only be found in the variation, development, and combination of now-familiar themes.

The tension caused by father–son relationships in this generation has been noticeable: it perhaps results in part from the strange fear that both Wolfgang and Wieland experienced about the very idea of having a son. It is difficult to tell whether this was a reaction against the excessive burden that had been placed on them, as male successors to the dynasty; both brothers probably subconsciously wished to avoid re-experiencing their own masculine dilemmas in their sons. The fundamental ambivalence of their fathers was bound to make life difficult for Wolf Siegfried and Gottfried. They would experience a classic double-bind: expected to be exactly like their fathers, with the same talents, and yet at the same time, to be themselves – to be 'more free than I, the god', in Wotan's words.

Even Wolf Siegfried's name is an indication that his parents – so refreshingly Graecophile in their other choices – did not quite know what to do with him; their choice seemed to tether him to his uncle and father, rather than promising an independent destiny. It took a while for this to become apparent. During his wild childhood years at the restored Wahnfried, he was always the boldest of the Bayreuth boys, neither brought up as a Wagner, nor spoilt as one; as a teenager, he was generous and imaginative but also somewhat lazy and feckless – tendencies watched anxiously by his father who, in this respect, was rather conventional. Like many uncertain fathers, Wieland frequently buried himself in his work as a strategy for shirking his parental responsibilities. At first he found it difficult to accept that his son was different from him: not an introverted workaholic or brilliant intellectual, but a ladies' man fond of fast cars and expensive living. He felt happier with his daughters, who always returned from school with top grades as he had done. A problematic psychological pattern of unspoken expectations and disappointed hopes was set in train.

With phrases such as 'It's up to you what we make of the father–son situation', Wieland merely passed the buck to his son, who consequently suffered from unjustified and undefinable feelings of guilt, as if being the son of a celebrity was not enough pressure for him already. On certain occasions, however, the mask of the omnipotent father began to crack, and when Wieland's life threatened to run out of control because of the Anja Silja situation, he was suddenly glad to have a young man he could rely on at his side. He engaged the twenty-two-year-old Wolf Siegfried at the Festspielhaus and began to appreciate his artistic and practical skills.

It is remarkable that Wieland, who had always been so sceptical about the value of dynastic tradition, should have acted to preserve family continuity at this time of crisis; it reveals more of the 'inner Cosima' in him than he would have cared to admit. He himself was generally quick to see the dangers of nepotism: Gertrud had great difficulty in persuading him to let the daughters – first Iris, and later Nike and Daphne – dance in the choreographic sequences she designed for the festival productions. Wieland's sensitivities about the use of family privilege were understandable: this was, after all, the first time that a family member would appear on the Festspielhaus stage, as distinct from the conductor's podium. Nonetheless, Gertrud prevailed and Iris appeared among the girls from Fürth in *Die Meistersinger* in 1957, while Nike and Daphne appeared between 1963 and 1965 as Bacchantes in *Tannhäuser,* flower maidens in *Parsifal,* and festival Muses in the final scene of *Die Meistersinger.*

Wolf Siegfried's brief apprenticeship to his father was not enough to give him any leverage in festival politics when Wieland died: with his death, the ritual of passing the Wagner crown from father to son came to an abrupt end. Paradoxically, it was Wolfgang – now seen as the guarantor of tradition – who brought about this infringement of the dynastic principle; the discontinuity which his assumption of power embodied is now itself established as tradition, such has been the unending nature of his reign. Meanwhile, Wummi – his childhood nickname has caught on with the public – made a timely escape to the United States, where he developed his skills as an opera director by working with student companies, then returned to Hamburg, where he spent over ten years as a freelance opera director and stage designer. He was mainly offered work on Wagner

287

productions, not surprisingly, but he also directed Puccini and Heiner Müller; he directed as a guest in several German opera houses, but also worked in Italy, Portugal, the United States and even Iran. Malicious observers often claimed that he was merely walking in his father's footsteps, interpreting this as the sign of a weak ego, but his choice of career should really be seen in the opposite light: it takes a great deal of confidence to accept such a heritage, rather than walking away completely. Like his grandfather and near-namesake, Wolf Siegfried was strong enough to take his historical mission seriously; it was characteristic of both Siegfrieds that they would eventually escape from their fathers' all-pervading shadows.

After more than forty productions, however, Wolf Siegfried overplayed his hand: in 1984, the year in which Wolfgang reached pensionable age, he publicly announced his claim to the Bayreuth succession. His quest for the Grail was hopeless, because of the legal provisions which now determined the succession of the directorship. He accepted the logic of the reality principle, which suggested that he should abandon his own aspirations before they led him into delusion and madness: he gave up the world of the theatre, and went south to the island of Mallorca. There, he has become Señor Wagner, proprietor of a building firm and owner of land, sheep and dogs; he is as popular with the farm labourers as he had once been with opera singers. He has been consoled for the loss of position in Bayreuth by the chance to return to his first dream of being an architect – unlike Siegfried Wagner, who never found his way back to that same early ambition. Wolf Siegfried now builds houses, villas, gardens, even fairy-tale palaces. He holds court at his own country estate for numerous visitors, particularly his sisters, who adore him in the same way as the Liszt sisters had adored their only brother Daniel, and Cosima's daughters their only brother Siegfried. The patterns are repeating themselves in a Wahnfried of the south . . .

Gottfried, too, made his escape southwards – as though both cousins were following Nietzsche's argument that the Mediterranean was the best antidote to the Nordic gloom of Wagner. He is in Milan, and his destiny has proved very different from what his name might have led him to expect: he has not become the young saviour of the empire, the successor of Lohengrin on the throne of Brabant. Unlike Wummi, he curses his childhood: 'I wouldn't want to relive a single day of it!' His memories are not of an aesthetically privileged childhood in the 'cloudy heights' of Wahnfried, nor of any boyish freedom to explore the world. He recalls only commands and prohibitions; images of fences and prisons dominate his thoughts about that period. His father was often absent, but was authoritarian when at home, his mother became excessively dependent on his support, and his domineering sister enjoyed all their father's favours. He was frequently moved between different boarding schools, which made it impossible for him to form any lasting friendships and engendered a defensive attitude. Gottfried's angry, helpless outbursts of childhood frustration were no more understood by his parents than his later hero-worship of Uncle Wieland. How did it benefit him if, to everyone else's delight, he looked just like the young revolutionary Richard Wagner? He found it impossible to gain his father's love and respect, no matter what his achievements: his degree in musicology, his debut production (*Fidelio* in Bonn in 1967), a film version of extracts from *The Ring*, his doctorate on Kurt Weill and numerous other academic distinctions. Though he was allowed to act as assistant director for the centenary *Ring*, Gottfried could not reconcile himself to his father, particularly after his acrimonious divorce. He left the house of the newlywed Wolfgang and Gudrun – according to him, his father 'put our furniture out of the door' – and with it the Festspielhaus. No doubt it had been his goal, no less than Wummi's, to take it over one day.

Up to this point there are striking parallels between the lives of Gottfried and Wummi – the two cousins were only four years apart in age, and were frequently confused by the press, as their fathers had been. However, the way in which they reacted to the critical event of leaving Bayreuth was very different: their different strategies of survival reveal that they are in many respects polar opposites.

Even as a boy, Wummi had loved blonde women and the good things of life: anything that was extravagant, amusing or bizarre was irresistible to him. He had inherited, along with a certain cynicism, a touch of the grand manner. While he felt an instinctive social allegiance with the fast-living upper classes, his artistic sympathies found their natural home in the experimental wing of contemporary art. His first marriage to the blonde daughter of a Bielefeld industrialist took him for a while into a bourgeois milieu, but despite the birth of a (blonde) daughter, Joy Olivia, he soon took flight. The pretty Malo Osthoff, who had always supplied her husband with good food and cosy domesticity, suffered the fate of Minna Wagner. Wolf Siegfried found his ideal in Eleonore, Countess Lehndorff: another blonde, with an aristocratic bearing and that touch of masculinity in her good looks that his father had also liked. 'But Herr Wagner, the one is a blonde and the other is a blonde – so why all these complications?' the family banker asked with bemusement, when Wummi approached him for an advance against his future inheritance in order to buy his freedom from his first marriage.

Over the years, Wolf Siegfried was gradually assimilated into the Lehn-dorff family, who were well known for their involvement in the '20 July', the conspiracy to kill Hitler; they belonged to the former Prussian elite, who had regained their old position of power and influence after their temporary expulsion. There were certain structural parallels with Wummi's own family: the Lehndorffs, like the Wagners, had a 'lost utopia' in the shape of their East Prussian estates. The difference was that the Lehndorffs had preserved the integrity of their extended family, owing to their longstanding traditions and their shared fate, while the rapidly fragmenting Wagners had not. The other main difference from Wummi's upbringing was that here, art was not taken too seriously: as the old saying had it, it was the art of living that was important.

Life with the countess had an added psychological benefit for Wolf Sieg-fried, besides allowing him to move on that higher social level to which his great-grandmother, old Cosima, had also been attracted. Because Eleonore was the daughter of a man who had been executed by the Nazis for his part in the assassination attempt on Hitler, and had herself experienced life in a concentration camp because of her family's culpability, his alliance with her allowed Winifred's grandson to feel that he had finally, if a little belatedly, landed on the 'good side' of German history. The couple took a provocative pleasure in their occasional dinners with the Nazi grandmother at Wahn-fried. As a result of this alliance, Wummi – who was not politically engaged himself, unlike Gottfried – had outflanked his generation's obsession with 'penitence' and 'reparation', by aligning himself with those who had nothing to repent. And yet his motivation was love, not politics.

Wolf Siegfried's position was in marked contrast to that of Gottfried. Whereas the former had successfully put a wall between the family's Nazi past and his own life, the latter continued to be troubled by the legacy of the Third Reich. He continued to revolt against his family. His attachment to Bayreuth remained strong, paradoxically, because of its negative energy; in attempting to break out, he had ended up crashing into his own walls. His early life was spent in left-wing politics and in an unsuccessful marriage to the lawyer Beatrix Kraus, who did not let herself be turned into a Minna, but pursued her own career with great success. It was only towards the end of the 1980s that he found the appropriate means through which to work out his unresolved Oedipal issues. He became interested in Wagner's attitude to Judaism – an issue which commanded increasing academic interest – and he developed his thoughts into a complete ideological critique of the institution of Bayreuth. This provided him with a context in which the question of guilt could be discussed with a certain degree of objectivity. Though the impulsiveness of the irascible child was still recognisable in the fifty-year-old Gottfried, his attack on his family's actions had been refined by a lifetime's experience of identifying with the victims. (There was a persistent family rumour that his maternal grandmother, Thora, had been of Jewish origin: this may have intensified his feelings of personal involvement.)

Gottfried's identity as the family outsider and outcast, and his desire to have this role confirmed, are proved by his recent public declarations. For example, he stated that after lecturing at the University of Tel Aviv he had been declared 'fair game' at Bayreuth: attacks on his person and views were positively encouraged. His crime was not so much his discussion of Wagner's anti-Semitism – this was already well known – as his criticism of the commercial and political machinations of Wolfgang's Bayreuth. He had described the festival as 'Salvation Incorporated', an 'investment exchange' whose 'untrustworthy processing of the past' he could not tolerate. He is the most recent manifestation of that political rebellion against Bayreuth that was inaugurated before the war by his Aunt Friedelind. His philosophical resolution to be a 'good Wagner', a 'reparation Wagner' – the only way to see his penitent appearances in Israel and Auschwitz – is touchingly matched by his attempts to ease human suffering on a personal level. In 1990, with his Italian wife Teresa, he rescued a five-year-old boy from an orphanage in Ceausescu's Romania. With an unplanned irony, the day on which the adoption of Eugenio was confirmed was his father's birthday. Gottfried observed that this tortured young child, now destined to enjoy a happy childhood, would become the 'first free Italian Wagner' – as though he were a Mediterranean version of the young Siegfried. Gottfried's emphasis on his paternal role is part of an attempt to become a counter-image of his own father: he is trying to rewrite his own unhappy childhood through his son, as if to say, 'this is how it could have been . . .'

The surname Lafferentz seemed to send Verena's children off in a different direction altogether. This was not entirely accidental – their mother admitted that she had deliberately brought them up 'away from Bayreuth'. The negative expression is telling: it defines the children's identity as 'not Bayreuth' rather than anything more positive. This attitude has coloured their upbringing, giving them a sense of 'not belonging', perhaps of being 'inauthentic'. This consciousness was strongest in the two oldest children, Amélie and Manfred, since their formative years were the period in which their mother's sense of exclusion from Bayreuth was at its strongest. Manfred, when he went to the festival as a little boy, always regarded Wahnfried as a 'dark castle', where one could not really live. The strange unreality of the Wagners worried him, accustomed as he was to the small and straightforward world of Lake Constance. An early attachment to Uncle Wieland soon foundered, to his disappointment – either because Wieland had no time for him, or because the dead hand of Winifred intervened to discourage the allegiance. The young Lafferentzes were only allowed to attend one act of a performance at a time, then they were swiftly removed to their grandmother's home at Oberwarmensteinach, where they were taken by the old family nanny, Emma. The things she whispered to them while she sieved her famous mashed potatoes were scarcely likely to soothe childish fears: she told them that there was a 'curse' on the Wagner family and that nothing good could ever come of them. With her callused hands and feet and her snow-white hair, Emma herself seemed like a character from a gloomy fairy tale. To Manfred, who had inherited his mother's delicately moulded Wagner features, the family atmosphere was 'cold'. How could one become friendly with any of them, when they all plotted behind each other's backs? A delicate and sickly child, the future engineering graduate was soon labelled as a 'weakling' in a household where the ideals of the master race had not disappeared with the Third Reich: he was mocked as 'our intellectual with the Jewish curls'. The second son, named Wieland after his uncle, fared better. Because he was his mother's favourite, and because he resembled his great-great-grandfather Liszt, his musical gifts were encouraged from an early age. He married young and moved to Salzburg: the softer Austrian lifestyle seemed to suit his dandyish nature better than the more brutal atmosphere of Germany.

If Bayreuth was unappealing to the young Lafferentzes, then their own childhood environment on Lake Constance was not exactly joyful. Manfred is still reluctant to recall the nihilistic defeatism that dominated his parental home, though this attitude would scarcely be a surprising one for a household of former Nazis in the 1940s and 1950s. Added to this political depression, there was the domestic depression caused by the family's enforced absence from Bayreuth. As is commonplace in these situations, the family dealt with its adversity by reversal, by emphasising the qualities of the new way of life that differ most from the life left behind. There was therefore little effort to remedy the peasant-like and basic conditions of the family's life in Nussdorf: this was in any case a return to roots for Bodo Lafferentz, who had grown up on a farm near Kiel. Manfred soon left this narrow world and moved into the opposite environment of left-wing West Berlin; today he works in the Berlin city and regional planning office.

'Little Wieland' chose a different course through life, always remaining on what his family considered to be the 'correct' path. He studied at the Mozarteum in Salzburg, then drifted – through Winifred's influence – into the Karajan circle in Berlin and Vienna. His family connections did not ultimately benefit his musical career: discussing his conducting experiences in a recent interview, he recalled that there were always imme- diate problems with orchestras whenever the topic of his family heritage came up, and like his cousins, he was never admitted to his uncle's Festspielhaus, either as a musician or an administrator. Although he was a talented conductor, he eventually chose to make his career in arts administration. He was appointed administrative director of the Philharmonic Orchestra in Dresden: the scene of his great-grandfather's revolutionary activities, and the city where *Rienzi* and *The Flying Dutchman* had been premiered. In the mid-1990s, he returned to the city where his adult life had begun, as adminstrative director of the Salzburg Mozarteum. A Mozartian of very high repute, he is now managing a Mozart empire of great diversity, and it is understandable that he should take some pride in the contrast with Bayreuth: Wagner and nothing but Wagner is 'not his line at all'.

It was not uncommon for German children of this era to fight a bitter generational conflict with their parents, particularly if they felt they had been born 'on the wrong side'. The Lafferentzes, children of a prominent Nazi functionary, seemingly had more reason than most of the Wagners to take this line. Their dilemma, though, was a classic reflection of the inner dichotomy of the immediate post-war generation. They found it difficult to reject their father, Bodo: they viewed him as a good and strong parent, one who (in line with the stereotype) had 'never done anything bad', who had 'only organised' for the Nazis. Post-war life was difficult for Bodo: he tried to use his contacts with his former research institutes to obtain a post where he could develop his interest in technology, but it was an unrealistic ambition for a man born in 1897.

The fact that their mother, Verena, was not prepared to renounce her nostalgic view of the Nazi era – this was the time of her golden youth – probably added to the children's inner dilemma. To this day, she remembers with pleasure the 'childlike laughter' that made Joseph Goebbels so charming. The children's close ties to the spirit of their grandmother Winifred can scarcely have helped them to see the family's involvement with the criminal regime in its true light. What, then, could they do? Verena's eldest daughter, living in Munich, has more or less broken with her family; the middle daughter has established her own family life in Montreal with her mathematician husband, and visits Lake Constance and the Bayreuth festival only during holidays. It is only the youngest child, Verena, who has avoided breaking from her family, remaining near her mother in Überlingen.

Meanwhile, back in Bayreuth, Wolfgang was busy consolidating his position of supremacy, making use of his managerial skills and acute sensitivity to the political climate of the moment. He was further blessed with rude health and vigorous powers of endurance. He enjoyed his position, and this enjoyment further stimulated his work; reporters admired his growing authority at the Festspielhaus, and the fact that he seemed to be omnipresent. Every plan, every strategy seemed to succeed – Wolfgang is like an astonishing administrative machine. If one were to ask what had kept him in ceaseless motion, besides his strong masculine ego, one crucial factor would emerge. This is his ability to distance himself from his family, paradoxical though it may seem, for this man who has lived and worked all his life in the town of his ancestors.

His crucial break had come in 1955, when he moved into his own villa in Bayreuth, thereby separating himself from Wahnfried. It had long been his dream to free himself from his family: it is unclear whether this was the result of an unconscious psychological trait, or because he believed it to be a recipe for career success. It certainly proved to be the latter. Removing himself physically from Wahnfried must have been relatively easy, compared to the later task of eliminating all competition from the Festspielhaus. But he has succeeded in that too, step by step.

The first phase in the process was achieved by the transfer of the family inheritance to the Richard Wagner Foundation in 1973. Though this was a necessary condition for later developments, it did not guarantee Wolfgang's financial security. He was not exactly poor – his share of the sale of the estate was two and a half million marks, and the festival director's salary ran into five figures – but there was still no provision for his old age. In 1984, when Wolfgang reached the age of sixty-five, it was decided at a special session of the Bayreuth council that he should be employed on a level of pay equivalent to that of an assistant minister, a general of the second rank, or a local functionary such as the mayor of Bayreuth. The same meeting also agreed a one-off payment of eight hundred thousand marks for the transfer of the Festspielhaus archive (now known as *Zustiftung Wolfgang Wagner*) to the Foundation. As his sharp-tongued sister Verena observed, 'He just can't gobble enough up.'

However, these generous pension arrangements included a condition. The town, with only one vote on the Foundation Board, felt under-represented, and demanded three more seats – which could make a crucial difference to the election of a successor. Hans Walter Wild, the mayor of

Bayreuth and a close associate of Wolfgang, had been worrying about the succession ever since his friend reached pensionable age. His insistence on the town's rights was prompted by the fear that the state, which controlled half the votes on the Foundation Board, might impose an Intendant from outside.

The final stage in Wolfgang's assumption of absolute power took place in 1986. Although Wolfgang's financial position, and that of his second wife and eight-year-old daughter, was now secure, there were still some areas of festival organisation that concerned him. To solve these problems, the entire assets of the festival were transferred to a limited liability company, the Festspiel GmbH, and Wolfgang was appointed as its only director and only shareholder. He was thereby relieved of the nominal risks that he had undergone as a private entrepreneur, without having to sacrifice anything of his personal power or artistic freedom. He pulled off a final trick by establishing his right to determine his own date of departure. The negotiators hesitated at this, but he bullied them into submission. Perhaps they did not realise the full consequences of their action: that the entire future of the Festspielhaus was now irrevocably tied to the person of Wolfgang Wagner. Perhaps they assumed that old age would soon cause him to bow out gracefully. If so, then they vastly underestimated the endurance of the man who had once been toughened up by the Wehrmacht. Even ten years later, in 1996, the old gentleman felt strong enough to dismiss the question of succession with a joke, proposing the 'zoological solution' that the candidate who most resembled Richard Wagner should be chosen. This, of course, would have been his rejected son, Gottfried – such an unlikely candidate that Wolfgang knew that no one would take his suggestion seriously.

In any case, Wolfgang's successor would now be a pure manager, without any personal financial stake. The shares of the former partners would revert to the Federal Republic, the Land of Bavaria, the town of Bayreuth and the Society of Friends. As the festival press spokesman observed at the time, all the legal provisions for the succession had now been made. The age of management, virtually personified already by Wolfgang, had been codified as the model for the future. In the words of the *Stuttgarter Zeitung*, 'That would therefore mean the end of the family business that has operated for more than a century.'

So Wolfgang stands at the head of the Bayreuth festival for life – alone at last, unchallenged, '*sans famille*'. Would anyone in the family have believed the 'kid brother' capable of this? The public adulation of the 'oldest serving Intendant in the world' increased with every significant anniversary: on his seventieth birthday he was hailed as a 'genius' by Joachim Kaiser, while on his seventy-fifth, the Richard Wagner Association described him as the 'last great father figure in the theatre'. Ironically, the man who obtained his position through pragmatism has now become a figure of myth. Even the mere dates of his reign fascinate the public – how is it possible for a man whose grandfather was born almost two hundred years ago still to be working in the same theatre? Germany watches the spectacle of power, gilded by the setting sun; her people enjoy it as a manifestation of their rich cultural tradition.

With her elder brother and mother now only distant memories, Friedelind was the next member of the family to die, in 1991. She stubbornly refused to let a doctor near her when she fell ill, tortured by the starvation to which she had subjected herself all her life: a residue of the childhood experience of having unwanted food forced down her throat by her mother. Her final refuge was a sanatorium in Herdecke, Westphalia. Obituaries praised her witty, uncompromising, unprejudiced and selfless nature. She was one of the few members of the family to emerge with credit from the 1930s and 1940s, even if her flight from Nazi Germany resulted from personal rather than political motivations.

Had Mausi made her peace with the world? It almost seemed that she had. When people visited her, she would generally be lying in her loose-fitting Hawaiian dress on the terrace of her villa in Lucerne, with its view of the peninsula on which Tribschen stood – the house where her father had been born and where Richard Wagner's family of exiles had been happy. She had made her last 'sentimental journey' to Siegfried's birth-place in 1984, four years after her mother's death. Her only real failure now seemed to be her inability to order her personal archive, which was scattered through the world, owing to her itinerant existence. Her main historical resource was her accurate memory, from which she extracted names, dates and incidents as though from a bottomless drawer. Without any bitterness, she maintained her distance from Verena: the opposed ideological positions of the two sisters had not changed since her emigration. Her views on Wolfgang were expressed with less reserve: she did not have a single good word to say for him. Her last visit to Bayreuth was made in 1990, when she took her friend Leonard Bernstein to see Wahnfried, the synagogue and the Festspielhaus; she was deeply disappointed when Wolfgang avoided this distinguished visitor.

No doubt her siblings had reason to be exasperated with Friedelind, with her wild idealism and her childlike approach to life. This often condemned her to beating her head grandly against the wall of reality, but it also gave her the ability to work to improve that reality. The family must have been surprised when she quoted Mahatma Gandhi during disputes over the inheritance – but it was her determination to see fair play that often allowed unity to be restored. When Winifred's will unfairly favoured the Lafferentz family, for example, Friedelind offered compensation from her own resources that satisfied all parties concerned. Having experienced poverty, she was generous in handing out money to others, as soon as her inheritance allowed her to do so. The family member most victimised by her relatives was also the one who had the most positive idea of what a family should be. And the one who had no children of her own was invariably willing to help the children and grandchildren of the others. She was an aunt quite different from the general run of adults: cheerful, unconventional and full of fantasy. The family motif of the 'childless aunt', represented first of all by Aunt Lulu and Eva Chamberlain, had been heard again in a more cheerful key. In terms of family politics, her death meant the disappearance of the last effective opposition to Wolfgang, and the loss of an incorruptible family memory.

Just as she had learnt to live and think independently, so Friedelind was determined to die without compromise. Her refusal to be buried among the family in Bayreuth was impressively consistent: she wanted instead to have her ashes scattered in the garden of her Lucerne home. This last wish was carried out by the Englishman Neill Thornborrow, a former masterclass student who had become like an adopted son to her, and whom she had made her sole heir. (By chance – or fate – Neill's profile has something of the Wagners about it, though it is more delicate, as if drawn with a silver pencil.) The death of the outsider was marked at Bayreuth only by a 'memorial hour'. As with Winifred's more elaborate funeral, the family turned up in full strength. Songs by her father and grandfather were performed in the parental home; Wolfgang gave a judicious oration. And yet something was missing. What did Goethe say about the suicide Werther? – 'No priest accompanied him.' The passing of Friedelind, refugee from Hitler, received no acknowledgement from either town or state.

19

1990–2000: the battle for succession

THE DEATH OF FRIEDELIND MARKED YET ANOTHER SYMBOLIC break in history for the Wagner family: a year too late, the 1990s had arrived. The present chronicle has reached its final episode, but its ending cannot be a satisfying one. While it is brought to an artificial close on the stroke of the millennium, the history of the festival does not fit so obligingly into chronological packets. The next act is about to start, and the players are beginning to assemble . . .

Let us begin by considering the offspring of Wieland. They had barely come of age when they were orphaned in 1966, and the process of emancipation and self-discovery was forcibly accelerated by the traumatic events that followed. The courses that the siblings followed were individual and divergent, but the shared experience of a stormy family life in the last years of Wahnfried meant that there was some common ground in their decisions. They did not feel restricted, as previous generations had done, in their choice of friends, partner, career or location. The story of Wolf Siegfried, the only son, has already been related. Of the daughters, Daphne, the youngest, chose to be an actress; Nike studied German literature and moved from academia to a freelance career as a writer; Iris became a photographer, author and scriptwriter. Munich, Vienna and Berlin are the cities in which the lives of the three sisters are anchored: three points of a triangle, in which Bayreuth is at the centre. This is of course a geographical fluke, but it could also be interpreted symbolically: it suggests troops strategically surrounding a city in preparation for an assault.

After their father's death, Wolf Siegfried became the accepted champion of the family's hopes to regain influence at the festival; when he decided to turn his back on his uncle's fortress, none of the three sisters was ready to pick up the baton, and even less did they work together. Mythological models, the bread and butter of intra-family jokes, no longer provided suitable images. To describe the sisters as Valkyrie orphans was nonsense, and it was a little early for them to think of themselves as the three Norns: neither their age or knowledge qualified them for that. There remained perhaps another source of inspiration, one from which Wieland had already drawn for his work as well as for his daughter's names. This was the spirit of Greece, carried on the Mediterranean air, which the brother had chosen to go and breathe. Uncle Wolfgang could easily be thought of as an Agamemnon, sacrificing his daughter Eva/Iphigenia. And the family had always thought of Friedelind as an Elektra laying siege to Wolfgang's Aegisthus. Since her death, the role was vacant: it clearly required someone with a militant spirit, something that Nike's promising Christian name seemed to suggest. A fanciful interpretation, of course, but not without a certain appeal. Let us return to Argos and summarise the state of play.

The official honours due to the tyrant are now exhausted. In marked contrast to the ceremonies that accompanied previous anniversaries, Wolfgang Wagner celebrated his eightieth birthday in 1999 with no other public commemoration than a few articles in the press. These expressed not so much admiration as astonishment – not to say alarm – at the inexhaustible physical strength of the octogenarian. The *Neue Musikzeitung* had already set the tone back in 1995 when it described Wolfgang as 'an obstinate old mayor who only thinks about hanging on to power'. As all parties recognised, while Wolfgang's artistic capabilities could be – and frequently are – criticised, his commercial management of the enterprise is hugely successful. The demand for tickets always exceeds what is available by a factor of ten; the town and the sponsors remain delighted with their festival; the cultural authorities, with a few pointed exceptions, remain neutral, and are in any case powerless to change anything. Wolfgang remains free to extend his period of office for as long as he wants, despite the fact that he has probably already broken all the records in the history of opera: of the hundreds of performances of Wagner given in Bayreuth, Wolfgang has presided over far more than all his predecessors put together.

Ironically, given his determination at the beginning of his reign to detach himself from his family, his personal power has served to strengthen the mystique of the family name, creating the impression that only a Wagner is capable of maintaining the flame. Yet this is a double-edged sword for Wolfgang. The contract that enshrines his right to indefinite power is also the document that gives the lie to his claim to be the last Wagner to exercise this power. The clause allowing Wagner's biological descendants a moral advantage over any other candidate is still in place: indeed, it becomes ever more relevant as the date approaches when the succession must be decided, and the story of Bayreuth becomes ever more like a soap opera. The rivalries between the candidates serve to increase public interest in the issue, but they do not invalidate the conditions foreseen by the statutes of the foundation. These dictate that, in the event of the entire family not being able to agree on a single candidate, each of the heirs to Siegfried's estate is permitted to nominate their own contender. The final decision is the responsibility of the full assembly of the council.

The heirs of Siegfried, numbering five at the time when the arrangements were drawn up in 1973, have dwindled to three after the deaths of Winifred and Friedelind. Although the latter left a representative in the person of her heir Neill Thornborrow, the adoption of him that Friedelind would have liked to bring about had never been ratified in court. His right to cast her vote would probably have been contested by the family, had he not already taken the initiative by withdrawing from the current struggle; his overriding concern was to maintain his excellent relationship with Wolfgang, whom he serves in his professional role as an artistic agent. Three strands of the family remain, therefore: the dead Wieland is represented by his four children, and the two octagenarians Wolfgang and Verena represent themselves.

*

The distinction between witness and participant has been a difficult one for the present author to preserve, but the point has now been reached where her personal involvement in events has become impossible to hide. Of course, the author's presentation of events is inevitably coloured by the desire to defend her own interests, but in order to preserve the historian's tone for as long as possible, explicit statement of a personal position is deferred until the end of the book – where there is an open plea linked to a number of proposals. Of the rival contenders for the festival directorship, Nike Wagner will be presented last, and not only for rhetorical reasons. Since it is the idea of change that is at issue, it is appropriate to begin by considering the vote of the one who wants to change nothing, who even denies the propriety of the debate, and has never missed an opportunity to defer it.

Wolfgang has been consistent in his refusal to consider any alternative to his own regime, ever since 1951, when he declared that no members of the family other than he and his brother were capable of taking on the demands of the festival. As his reign continued, his resistance to the presumption that younger members of the family would seek to replace him became increasingly pathological: what was initially only a sensitive point became a burning source of rage. He fought the question with a number of arguments, none of which stood up to much scrutiny. First of all he claimed that the young Wagners lacked the necessary professional skill, that only someone who had worked their way up from the bottom in the theatre could do the job properly. Next, he decided to mock their commitment: just let the young ones try, he sneered – that would teach them something about the drudgery of the theatre. After that, he increased the number of possible contenders to ridiculous proportions in order to make a rhetorical point. 'I can't use all twelve of them,' he would complain, when there were in reality only two or three candidates. His final strategy was to patronise them: 'The Festspielhaus is not an educational establishment for Wagner great-grandchildren,' he declared, conveniently forgetting that most of the candidates were in their late forties by this time.

No hint that Wolfgang had even considered the idea of passing on power surfaced until 1996, when he gave a rather surprising press conference. It was not called to announce that he had at last seen the merits of any of the pretenders to his throne: on the contrary, he announced his intentions of 'outliving a generation', so that by the time he did choose to retire, all the natural contenders would themselves be 'too old'! However, the patriarch also took the opportunity to introduce his family to the public. His wife Gudrun was already familiar to the Bayreuth 'insiders', of course, but she now appeared in a new light, allowed to speak for herself rather than mutely serving her husband's will. By her side – or rather towering over her, like a radiant, blonde Valkyrie – stood Katharina Friderike Wagner, then aged eighteen. The press learnt that she would be initiated into operatic management through a series of work placements in great opera houses of the world, beginning with the State Opera in Berlin, which was headed by Daniel Barenboim who had also been the chief conductor in Bayreuth for the last eighteen years. Gudrun commented that 'the child adores her father, and it is astonishing to see how quickly she learns from him'; in the same interview, she hinted at her own readiness to take over the festival. 'I am a doer,' she declared, with unmistakable intent.

If this press conference suggested that the ageing Wolfgang had at last devised a plan for the succession, then this impression was confirmed three years later, on the threshold of the new millennium, when Wolfgang and Gudrun gave an interview to *Der Spiegel* in which nothing remained hidden. The headline given by the magazine summed up the essential message: 'I am not moving from here'. But the interest does not lie in yet another declaration of his own immortality, but in the explanation of the conditions that would surround his voluntary abdication, if it eventually came. There was of course no question of it in the immediate future. Had not the Federal State just reduced its subsidies for the 2000 Festival, and who could resist this act of financial aggression better than the old accountant who had been guarding the cash boxes of Bayreuth for fifty years? His artistic power, too, would not change: those of his productions which were currently in the repertoire would stay there for some years yet, and they required his continuing personal attention. Unless, unless . . . – unless a new director could be found who would work harmoniously with the old regime. And who could do that better than Wolfgang's wife and collaborator of the last quarter of a century? Gudrun, when asked, claimed that she was entirely capable of taking on the double task, artistic and administrative, if it were entrusted to her. Wolfgang made it known, unofficially of course, that this would be the option that would get his vote. And later Katharina, perhaps. 'Music of the future', quipped Gudrun. 'Absolutely too soon to speak about it', the head of the family judiciously concluded.

Without for a moment wanting this happy ending to become a reality, we must concede its dramatic force. A family has appeared to exhaust itself with the last bearer of its name, who is fiercely determined that it should die with him. But then, with one bound, and showing no fear of the approaching Siegfrieds, Fafner draws himself up to his full height and slips the ring on the finger of his daughter – just when one was least expecting it. At the back of the stage, the duped onlookers can only stand and stare.

Let us wake up from this fairy story and count the votes again. Wolfgang's has clearly already been committed to Gudrun. Wieland's vote has been entrusted to Nike, who will naturally support her own cause. That makes two cases settled: there remains Verena.

Until very recently, she had yet to cast her vote: torn between loyalty to her elder brother and her natural maternal feelings, she seemed to hesitate for a long time. But everything depended on her, for only with her vote could a majority be formed. A whispering game began, attempts to exert influence were made, and the tension rose: would Verena at last proclaim her son's status as an adult by declaring that she believed him capable of directing the festival? For on close examination Wieland Lafferentz proved to have the ideal training, the background of which the Foundation dreams. Having been a professional musician himself, he was now, in Salzburg, steering a great musical organisation for the second time through all the perils caused by the state policy of cutting subsidies. However, there was a slight drawback – he was not a prominent figure as far as the media were concerned. What use was his obvious likeness to Franz Liszt? And there was yet another drawback to this good-looking man of the right age for the post: he had the 'wrong' surname. He joked that people had suggested he might stand a better chance if he applied to Bayreuth as 'Wieland Wagner' – archaic requirements clearly override the criteria of good taste. No, he repeatedly insisted, he was grateful to his surname for its protective function, under cover of which he had been able to develop less stressfully as a musician. But now he intended to emerge from cover of any kind, and for that he needed his mother: would her protective instincts leave him alone, would she overcome her fear of seeing her son torn to pieces in the shark-pool of Bayreuth?

The time had come for political wheeling and dealing – and for the lawyers. In the comfortable and prestigious office of the Munich solicitors consulted by the 'young' Wagners, a wonderfully utopian scene was played out. After decades of exclusion from Bayreuth, three former playmates met as candidates for the succession to the Bayreuth throne, and were obliged to recognise that only as a self-contained team, a trio, could they come into their inheritance: there had to be harmony or none of them would have a chance. Wieland was there, smoking nervously, obviously his mother's candidate; Nike was there, representing her siblings – and finally there was Eva. For Eva would play a key part in the game of roulette that was just beginning. Irrespective of whether or not she was presented as a candidate from the heart of the family, there had always been a kind of tacit understanding that this daughter of Wolfgang would be awarded the laurel wreath. She has never openly criticised her father, good conduct which has won her the confidence of Bavarian government ministers, the city fathers, and the conservative patrons of the festival. While her brother Gottfried walked away from the family universe, Eva always clung on, though whether this was due to ambition or to loyalty it is hard to say. Anyway, nothing could be done without Eva: the other two had to secure her presence as part of the triumvirate, and they had to win Verena's approval for this project. The proposal that three of the composer's great-grandchildren from three different branches of the family should direct the festival would be impossible for the trustees of the Foundation to resist, if only for historical reasons.

For the time being, the trio condemned to exist in harmony did at least share a negative aim: anything was preferable to Gudrun. But did the three cousins know if they could work together on the battlefield left to them by their fathers? Positive aims appeared harder to achieve. No sooner had the first demonstrations of solidarity been called for, in the form of written undertakings, than the first quarrel broke out, soon to be followed by a second. Eva dropped out of the alliance and applied directly to the Richard Wagner Foundation on her own behalf, aware of her proven strengths after many years working in opera management, and aware too of her good political connections. Her application seemed to contravene the constitution, but – as we know from politics – rules can be bent when the will to enforce a decision is there.

Nike more than anyone now had to look around for help. She could hardly count on getting the half of Verena's vote that would place her on a par with Wieland. Her years of sharp criticism of the direction of the festival have won her not only the furious antagonism of her uncle, whom her aunt loves because he is her brother, but also the hostility of those political circles which are anxious to maintain the status quo, convinced that Bayreuth can rest on the laurels of its traditions. And the Richard Wagner Foundation consists of people with such convictions. Nike, who was considered an 'intellectual', had to look for a partner with practical experience of the way in which the theatre functions, of theatrical administration and finance. An experienced white knight of this kind was actually found, and the first steps in their campaign were taken. But could the champion be expected to commit himself to so nebulous a long-term aim as Bayreuth, a position humiliatingly dependent on an old man's physical stamina? After all, the Wagnerian paradise in Bayreuth is not the only Eden: the Salzburg festival was also looking out for a new artist director, and promptly snapped up Nike's high-profile colleague. She would have to look elsewhere . . .

Valuable time had passed, but at last Verena's decision was announced: she was splitting her vote equally between her son Wieland and her niece Eva. Eva's position was legally safeguarded now that she had half a vote from within the family circle, and Wieland's own position was reinforced as the colleague of the candidate who held the best cards. Finally, in February 2000, the Richard Wagner Foundation fixed a date on which the various candidates would have an opportunity to introduce themselves to the assembled representatives of Bayreuth and Upper Franconia, and to the patrons as well. It was to be a kind of examination, then, of an obviously comic and indeed farcical character: there sat the old head of the family firm, surrounded by politicians, and his wife, his daughter, his nephew and his niece were to appear before him to give evidence of their ability to replace him. The outcome of this procedure was obvious from the first: if the Foundation chose anyone but his wife Gudrun, Wolfgang

Wagner would simply fall back on the terms of the contract granted him by the Foundation itself, a contract for life. Nothing and no one could make the patriarch abdicate. He only had to sit and wait. This absurd scenario became a subject of public discussion in cultural circles, arousing disapproval, merriment or repugnance, depending on one's temperament and one's point of view.

However, it was necessary to keep up appearances: despite its inability to do anything, the Foundation acted as if it could, and invited the candidates to face questioning in the Bayreuth Town Hall. They were asked in turn who they were and what ideas they had for the future direction of the festival. The answers of the two opposing sets of candidates who were the most likely prospects – Gudrun on the one hand, Wieland and Eva on the other – had one factor in common, a factor which determines everything else: nothing at Bayreuth must be changed – why should it be, when it is all going so very well and so successfully? Gudrun discreetly utters the innocuous word 'evolution', with a view to nipping in the bud any idea of 'revolution' – not that such an idea would have occurred to anyone. And we hear the familiar note struck, in the conformist jargon that suits all political temperaments: Wagner's work is inexhaustible, eternal, although of course one does not shrink from new initiatives which might be proposed by talented colleagues, but just because such talents can be so diverse and contrasting, a firm, experienced hand is required to hold the whole thing together, and she, Gudrun, is that hand.

Formally, Eva and Wieland were in a different position, since there were two of them. The tried and tested idea of division into artistic and administrative direction surfaced, along with the pecking order proper to it. Eva made a firm stand, putting her claim to become chief artistic director. Wieland seemed to go along with her, and restricted himself to remarks about the organisational and financial aspects of the festival. His ideas for Bayreuth were determined by the marketing principle that decrees that only a 'clearly defined product' is guaranteed to succeed. So there would be no blurred edges, no changes to the traditional repertory, they would stick to the ten familar works – at the very outside, there might be a concert performance of *Rienzi*. The members of the family felt some surprise. Was Wieland really ready to put his musical abilities on the back burner, confining himself to the less prestigious administrative role in Bayreuth? His mother for one was not happy with this prospect; she claimed that he should be involved in the artistic direction. The Foundation hesitated: only a moment ago these two candidates seemed ideal, with their neat division of responsibilities. Like Gudrun, Eva and Wieland could have been represented as 'new blood' in order to give the appearance of change at the top.

Sometimes earthquakes begin with small cracks in the ground, and then whole edifices suddenly collapse. Such was the case here: the other family members, and the board of the Foundation itself, were surprised by a sudden press release only a few months later. Just before the day on which the two of them would have been named the winners, Wieland broke off his connection with Eva, publicly and in harsh language. It seemed difficult to understand this, for was it not only just and fair for the Lafferentz branch to have its rights in Bayreuth at last? A closer look, however, explains what had happened. The idea of taking second place to his cousin would have been intolerable to Wieland – both professionally and as a matter of male pride. And incompatibilities between them which had gone unnoticed in the haste of the early stages of the competition now appeared; the saying that relations sometimes know very little about each other had been proved true. The Lafferentz family had become cautious through their long history of injuries suffered at the hands of the Bayreuth establishment. Now, so close to the point where justice was at last to be done, Wieland withdrew before coming up against the old barriers and perhaps suffering further injury. There is undoubtedly a hidden, tragic aspect to this apparently stormy dissolution of a brief union of interests. However, the last word has not yet been spoken, and Wieland will offer himself as a candidate on his own account in the next round. So, it seems, will Eva.

Candidate number three at least benefitted from the change in the landscape after this storm. Although she had appeared to be routed already, Nike had now gained time. Moreover, a new Lohengrin had been found, one whose combination of artistic and business abilities would make him a convincing partner for her in front of the tribunal which was to decide on the succession. This was Dr Elmar Weingarten, general manager of the Berlin Philharmonic Orchestra. The charge that she lacked managerial expertise would be invalidated by a partnership with Wein-garten, who supplied the administrative expertise that she needed. And there were no conflicts inherent in the division of labour between a woman who, in many literary essays, had given evidence of her knowledge of the theatre, and a man who was used to administering a budget of millions for a musical institution. Their complementary abilities seemed to provide a promising chance of smooth and successful day-to-day man-agement, founded on the basis of a shared aesthetic culture. It was in this light that the team presented itself at the curious show-jumping trials which were held in front of the board of the Foundation in February 2000. The alliance expressly emphasised its desire to revive and open up the Bayreuth Festival – an idea which fell on deaf ears, as was only to be expected, since no one was prepared to acknowledge the insight of a famous writer who said that 'If you want everything to stay as it is, then you must change everything.'

Here, however, the present author must abandon her pose of being an objective chronicler of events, for the story has now reached the present day. Candidate number three must show herself in her true colours, as a figure involved with and indeed committed to those events, and must state, directly and in the first person, how she would like Bayreuth to develop. The family history recounted above will therefore conclude with a personal credo. One might call it a special kind of profession of belief, one which expresses the family spirit in so far as that spirit aims to win a new future for Wagner by disturbing the hallowed ground of Bayreuth. *Zukunft* – 'future' – was a favourite word in the vocabulary of the com-poser himself, and we should give it its due here.

My plan for the restructuring of the festival has been drawn up together with Elmar Weingarten. If my candidature was successful, we would share the artistic direction of the festival: Elmar Weingarten would take charge of its financial affairs and public relations, and I would be concerned principally with programming and the detail of the productions.

Our proposals are made in reaction to the increasingly museum-like approach of the festival in recent years. The changes that are necessary cannot be made through the introduction of a new management alone; they must involve the further artistic development of the Wagnerian legacy. Without basic reflection on the place of musical theatre and art today, the Festspielhaus runs the danger of redundancy, of falling back on its dowry. If Bayreuth wants to be seen as more than a business enterprise, as a place where artistic sensibility takes priority, then it must seek to redesign its future. Wagner's modernity must always be tested and discovered anew.

The paradox of a 'break in tradition faithful to Wagner', achieved at different times both by Wieland Wagner and Patrice Chéreau, has shown how successful reform can be. Bayreuth has nothing to fear from reform, because the weight of tradition dominates in any case. The rearguard is always there. But Bayreuth must also take its place in the context of general changes in the international opera scene. Within that context, it must, where the production of Wagner is concerned, exercise a role appropriate to its special circumstances, providing an authoritative and contemporary view of Wagner, and establishing his relevance to the twenty-first century. The privileged position of Bayreuth constitutes a challenge to which the festival must respond with performances that are unlike any that a repertory house could produce. This is not always easy today: the constant presence of the same few star singers, conductors and directors tends to impose an unwanted homogeneity on opera pro-ductions. It is neither possible nor desirable for Bayreuth to jump off this international merry-go-round, but it can by virtue of its festival status seek out collaborators with special care, and combine musicians and directors with great imagination. It also has a particular responsibility to discover and nurture new talent.

There must also be some structural changes to the programme of the festival. The Festspielhaus was built to allow *The Ring* to be presented as a totality, yet only *Parsifal* was composed for its peculiar acoustic. The other works performed, beginning with *The Flying Dutchman*, through *Tannhäuser*, *Lohengrin*, and *Tristan*, to *Die Meistersinger*, were actually added to the festival by Cosima. As a result of this gradual incorporation of works, more haphazard than is generally realised, no repertory or dramatic theory has ever been established. *The Ring* is generally kept in the repertory for four years, and one other work is changed each year, so that there is at least the possibility of one new production.

The specific acoustic makeup and the unchanging repertory distinguish Bayreuth, to be sure, but they also pose a danger. Both factors tend towards stagnation. The architecture of the Festspielhaus commits every work performed there, musically and acoustically, to an opaque sonic mix, which only a few conductors can really penetrate, and which is a principal component of the 'Wagner mystique' whose essence has not changed since the nineteenth century.

We need a new direction: the repertory must be expanded. After all, there is no reason for anything decreed by Wagner's widow to be considered as sacrosanct: she herself took the liberty of expanding the repertory beyond what the Master had imagined because the house was not paying for itself. That criterion fortunately no longer applies today, but there is still good reason to broaden the range. Wagner's early works, *Die Feen, Das Liebesverbot* and *Rienzi*, should certainly be performed. While directors seem, for the moment, almost to have exhausted the potential of the mature works – exceptions only serve to prove the rule – the early works are ripe for contemporary re-exploration. Moreover, their inclusion would provide the opportunity for audiences to trace the arc from the composer's early works to his maturity, and thus to gain a fuller understanding of Wagner's astonishing development throughout his career. The handful of non-operatic works could also be presented – other performing facilities are available – and then we would have the 'complete Wagner'. Only Bayreuth can provide that.

The works must be presented in new combinations, rather than being routinely rotated, as is the case at the moment. There are unrealised possibilities for fascinating juxtapositions and harmonious successions. Sequences could be devised which would allow familiar works to be seen from a new perspective. For example, 'On the Trail of Grand Opera': *Rienzi, Dutchman, Götterdämmerung.* 'Forbidden Love': *Das Liebesverbot, Dutchman, Tannhäuser, Das Rheingold.* 'The Medieval and the Modern': *Tannhäuser, Lohengrin, Tristan, Parsifal.* 'Tragedy and Satyr Plays': *Tannhäuser, Tristan, Meistersinger.* 'Politics versus Myth': *Lohengrin, The Ring.* 'The Sound of Space and the Space of Sound': *Tristan, Parsifal.* 'Beginning and End': *Die Feen, Parsifal.*

The relationship between stage and orchestra must be co-ordinated with great sensitivity. It is not enough simply to throw together famous and proven artists. It is necessary to ensure that conductor and director share a conception beforehand and work it out together. The stage and the orchestra should not trip each other up. For example, a steely, futuristic staging should not be entrusted to a romantically minded and over-reverential conductor, as has often happened in the past. The meaning of the term *Gesamtkunstwerk* must be precisely observed.

At the reopening of the festival after the war, Beethoven's Ninth Symphony was played; this idea could be revived, as a homage to Wagner's musical heritage as well as a declaration of brotherhood. Perhaps the work of other precursors of Wagner could also be introduced: Carl Maria von Weber, perhaps? Other variations could be explored to extend the repertory, to draw interesting and refreshing connections. Even the Wagner family provides a source of inspiration: neighbouring concert halls and theatres could easily perform works by Franz Liszt, Siegfried Wagner and possibly Hans von Bülow.

And if Bayreuth's connection to musical history is to be explored, then why not also its connection to our time and to the future? There are numerous works that can be considered as a homage to Wagner, from Bruckner and Berg through to Hans Werner Henze, Klaus Huber and Dieter Schnebel. Others are still to be created. There is no reason why Bayreuth should not give premieres as part of a season of music that relates to Wagner or takes its inspiration from Bayreuth's acoustical makeup and recessed orchestra. The association of Wagner with contemporary composers would show him to be 'a contemporary of the future'.

But a new era also requires new methods. Alongside this development of the repertoire, there must be related measures to pursue Wagner's ideas in a broader sphere: intellectually, choreographically, or in the new electronic media, to draw Wagner into the present context of social discourse. Commissions could be conferred on artists, encouraging them to consider a particular theme in relation to the Festspielhaus site: they could institute installations, projects, topographical evocations or acoustic experiments. The 'search for the Grail' could provide a suitable theme, as could the place of art in a modern community. Symposia joining scholarship with artistic productions would accompany these projects, helping to link Wagner to the arts of today.

This 'new dramaturgy' must always be grounded in an idea of why we perform Wagner, and why we seek to interest emerging generations and inspire them with his work. It concerns the audiences as well as the performers of the future. In this spirit a Bayreuth summer school would be established in close affiliation with the Munich Theatre Academy. Masterclasses in Wagner singing could be provided by the present artists, and projects by young directors and designers could be linked with festival activities. Because it would continue the tradition that Friedelind Wagner founded with her masterclasses, the summer academy would be named after this Wagner granddaughter.

The new Bayreuth dramaturgy also makes possible a stronger relationship with the city. Bayreuth offers many performance spaces, conference halls and stages in addition to the Festspielhaus: for example, the Margraves' Opera House, the Villa Wahnfried and the Eremitage. In addition, taking its lead from the Salzburg and Munich festivals and from Covent Garden, it should offer live open-air telecasts of productions in the city's public spaces. The previous role of the Bayreuth public as mere onlookers must be changed. An extension of these activities to the performing sites and theatres of the Oberfranken region – Bamberg, Nuremberg, Hof – is also a possibility.

The notorious discrepancy between ticket availability and demand gives constant cause for complaint. For this reason, and also to further the desired expansion of the repertory, an additional Whitsun season with reduced ticket prices would be proposed. This could profitably make use of young orchestras and conductors: the Junge Deutsche Philharmonie, for example, or the Gustav Mahler Youth Orchestra. Young singers could be given invaluable experience by preparing concert performances of Wagner on the Festspielhaus stage, perhaps just with a piano accompaniment. The main purpose of a second season would be to open the Festspielhaus to a younger public and young interpreters. In addition, it could also consider inviting outstanding Wagner productions from other houses.

The existing financial structures of the core events in the Festspielhaus would be fundamentally preserved. The public agencies would not be relieved of their obligations, but the principle of general thrift would be observed where honoraria are concerned! The new management would also try to achieve closer co-operation with the sponsors' organisation, the Friends of Bayreuth. The reductions in subsidies announced by the state suggest a restructuring of ticket prices in the foreseeable future. The main priority of such restructuring would be to ensure that prices remained stable at the bottom end of the price range. But ticket sales would not be the only source of income: improved contacts with the media would be sought to achieve a larger revenue from broadcasting and merchandising. The artistic activities taking place outside the festival stage should aim to be self financing, through sponsorship of individual projects and co-operation with relevant corporations.

Finally, future directors of the Bayreuth Festival would be restricted to a term of office of no more than ten years.

So, a manifesto to round off a family story? It was not premeditated that it should appear, either in this form or at this point, and by the time this book is published it will already have been overtaken by events. The cemetery that was referred to at the beginning of this family history is not closing itself up again; the shaken stones will not be put back into place. From an older tomb, outside the cemetery, a playful, almost mocking voice can still be heard: 'The new, my children,' it says, 'always try the new.'

The word 'end' can be erased from this history before it is even inscribed. So how should we conclude? 'To be continued' would be too much to promise, and too much to expect of public curiosity, which could easily become weary of having its attention bounced back between rival claims, on a timetable that is endlessly deferred. The soap opera could simply become a document, put back in its folder. But if this seems a doleful prospect for the family deities, then one final incident should give pleasure to the Norns, whose sense of humour has been clear throughout the course of this account. Wolfgang Wagner has just contracted the conductors for a new *Ring* cycle in 2006. And he has not ruled out the possibility of directing it himself.

INDEX